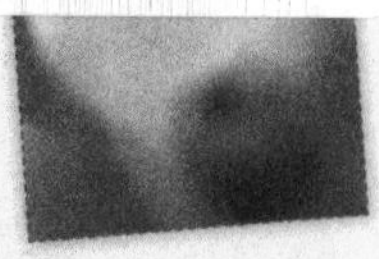

I'm sorry. I said I liked Iwase in volume 2 but I'm now an Aoki fan. I feel really bad about it. Sorry, Iwase...

—Tsugumi Ohba

I like old people, so I drew a manga with an old man as the main character. I was in third grade. It was my second manga series in the school newspaper.

—Takeshi Obata

Tsugumi Ohba

Born in Tokyo, Tsugumi Ohba is the author of the hit series *Death Note*. His current series *Bakuman。* is serialized in *Weekly Shonen Jump*.

Takeshi Obata

Takeshi Obata was born in 1969 in Niigata, Japan, and is the artist of the wildly popular SHONEN JUMP title *Hikaru no Go*, which won the 2003 Tezuka Osamu Cultural Prize: Shinsei "New Hope" award and the 2000 Shogakukan Manga award. Obata is also the artist of *Arabian Majin Bokentan Lamp Lamp*, *Ayatsuri Sakon*, *Cyborg Jichan G.*, and the smash hit manga *Death Note*. His current series *Bakuman。* is serialized in *Weekly Shonen Jump*.

BAKUMAN。

Volume 6

SHONEN JUMP Manga Edition

Story by **TSUGUMI OHBA**
Art by **TAKESHI OBATA**

Translation | **Tetsuichiro Miyaki**
English Adaptation | **Hope Donovan**
Touch-up Art & Lettering | **James Gaubatz**
Design | **Fawn Lau**
Editor | **Alexis Kirsch**

Printed in the U.S.A.

Published by VIZ Media, LLC
P.O. Box 77010
San Francisco, CA 94107

10 9 8 7 6 5 4 3 2 1
First printing, August 2011

viz media
www.viz.com

SHONEN JUMP
www.shonenjump.com

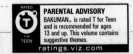

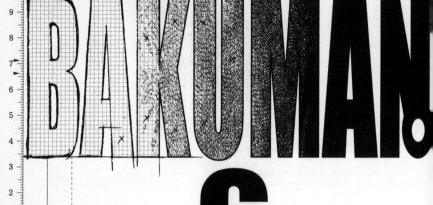

BAKUMAN.

6

RECKLESSNESS
and
GUTS

STORY BY
TSUGUMI OHBA

ART BY
TAKESHI OBATA

MAN。 バクマン。 vol. 6

F
G
H
LOVE

EIJI
Nizuma

A manga prodigy and Tezuka Award winner at the age of 15. One of the most popular creators in *Jump*.

Age: 18

KAYA
Miyoshi

Miho's friend and Akito's girlfriend. A nice girl who actively works as the interceder between Moritaka and Azuki.

Age: 17

AKITO
Takagi

Manga writer. An extremely smart guy who gets the best grades in his class. A cool guy who becomes very passionate when it comes to manga.

Age: 17

MIHO
Azuki

A girl who dreams of becoming a voice actress. She promised to marry Moritaka under the condition that they not see each other until their dreams come true.

Age: 17

MORITAKA
Mashiro

Manga artist. An extreme romantic who believes that he will marry Miho Azuki once their dreams come true.

Age: 17

*These ages are from June 2011.

STORY In order to attain the glory that only a handful of people can, two young men decide to walk the rough "path of manga" and become professional manga creators. This is the story of a great artist, Moritaka Mashiro, a talented writer, Akito Takagi, and their quest to become manga legends!

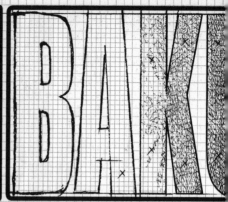

The characters with this mark appear for the first time in volume 6.

WEEKLY SHONEN JUMP

Editorial Office

1	Editor in Chief Sasaki	Age: 48
2	Deputy Editor in Chief Heishi	Age: 42
3	Soichi Aida	Age: 35
4	Yujiro Hattori	Age: 29
5	Akira Hattori	Age: 31
6	Koji Yoshida	Age: 32
7	Goro Miura	Age: 24

UP AND COMING MANGA ARTISTS

A	SHINTA FUKUDA	Age: 20
B	TAKURO NAKAI	Age: 35
C	KO AOKI	Age: 21
D	KOJI MAKAINO	Age: 30
E	KAZUYA HIRAMARU	Age: 26

F Ogawa G Takahama H Kato I Yasuoka

Muto Ashirogi's Assistants

BAKUMAN. Vol.6

(RECKLESSNESS AND GUTS)

CONTENTS

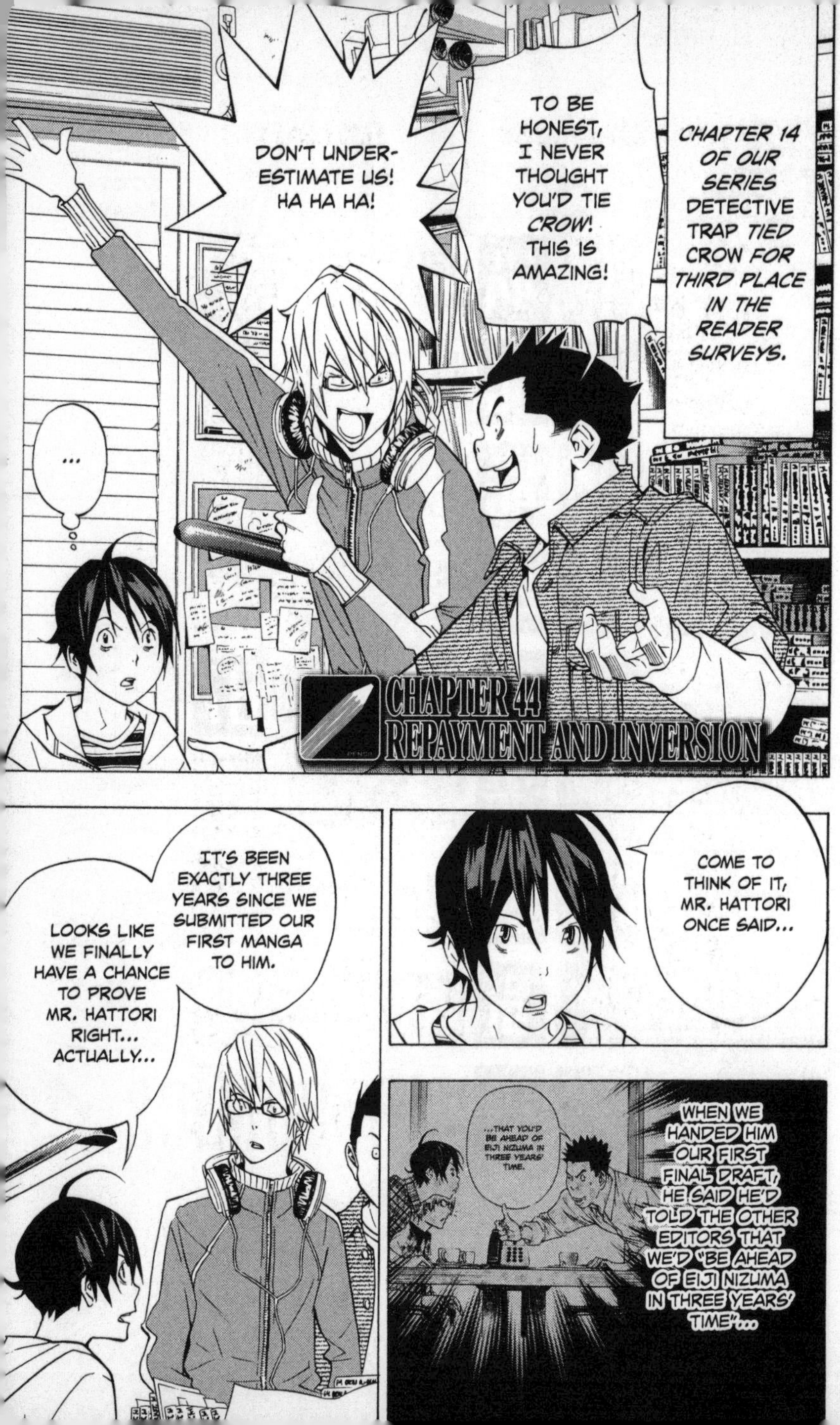
CHAPTER 14 OF OUR SERIES DETECTIVE TRAP TIED CROW FOR THIRD PLACE IN THE READER SURVEYS.
TO BE HONEST, I NEVER THOUGHT YOU'D TIE CROW! THIS IS AMAZING!
DON'T UNDER-ESTIMATE US! HA HA HA!
...
CHAPTER 44 REPAYMENT AND INVERSION
COME TO THINK OF IT, MR. HATTORI ONCE SAID...
WHEN WE HANDED HIM OUR FIRST FINAL DRAFT, HE SAID HE'D TOLD THE OTHER EDITORS THAT WE'D "BE AHEAD OF EIJI NIZUMA IN THREE YEARS' TIME"...
...THAT YOU'D BE AHEAD OF EIJI NIZUMA IN THREE YEARS' TIME.
IT'S BEEN EXACTLY THREE YEARS SINCE WE SUBMITTED OUR FIRST MANGA TO HIM.
LOOKS LIKE WE FINALLY HAVE A CHANCE TO PROVE MR. HATTORI RIGHT... ACTUALLY...

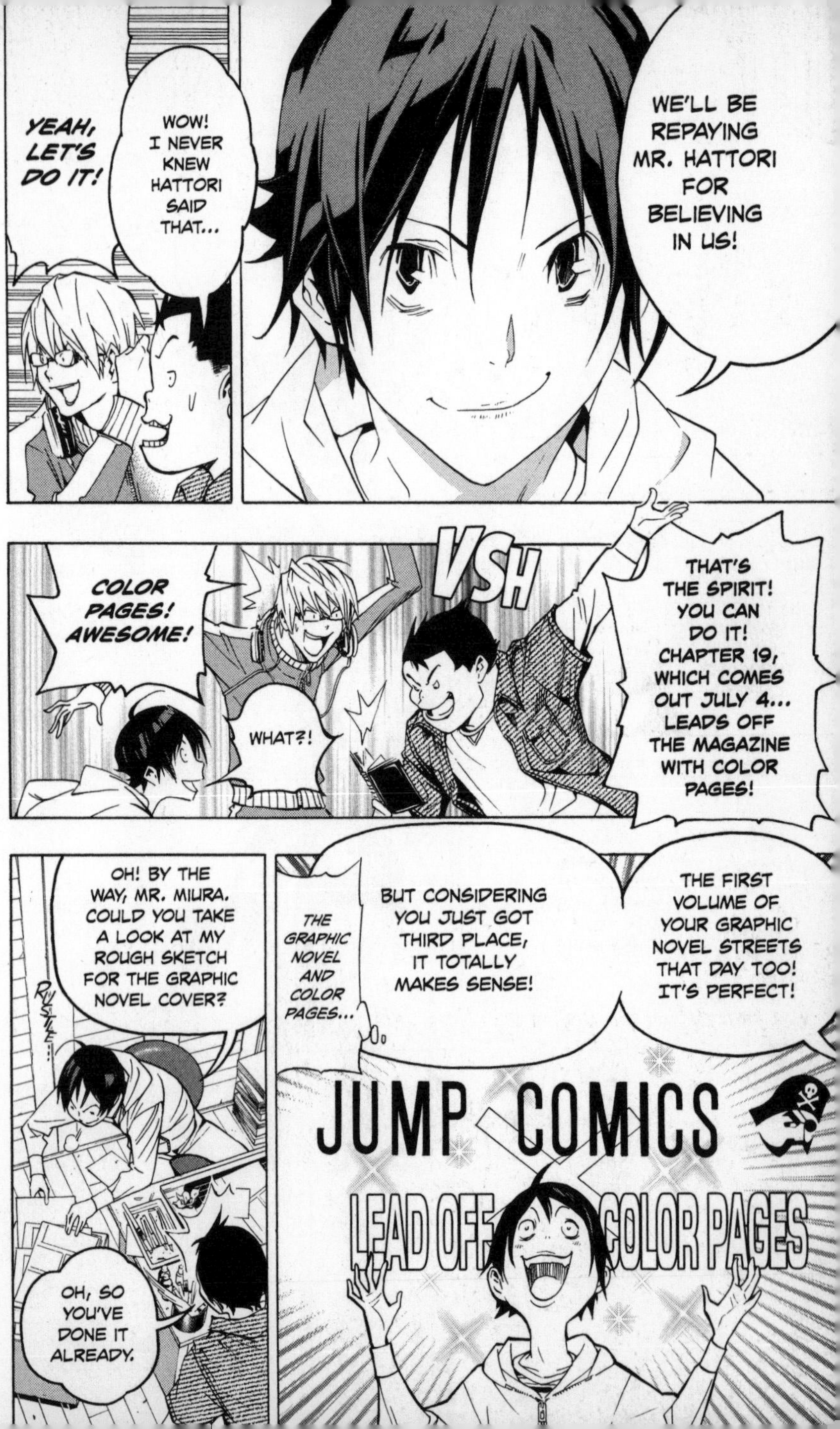
WE'LL BE REPAYING MR. HATTORI FOR BELIEVING IN US!
WOW! I NEVER KNEW HATTORI SAID THAT...
YEAH, LET'S DO IT!
THAT'S THE SPIRIT! YOU CAN DO IT! CHAPTER 19, WHICH COMES OUT JULY 4... LEADS OFF THE MAGAZINE WITH COLOR PAGES!
VSH
COLOR PAGES! AWESOME!
WHAT?!
THE FIRST VOLUME OF YOUR GRAPHIC NOVEL STREETS THAT DAY TOO! IT'S PERFECT!
BUT CONSIDERING YOU JUST GOT THIRD PLACE, IT TOTALLY MAKES SENSE!
THE GRAPHIC NOVEL AND COLOR PAGES...
JUMP COMICS
LEAD OFF
COLOR PAGES
OH! BY THE WAY, MR. MIURA. COULD YOU TAKE A LOOK AT MY ROUGH SKETCH FOR THE GRAPHIC NOVEL COVER?
RUSTLE
OH, SO YOU'VE DONE IT ALREADY.

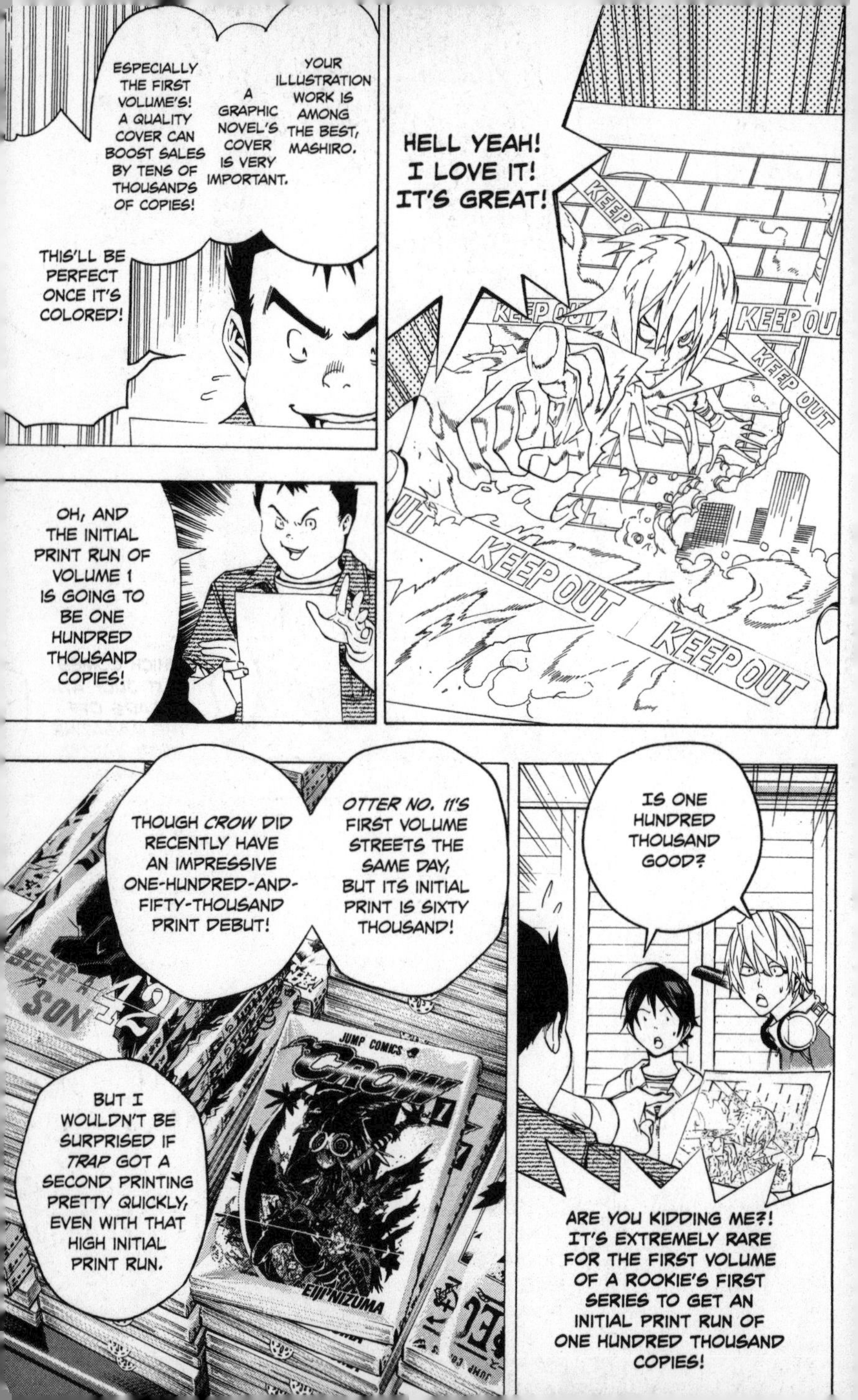
HELL YEAH! I LOVE IT! IT'S GREAT!
KEEP OUT
YOUR ILLUSTRATION WORK IS AMONG THE BEST, MASHIRO.
A GRAPHIC NOVEL'S COVER IS VERY IMPORTANT.
ESPECIALLY THE FIRST VOLUME'S! A QUALITY COVER CAN BOOST SALES BY TENS OF THOUSANDS OF COPIES!
THIS'LL BE PERFECT ONCE IT'S COLORED!
OH, AND THE INITIAL PRINT RUN OF VOLUME 1 IS GOING TO BE ONE HUNDRED THOUSAND COPIES!
IS ONE HUNDRED THOUSAND GOOD?
ARE YOU KIDDING ME?! IT'S EXTREMELY RARE FOR THE FIRST VOLUME OF A ROOKIE'S FIRST SERIES TO GET AN INITIAL PRINT RUN OF ONE HUNDRED THOUSAND COPIES!
OTTER NO. 11'S FIRST VOLUME STREETS THE SAME DAY, BUT ITS INITIAL PRINT IS SIXTY THOUSAND!
THOUGH *CROW* DID RECENTLY HAVE AN IMPRESSIVE ONE-HUNDRED-AND-FIFTY-THOUSAND PRINT DEBUT!
BUT I WOULDN'T BE SURPRISED IF *TRAP* GOT A SECOND PRINTING PRETTY QUICKLY, EVEN WITH THAT HIGH INITIAL PRINT RUN.
JUMP COMICS
EIJI NIZUMA

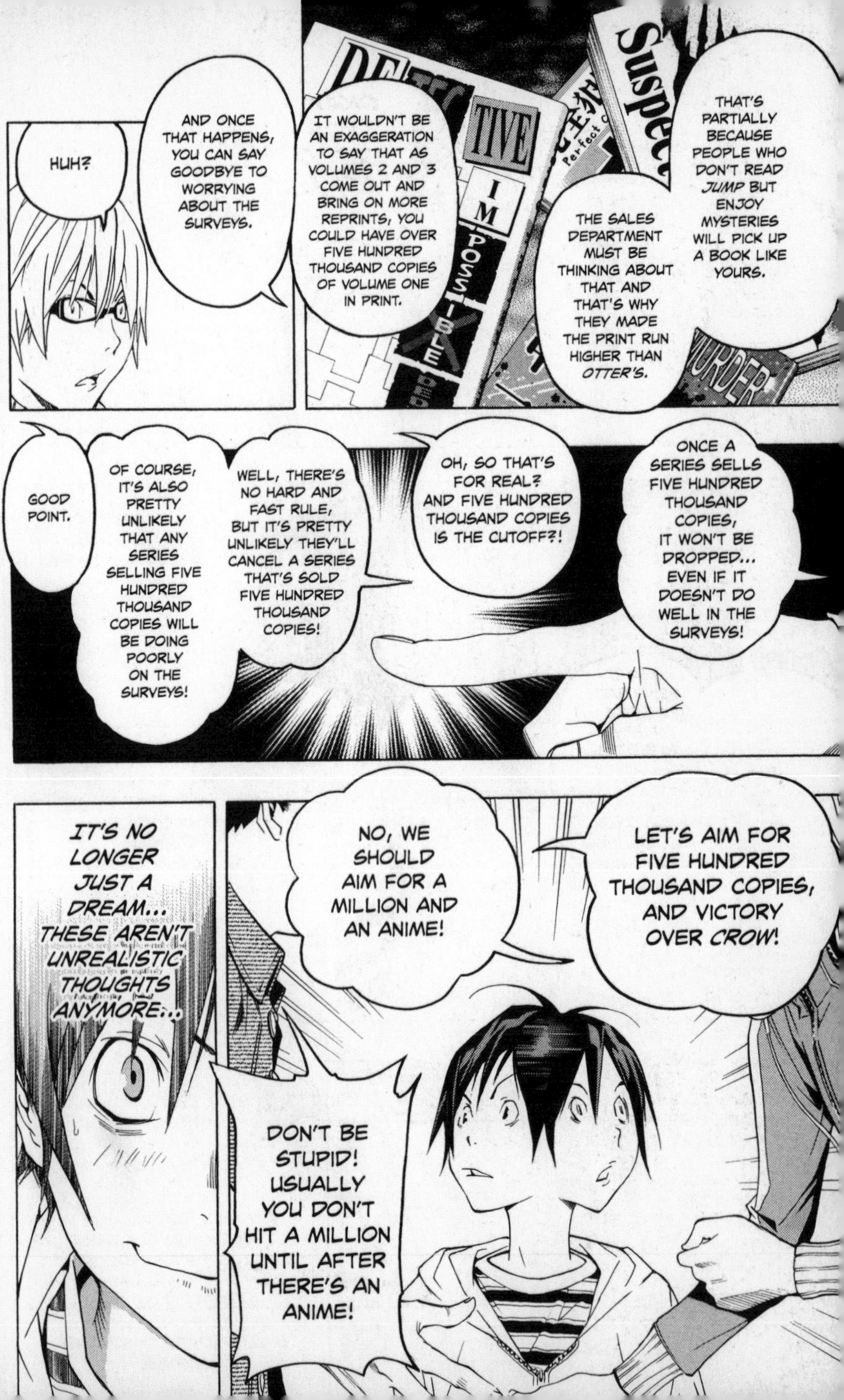
THAT'S PARTIALLY BECAUSE PEOPLE WHO DON'T READ *JUMP* BUT ENJOY MYSTERIES WILL PICK UP A BOOK LIKE YOURS.
THE SALES DEPARTMENT MUST BE THINKING ABOUT THAT AND THAT'S WHY THEY MADE THE PRINT RUN HIGHER THAN *OTTER'S*.
IT WOULDN'T BE AN EXAGGERATION TO SAY THAT AS VOLUMES 2 AND 3 COME OUT AND BRING ON MORE REPRINTS, YOU COULD HAVE OVER FIVE HUNDRED THOUSAND COPIES OF VOLUME ONE IN PRINT.
AND ONCE THAT HAPPENS, YOU CAN SAY GOODBYE TO WORRYING ABOUT THE SURVEYS.
HUH?
ONCE A SERIES SELLS FIVE HUNDRED THOUSAND COPIES, IT WON'T BE DROPPED... EVEN IF IT DOESN'T DO WELL IN THE SURVEYS!
OH, SO THAT'S FOR REAL? AND FIVE HUNDRED THOUSAND COPIES IS THE CUTOFF?!
WELL, THERE'S NO HARD AND FAST RULE, BUT IT'S PRETTY UNLIKELY THEY'LL CANCEL A SERIES THAT'S SOLD FIVE HUNDRED THOUSAND COPIES!
OF COURSE, IT'S ALSO PRETTY UNLIKELY THAT ANY SERIES SELLING FIVE HUNDRED THOUSAND COPIES WILL BE DOING POORLY ON THE SURVEYS!
GOOD POINT.
LET'S AIM FOR FIVE HUNDRED THOUSAND COPIES, AND VICTORY OVER *CROW*!
NO, WE SHOULD AIM FOR A MILLION AND AN ANIME!
DON'T BE STUPID! USUALLY YOU DON'T HIT A MILLION UNTIL AFTER THERE'S AN ANIME!
IT'S NO LONGER JUST A DREAM... THESE AREN'T UNREALISTIC THOUGHTS ANYMORE...

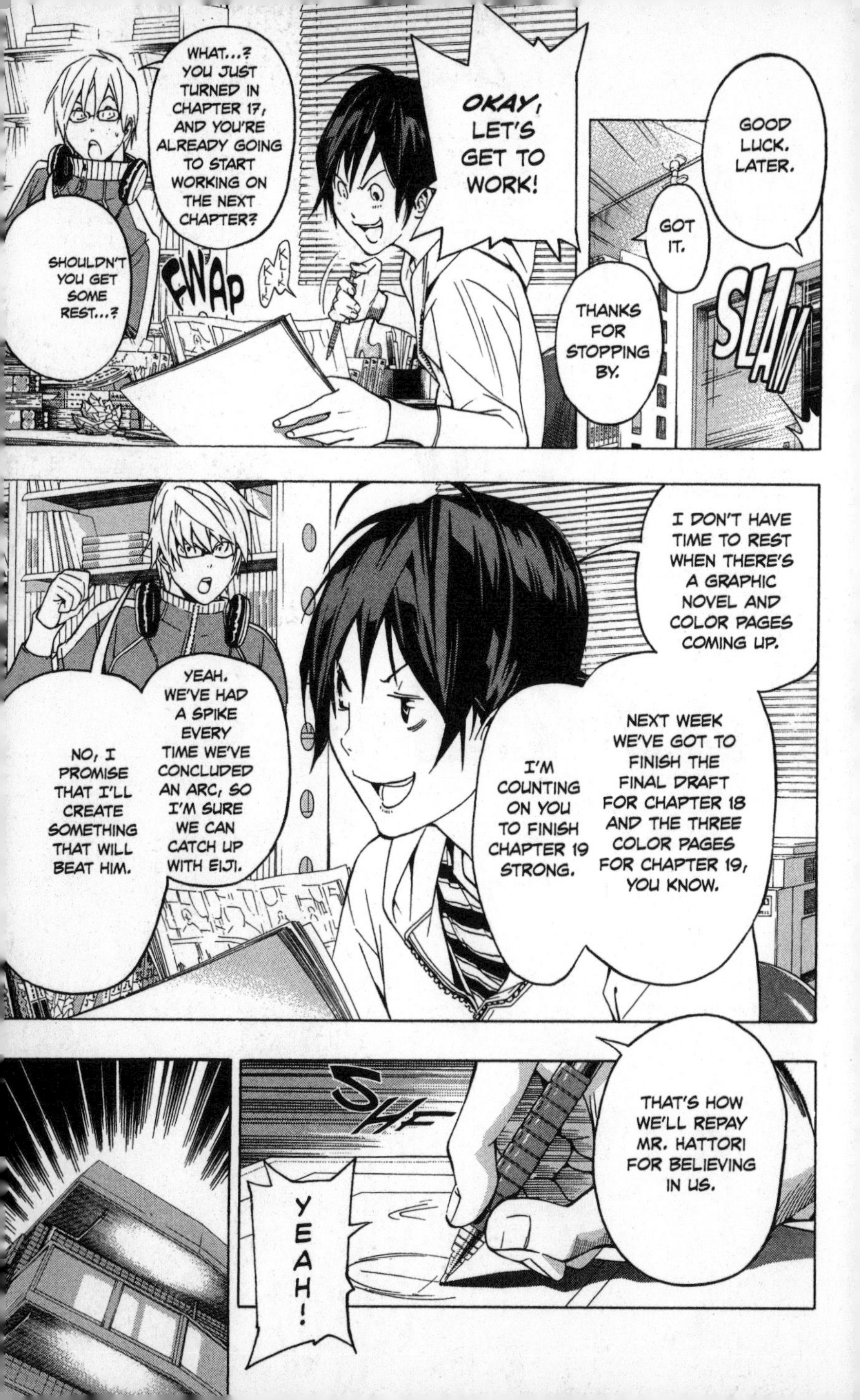
GOOD LUCK. LATER.
GOT IT.
THANKS FOR STOPPING BY.
SLAM
OKAY, LET'S GET TO WORK!
WHAT...? YOU JUST TURNED IN CHAPTER 17, AND YOU'RE ALREADY GOING TO START WORKING ON THE NEXT CHAPTER?
KLIK KLIK
FWAP
SHOULDN'T YOU GET SOME REST...?
I DON'T HAVE TIME TO REST WHEN THERE'S A GRAPHIC NOVEL AND COLOR PAGES COMING UP.
NEXT WEEK WE'VE GOT TO FINISH THE FINAL DRAFT FOR CHAPTER 18 AND THE THREE COLOR PAGES FOR CHAPTER 19, YOU KNOW.
I'M COUNTING ON YOU TO FINISH CHAPTER 19 STRONG.
YEAH. WE'VE HAD A SPIKE EVERY TIME WE'VE CONCLUDED AN ARC, SO I'M SURE WE CAN CATCH UP WITH EIJI.
NO, I PROMISE THAT I'LL CREATE SOMETHING THAT WILL BEAT HIM.
THAT'S HOW WE'LL REPAY MR. HATTORI FOR BELIEVING IN US.
SHF
YEAH!

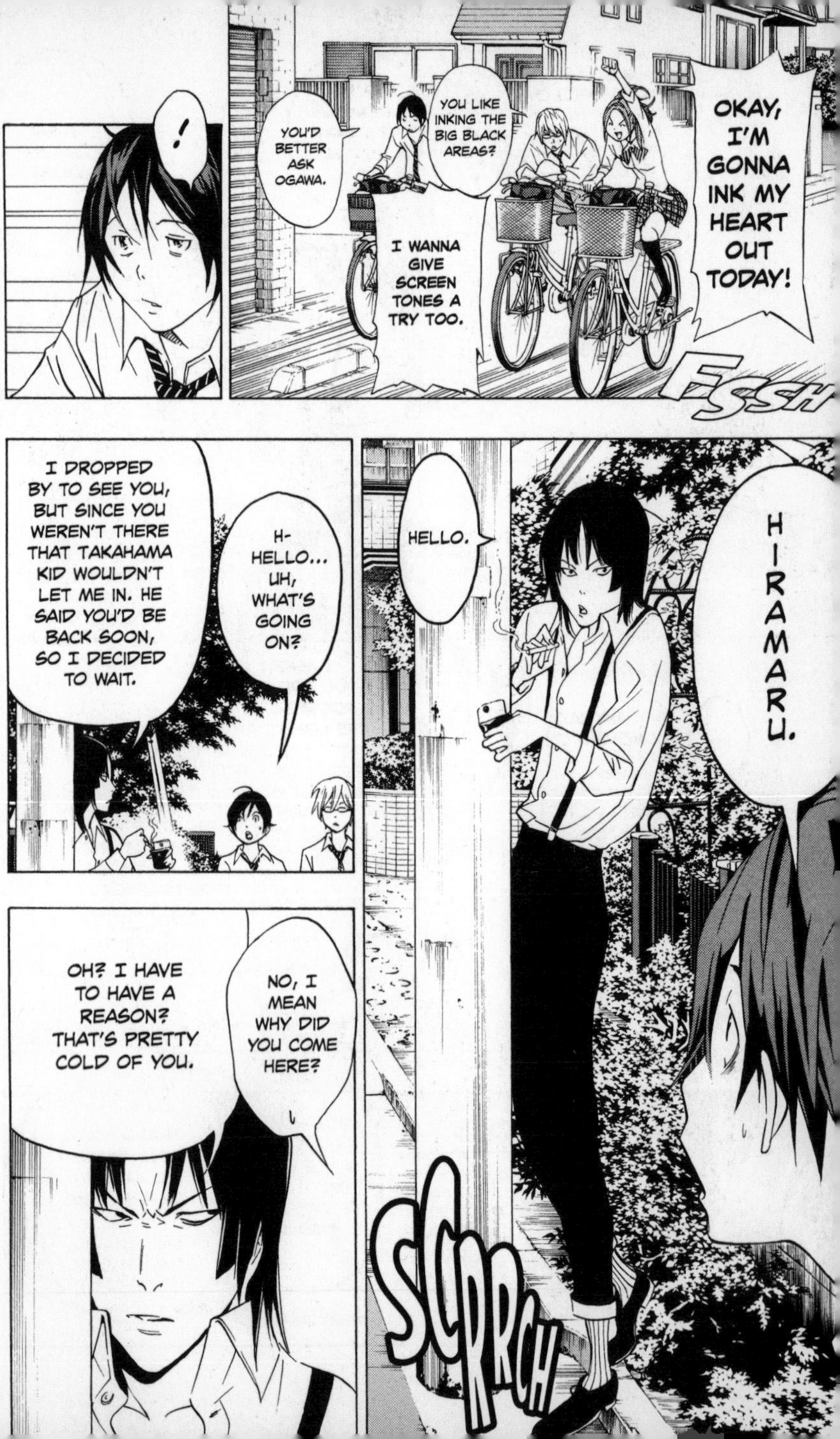

OKAY, I'M GONNA INK MY HEART OUT TODAY!
YOU LIKE INKING THE BIG BLACK AREAS?
I WANNA GIVE SCREEN TONES A TRY TOO.
YOU'D BETTER ASK OGAWA.
FSSH
!
HIRAMARU.
HELLO.
SCRCH
H- HELLO... UH, WHAT'S GOING ON?
I DROPPED BY TO SEE YOU, BUT SINCE YOU WEREN'T THERE THAT TAKAHAMA KID WOULDN'T LET ME IN. HE SAID YOU'D BE BACK SOON, SO I DECIDED TO WAIT.
NO, I MEAN WHY DID YOU COME HERE?
OH? I HAVE TO HAVE A REASON? THAT'S PRETTY COLD OF YOU.

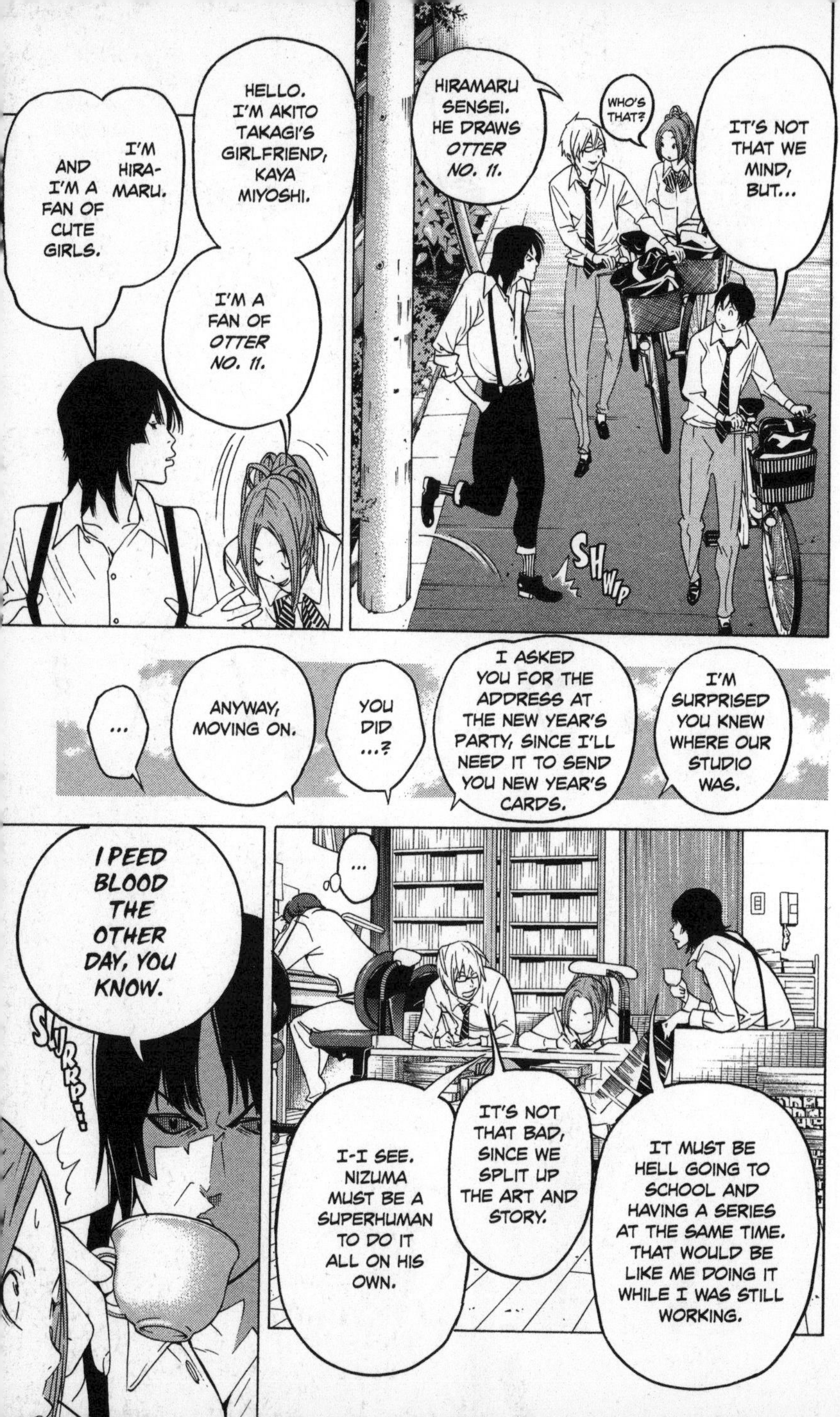
IT'S NOT THAT WE MIND, BUT...
WHO'S THAT?
HIRAMARU SENSEI. HE DRAWS OTTER NO. 11.
SHWIP
HELLO. I'M AKITO TAKAGI'S GIRLFRIEND, KAYA MIYOSHI.
I'M A FAN OF OTTER NO. 11.
I'M HIRA-MARU.
AND I'M A FAN OF CUTE GIRLS.
I'M SURPRISED YOU KNEW WHERE OUR STUDIO WAS.
I ASKED YOU FOR THE ADDRESS AT THE NEW YEAR'S PARTY, SINCE I'LL NEED IT TO SEND YOU NEW YEAR'S CARDS.
YOU DID ...?
ANYWAY, MOVING ON.
...
...
IT MUST BE HELL GOING TO SCHOOL AND HAVING A SERIES AT THE SAME TIME. THAT WOULD BE LIKE ME DOING IT WHILE I WAS STILL WORKING.
IT'S NOT THAT BAD, SINCE WE SPLIT UP THE ART AND STORY.
I-I SEE. NIZUMA MUST BE A SUPERHUMAN TO DO IT ALL ON HIS OWN.
I PEED BLOOD THE OTHER DAY, YOU KNOW.

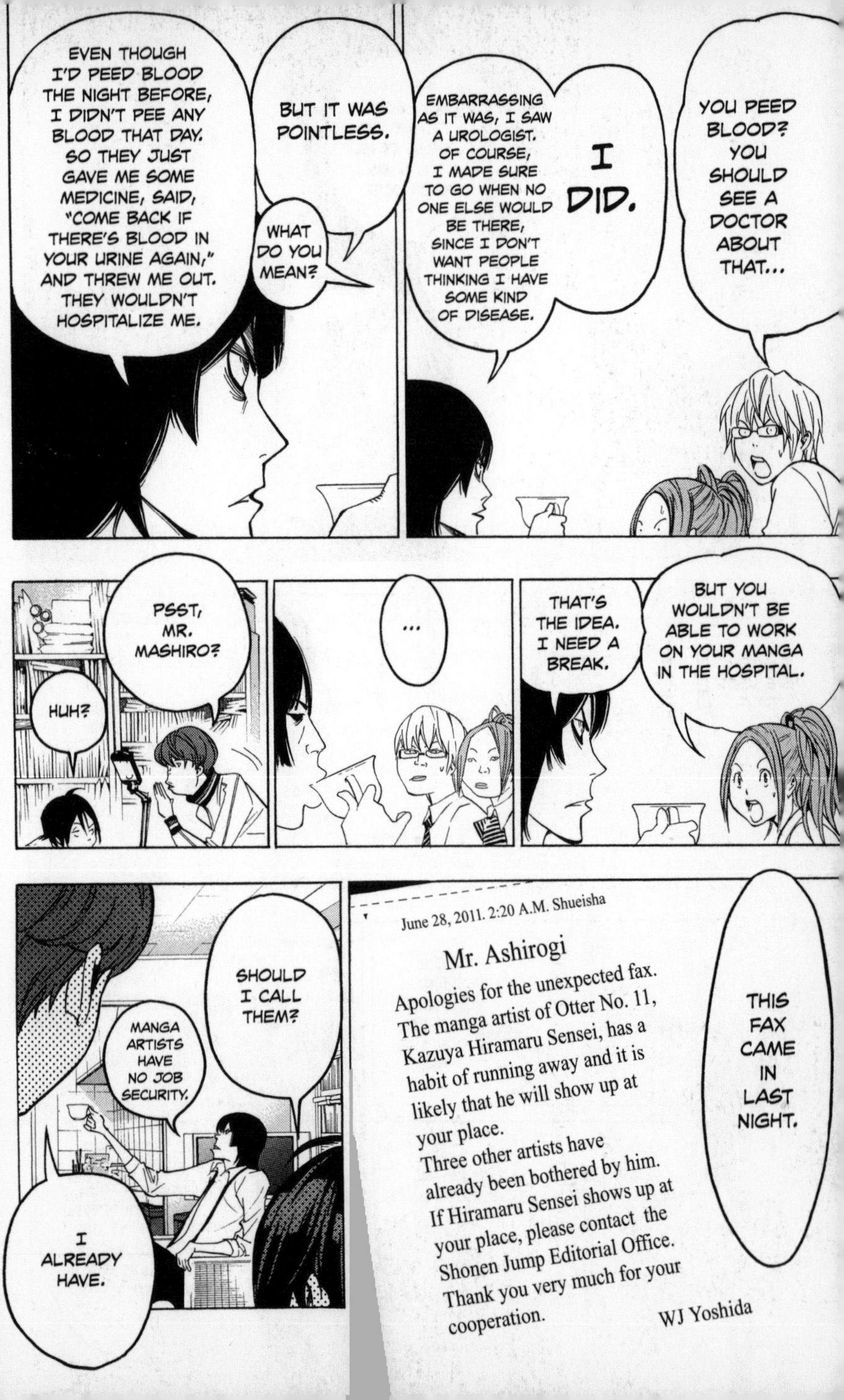
YOU PEED BLOOD? YOU SHOULD SEE A DOCTOR ABOUT THAT...
I DID.
EMBARRASSING AS IT WAS, I SAW A UROLOGIST. OF COURSE, I MADE SURE TO GO WHEN NO ONE ELSE WOULD BE THERE, SINCE I DON'T WANT PEOPLE THINKING I HAVE SOME KIND OF DISEASE.
BUT IT WAS POINTLESS.
WHAT DO YOU MEAN?
EVEN THOUGH I'D PEED BLOOD THE NIGHT BEFORE, I DIDN'T PEE ANY BLOOD THAT DAY. SO THEY JUST GAVE ME SOME MEDICINE, SAID, "COME BACK IF THERE'S BLOOD IN YOUR URINE AGAIN," AND THREW ME OUT. THEY WOULDN'T HOSPITALIZE ME.
BUT YOU WOULDN'T BE ABLE TO WORK ON YOUR MANGA IN THE HOSPITAL.
THAT'S THE IDEA. I NEED A BREAK.
...
PSST, MR. MASHIRO?
HUH?
THIS FAX CAME IN LAST NIGHT.
June 28, 2011. 2:20 A.M. Shueisha
Mr. Ashirogi
Apologies for the unexpected fax.
The manga artist of Otter No. 11, Kazuya Hiramaru Sensei, has a habit of running away and it is likely that he will show up at your place.
Three other artists have already been bothered by him.
If Hiramaru Sensei shows up at your place, please contact the Shonen Jump Editorial Office.
Thank you very much for your cooperation.
WJ Yoshida
SHOULD I CALL THEM?
MANGA ARTISTS HAVE NO JOB SECURITY.
I ALREADY HAVE.

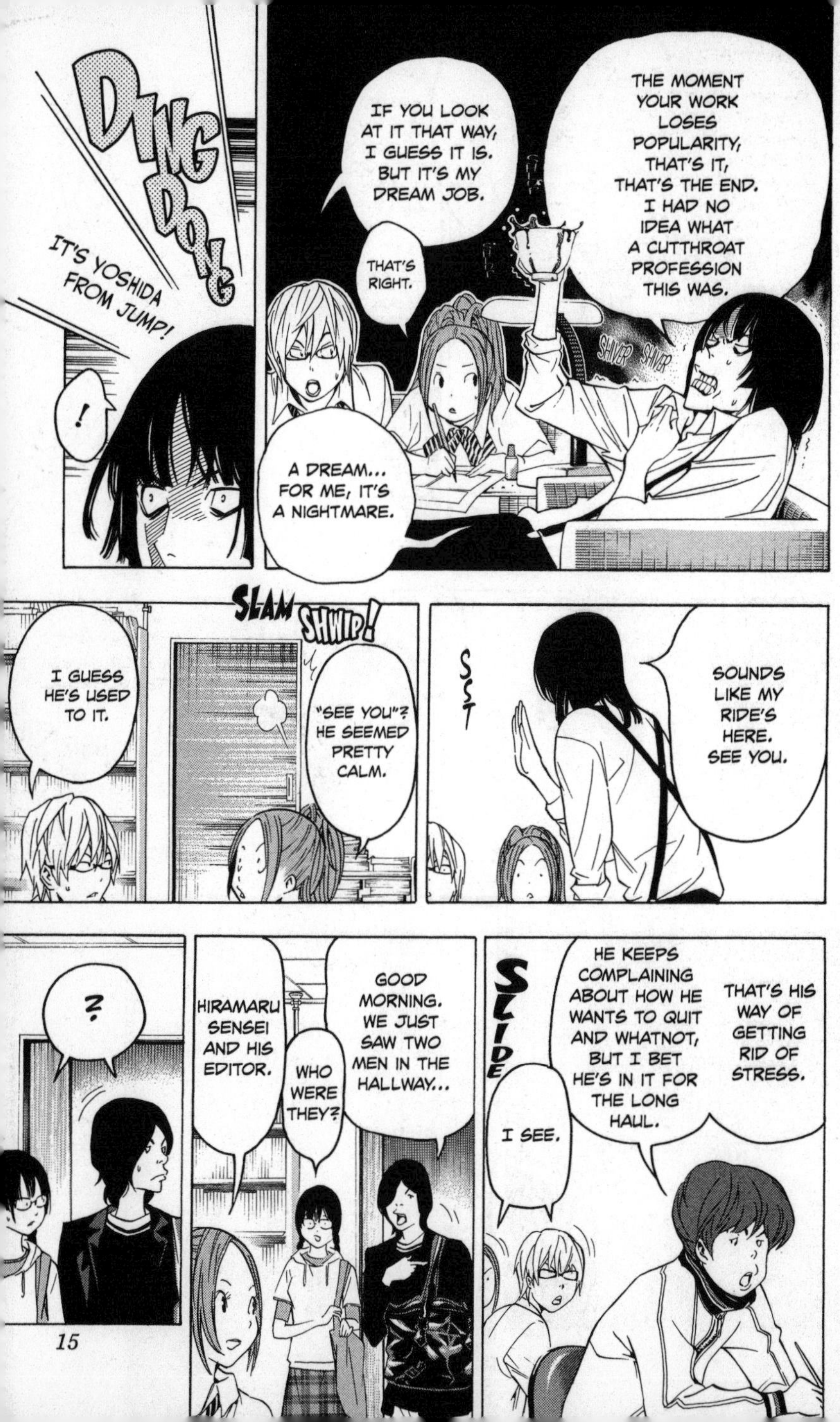
THE MOMENT YOUR WORK LOSES POPULARITY, THAT'S IT, THAT'S THE END. I HAD NO IDEA WHAT A CUTTHROAT PROFESSION THIS WAS.
SHIVER SHIVER
IF YOU LOOK AT IT THAT WAY, I GUESS IT IS. BUT IT'S MY DREAM JOB.
THAT'S RIGHT.
A DREAM... FOR ME, IT'S A NIGHTMARE.
DING DONG
IT'S YOSHIDA FROM JUMP!
!
SOUNDS LIKE MY RIDE'S HERE. SEE YOU.
SST
SLAM
SHWIP!
"SEE YOU"? HE SEEMED PRETTY CALM.
I GUESS HE'S USED TO IT.
SLIDE
THAT'S HIS WAY OF GETTING RID OF STRESS.
HE KEEPS COMPLAINING ABOUT HOW HE WANTS TO QUIT AND WHATNOT, BUT I BET HE'S IN IT FOR THE LONG HAUL.
I SEE.
GOOD MORNING. WE JUST SAW TWO MEN IN THE HALLWAY...
WHO WERE THEY?
HIRAMARU SENSEI AND HIS EDITOR.
?

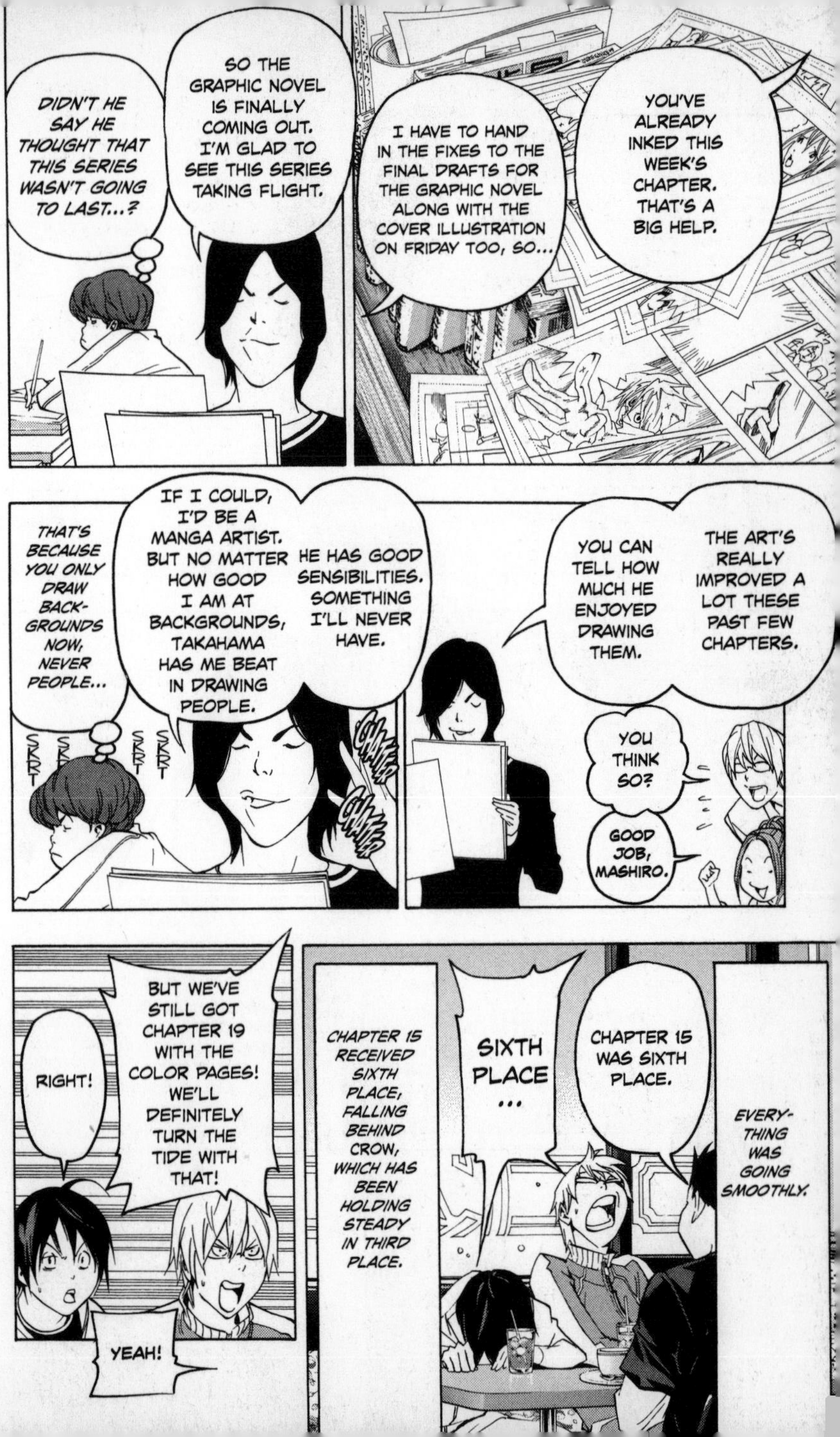
YOU'VE ALREADY INKED THIS WEEK'S CHAPTER. THAT'S A BIG HELP.
I HAVE TO HAND IN THE FIXES TO THE FINAL DRAFTS FOR THE GRAPHIC NOVEL ALONG WITH THE COVER ILLUSTRATION ON FRIDAY TOO, SO...
SO THE GRAPHIC NOVEL IS FINALLY COMING OUT. I'M GLAD TO SEE THIS SERIES TAKING FLIGHT.
DIDN'T HE SAY HE THOUGHT THAT THIS SERIES WASN'T GOING TO LAST...?
THE ART'S REALLY IMPROVED A LOT THESE PAST FEW CHAPTERS.
YOU CAN TELL HOW MUCH HE ENJOYED DRAWING THEM.
YOU THINK SO?
GOOD JOB, MASHIRO.
HE HAS GOOD SENSIBILITIES. SOMETHING I'LL NEVER HAVE.
IF I COULD, I'D BE A MANGA ARTIST. BUT NO MATTER HOW GOOD I AM AT BACKGROUNDS, TAKAHAMA HAS ME BEAT IN DRAWING PEOPLE.
SKRT SKRT
THAT'S BECAUSE YOU ONLY DRAW BACKGROUNDS NOW, NEVER PEOPLE...
SKRT SKRT
EVERYTHING WAS GOING SMOOTHLY.
CHAPTER 15 WAS SIXTH PLACE.
SIXTH PLACE...
CHAPTER 15 RECEIVED SIXTH PLACE, FALLING BEHIND CROW, WHICH HAS BEEN HOLDING STEADY IN THIRD PLACE.
BUT WE'VE STILL GOT CHAPTER 19 WITH THE COLOR PAGES! WE'LL DEFINITELY TURN THE TIDE WITH THAT!
RIGHT!
YEAH!

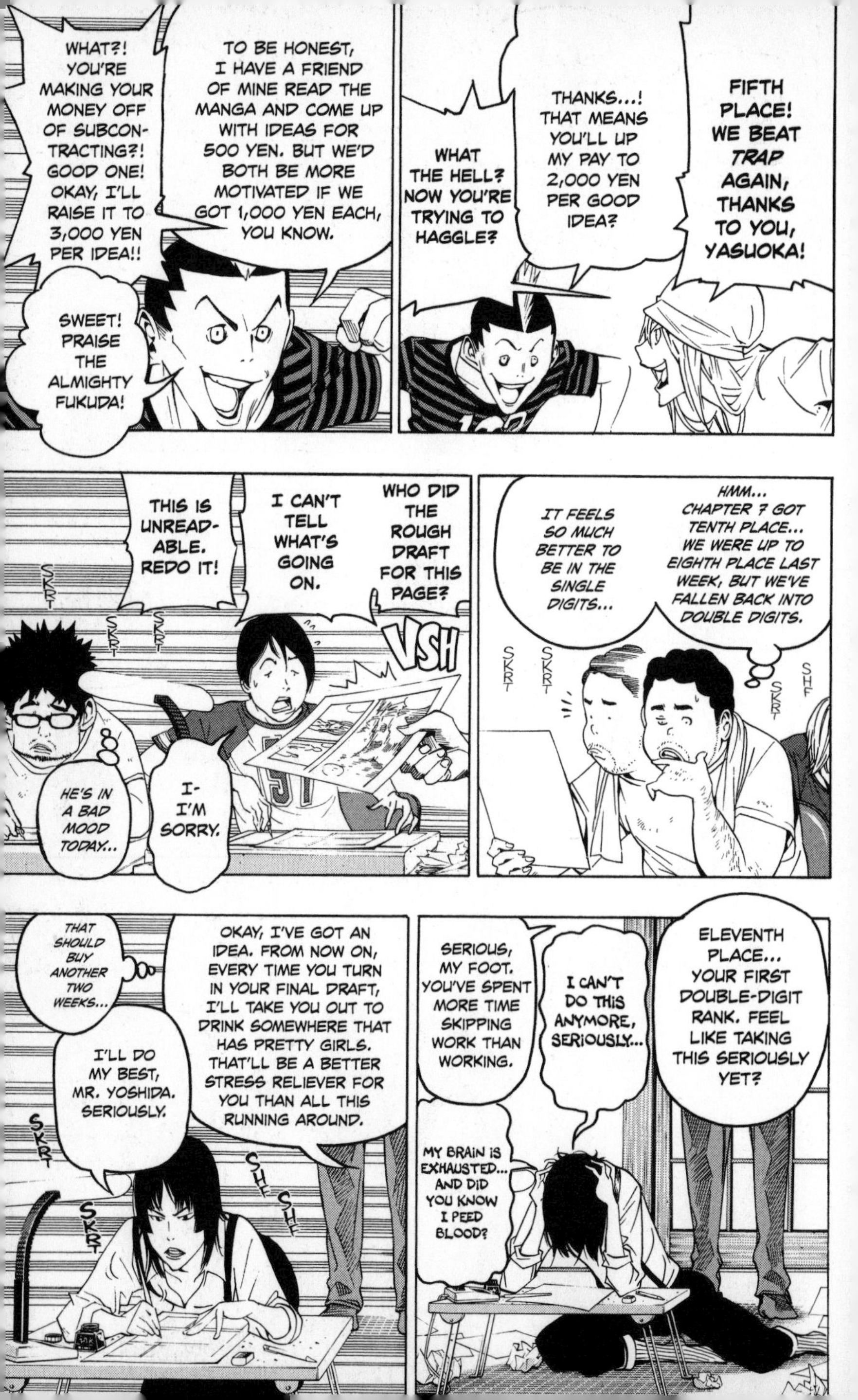
FIFTH PLACE! WE BEAT *TRAP* AGAIN, THANKS TO YOU, YASUOKA!
THANKS...! THAT MEANS YOU'LL UP MY PAY TO 2,000 YEN PER GOOD IDEA?
WHAT THE HELL? NOW YOU'RE TRYING TO HAGGLE?
TO BE HONEST, I HAVE A FRIEND OF MINE READ THE MANGA AND COME UP WITH IDEAS FOR 500 YEN. BUT WE'D BOTH BE MORE MOTIVATED IF WE GOT 1,000 YEN EACH, YOU KNOW.
WHAT?! YOU'RE MAKING YOUR MONEY OFF OF SUBCON-TRACTING?! GOOD ONE! OKAY, I'LL RAISE IT TO 3,000 YEN PER IDEA!!
SWEET! PRAISE THE ALMIGHTY FUKUDA!
HMM... CHAPTER 7 GOT TENTH PLACE... WE WERE UP TO EIGHTH PLACE LAST WEEK, BUT WE'VE FALLEN BACK INTO DOUBLE DIGITS.
IT FEELS SO MUCH BETTER TO BE IN THE SINGLE DIGITS...
SHF
SKRT
SKRT
SKRT
WHO DID THE ROUGH DRAFT FOR THIS PAGE?
VSH
I CAN'T TELL WHAT'S GOING ON.
THIS IS UNREADABLE. REDO IT!
SKRT
SKRT
SKRT
I- I'M SORRY.
HE'S IN A BAD MOOD TODAY...
ELEVENTH PLACE... YOUR FIRST DOUBLE-DIGIT RANK. FEEL LIKE TAKING THIS SERIOUSLY YET?
I CAN'T DO THIS ANYMORE, SERIOUSLY...
SERIOUS, MY FOOT. YOU'VE SPENT MORE TIME SKIPPING WORK THAN WORKING.
MY BRAIN IS EXHAUSTED... AND DID YOU KNOW I PEED BLOOD?
OKAY, I'VE GOT AN IDEA. FROM NOW ON, EVERY TIME YOU TURN IN YOUR FINAL DRAFT, I'LL TAKE YOU OUT TO DRINK SOMEWHERE THAT HAS PRETTY GIRLS. THAT'LL BE A BETTER STRESS RELIEVER FOR YOU THAN ALL THIS RUNNING AROUND.
THAT SHOULD BUY ANOTHER TWO WEEKS...
I'LL DO MY BEST, MR. YOSHIDA. SERIOUSLY.
SHF
SHF
SKRT
SKRT

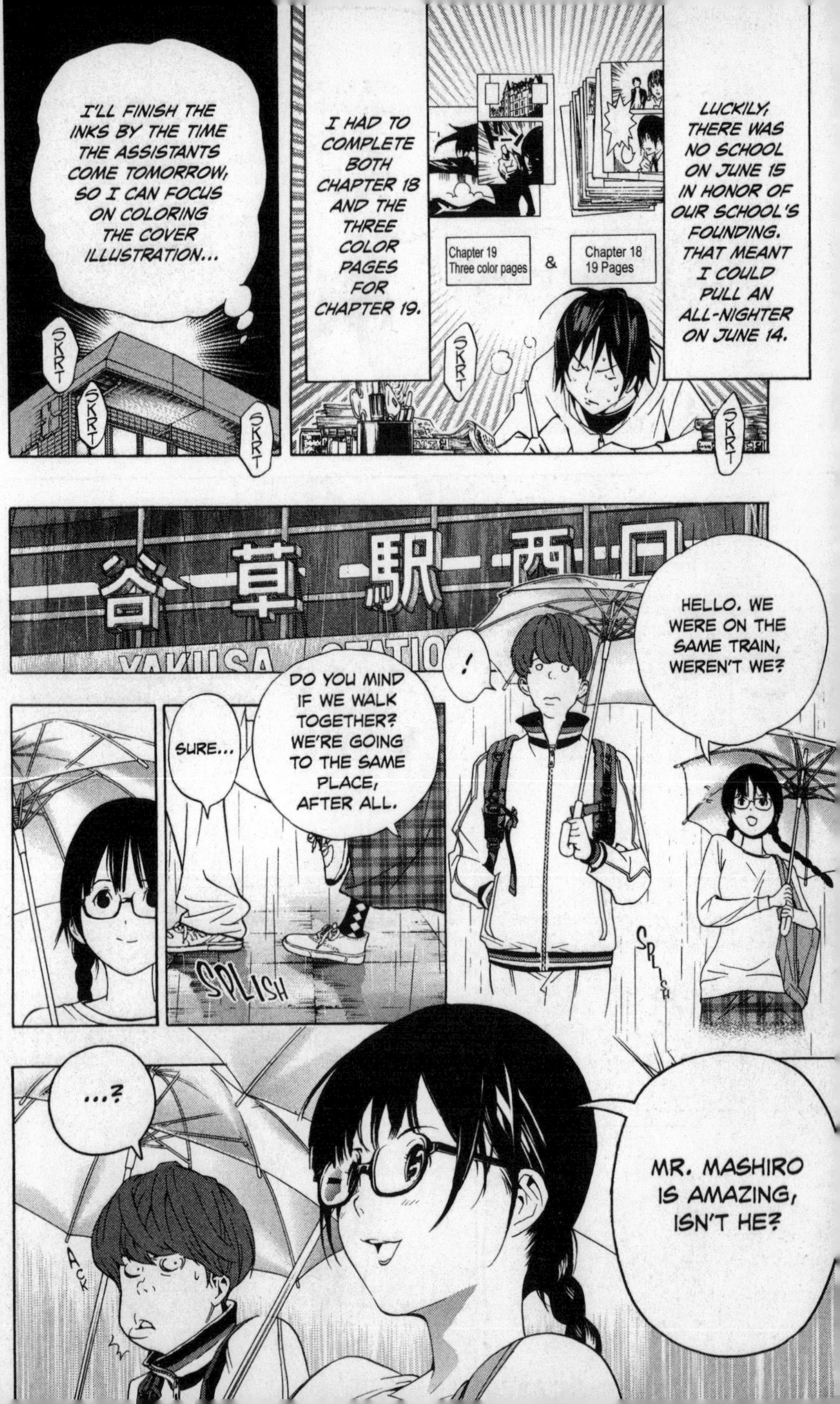

LUCKILY, THERE WAS NO SCHOOL ON JUNE 15 IN HONOR OF OUR SCHOOL'S FOUNDING. THAT MEANT I COULD PULL AN ALL-NIGHTER ON JUNE 14.
I HAD TO COMPLETE BOTH CHAPTER 18 AND THE THREE COLOR PAGES FOR CHAPTER 19.
Chapter 18 19 Pages
&
Chapter 19 Three color pages
SKRT
SKRT
I'LL FINISH THE INKS BY THE TIME THE ASSISTANTS COME TOMORROW, SO I CAN FOCUS ON COLORING THE COVER ILLUSTRATION...
SKRT
SKRT
SKRT
谷草駅西口
HELLO. WE WERE ON THE SAME TRAIN, WEREN'T WE?
!
SPLISH
DO YOU MIND IF WE WALK TOGETHER? WE'RE GOING TO THE SAME PLACE, AFTER ALL.
SURE...
SPLISH
MR. MASHIRO IS AMAZING, ISN'T HE?
...?
ACK

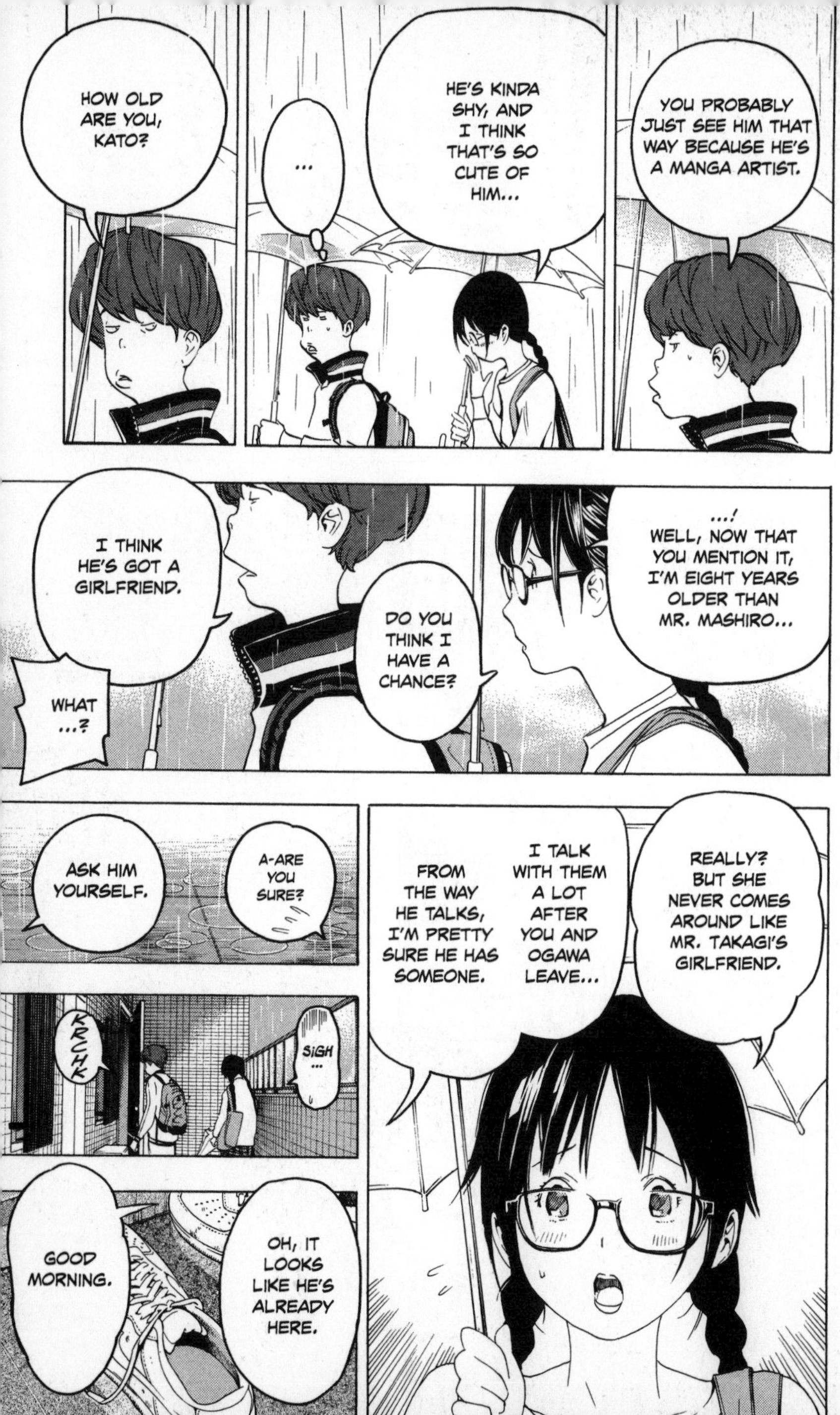
YOU PROBABLY JUST SEE HIM THAT WAY BECAUSE HE'S A MANGA ARTIST.
HE'S KINDA SHY, AND I THINK THAT'S SO CUTE OF HIM...
...
HOW OLD ARE YOU, KATO?
...! WELL, NOW THAT YOU MENTION IT, I'M EIGHT YEARS OLDER THAN MR. MASHIRO...
DO YOU THINK I HAVE A CHANCE?
I THINK HE'S GOT A GIRLFRIEND.
WHAT ...?
REALLY? BUT SHE NEVER COMES AROUND LIKE MR. TAKAGI'S GIRLFRIEND.
I TALK WITH THEM A LOT AFTER YOU AND OGAWA LEAVE...
FROM THE WAY HE TALKS, I'M PRETTY SURE HE HAS SOMEONE.
A-ARE YOU SURE?
ASK HIM YOURSELF.
SIGH...
KRCHK
OH, IT LOOKS LIKE HE'S ALREADY HERE.
GOOD MORNING.

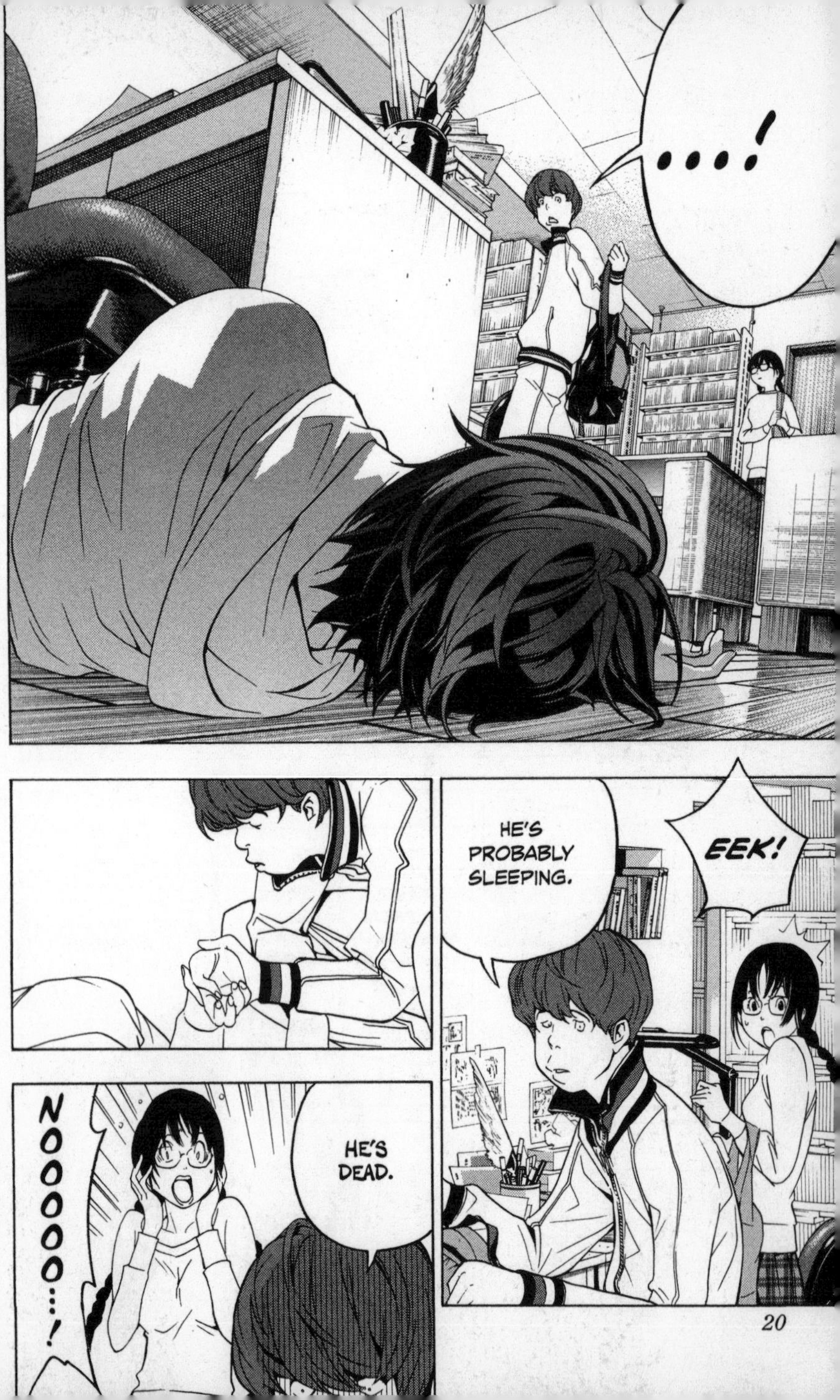

...!
EEK!
HE'S PROBABLY SLEEPING.
HE'S DEAD.
NOOOOOO...!

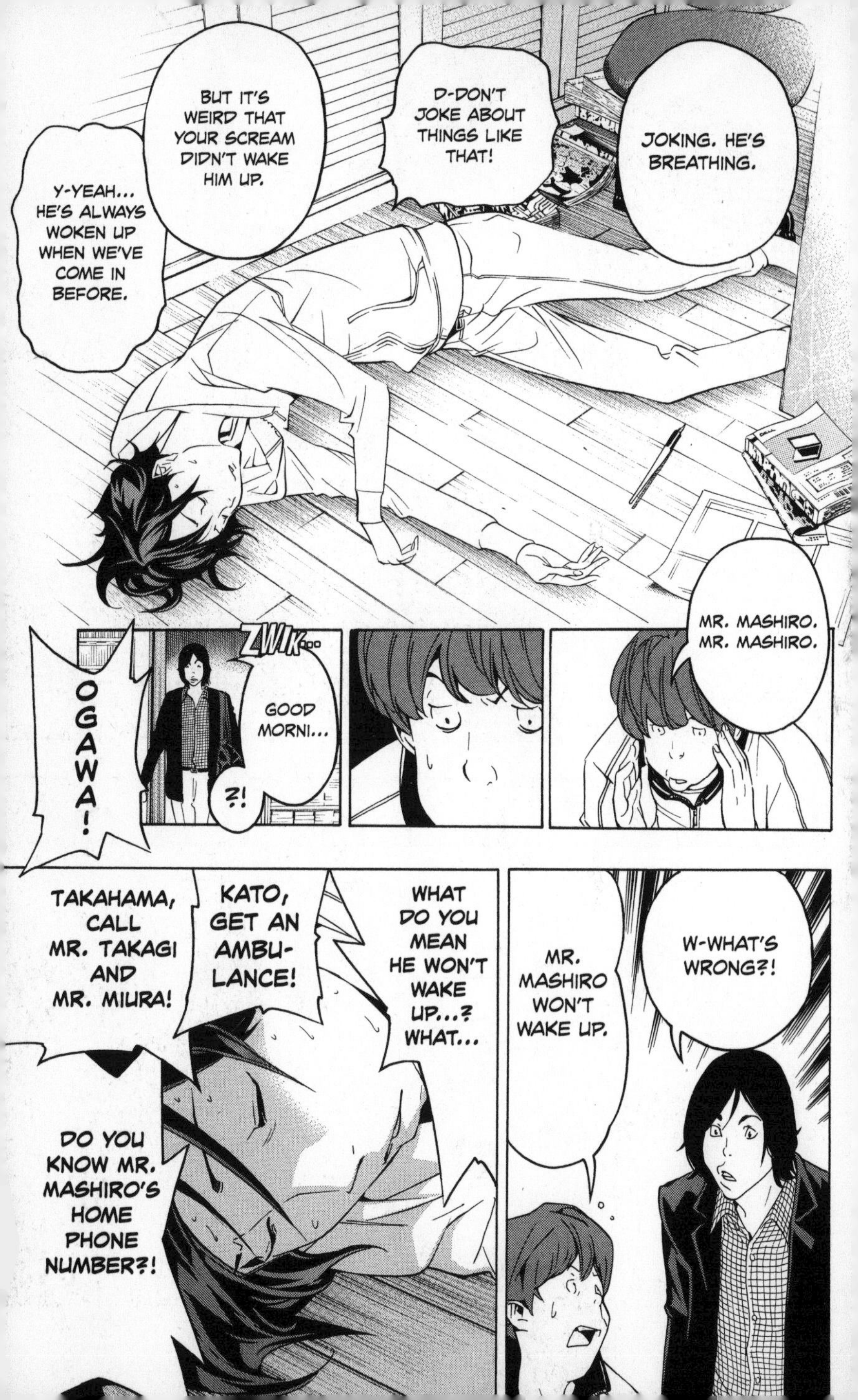
JOKING. HE'S BREATHING.
D-DON'T JOKE ABOUT THINGS LIKE THAT!
BUT IT'S WEIRD THAT YOUR SCREAM DIDN'T WAKE HIM UP.
Y-YEAH... HE'S ALWAYS WOKEN UP WHEN WE'VE COME IN BEFORE.
MR. MASHIRO. MR. MASHIRO.
ZWIK...
GOOD MORNI...
?!
OGAWA!
W-WHAT'S WRONG?!
MR. MASHIRO WON'T WAKE UP.
WHAT DO YOU MEAN HE WON'T WAKE UP...? WHAT...
KATO, GET AN AMBULANCE!
TAKAHAMA, CALL MR. TAKAGI AND MR. MIURA!
DO YOU KNOW MR. MASHIRO'S HOME PHONE NUMBER?!

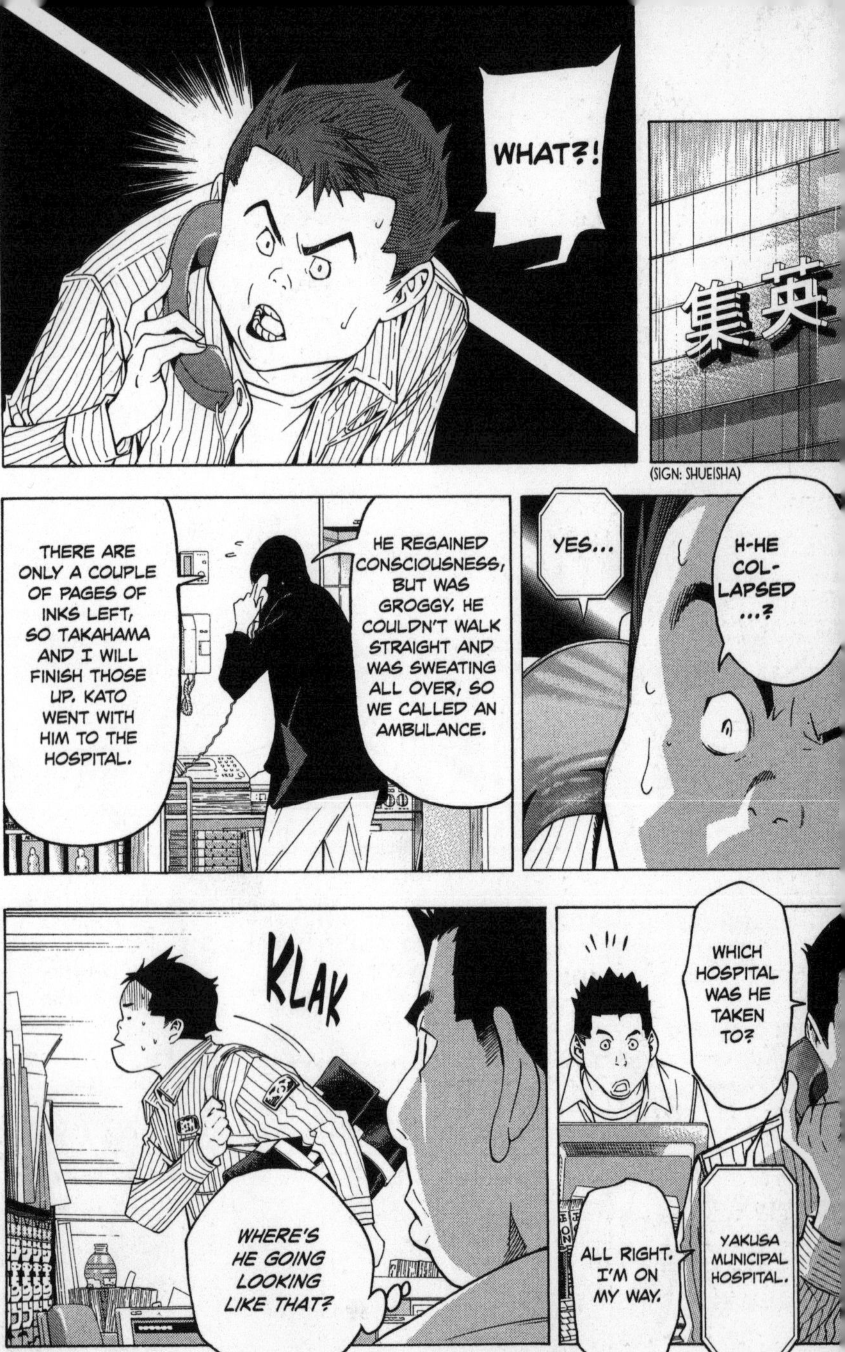
集英
(SIGN: SHUEISHA)
WHAT?!
H-HE COL-LAPSED...?
YES...
HE REGAINED CONSCIOUSNESS, BUT WAS GROGGY. HE COULDN'T WALK STRAIGHT AND WAS SWEATING ALL OVER, SO WE CALLED AN AMBULANCE.
THERE ARE ONLY A COUPLE OF PAGES OF INKS LEFT, SO TAKAHAMA AND I WILL FINISH THOSE UP. KATO WENT WITH HIM TO THE HOSPITAL.
WHICH HOSPITAL WAS HE TAKEN TO?
YAKUSA MUNICIPAL HOSPITAL.
ALL RIGHT. I'M ON MY WAY.
KLAK
WHERE'S HE GOING LOOKING LIKE THAT?

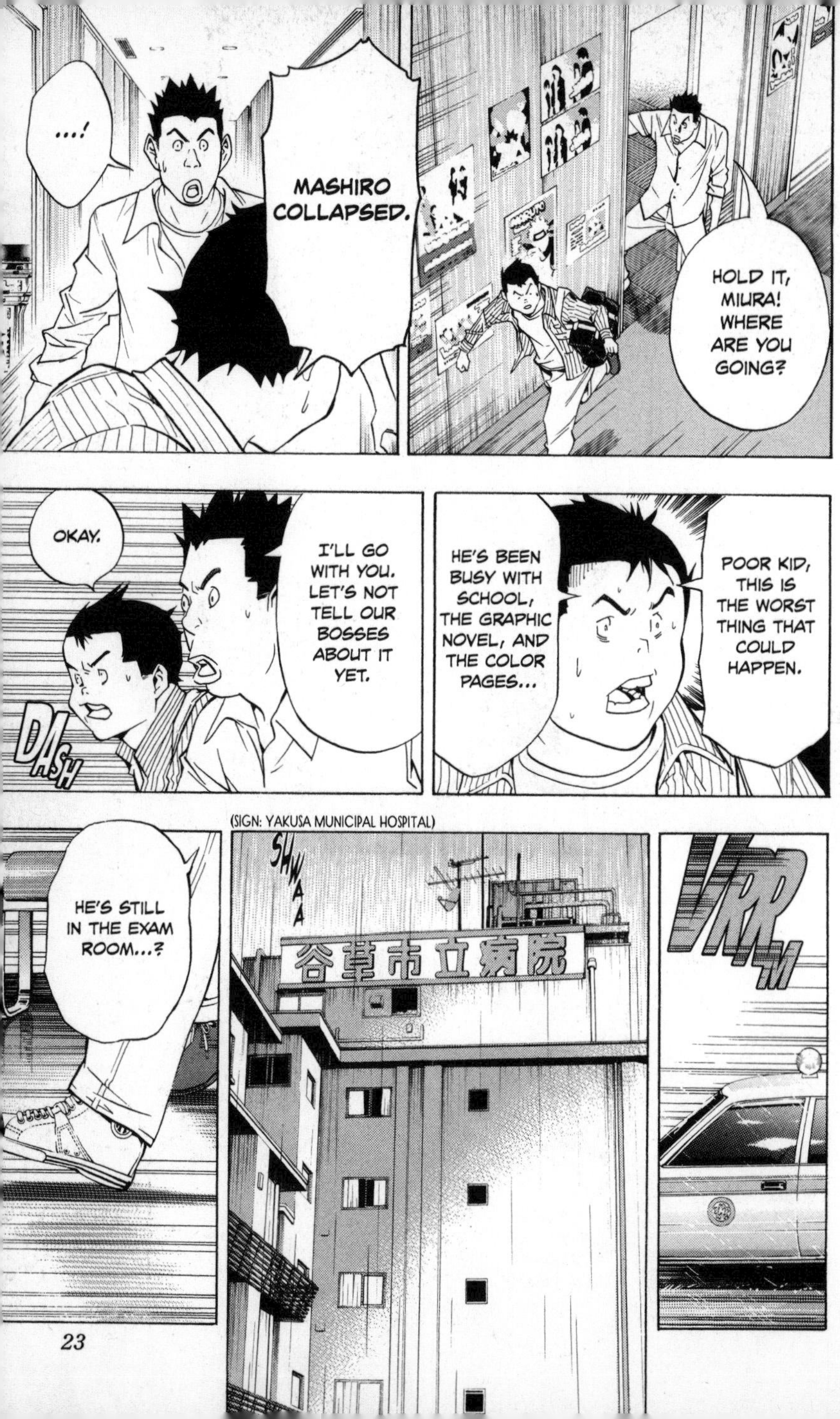
HOLD IT, MIURA! WHERE ARE YOU GOING?
MASHIRO COLLAPSED.
...!
POOR KID, THIS IS THE WORST THING THAT COULD HAPPEN.
HE'S BEEN BUSY WITH SCHOOL, THE GRAPHIC NOVEL, AND THE COLOR PAGES...
I'LL GO WITH YOU. LET'S NOT TELL OUR BOSSES ABOUT IT YET.
OKAY.
DASH
VRRM
(SIGN: YAKUSA MUNICIPAL HOSPITAL)
SHWAA
谷草市立病院
HE'S STILL IN THE EXAM ROOM...?

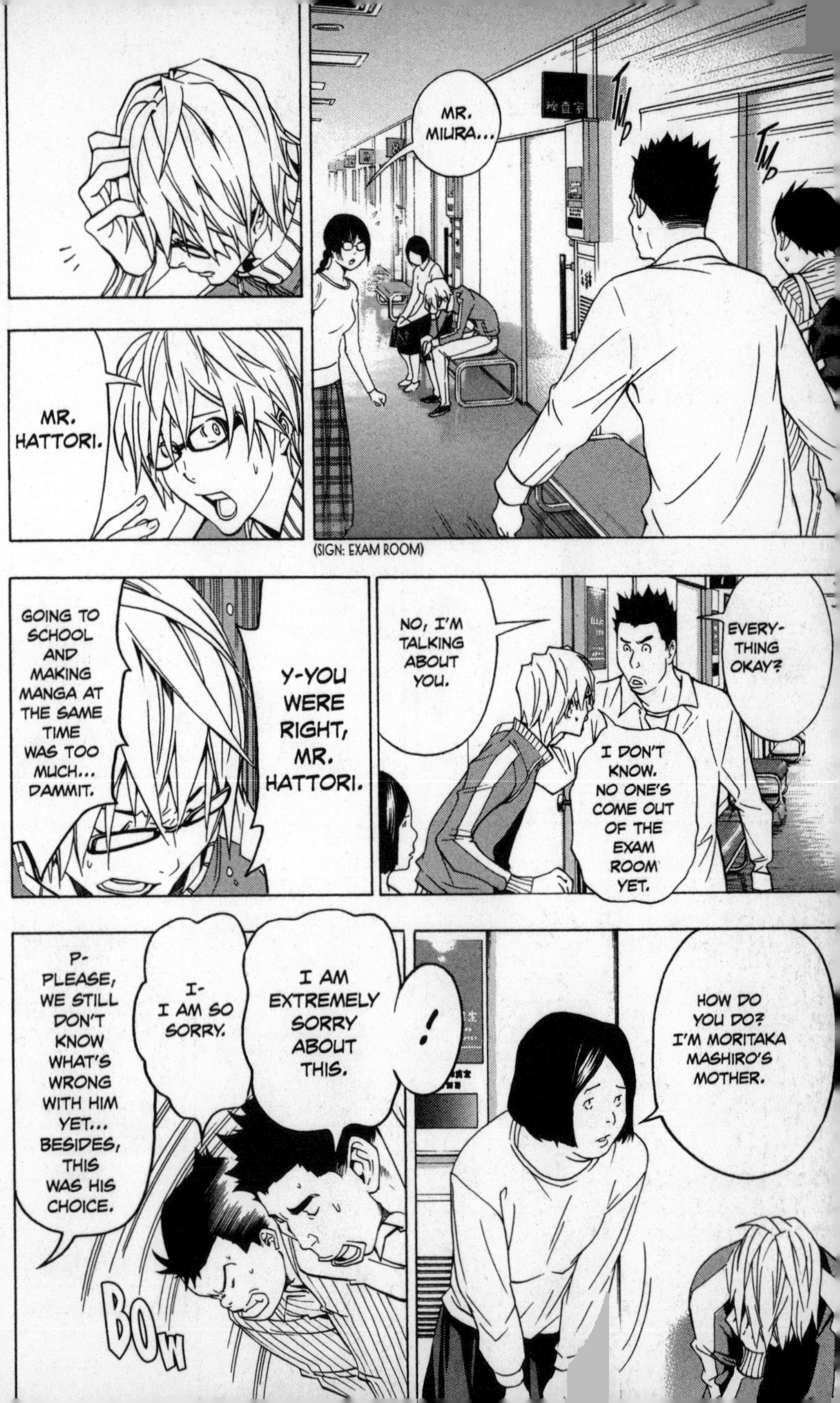
MR. MIURA...
TMP
TMP
MR. HATTORI.
EVERY-THING OKAY?
NO, I'M TALKING ABOUT YOU.
I DON'T KNOW. NO ONE'S COME OUT OF THE EXAM ROOM YET.
Y-YOU WERE RIGHT, MR. HATTORI.
GOING TO SCHOOL AND MAKING MANGA AT THE SAME TIME WAS TOO MUCH... DAMMIT.
HOW DO YOU DO? I'M MORITAKA MASHIRO'S MOTHER.
!
I AM EXTREMELY SORRY ABOUT THIS.
I- I AM SO SORRY.
P-PLEASE, WE STILL DON'T KNOW WHAT'S WRONG WITH HIM YET... BESIDES, THIS WAS HIS CHOICE.
BOW
(SIGN: EXAM ROOM)

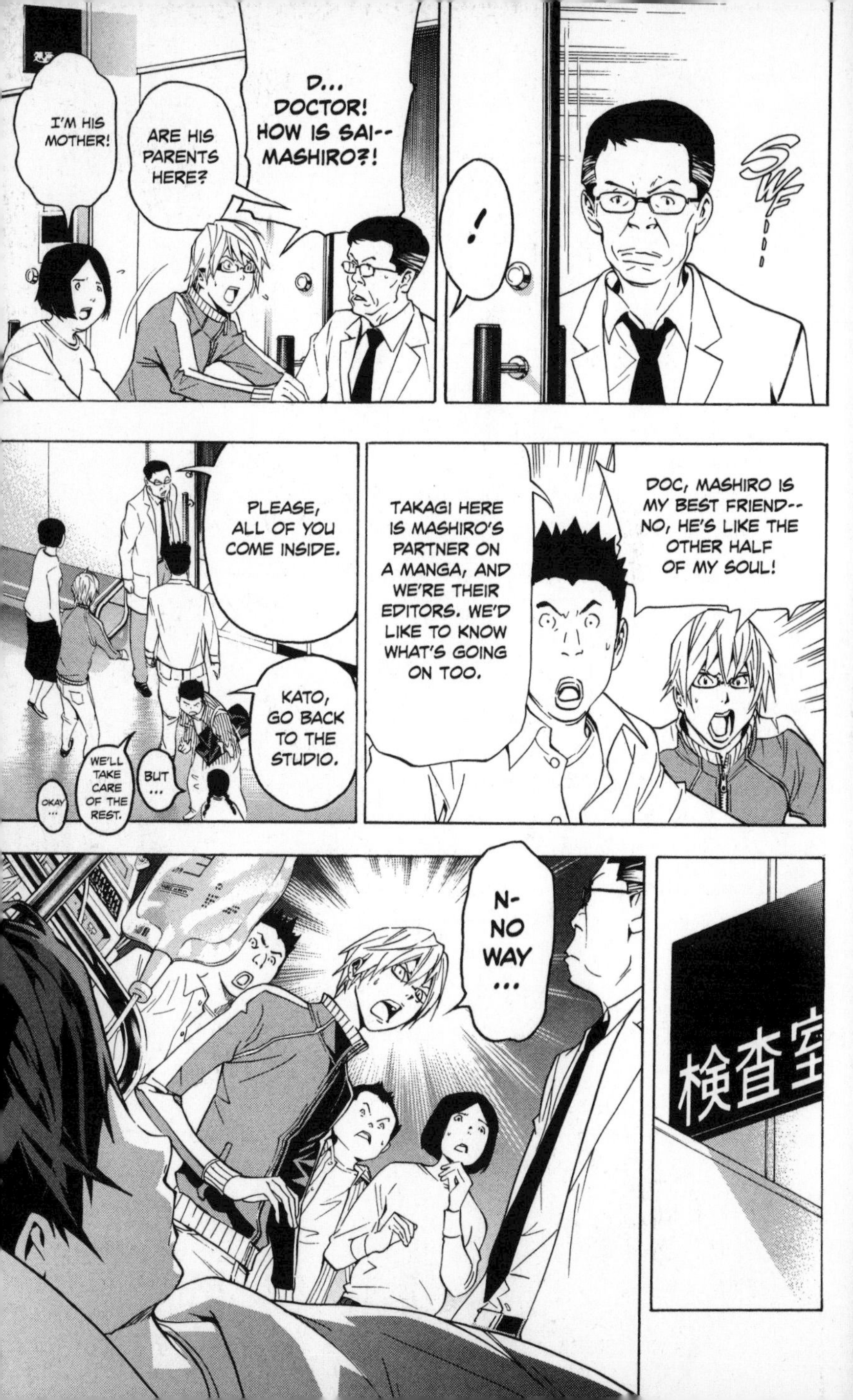
SWF
!
D... DOCTOR! HOW IS SAI-- MASHIRO?!
ARE HIS PARENTS HERE?
I'M HIS MOTHER!
DOC, MASHIRO IS MY BEST FRIEND-- NO, HE'S LIKE THE OTHER HALF OF MY SOUL!
TAKAGI HERE IS MASHIRO'S PARTNER ON A MANGA, AND WE'RE THEIR EDITORS. WE'D LIKE TO KNOW WHAT'S GOING ON TOO.
PLEASE, ALL OF YOU COME INSIDE.
KATO, GO BACK TO THE STUDIO.
BUT ...
WE'LL TAKE CARE OF THE REST.
OKAY ...
検査室
N- NO WAY ...

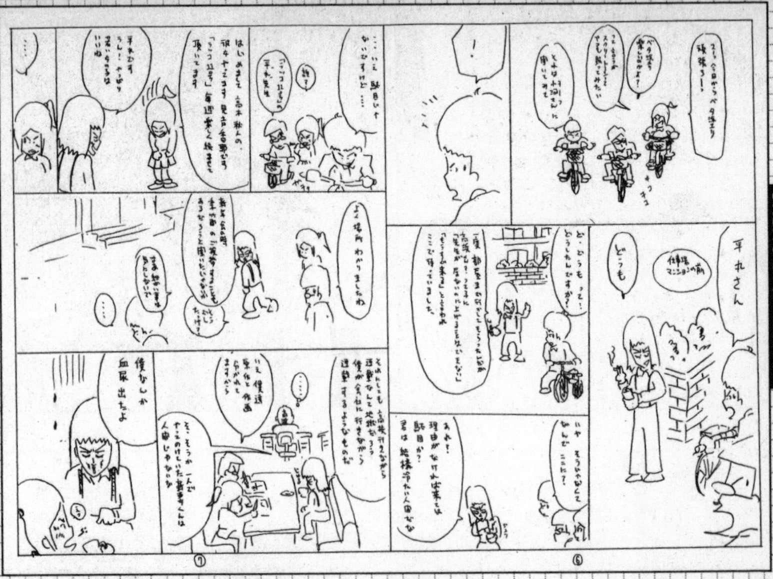

OHBA'S STORYBOARD

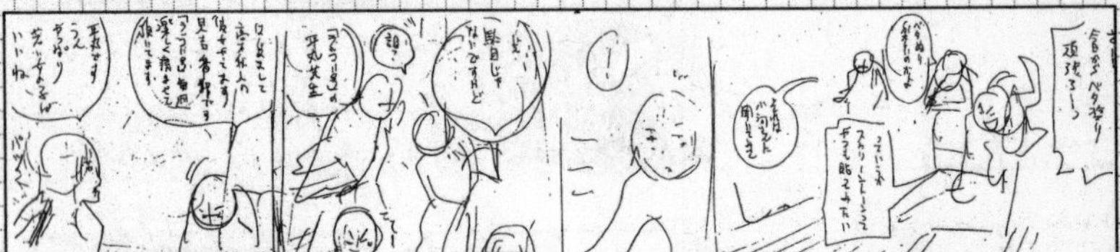

OBATA'S STORYBOARD

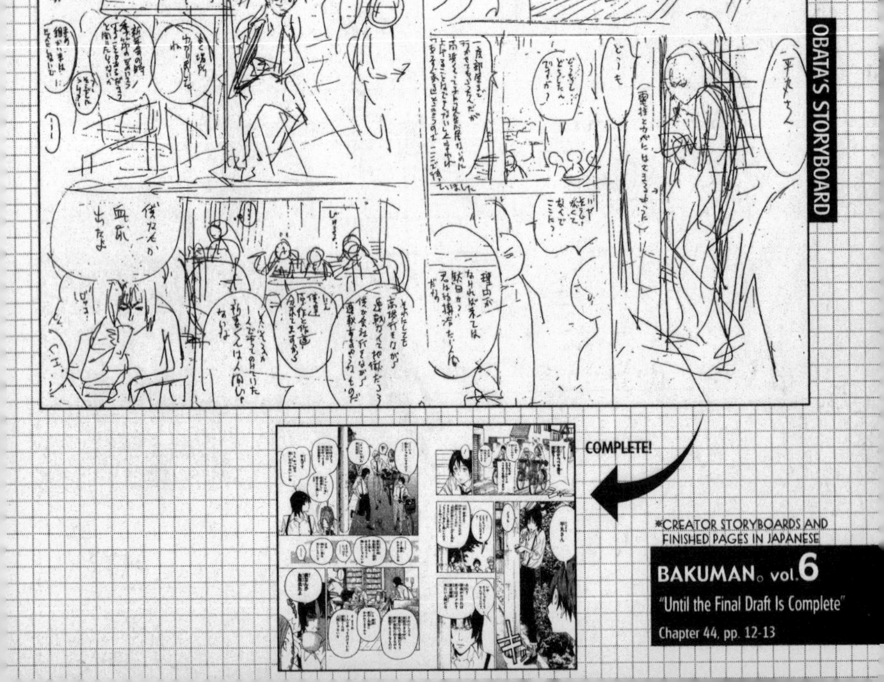

COMPLETE!

*CREATOR STORYBOARDS AND FINISHED PAGES IN JAPANESE

BAKUMAN。 vol.6

"Until the Final Draft Is Complete"

Chapter 44, pp. 12-13

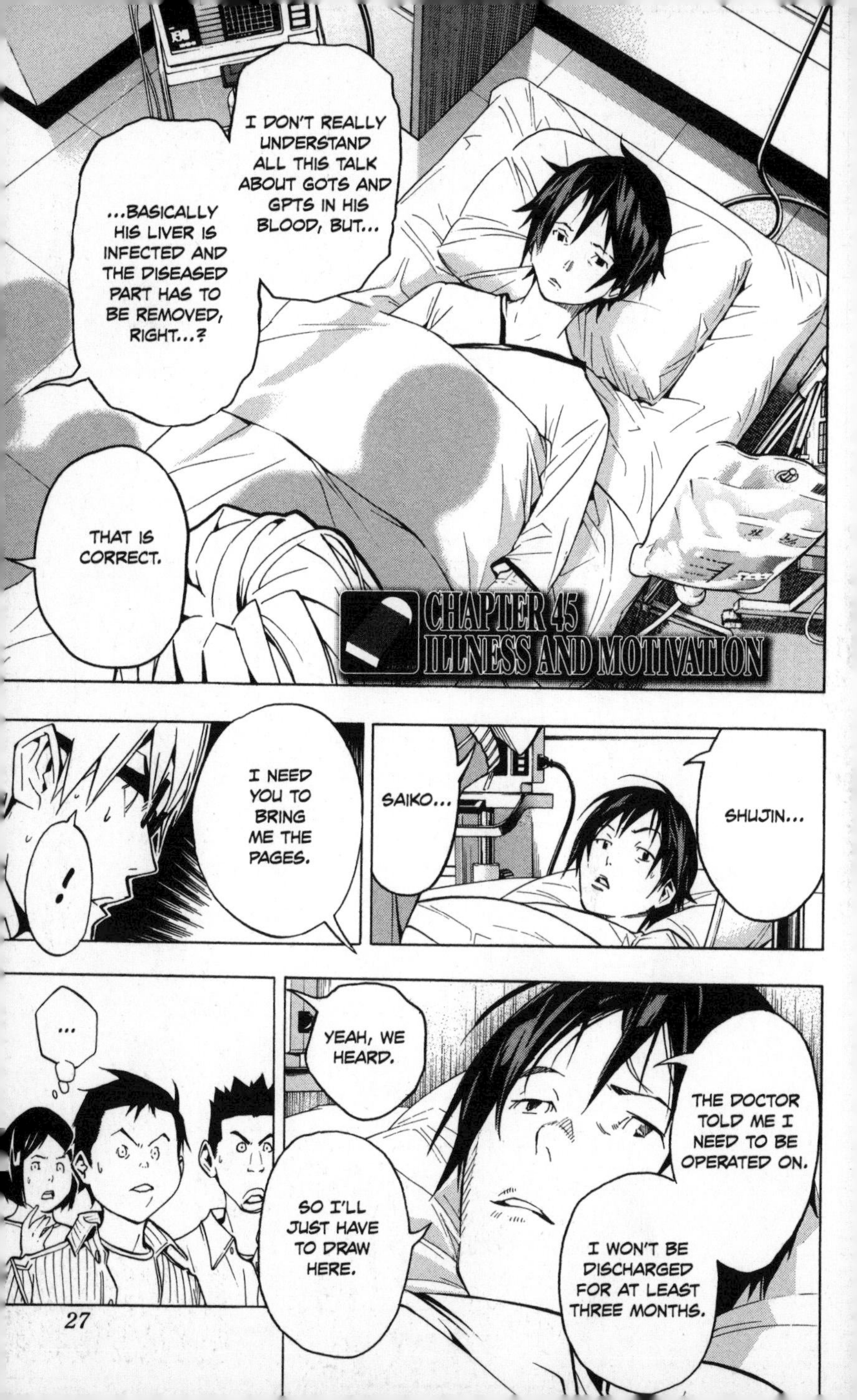
I DON'T REALLY UNDERSTAND ALL THIS TALK ABOUT GOTS AND GPTS IN HIS BLOOD, BUT...
...BASICALLY HIS LIVER IS INFECTED AND THE DISEASED PART HAS TO BE REMOVED, RIGHT...?
THAT IS CORRECT.
CHAPTER 45
ILLNESS AND MOTIVATION
SHUJIN...
SAIKO...
I NEED YOU TO BRING ME THE PAGES.
!
THE DOCTOR TOLD ME I NEED TO BE OPERATED ON.
I WON'T BE DISCHARGED FOR AT LEAST THREE MONTHS.
YEAH, WE HEARD.
SO I'LL JUST HAVE TO DRAW HERE.
...

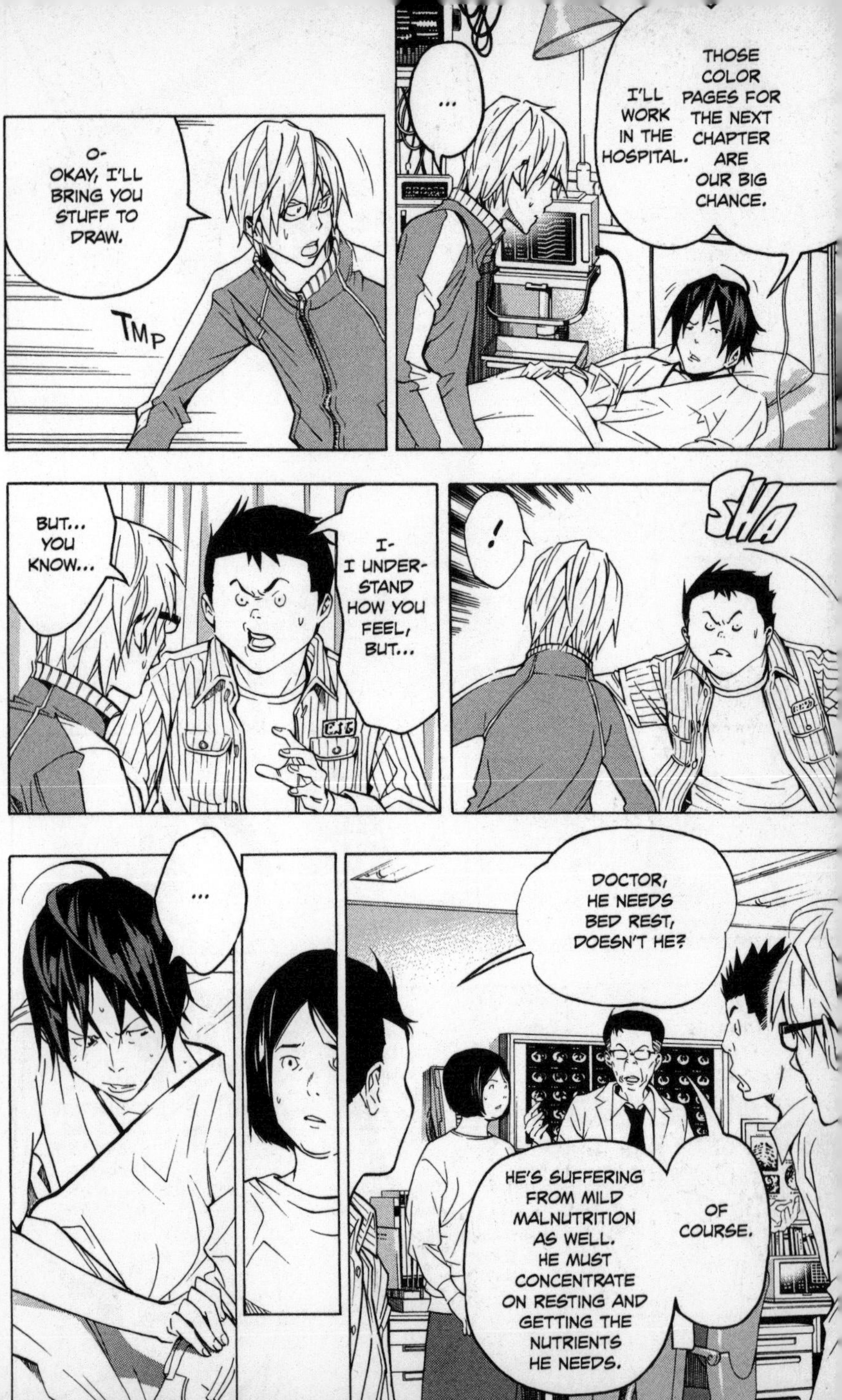
THOSE COLOR PAGES FOR THE NEXT CHAPTER ARE OUR BIG CHANCE.
I'LL WORK IN THE HOSPITAL.
...
O- OKAY, I'LL BRING YOU STUFF TO DRAW.
TMP
SHA
!
I- I UNDER-STAND HOW YOU FEEL, BUT...
BUT... YOU KNOW...
DOCTOR, HE NEEDS BED REST, DOESN'T HE?
OF COURSE.
HE'S SUFFERING FROM MILD MALNUTRITION AS WELL. HE MUST CONCENTRATE ON RESTING AND GETTING THE NUTRIENTS HE NEEDS.
...

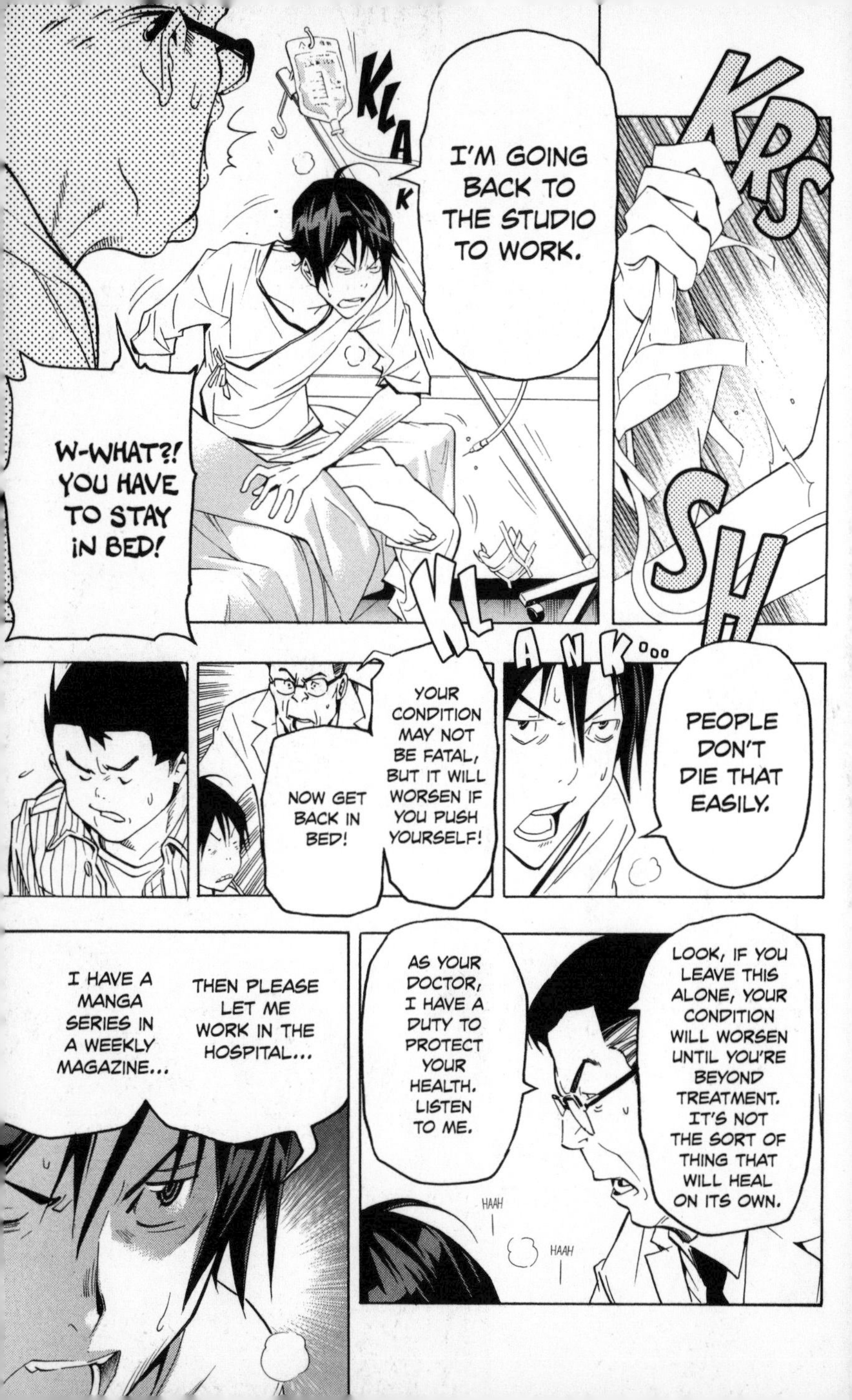
KRS
SH
KLAK
I'M GOING BACK TO THE STUDIO TO WORK.
W-WHAT?! YOU HAVE TO STAY iN BED!
KLANK...
PEOPLE DON'T DIE THAT EASILY.
YOUR CONDITION MAY NOT BE FATAL, BUT IT WILL WORSEN IF YOU PUSH YOURSELF!
NOW GET BACK IN BED!
LOOK, IF YOU LEAVE THIS ALONE, YOUR CONDITION WILL WORSEN UNTIL YOU'RE BEYOND TREATMENT. IT'S NOT THE SORT OF THING THAT WILL HEAL ON ITS OWN.
AS YOUR DOCTOR, I HAVE A DUTY TO PROTECT YOUR HEALTH. LISTEN TO ME.
HAAH
HAAH
THEN PLEASE LET ME WORK IN THE HOSPITAL...
I HAVE A MANGA SERIES IN A WEEKLY MAGAZINE...

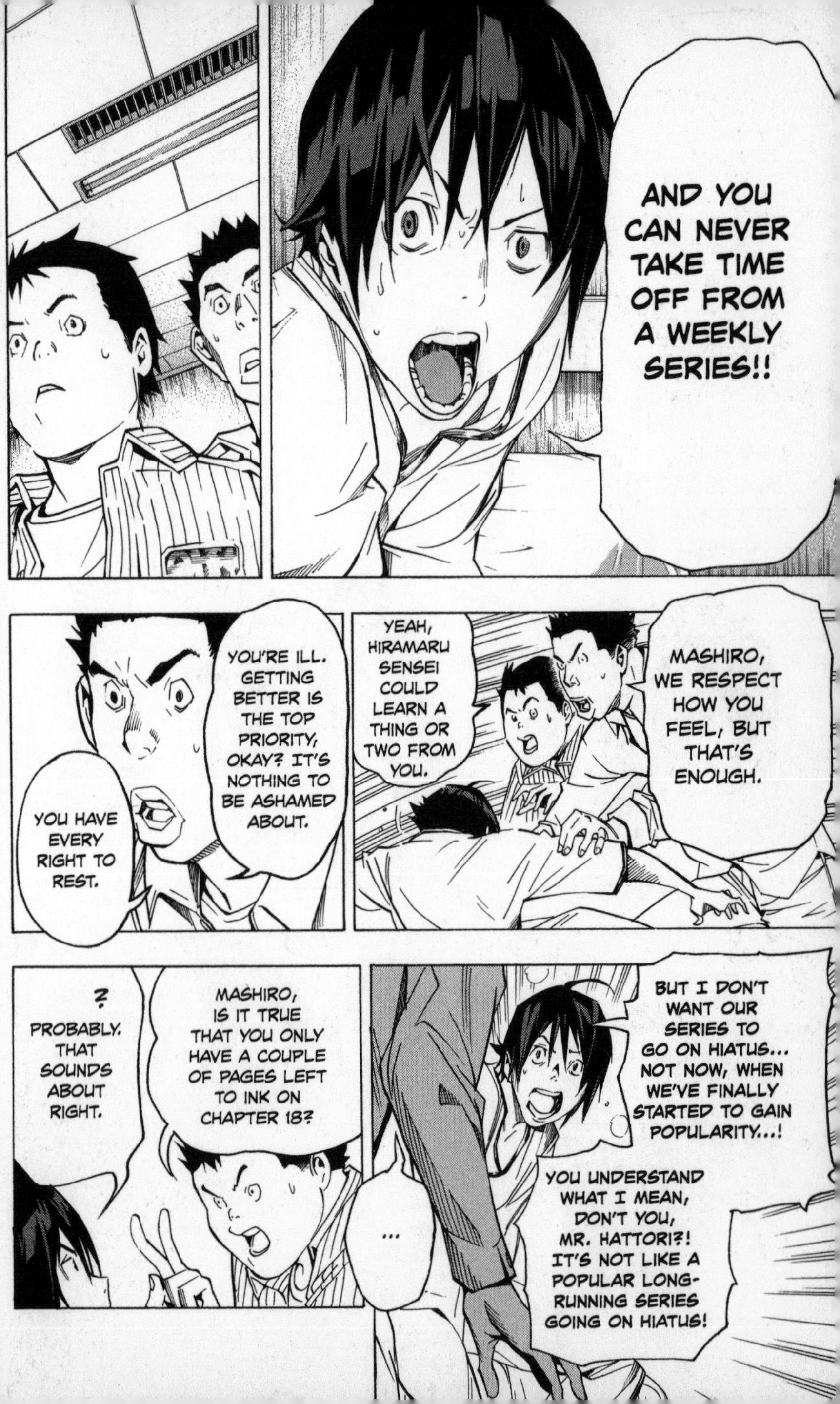
AND YOU CAN NEVER TAKE TIME OFF FROM A WEEKLY SERIES!!
MASHIRO, WE RESPECT HOW YOU FEEL, BUT THAT'S ENOUGH.
YEAH, HIRAMARU SENSEI COULD LEARN A THING OR TWO FROM YOU.
YOU'RE ILL. GETTING BETTER IS THE TOP PRIORITY, OKAY? IT'S NOTHING TO BE ASHAMED ABOUT.
YOU HAVE EVERY RIGHT TO REST.
BUT I DON'T WANT OUR SERIES TO GO ON HIATUS... NOT NOW, WHEN WE'VE FINALLY STARTED TO GAIN POPULARITY...!
YOU UNDERSTAND WHAT I MEAN, DON'T YOU, MR. HATTORI?! IT'S NOT LIKE A POPULAR LONG-RUNNING SERIES GOING ON HIATUS!
...
MASHIRO, IS IT TRUE THAT YOU ONLY HAVE A COUPLE OF PAGES LEFT TO INK ON CHAPTER 18?
? PROBABLY. THAT SOUNDS ABOUT RIGHT.

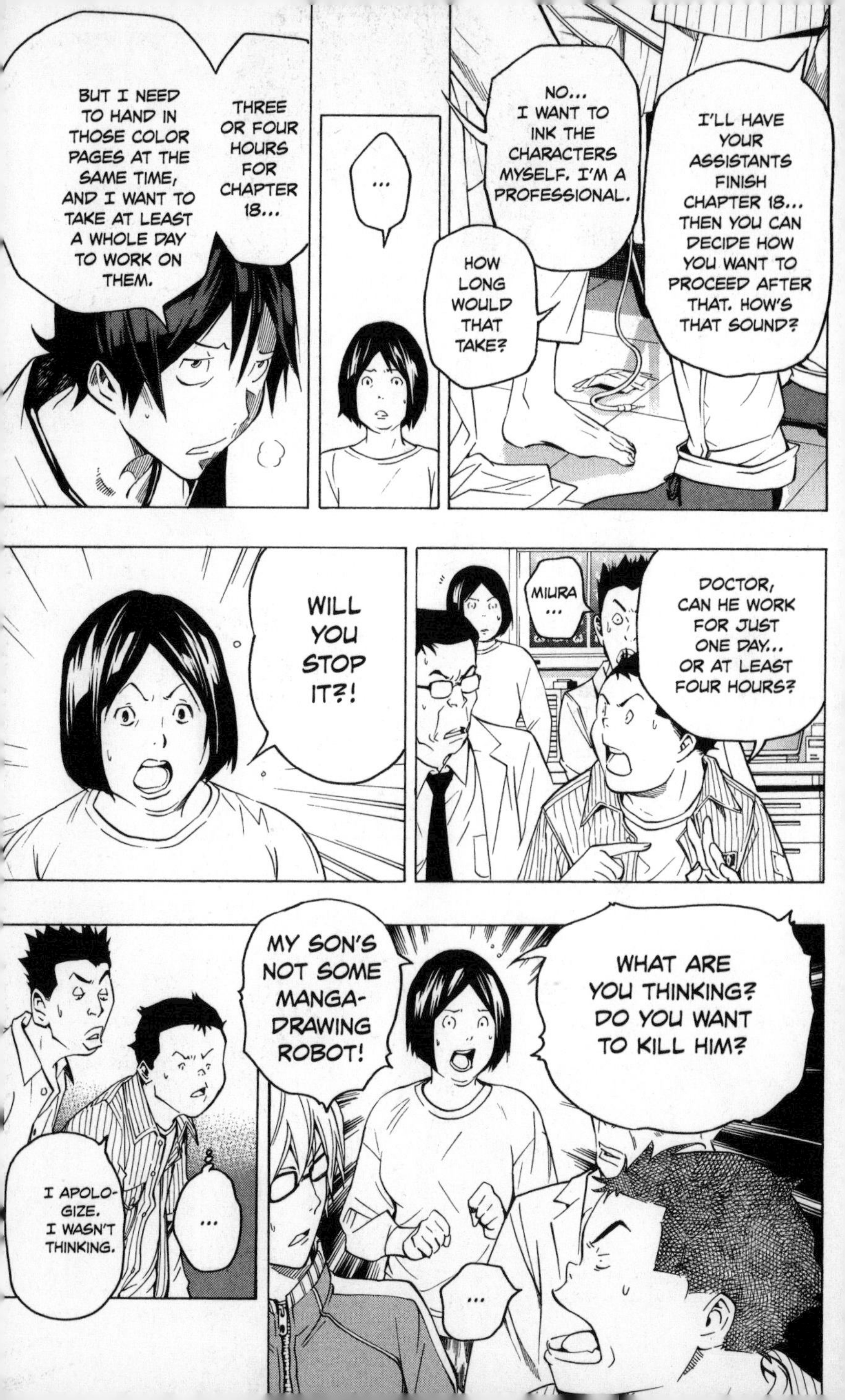
I'LL HAVE YOUR ASSISTANTS FINISH CHAPTER 18... THEN YOU CAN DECIDE HOW YOU WANT TO PROCEED AFTER THAT. HOW'S THAT SOUND?
NO... I WANT TO INK THE CHARACTERS MYSELF. I'M A PROFESSIONAL.
HOW LONG WOULD THAT TAKE?
...
THREE OR FOUR HOURS FOR CHAPTER 18...
BUT I NEED TO HAND IN THOSE COLOR PAGES AT THE SAME TIME, AND I WANT TO TAKE AT LEAST A WHOLE DAY TO WORK ON THEM.
DOCTOR, CAN HE WORK FOR JUST ONE DAY... OR AT LEAST FOUR HOURS?
MIURA ...
WILL YOU STOP IT?!
WHAT ARE YOU THINKING? DO YOU WANT TO KILL HIM?
MY SON'S NOT SOME MANGA-DRAWING ROBOT!
...
...
I APOLOGIZE. I WASN'T THINKING.

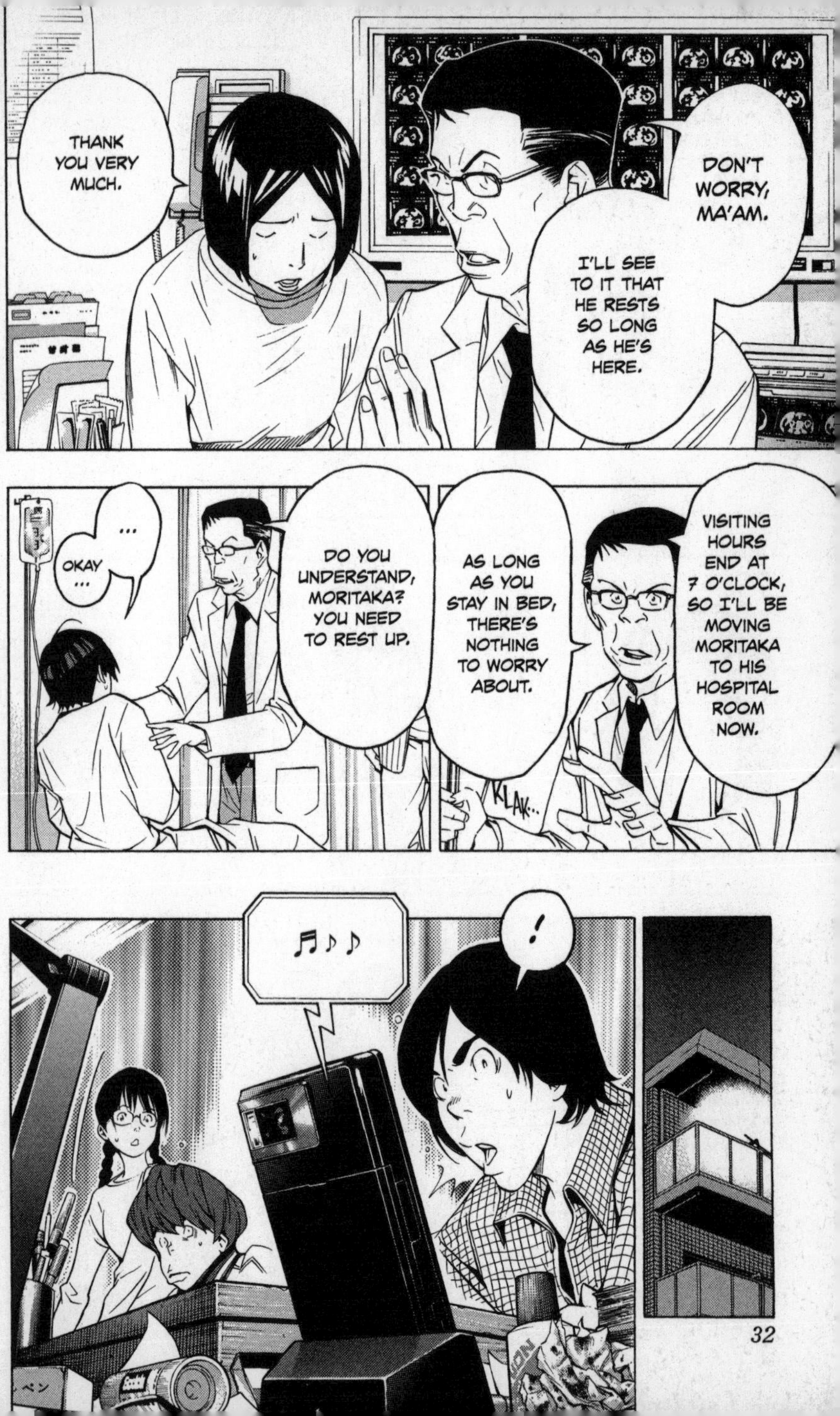
DON'T WORRY, MA'AM.
I'LL SEE TO IT THAT HE RESTS SO LONG AS HE'S HERE.
THANK YOU VERY MUCH.
VISITING HOURS END AT 7 O'CLOCK, SO I'LL BE MOVING MORITAKA TO HIS HOSPITAL ROOM NOW.
AS LONG AS YOU STAY IN BED, THERE'S NOTHING TO WORRY ABOUT.
KLAK...
DO YOU UNDERSTAND, MORITAKA? YOU NEED TO REST UP.
... OKAY ...
!
♬♪♪

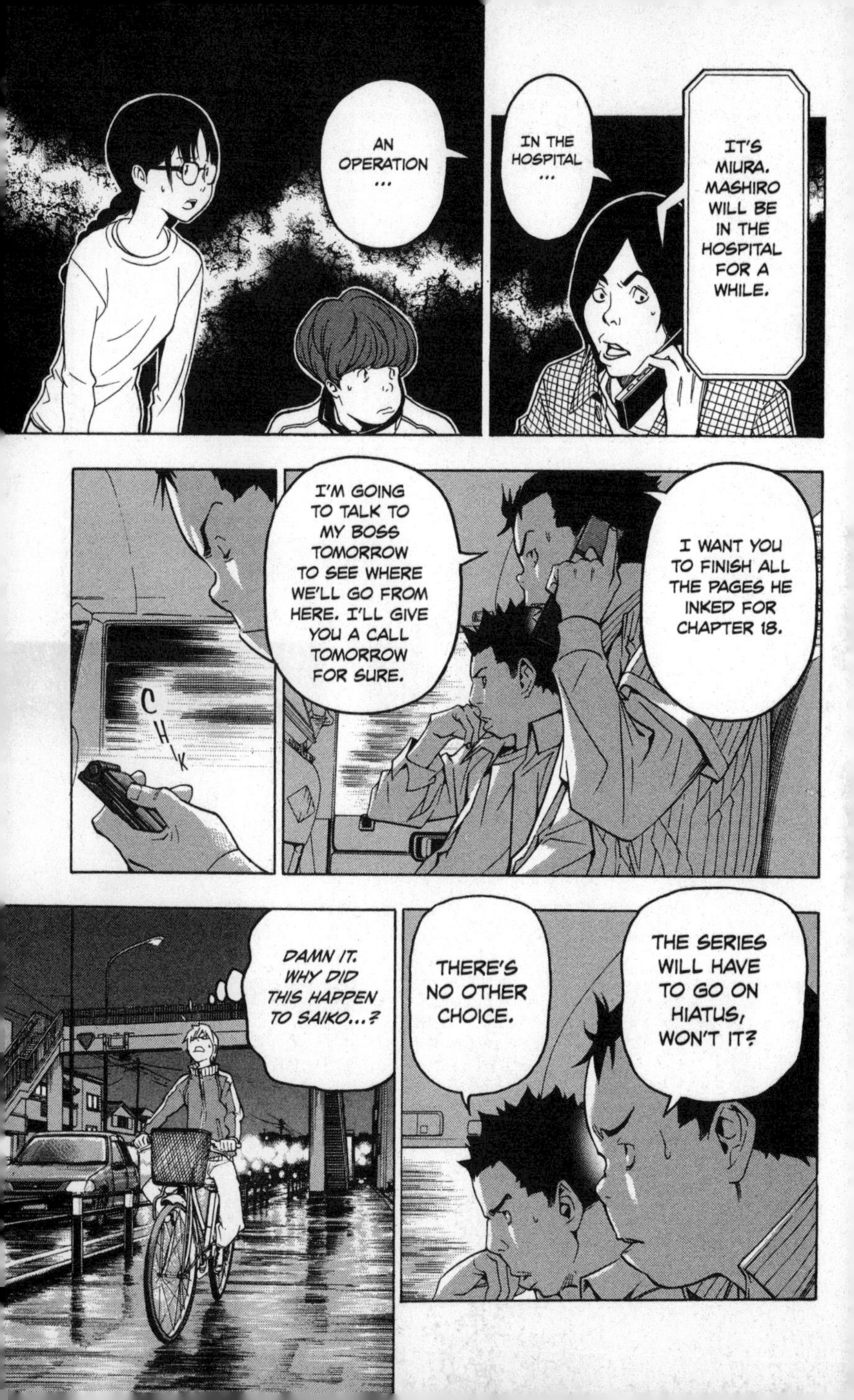
IT'S MIURA. MASHIRO WILL BE IN THE HOSPITAL FOR A WHILE.
IN THE HOSPITAL ...
AN OPERATION ...
I WANT YOU TO FINISH ALL THE PAGES HE INKED FOR CHAPTER 18.
I'M GOING TO TALK TO MY BOSS TOMORROW TO SEE WHERE WE'LL GO FROM HERE. I'LL GIVE YOU A CALL TOMORROW FOR SURE.
CHK
THE SERIES WILL HAVE TO GO ON HIATUS, WON'T IT?
THERE'S NO OTHER CHOICE.
DAMN IT. WHY DID THIS HAPPEN TO SAIKO...?

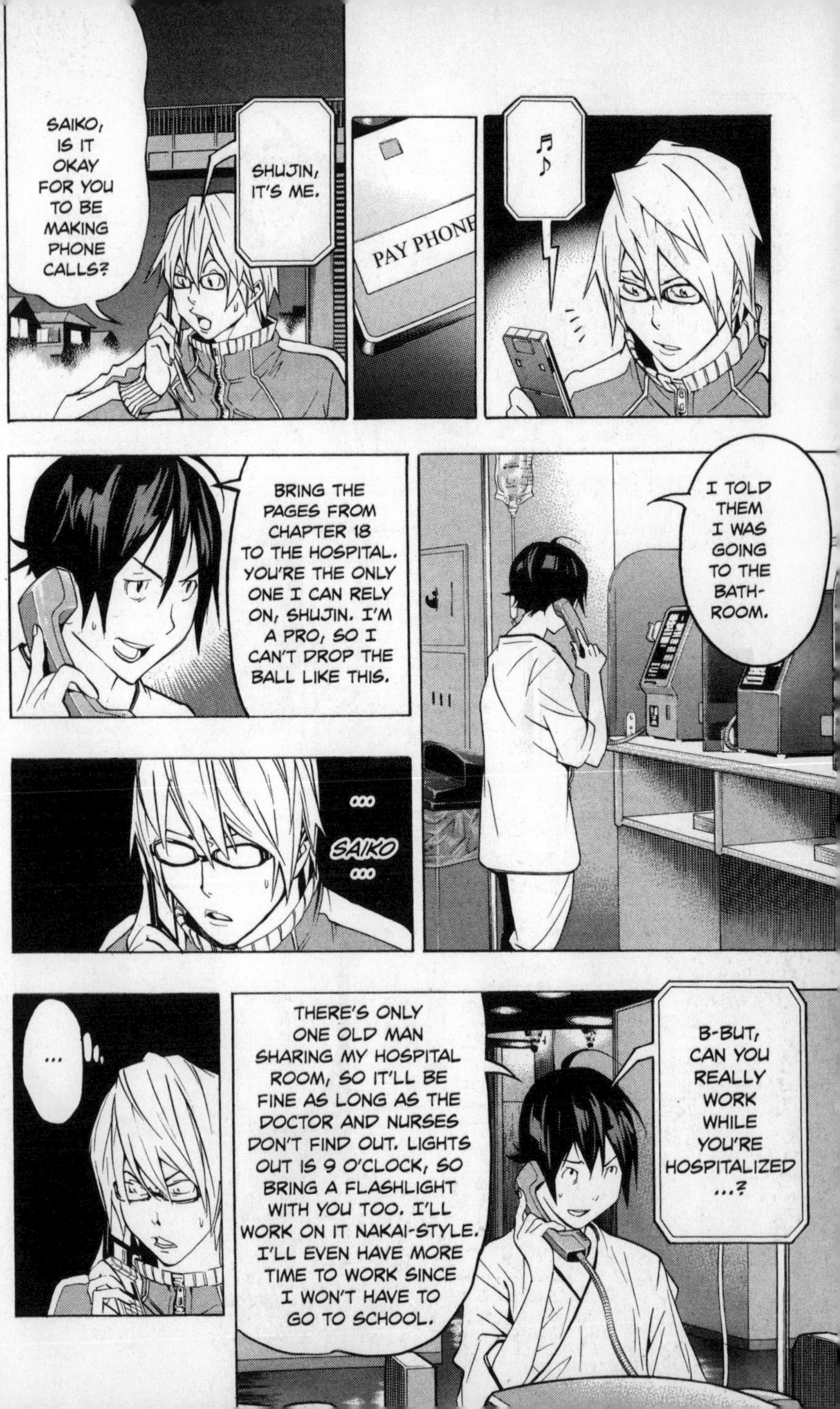
♬ ♪
PAY PHONE
SHUJIN, IT'S ME.
SAIKO, IS IT OKAY FOR YOU TO BE MAKING PHONE CALLS?
I TOLD THEM I WAS GOING TO THE BATH-ROOM.
BRING THE PAGES FROM CHAPTER 18 TO THE HOSPITAL. YOU'RE THE ONLY ONE I CAN RELY ON, SHUJIN. I'M A PRO, SO I CAN'T DROP THE BALL LIKE THIS.
... SAIKO ...
B-BUT, CAN YOU REALLY WORK WHILE YOU'RE HOSPITALIZED ...?
THERE'S ONLY ONE OLD MAN SHARING MY HOSPITAL ROOM, SO IT'LL BE FINE AS LONG AS THE DOCTOR AND NURSES DON'T FIND OUT. LIGHTS OUT IS 9 O'CLOCK, SO BRING A FLASHLIGHT WITH YOU TOO. I'LL WORK ON IT NAKAI-STYLE. I'LL EVEN HAVE MORE TIME TO WORK SINCE I WON'T HAVE TO GO TO SCHOOL.
...

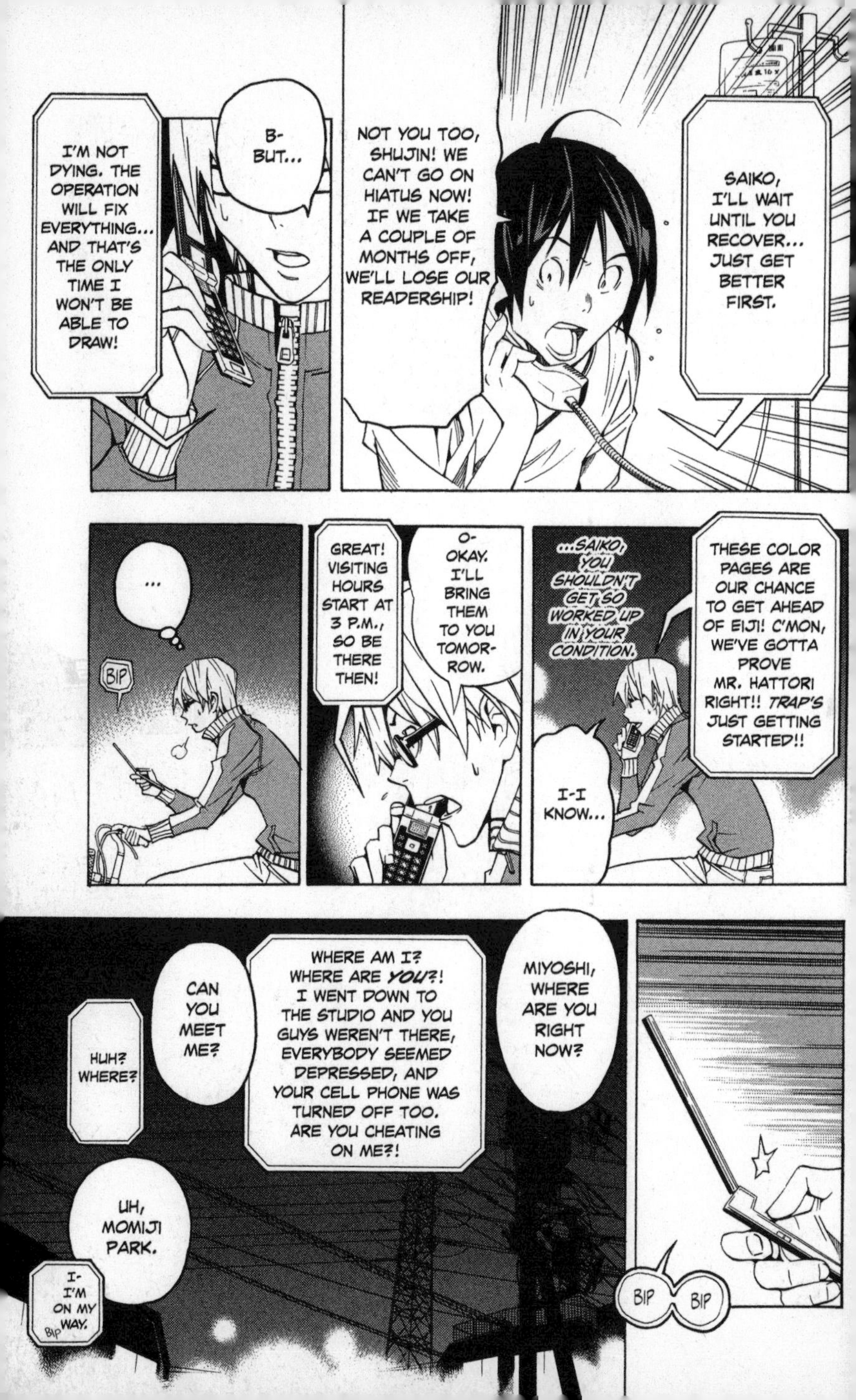
SAIKO, I'LL WAIT UNTIL YOU RECOVER... JUST GET BETTER FIRST.
NOT YOU TOO, SHUJIN! WE CAN'T GO ON HIATUS NOW! IF WE TAKE A COUPLE OF MONTHS OFF, WE'LL LOSE OUR READERSHIP!
B-BUT...
I'M NOT DYING. THE OPERATION WILL FIX EVERYTHING... AND THAT'S THE ONLY TIME I WON'T BE ABLE TO DRAW!
THESE COLOR PAGES ARE OUR CHANCE TO GET AHEAD OF EIJI! C'MON, WE'VE GOTTA PROVE MR. HATTORI RIGHT!! *TRAP'S* JUST GETTING STARTED!!
...SAIKO, YOU SHOULDN'T GET SO WORKED UP IN YOUR CONDITION.
I-I KNOW...
O-OKAY. I'LL BRING THEM TO YOU TOMORROW.
GREAT! VISITING HOURS START AT 3 P.M., SO BE THERE THEN!
...
BIP
BIP BIP
MIYOSHI, WHERE ARE YOU RIGHT NOW?
WHERE AM I? WHERE ARE *YOU*?! I WENT DOWN TO THE STUDIO AND YOU GUYS WEREN'T THERE, EVERYBODY SEEMED DEPRESSED, AND YOUR CELL PHONE WAS TURNED OFF TOO. ARE YOU CHEATING ON ME?!
CAN YOU MEET ME?
HUH? WHERE?
UH, MOMIJI PARK.
I-I'M ON MY WAY.
BIP

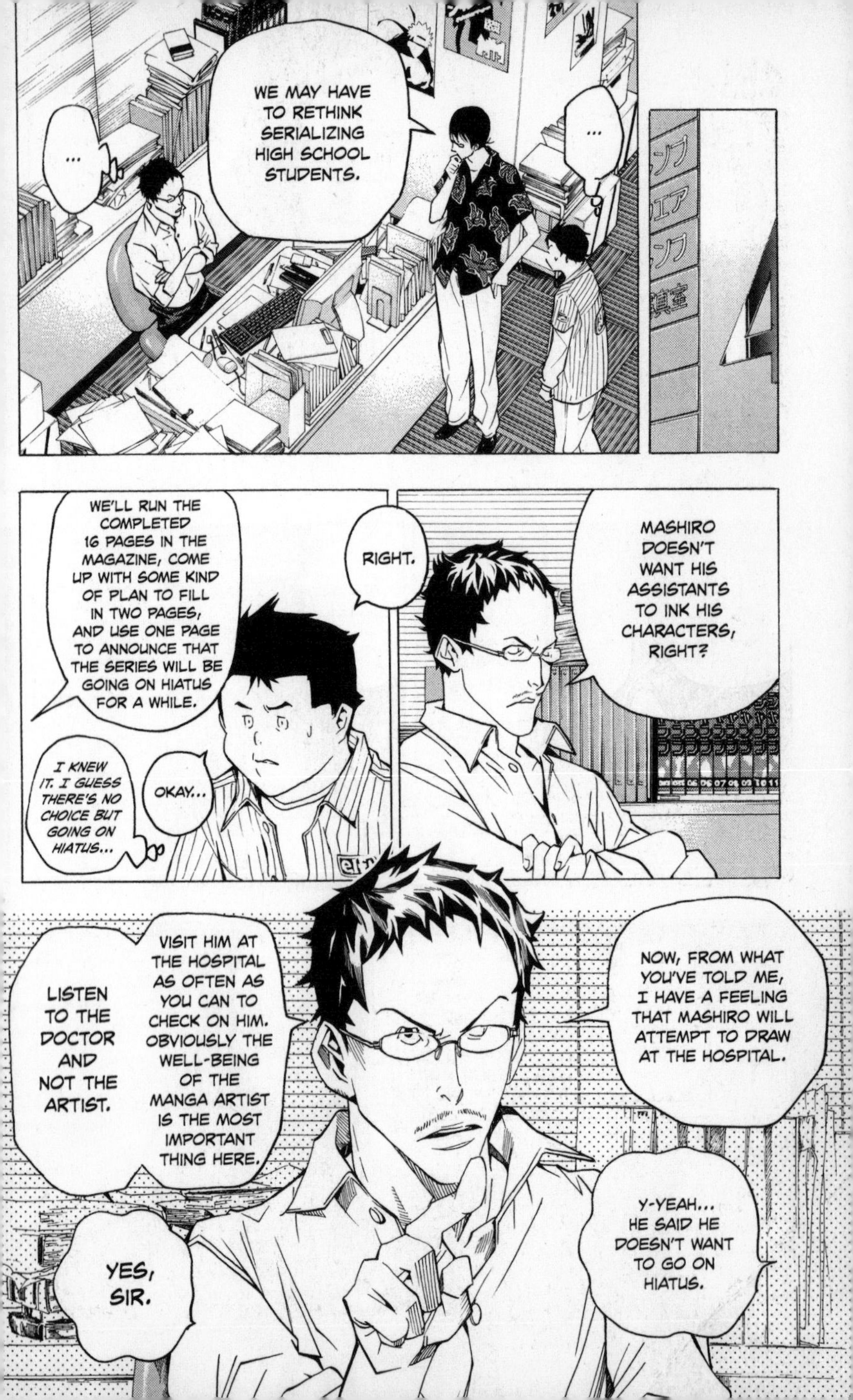
...
WE MAY HAVE TO RETHINK SERIALIZING HIGH SCHOOL STUDENTS.
...
MASHIRO DOESN'T WANT HIS ASSISTANTS TO INK HIS CHARACTERS, RIGHT?
RIGHT.
WE'LL RUN THE COMPLETED 16 PAGES IN THE MAGAZINE, COME UP WITH SOME KIND OF PLAN TO FILL IN TWO PAGES, AND USE ONE PAGE TO ANNOUNCE THAT THE SERIES WILL BE GOING ON HIATUS FOR A WHILE.
OKAY...
I KNEW IT. I GUESS THERE'S NO CHOICE BUT GOING ON HIATUS...
NOW, FROM WHAT YOU'VE TOLD ME, I HAVE A FEELING THAT MASHIRO WILL ATTEMPT TO DRAW AT THE HOSPITAL.
Y-YEAH... HE SAID HE DOESN'T WANT TO GO ON HIATUS.
VISIT HIM AT THE HOSPITAL AS OFTEN AS YOU CAN TO CHECK ON HIM. OBVIOUSLY THE WELL-BEING OF THE MANGA ARTIST IS THE MOST IMPORTANT THING HERE.
LISTEN TO THE DOCTOR AND NOT THE ARTIST.
YES, SIR.

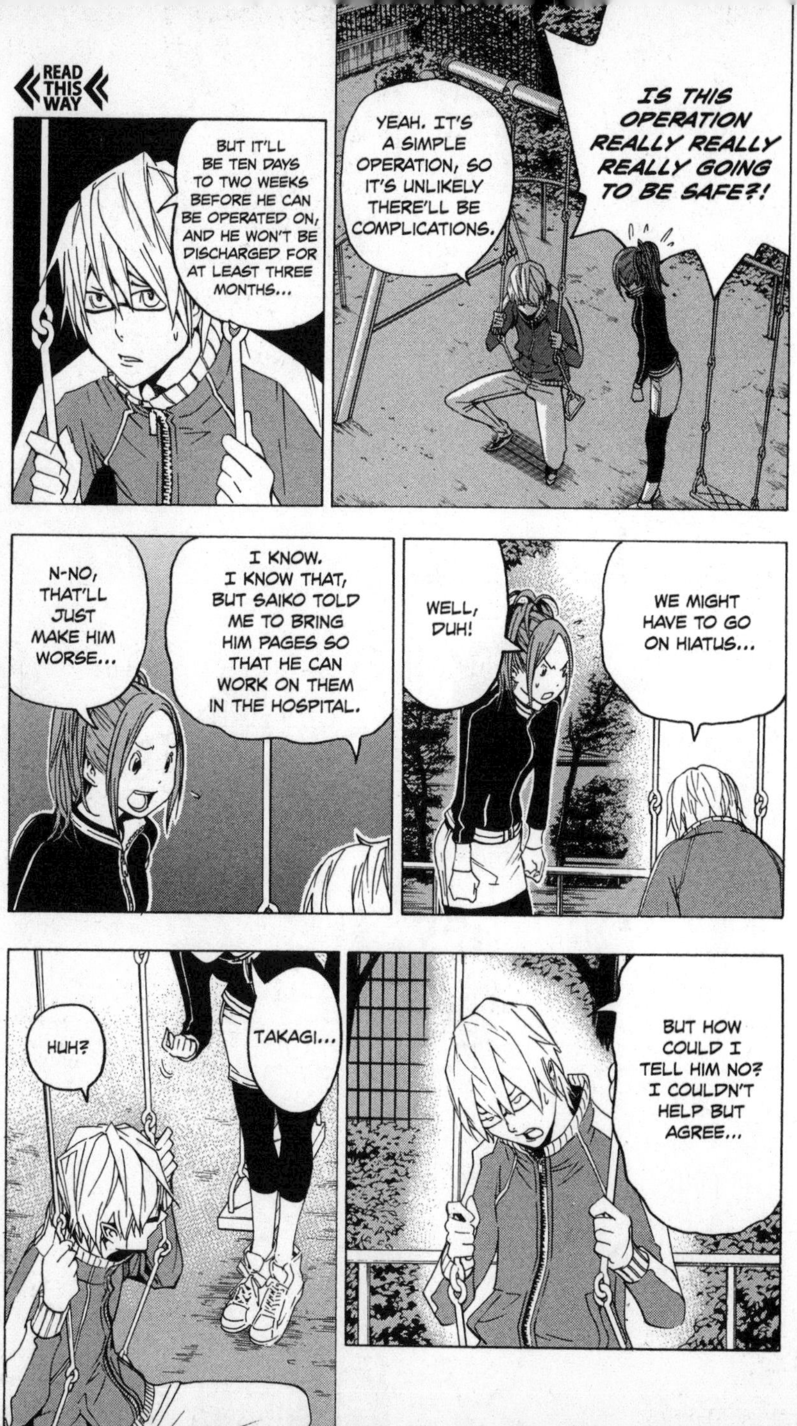
READ THIS WAY
YEAH. IT'S A SIMPLE OPERATION, SO IT'S UNLIKELY THERE'LL BE COMPLICATIONS.
IS THIS OPERATION REALLY REALLY REALLY GOING TO BE SAFE?!
BUT IT'LL BE TEN DAYS TO TWO WEEKS BEFORE HE CAN BE OPERATED ON, AND HE WON'T BE DISCHARGED FOR AT LEAST THREE MONTHS...
WE MIGHT HAVE TO GO ON HIATUS...
WELL, DUH!
I KNOW. I KNOW THAT, BUT SAIKO TOLD ME TO BRING HIM PAGES SO THAT HE CAN WORK ON THEM IN THE HOSPITAL.
N-NO, THAT'LL JUST MAKE HIM WORSE...
BUT HOW COULD I TELL HIM NO? I COULDN'T HELP BUT AGREE...
TAKAGI...
HUH?

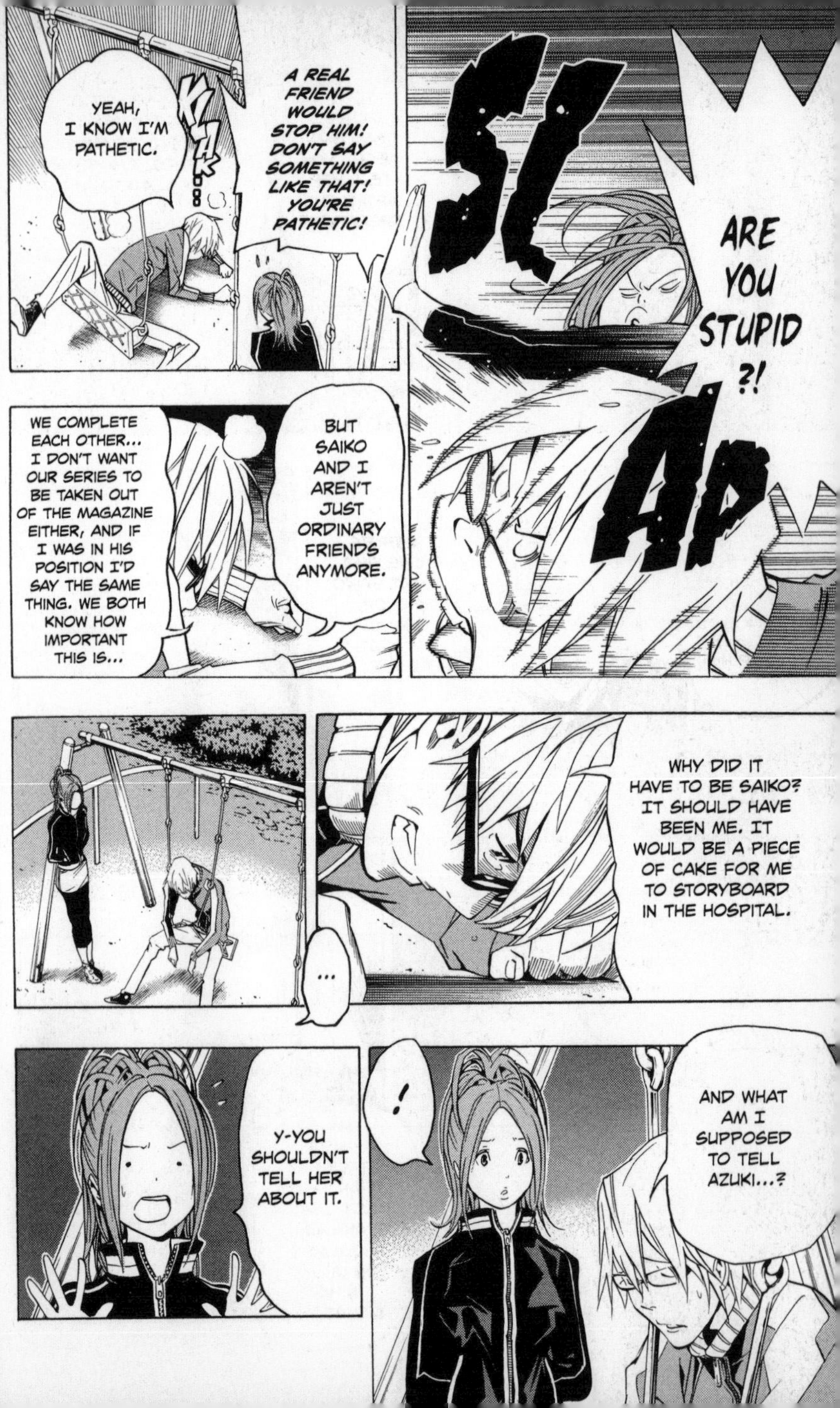
SLAP
ARE YOU STUPID?!
A REAL FRIEND WOULD STOP HIM! DON'T SAY SOMETHING LIKE THAT! YOU'RE PATHETIC!
KLAK
YEAH, I KNOW I'M PATHETIC.
BUT SAIKO AND I AREN'T JUST ORDINARY FRIENDS ANYMORE.
WE COMPLETE EACH OTHER... I DON'T WANT OUR SERIES TO BE TAKEN OUT OF THE MAGAZINE EITHER, AND IF I WAS IN HIS POSITION I'D SAY THE SAME THING. WE BOTH KNOW HOW IMPORTANT THIS IS...
WHY DID IT HAVE TO BE SAIKO? IT SHOULD HAVE BEEN ME. IT WOULD BE A PIECE OF CAKE FOR ME TO STORYBOARD IN THE HOSPITAL.
...
AND WHAT AM I SUPPOSED TO TELL AZUKI...?
!
Y-YOU SHOULDN'T TELL HER ABOUT IT.

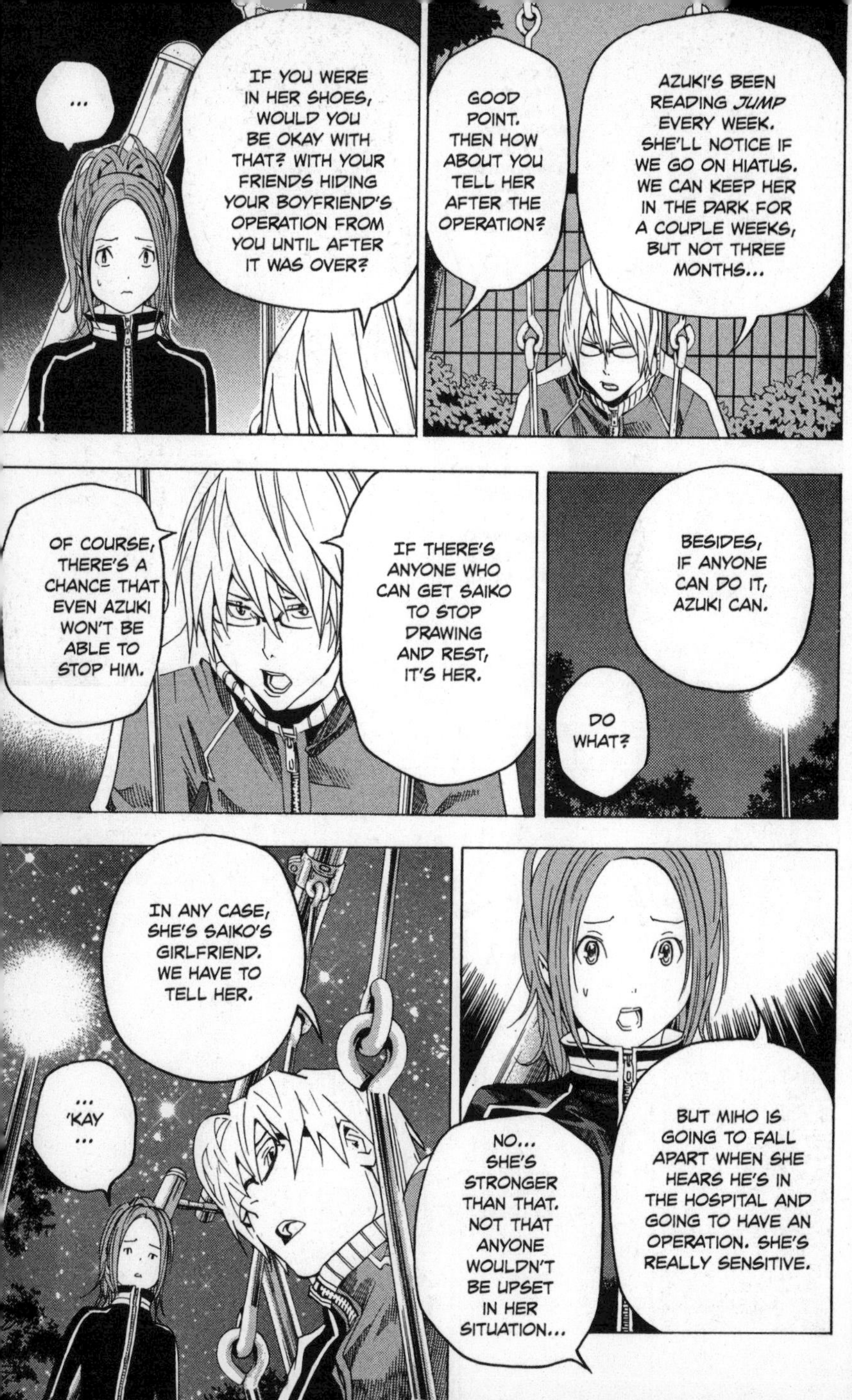
AZUKI'S BEEN READING *JUMP* EVERY WEEK. SHE'LL NOTICE IF WE GO ON HIATUS. WE CAN KEEP HER IN THE DARK FOR A COUPLE WEEKS, BUT NOT THREE MONTHS...
GOOD POINT. THEN HOW ABOUT YOU TELL HER AFTER THE OPERATION?
IF YOU WERE IN HER SHOES, WOULD YOU BE OKAY WITH THAT? WITH YOUR FRIENDS HIDING YOUR BOYFRIEND'S OPERATION FROM YOU UNTIL AFTER IT WAS OVER?
...
BESIDES, IF ANYONE CAN DO IT, AZUKI CAN.
DO WHAT?
IF THERE'S ANYONE WHO CAN GET SAIKO TO STOP DRAWING AND REST, IT'S HER.
OF COURSE, THERE'S A CHANCE THAT EVEN AZUKI WON'T BE ABLE TO STOP HIM.
BUT MIHO IS GOING TO FALL APART WHEN SHE HEARS HE'S IN THE HOSPITAL AND GOING TO HAVE AN OPERATION. SHE'S REALLY SENSITIVE.
NO... SHE'S STRONGER THAN THAT. NOT THAT ANYONE WOULDN'T BE UPSET IN HER SITUATION...
IN ANY CASE, SHE'S SAIKO'S GIRLFRIEND. WE HAVE TO TELL HER.
... 'KAY ...

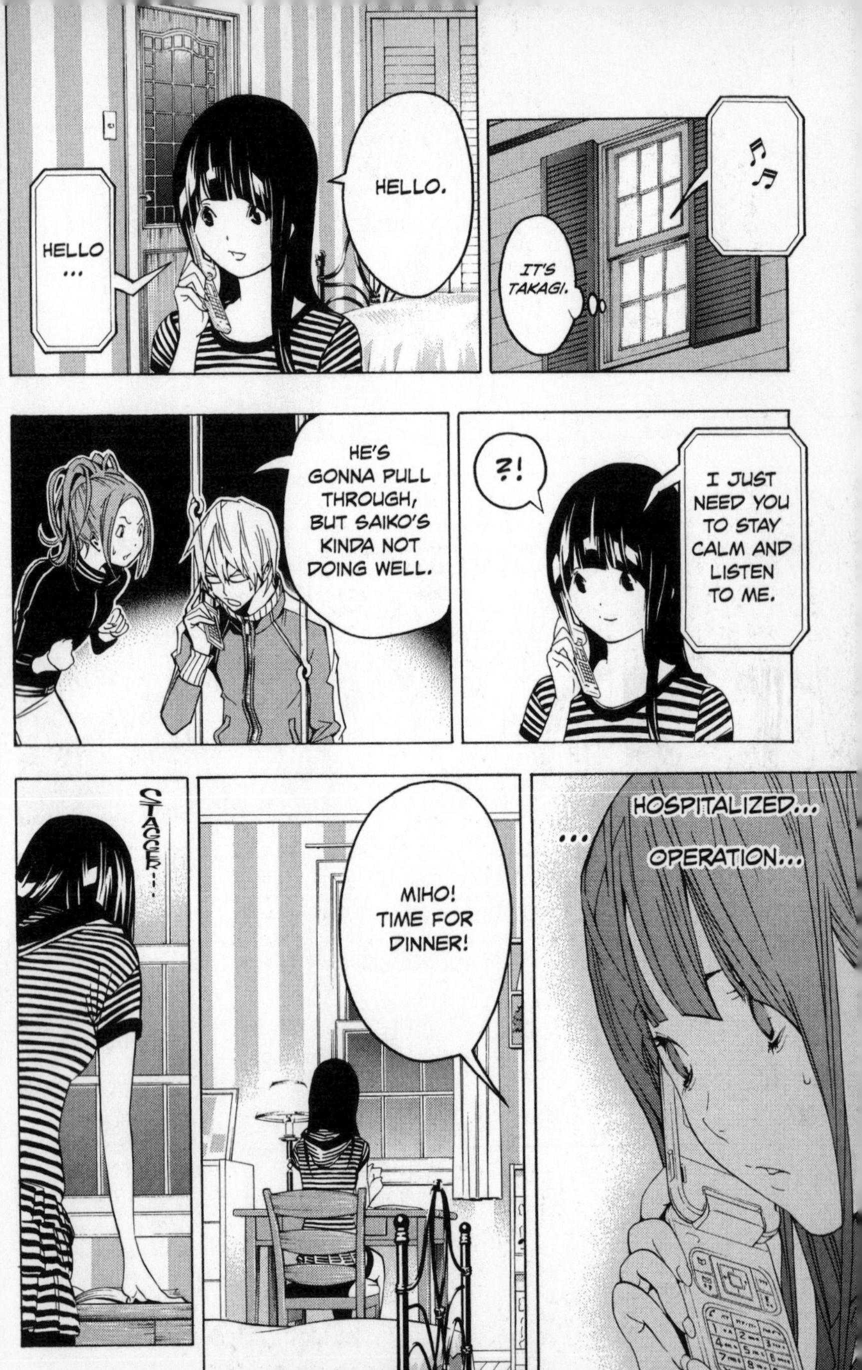
IT'S TAKAGI.
HELLO.
HELLO ...
I JUST NEED YOU TO STAY CALM AND LISTEN TO ME.
?!
HE'S GONNA PULL THROUGH, BUT SAIKO'S KINDA NOT DOING WELL.
HOSPITALIZED...
OPERATION...
...
MIHO! TIME FOR DINNER!
STAGGER...

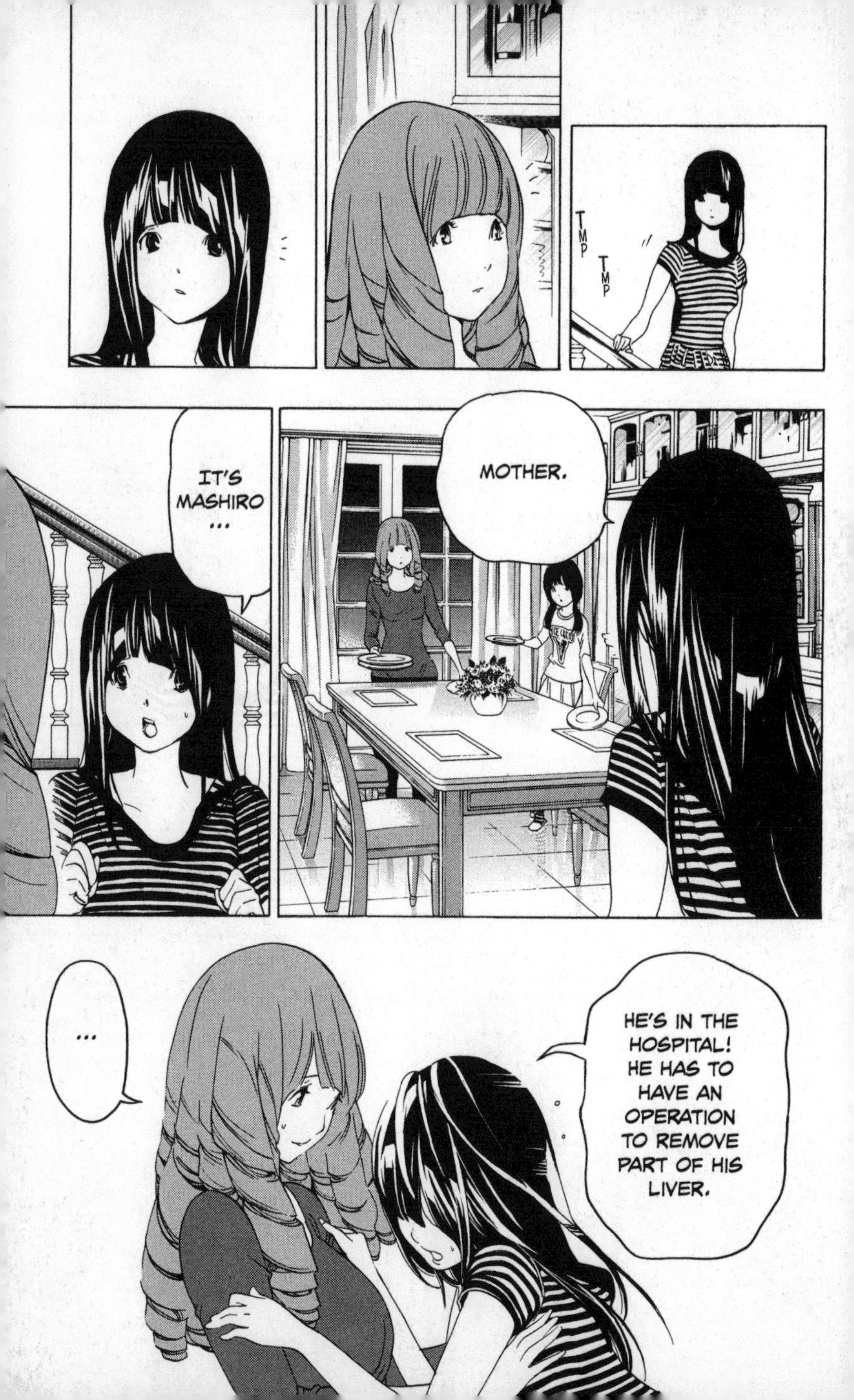
TMP TMP
MOTHER.
IT'S MASHIRO ...
HE'S IN THE HOSPITAL! HE HAS TO HAVE AN OPERATION TO REMOVE PART OF HIS LIVER.
...

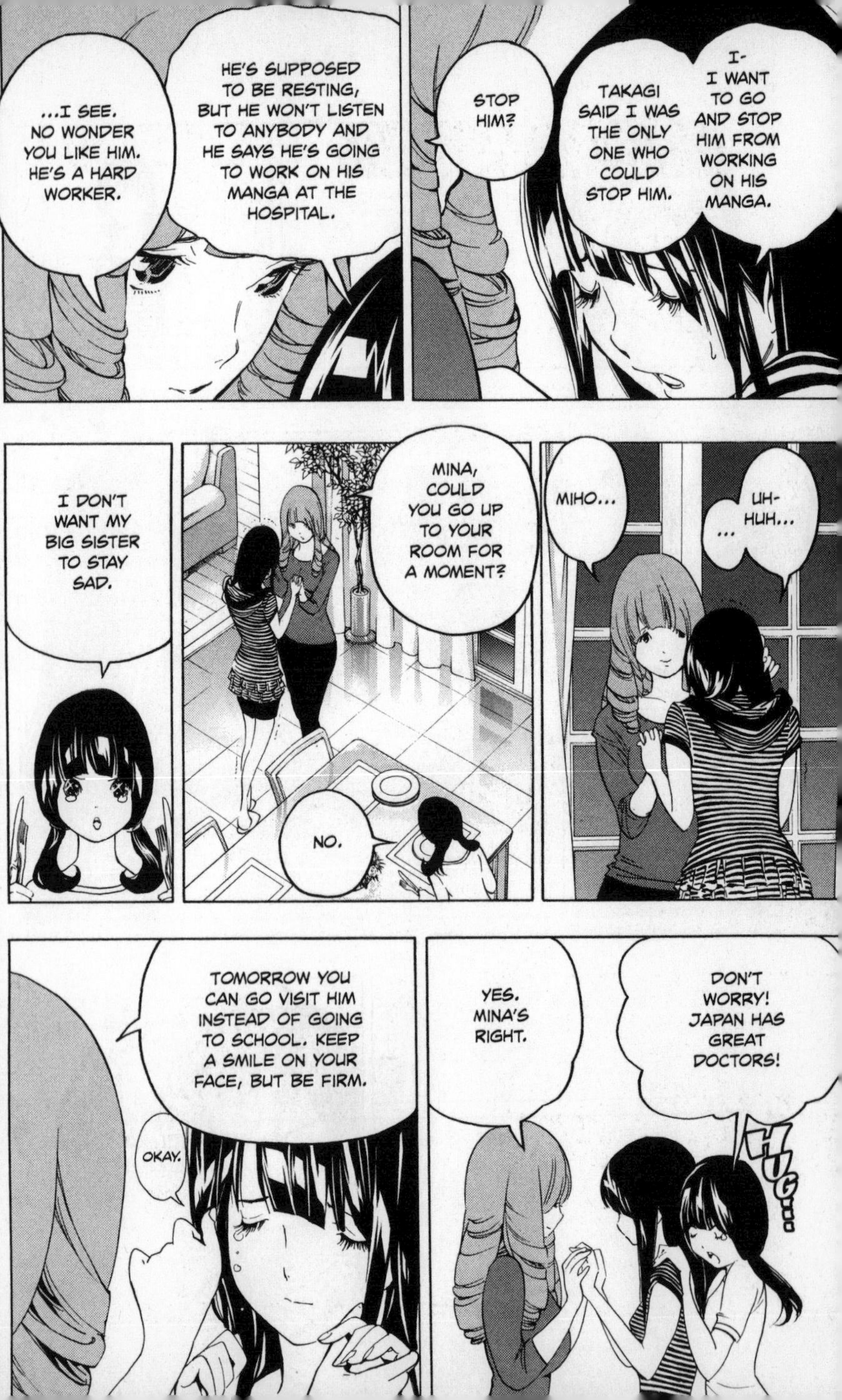
I- I WANT TO GO AND STOP HIM FROM WORKING ON HIS MANGA.
TAKAGI SAID I WAS THE ONLY ONE WHO COULD STOP HIM.
STOP HIM?
HE'S SUPPOSED TO BE RESTING, BUT HE WON'T LISTEN TO ANYBODY AND HE SAYS HE'S GOING TO WORK ON HIS MANGA AT THE HOSPITAL.
...I SEE. NO WONDER YOU LIKE HIM. HE'S A HARD WORKER.
UH-HUH...
...
MIHO...
MINA, COULD YOU GO UP TO YOUR ROOM FOR A MOMENT?
NO.
I DON'T WANT MY BIG SISTER TO STAY SAD.
DON'T WORRY! JAPAN HAS GREAT DOCTORS!
HUG...
YES. MINA'S RIGHT.
TOMORROW YOU CAN GO VISIT HIM INSTEAD OF GOING TO SCHOOL. KEEP A SMILE ON YOUR FACE, BUT BE FIRM.
OKAY.

2 0 1

Toichi Kitashita

Moritaka Mashiro

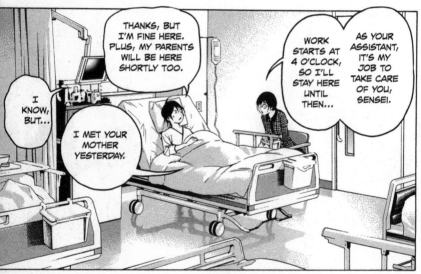

AS YOUR ASSISTANT, IT'S MY JOB TO TAKE CARE OF YOU, SENSEI.

WORK STARTS AT 4 O'CLOCK, SO I'LL STAY HERE UNTIL THEN...

THANKS, BUT I'M FINE HERE. PLUS, MY PARENTS WILL BE HERE SHORTLY TOO.

I KNOW, BUT...

I MET YOUR MOTHER YESTERDAY.

WHAT?!

MASHIRO.

KNOCK KNOCK

SHUJIN, WHAT'S TAKING YOU SO LONG...? I TOLD YOU TO BE HERE AT 3 O'CLOCK...

43

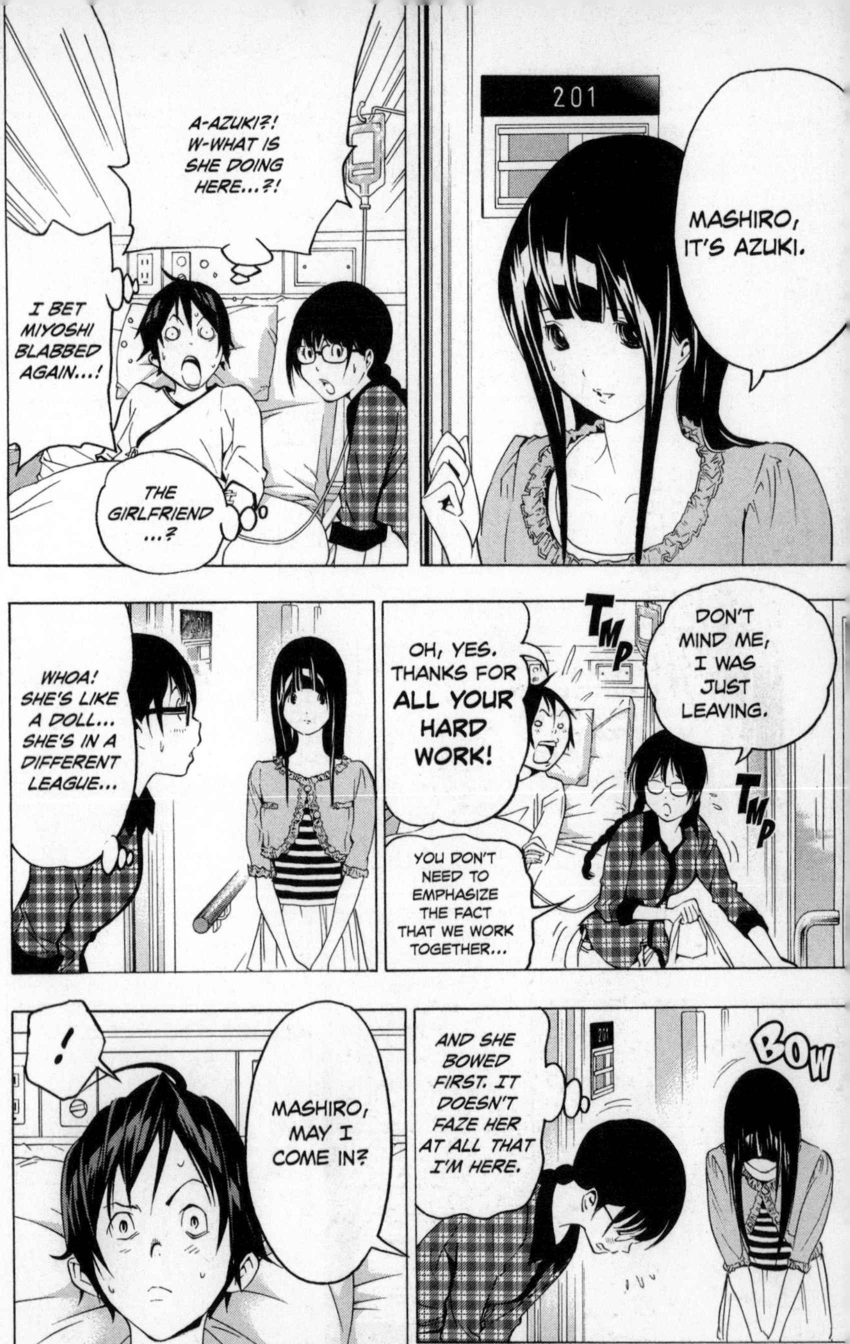
201
MASHIRO, IT'S AZUKI.
A-AZUKI?! W-WHAT IS SHE DOING HERE...?!
I BET MIYOSHI BLABBED AGAIN...!
THE GIRLFRIEND ...?
DON'T MIND ME, I WAS JUST LEAVING.
TMP
OH, YES. THANKS FOR **ALL YOUR HARD WORK!**
TMP
YOU DON'T NEED TO EMPHASIZE THE FACT THAT WE WORK TOGETHER...
WHOA! SHE'S LIKE A DOLL... SHE'S IN A DIFFERENT LEAGUE...
BOW
AND SHE BOWED FIRST. IT DOESN'T FAZE HER AT ALL THAT I'M HERE.
MASHIRO, MAY I COME IN?
!

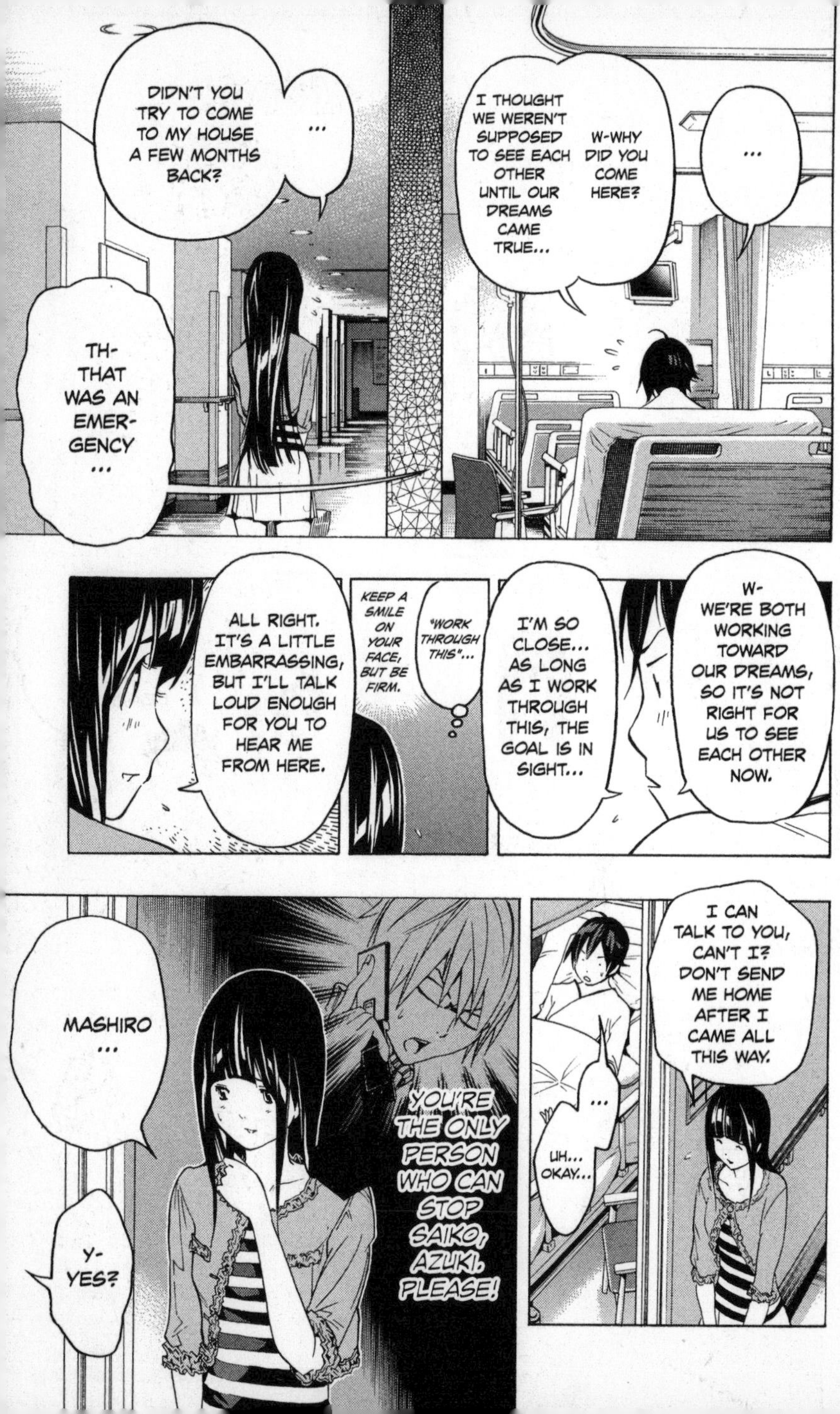
...
W-WHY DID YOU COME HERE?
I THOUGHT WE WEREN'T SUPPOSED TO SEE EACH OTHER UNTIL OUR DREAMS CAME TRUE...
...
DIDN'T YOU TRY TO COME TO MY HOUSE A FEW MONTHS BACK?
TH-THAT WAS AN EMERGENCY...
W- WE'RE BOTH WORKING TOWARD OUR DREAMS, SO IT'S NOT RIGHT FOR US TO SEE EACH OTHER NOW.
I'M SO CLOSE... AS LONG AS I WORK THROUGH THIS, THE GOAL IS IN SIGHT...
"WORK THROUGH THIS"...
KEEP A SMILE ON YOUR FACE, BUT BE FIRM.
ALL RIGHT. IT'S A LITTLE EMBARRASSING, BUT I'LL TALK LOUD ENOUGH FOR YOU TO HEAR ME FROM HERE.
I CAN TALK TO YOU, CAN'T I? DON'T SEND ME HOME AFTER I CAME ALL THIS WAY.
...
UH... OKAY...
YOU'RE THE ONLY PERSON WHO CAN STOP SAIKO, AZUKI. PLEASE!
MASHIRO...
Y-YES?

OHBA'S STORYBOARD

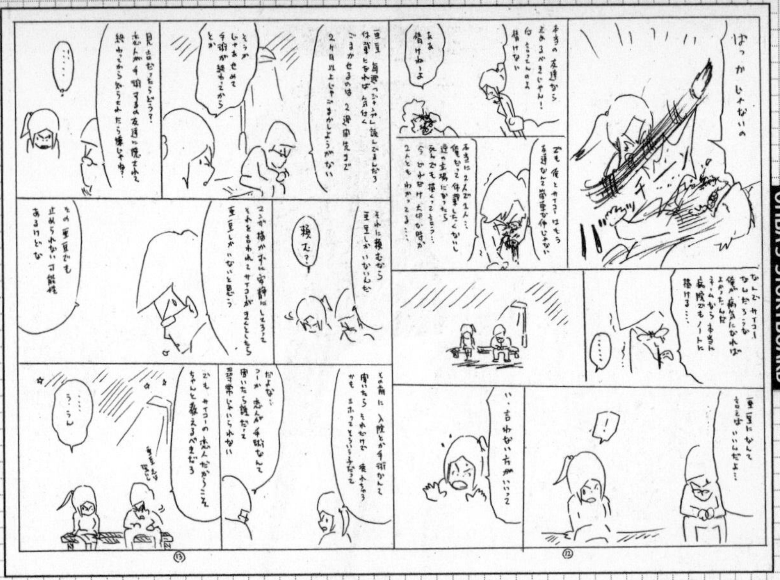

OBATA'S STORYBOARD

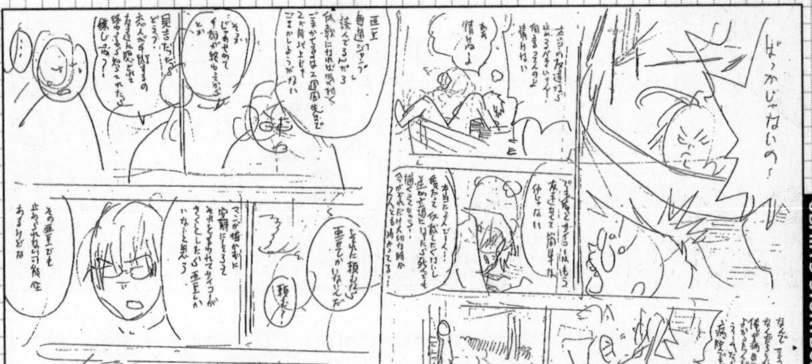

COMPLETE!

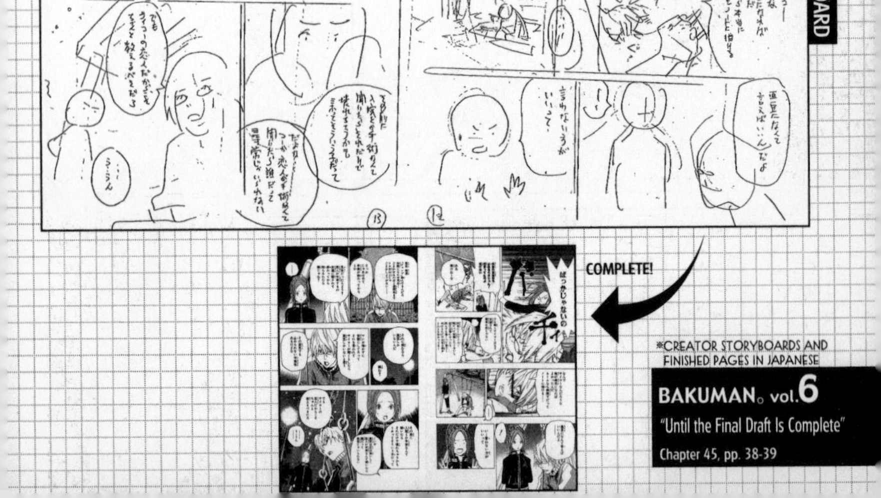

※CREATOR STORYBOARDS AND FINISHED PAGES IN JAPANESE

BAKUMAN。 vol.6

"Until the Final Draft Is Complete"

Chapter 45, pp. 38-39

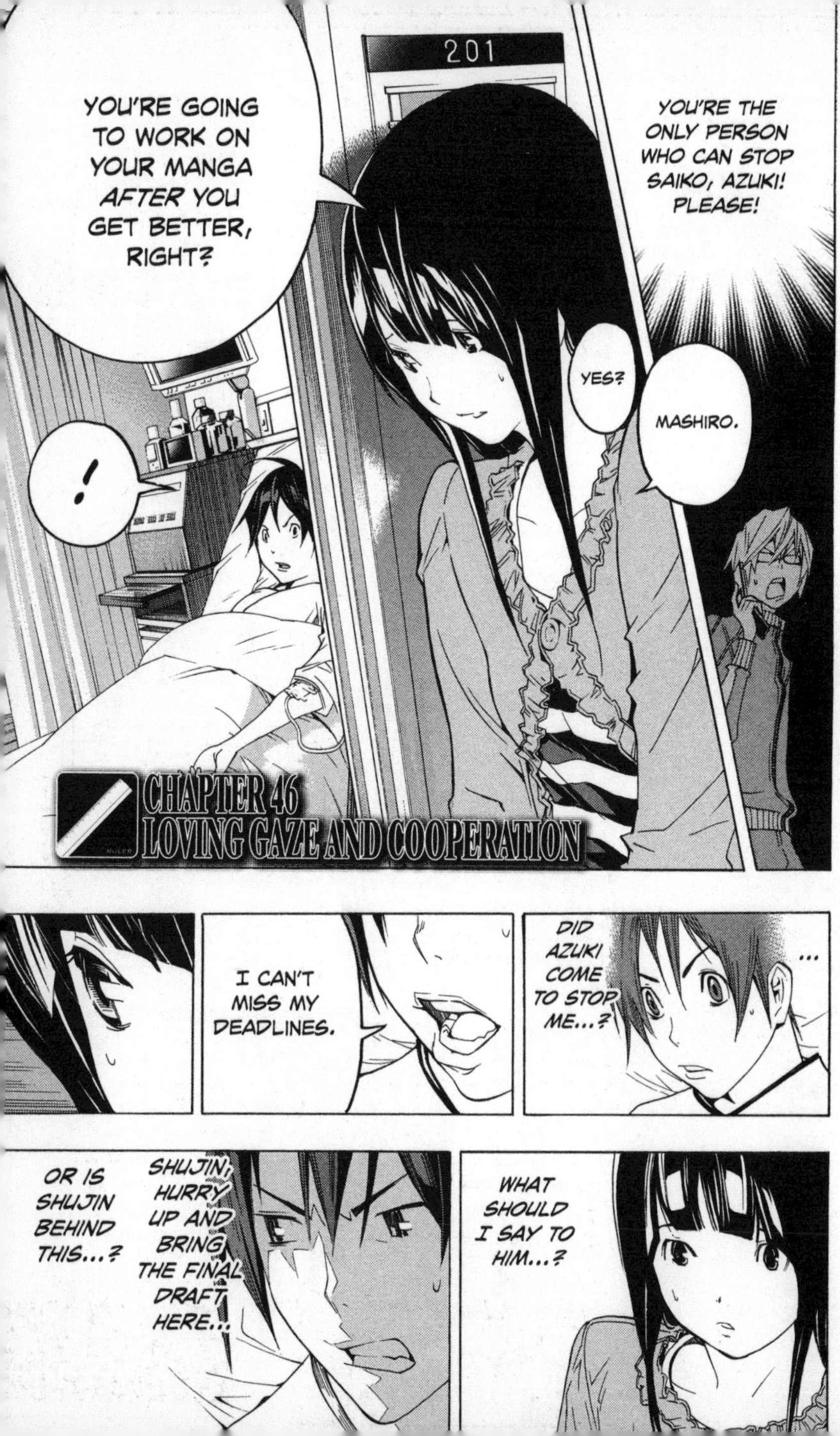

201
YOU'RE THE ONLY PERSON WHO CAN STOP SAIKO, AZUKI! PLEASE!
MASHIRO.
YES?
YOU'RE GOING TO WORK ON YOUR MANGA AFTER YOU GET BETTER, RIGHT?
!
CHAPTER 46
LOVING GAZE AND COOPERATION
...
DID AZUKI COME TO STOP ME...?
I CAN'T MISS MY DEADLINES.
WHAT SHOULD I SAY TO HIM...?
SHUJIN, HURRY UP AND BRING THE FINAL DRAFT HERE...
OR IS SHUJIN BEHIND THIS...?

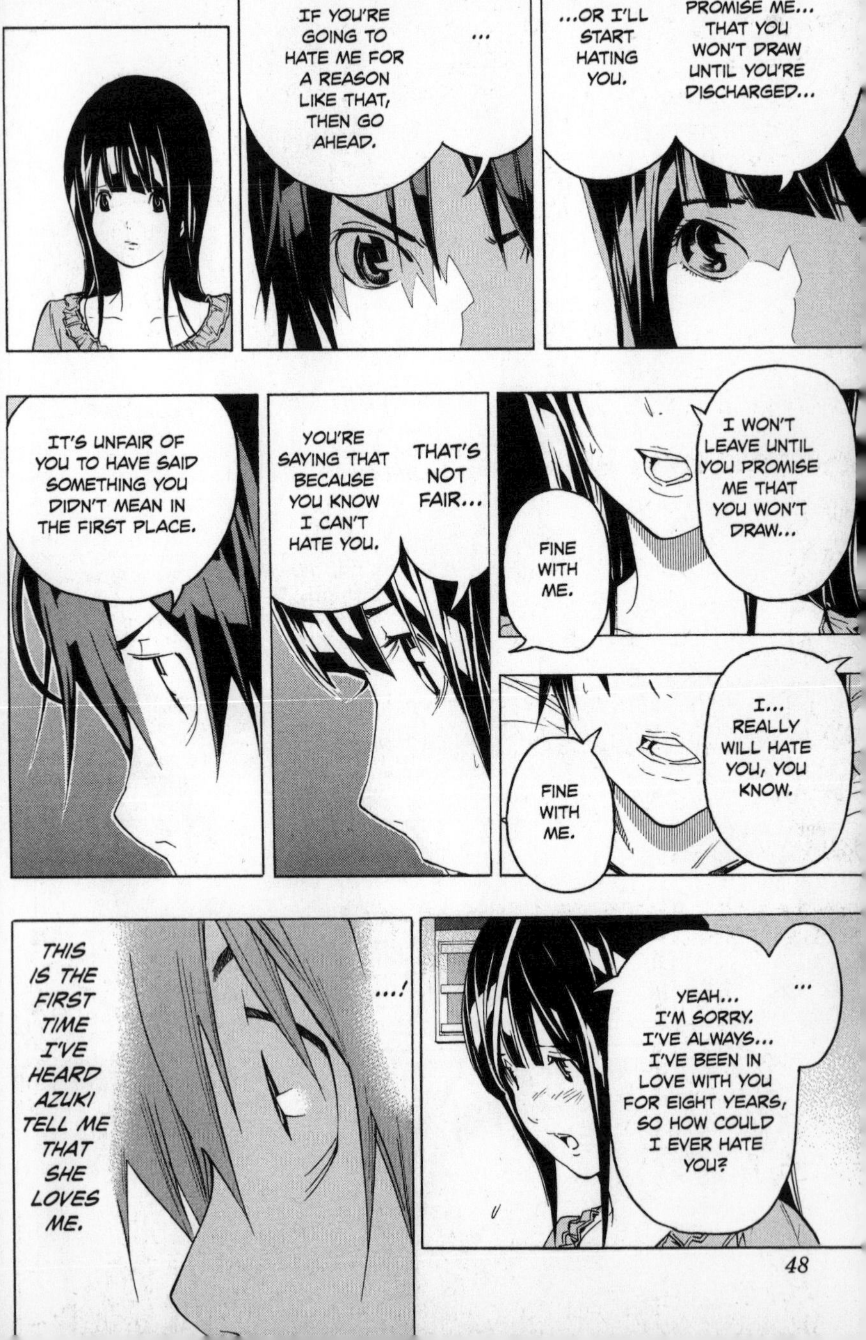
PROMISE ME... THAT YOU WON'T DRAW UNTIL YOU'RE DISCHARGED...
...OR I'LL START HATING YOU.
...
IF YOU'RE GOING TO HATE ME FOR A REASON LIKE THAT, THEN GO AHEAD.
I WON'T LEAVE UNTIL YOU PROMISE ME THAT YOU WON'T DRAW...
FINE WITH ME.
I... REALLY WILL HATE YOU, YOU KNOW.
FINE WITH ME.
THAT'S NOT FAIR...
YOU'RE SAYING THAT BECAUSE YOU KNOW I CAN'T HATE YOU.
IT'S UNFAIR OF YOU TO HAVE SAID SOMETHING YOU DIDN'T MEAN IN THE FIRST PLACE.
...
YEAH... I'M SORRY. I'VE ALWAYS... I'VE BEEN IN LOVE WITH YOU FOR EIGHT YEARS, SO HOW COULD I EVER HATE YOU?
...!
THIS IS THE FIRST TIME I'VE HEARD AZUKI TELL ME THAT SHE LOVES ME.

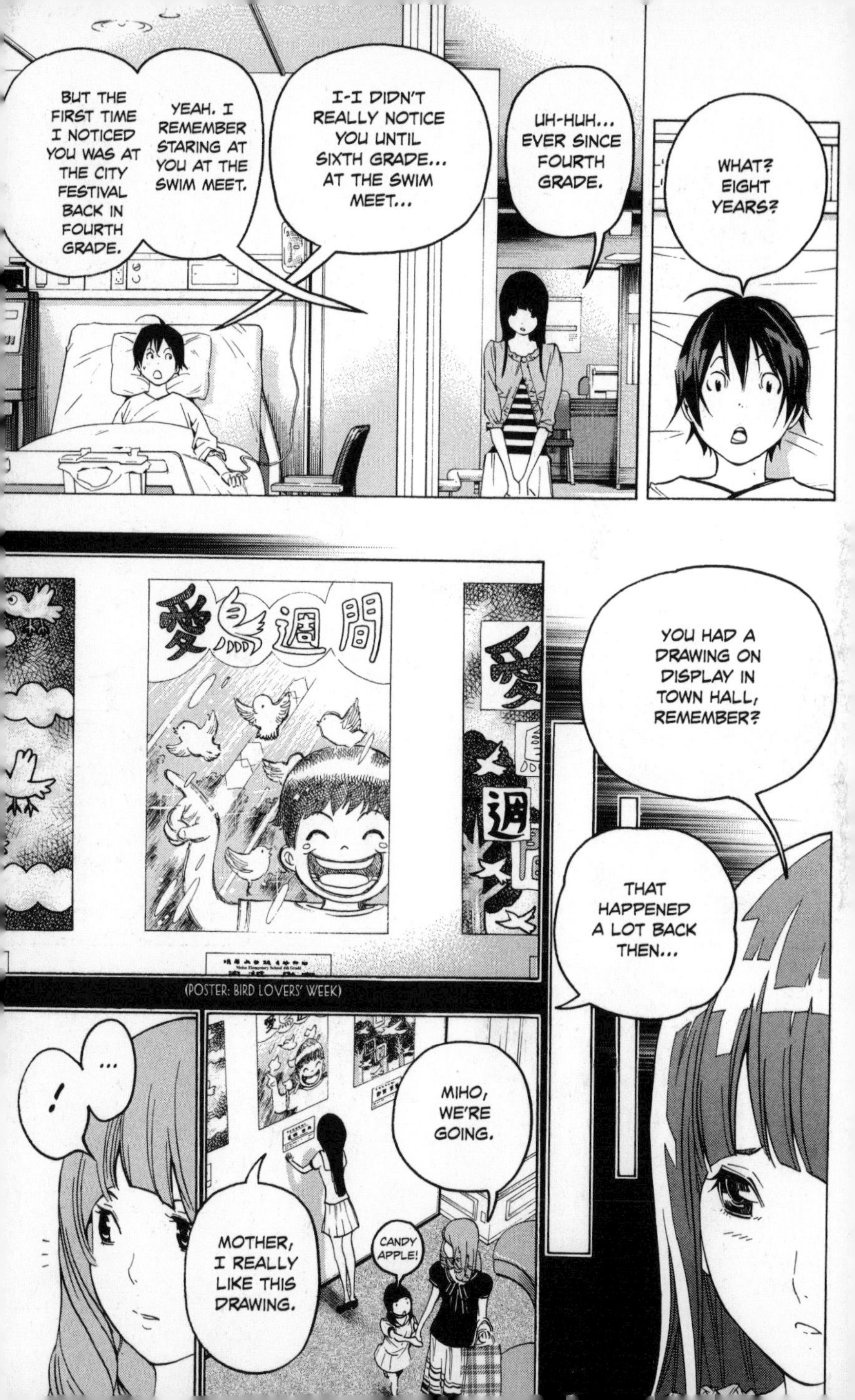
WHAT? EIGHT YEARS?
UH-HUH... EVER SINCE FOURTH GRADE.
I-I DIDN'T REALLY NOTICE YOU UNTIL SIXTH GRADE... AT THE SWIM MEET...
YEAH. I REMEMBER STARING AT YOU AT THE SWIM MEET.
BUT THE FIRST TIME I NOTICED YOU WAS AT THE CITY FESTIVAL BACK IN FOURTH GRADE.
YOU HAD A DRAWING ON DISPLAY IN TOWN HALL, REMEMBER?
THAT HAPPENED A LOT BACK THEN...
愛鳥週間
(POSTER: BIRD LOVERS' WEEK)
MIHO, WE'RE GOING.
CANDY APPLE!
MOTHER, I REALLY LIKE THIS DRAWING.
...
!

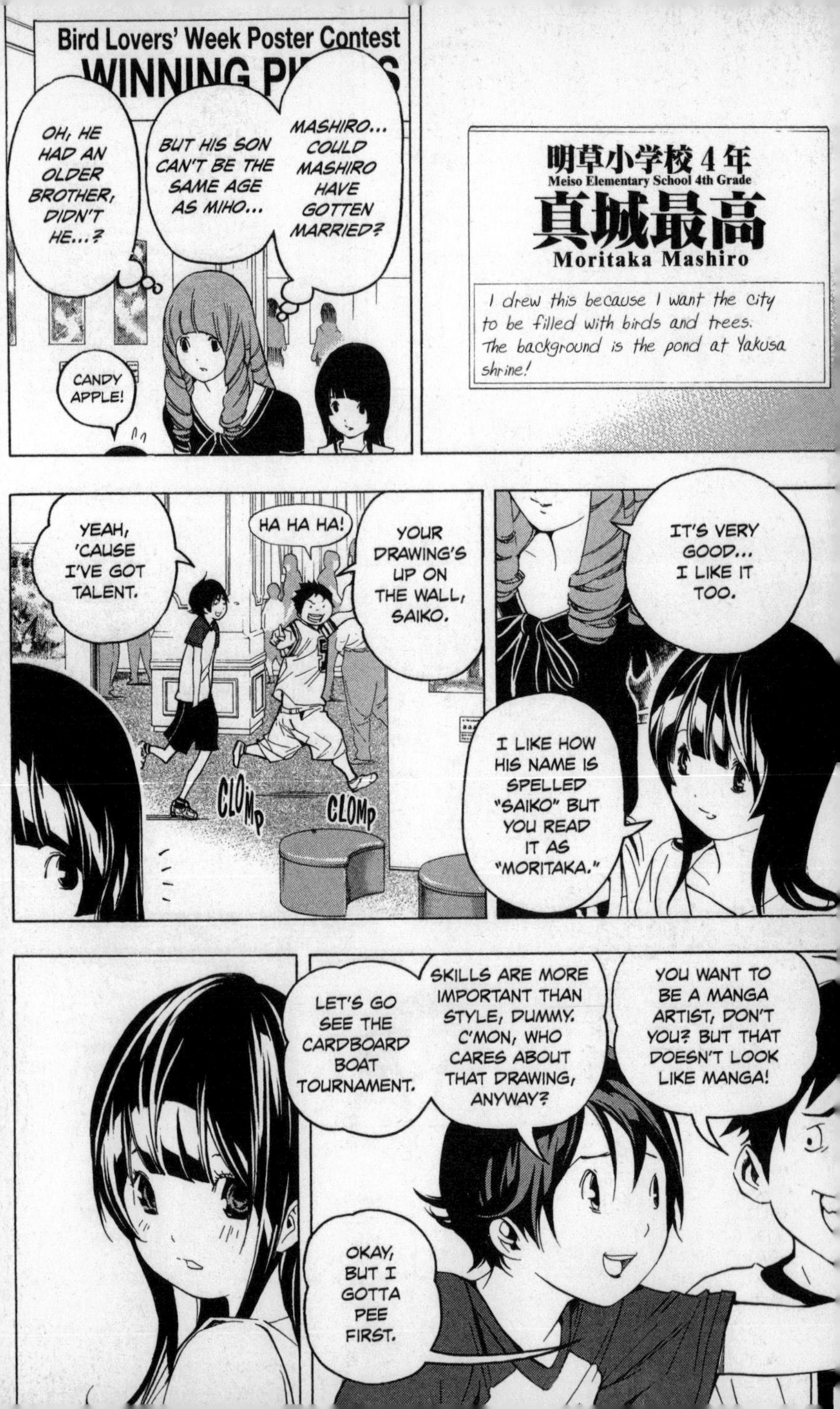
明草小学校４年
Meiso Elementary School 4th Grade
真城最高
Moritaka Mashiro
I drew this because I want the city to be filled with birds and trees. The background is the pond at Yakusa shrine!
Bird Lovers' Week Poster Contest
WINNING PI
MASHIRO... COULD MASHIRO HAVE GOTTEN MARRIED?
BUT HIS SON CAN'T BE THE SAME AGE AS MIHO...
OH, HE HAD AN OLDER BROTHER, DIDN'T HE...?
CANDY APPLE!
IT'S VERY GOOD... I LIKE IT TOO.
I LIKE HOW HIS NAME IS SPELLED "SAIKO" BUT YOU READ IT AS "MORITAKA."
YOUR DRAWING'S UP ON THE WALL, SAIKO.
HA HA HA!
YEAH, 'CAUSE I'VE GOT TALENT.
CLOMP
CLOMP
YOU WANT TO BE A MANGA ARTIST, DON'T YOU? BUT THAT DOESN'T LOOK LIKE MANGA!
SKILLS ARE MORE IMPORTANT THAN STYLE, DUMMY. C'MON, WHO CARES ABOUT THAT DRAWING, ANYWAY?
LET'S GO SEE THE CARDBOARD BOAT TOURNAMENT.
OKAY, BUT I GOTTA PEE FIRST.

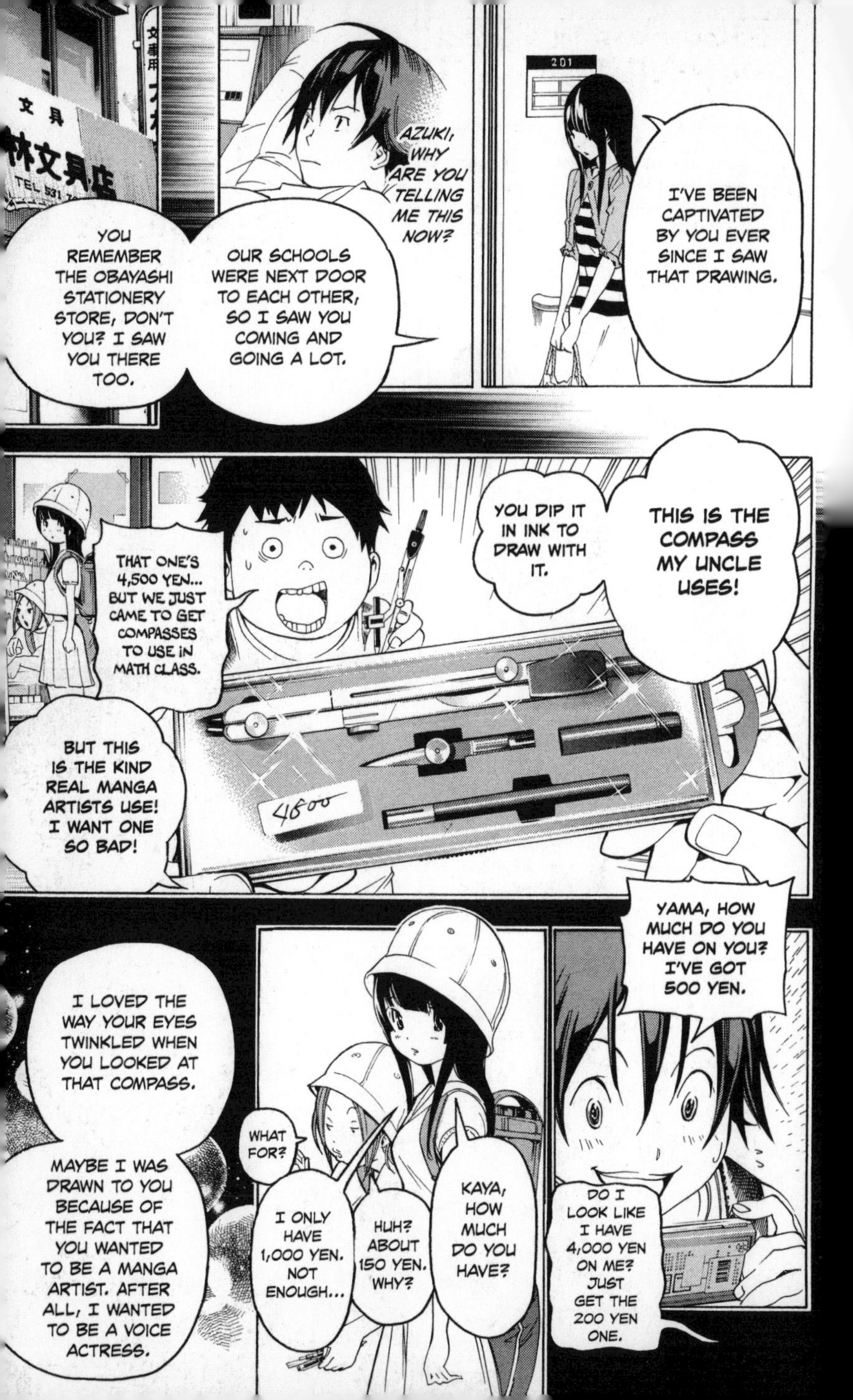
I'VE BEEN CAPTIVATED BY YOU EVER SINCE I SAW THAT DRAWING.
201
AZUKI, WHY ARE YOU TELLING ME THIS NOW?
OUR SCHOOLS WERE NEXT DOOR TO EACH OTHER, SO I SAW YOU COMING AND GOING A LOT.
YOU REMEMBER THE OBAYASHI STATIONERY STORE, DON'T YOU? I SAW YOU THERE TOO.
文具
林文具店
THIS IS THE COMPASS MY UNCLE USES!
YOU DIP IT IN INK TO DRAW WITH IT.
THAT ONE'S 4,500 YEN... BUT WE JUST CAME TO GET COMPASSES TO USE IN MATH CLASS.
BUT THIS IS THE KIND REAL MANGA ARTISTS USE! I WANT ONE SO BAD!
4800
YAMA, HOW MUCH DO YOU HAVE ON YOU? I'VE GOT 500 YEN.
DO I LOOK LIKE I HAVE 4,000 YEN ON ME? JUST GET THE 200 YEN ONE.
KAYA, HOW MUCH DO YOU HAVE?
HUH? ABOUT 150 YEN. WHY?
WHAT FOR?
I ONLY HAVE 1,000 YEN. NOT ENOUGH...
I LOVED THE WAY YOUR EYES TWINKLED WHEN YOU LOOKED AT THAT COMPASS.
MAYBE I WAS DRAWN TO YOU BECAUSE OF THE FACT THAT YOU WANTED TO BE A MANGA ARTIST. AFTER ALL, I WANTED TO BE A VOICE ACTRESS.

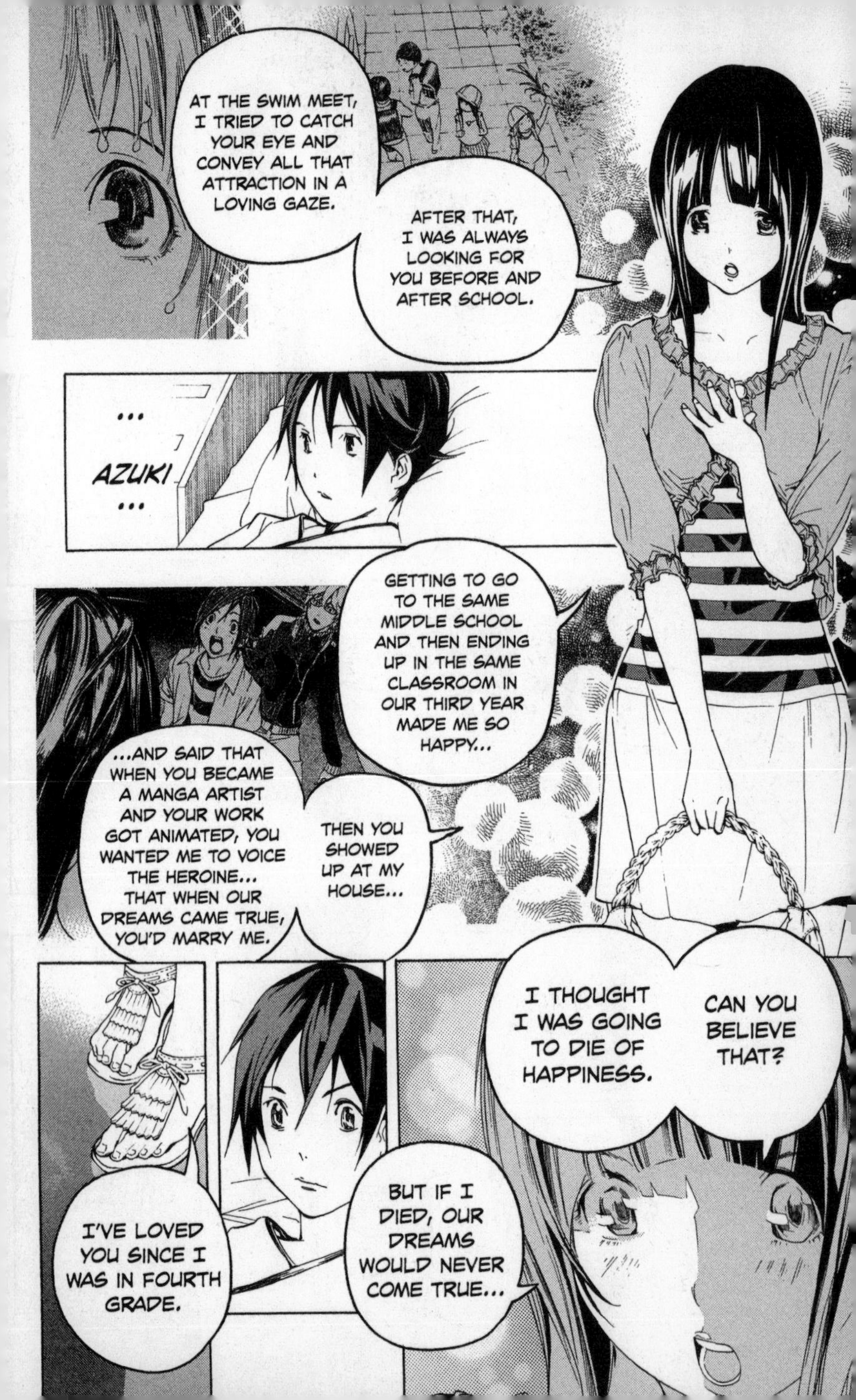
AT THE SWIM MEET, I TRIED TO CATCH YOUR EYE AND CONVEY ALL THAT ATTRACTION IN A LOVING GAZE.
AFTER THAT, I WAS ALWAYS LOOKING FOR YOU BEFORE AND AFTER SCHOOL.
... AZUKI ...
GETTING TO GO TO THE SAME MIDDLE SCHOOL AND THEN ENDING UP IN THE SAME CLASSROOM IN OUR THIRD YEAR MADE ME SO HAPPY...
THEN YOU SHOWED UP AT MY HOUSE...
...AND SAID THAT WHEN YOU BECAME A MANGA ARTIST AND YOUR WORK GOT ANIMATED, YOU WANTED ME TO VOICE THE HEROINE... THAT WHEN OUR DREAMS CAME TRUE, YOU'D MARRY ME.
CAN YOU BELIEVE THAT?
I THOUGHT I WAS GOING TO DIE OF HAPPINESS.
BUT IF I DIED, OUR DREAMS WOULD NEVER COME TRUE...
I'VE LOVED YOU SINCE I WAS IN FOURTH GRADE.

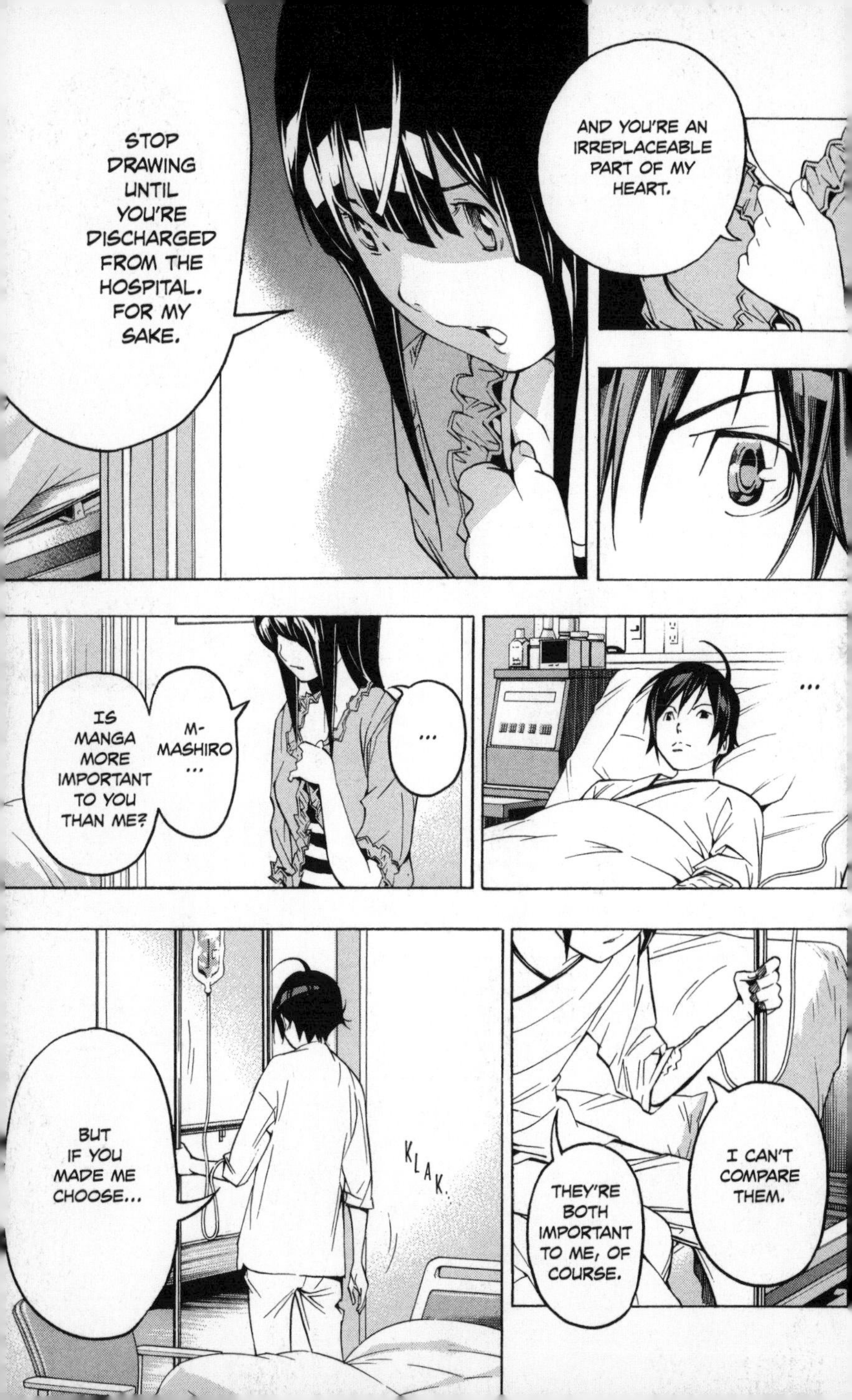
AND YOU'RE AN IRREPLACEABLE PART OF MY HEART.
STOP DRAWING UNTIL YOU'RE DISCHARGED FROM THE HOSPITAL. FOR MY SAKE.
...
...
M-MASHIRO...
IS MANGA MORE IMPORTANT TO YOU THAN ME?
I CAN'T COMPARE THEM.
THEY'RE BOTH IMPORTANT TO ME, OF COURSE.
KLAK.
BUT IF YOU MADE ME CHOOSE...

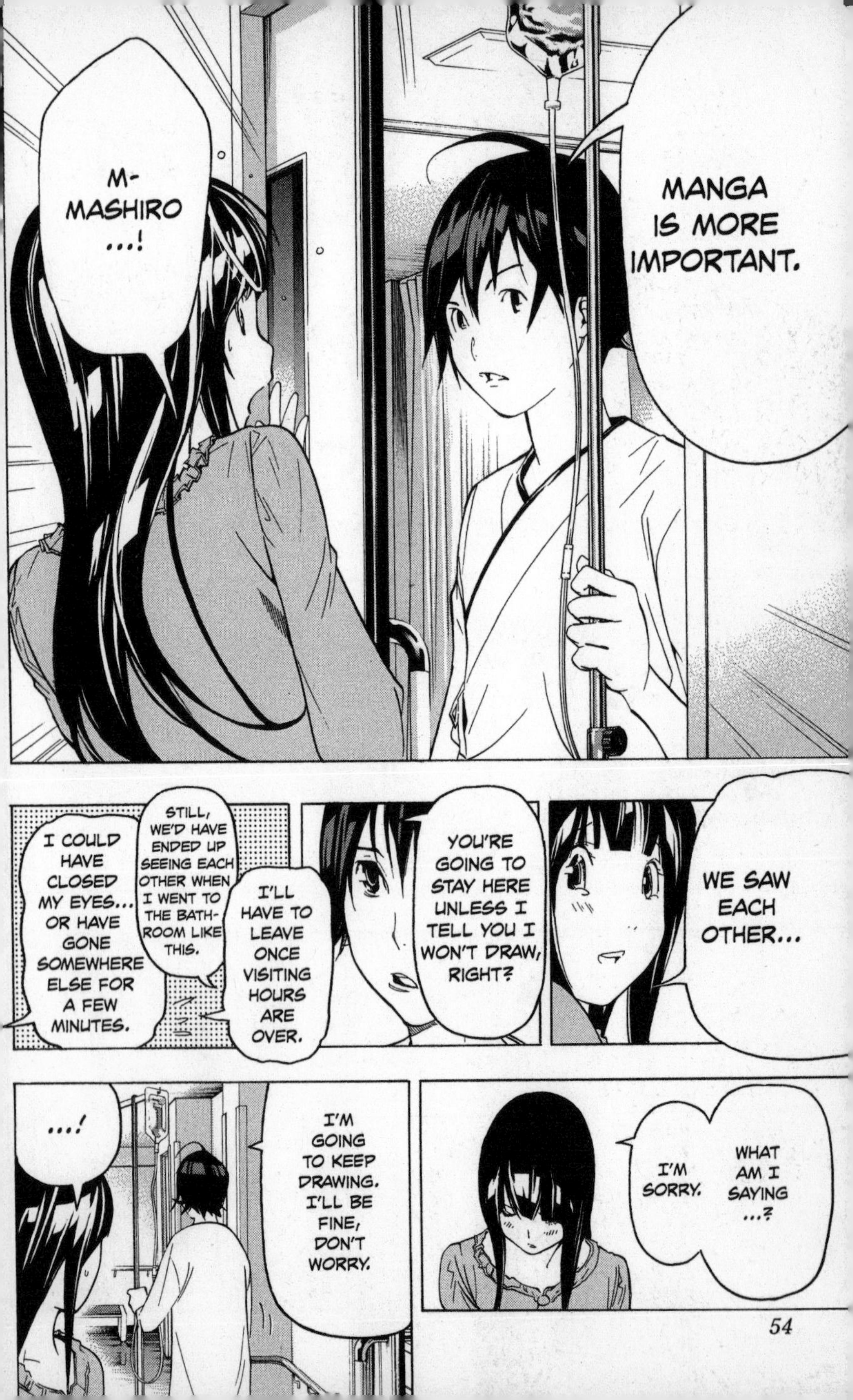

MANGA IS MORE IMPORTANT.
M-MASHIRO ...!
WE SAW EACH OTHER...
YOU'RE GOING TO STAY HERE UNLESS I TELL YOU I WON'T DRAW, RIGHT?
I'LL HAVE TO LEAVE ONCE VISITING HOURS ARE OVER.
STILL, WE'D HAVE ENDED UP SEEING EACH OTHER WHEN I WENT TO THE BATHROOM LIKE THIS.
I COULD HAVE CLOSED MY EYES... OR HAVE GONE SOMEWHERE ELSE FOR A FEW MINUTES.
WHAT AM I SAYING ...?
I'M SORRY.
I'M GOING TO KEEP DRAWING. I'LL BE FINE, DON'T WORRY.
...!

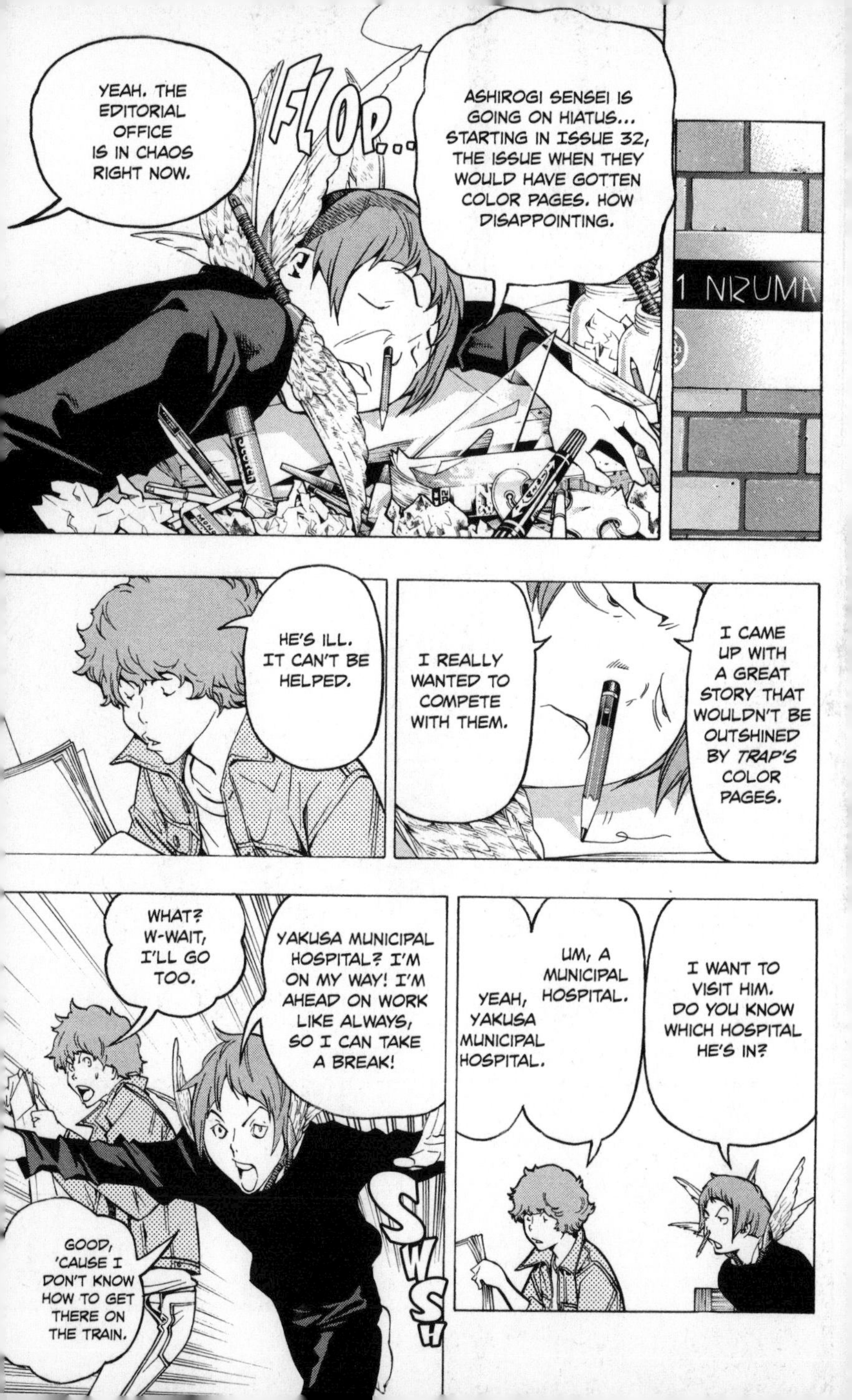
1 NIZUMA
ASHIROGI SENSEI IS GOING ON HIATUS... STARTING IN ISSUE 32, THE ISSUE WHEN THEY WOULD HAVE GOTTEN COLOR PAGES. HOW DISAPPOINTING.
FLOP...
YEAH. THE EDITORIAL OFFICE IS IN CHAOS RIGHT NOW.
I CAME UP WITH A GREAT STORY THAT WOULDN'T BE OUTSHINED BY *TRAP'S* COLOR PAGES.
I REALLY WANTED TO COMPETE WITH THEM.
HE'S ILL. IT CAN'T BE HELPED.
I WANT TO VISIT HIM. DO YOU KNOW WHICH HOSPITAL HE'S IN?
UM, A MUNICIPAL HOSPITAL.
YEAH, YAKUSA MUNICIPAL HOSPITAL.
YAKUSA MUNICIPAL HOSPITAL? I'M ON MY WAY! I'M AHEAD ON WORK LIKE ALWAYS, SO I CAN TAKE A BREAK!
WHAT? W-WAIT, I'LL GO TOO.
SWSH
GOOD, 'CAUSE I DON'T KNOW HOW TO GET THERE ON THE TRAIN.

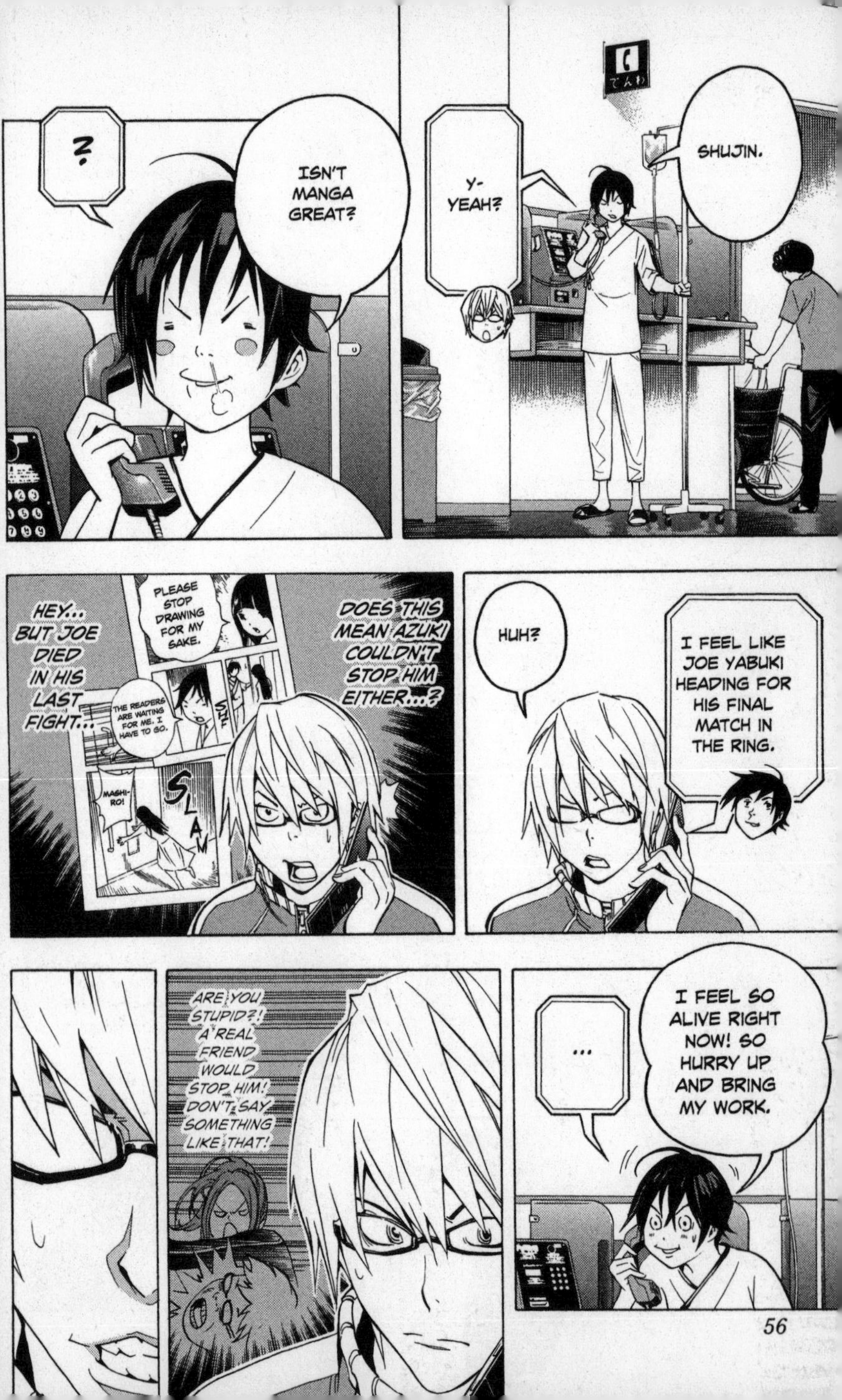
SHUJIN.
Y-YEAH?
ISN'T MANGA GREAT?
?
I FEEL LIKE JOE YABUKI HEADING FOR HIS FINAL MATCH IN THE RING.
HUH?
DOES THIS MEAN AZUKI COULDN'T STOP HIM EITHER...?
PLEASE STOP DRAWING FOR MY SAKE.
THE READERS ARE WAITING FOR ME. I HAVE TO GO.
SHF
MASHIRO!
SLAM
HEY... BUT JOE DIED IN HIS LAST FIGHT...
I FEEL SO ALIVE RIGHT NOW! SO HURRY UP AND BRING MY WORK.
...
ARE YOU STUPID?! A REAL FRIEND WOULD STOP HIM! DON'T SAY SOMETHING LIKE THAT!

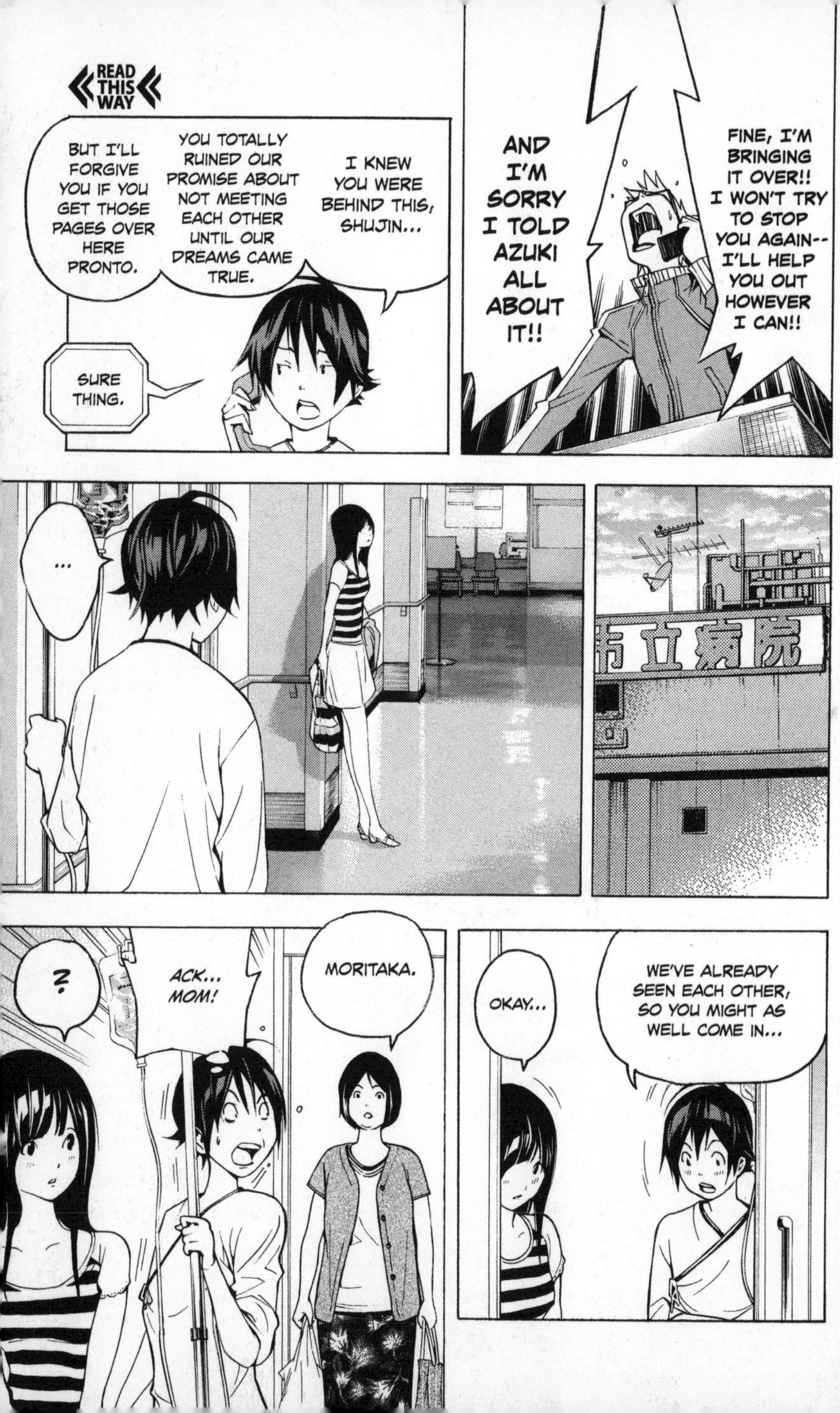
READ THIS WAY
FINE, I'M BRINGING IT OVER!! I WON'T TRY TO STOP YOU AGAIN-- I'LL HELP YOU OUT HOWEVER I CAN!!
AND I'M SORRY I TOLD AZUKI ALL ABOUT IT!!
I KNEW YOU WERE BEHIND THIS, SHUJIN...
YOU TOTALLY RUINED OUR PROMISE ABOUT NOT MEETING EACH OTHER UNTIL OUR DREAMS CAME TRUE.
BUT I'LL FORGIVE YOU IF YOU GET THOSE PAGES OVER HERE PRONTO.
SURE THING.
...
WE'VE ALREADY SEEN EACH OTHER, SO YOU MIGHT AS WELL COME IN...
OKAY...
MORITAKA.
ACK... MOM!
?

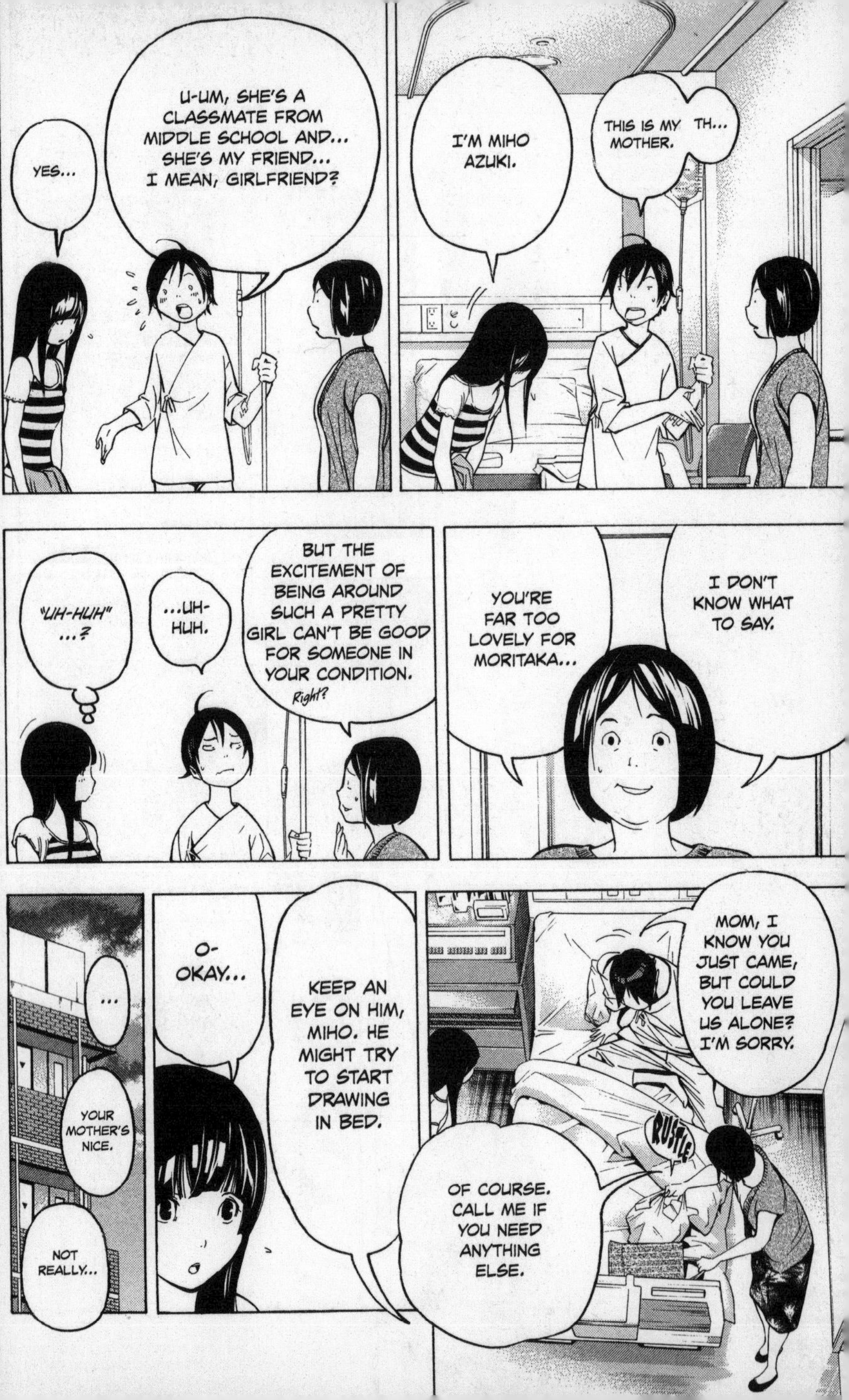
TH...
THIS IS MY MOTHER.
I'M MIHO AZUKI.
U-UM, SHE'S A CLASSMATE FROM MIDDLE SCHOOL AND... SHE'S MY FRIEND... I MEAN, GIRLFRIEND?
YES...
I DON'T KNOW WHAT TO SAY.
YOU'RE FAR TOO LOVELY FOR MORITAKA...
BUT THE EXCITEMENT OF BEING AROUND SUCH A PRETTY GIRL CAN'T BE GOOD FOR SOMEONE IN YOUR CONDITION.
Right?
...UH-HUH.
"UH-HUH" ...?
MOM, I KNOW YOU JUST CAME, BUT COULD YOU LEAVE US ALONE? I'M SORRY.
RUSTLE
OF COURSE. CALL ME IF YOU NEED ANYTHING ELSE.
KEEP AN EYE ON HIM, MIHO. HE MIGHT TRY TO START DRAWING IN BED.
O-OKAY...
...
YOUR MOTHER'S NICE.
NOT REALLY...

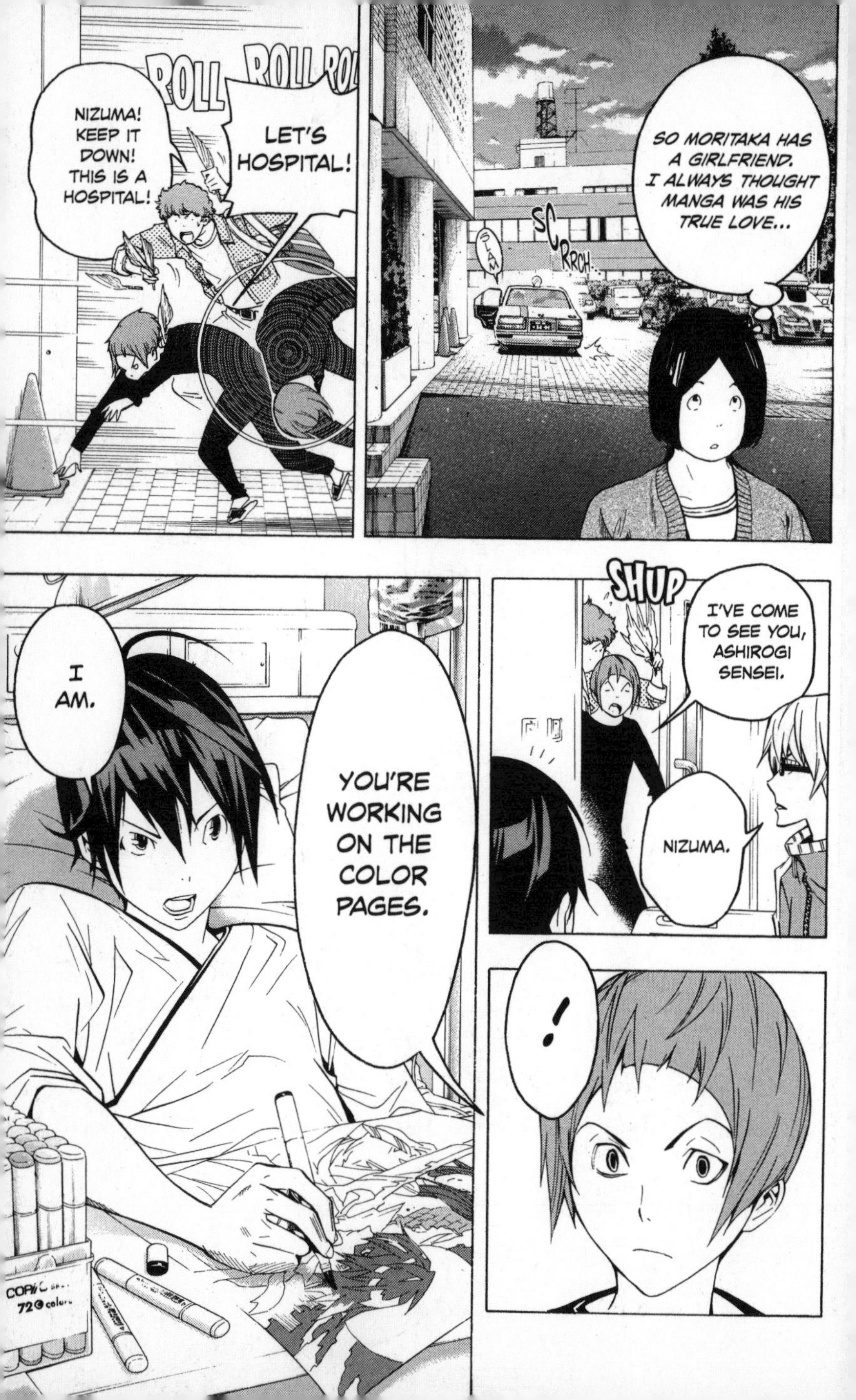
SO MORITAKA HAS A GIRLFRIEND. I ALWAYS THOUGHT MANGA WAS HIS TRUE LOVE...
SCRRCH
SLAM
ROLL ROLL ROL
LET'S HOSPITAL!
NIZUMA! KEEP IT DOWN! THIS IS A HOSPITAL!
SHUP
I'VE COME TO SEE YOU, ASHIROGI SENSEI.
NIZUMA.
!
YOU'RE WORKING ON THE COLOR PAGES.
I AM.

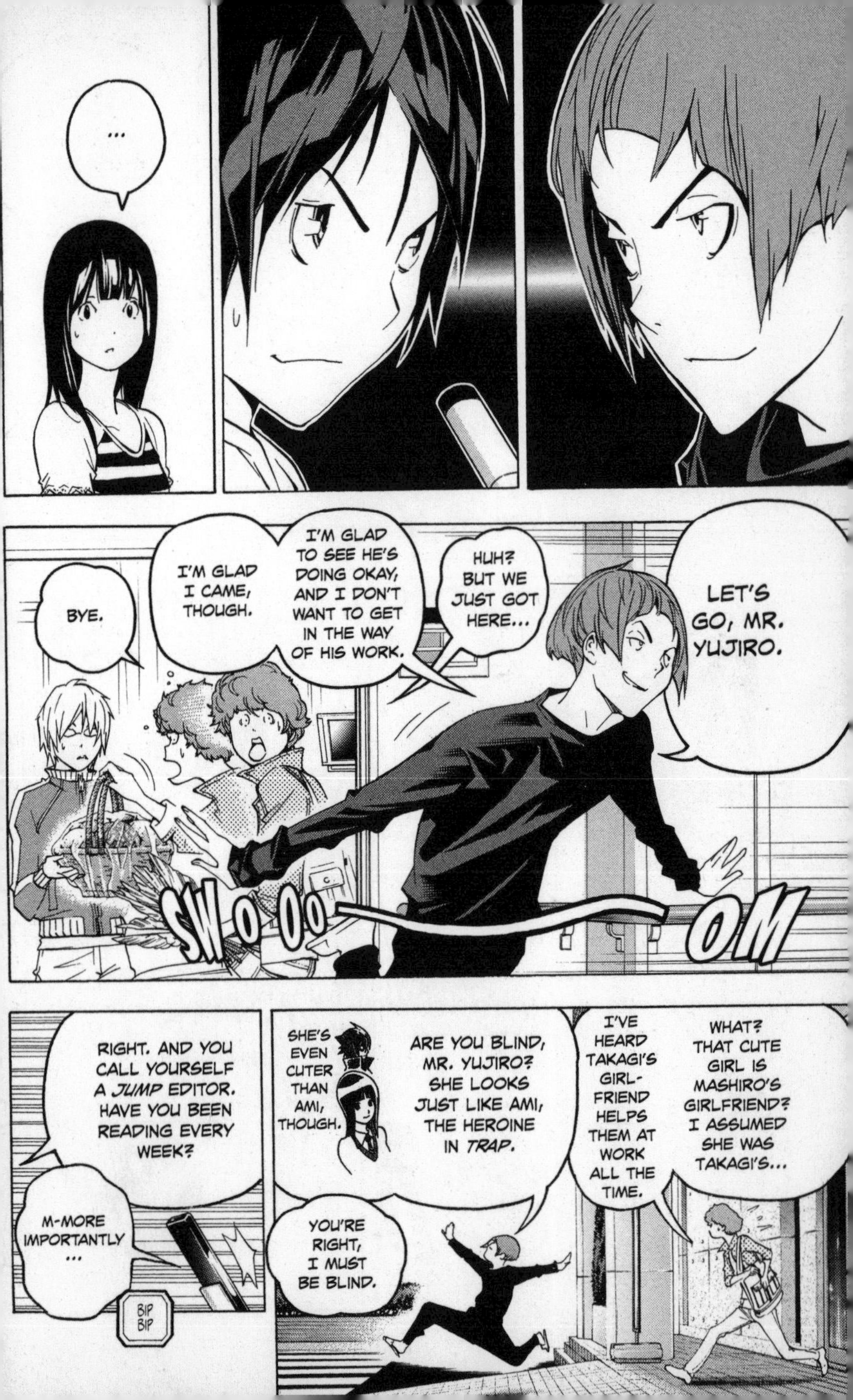
...
LET'S GO, MR. YUJIRO.
HUH? BUT WE JUST GOT HERE...
I'M GLAD TO SEE HE'S DOING OKAY, AND I DON'T WANT TO GET IN THE WAY OF HIS WORK.
I'M GLAD I CAME, THOUGH.
BYE.
SWOOOOM
WHAT? THAT CUTE GIRL IS MASHIRO'S GIRLFRIEND? I ASSUMED SHE WAS TAKAGI'S...
I'VE HEARD TAKAGI'S GIRLFRIEND HELPS THEM AT WORK ALL THE TIME.
ARE YOU BLIND, MR. YUJIRO? SHE LOOKS JUST LIKE AMI, THE HEROINE IN *TRAP*.
SHE'S EVEN CUTER THAN AMI, THOUGH.
YOU'RE RIGHT, I MUST BE BLIND.
RIGHT. AND YOU CALL YOURSELF A *JUMP* EDITOR. HAVE YOU BEEN READING EVERY WEEK?
M-MORE IMPORTANTLY...
BIP BIP

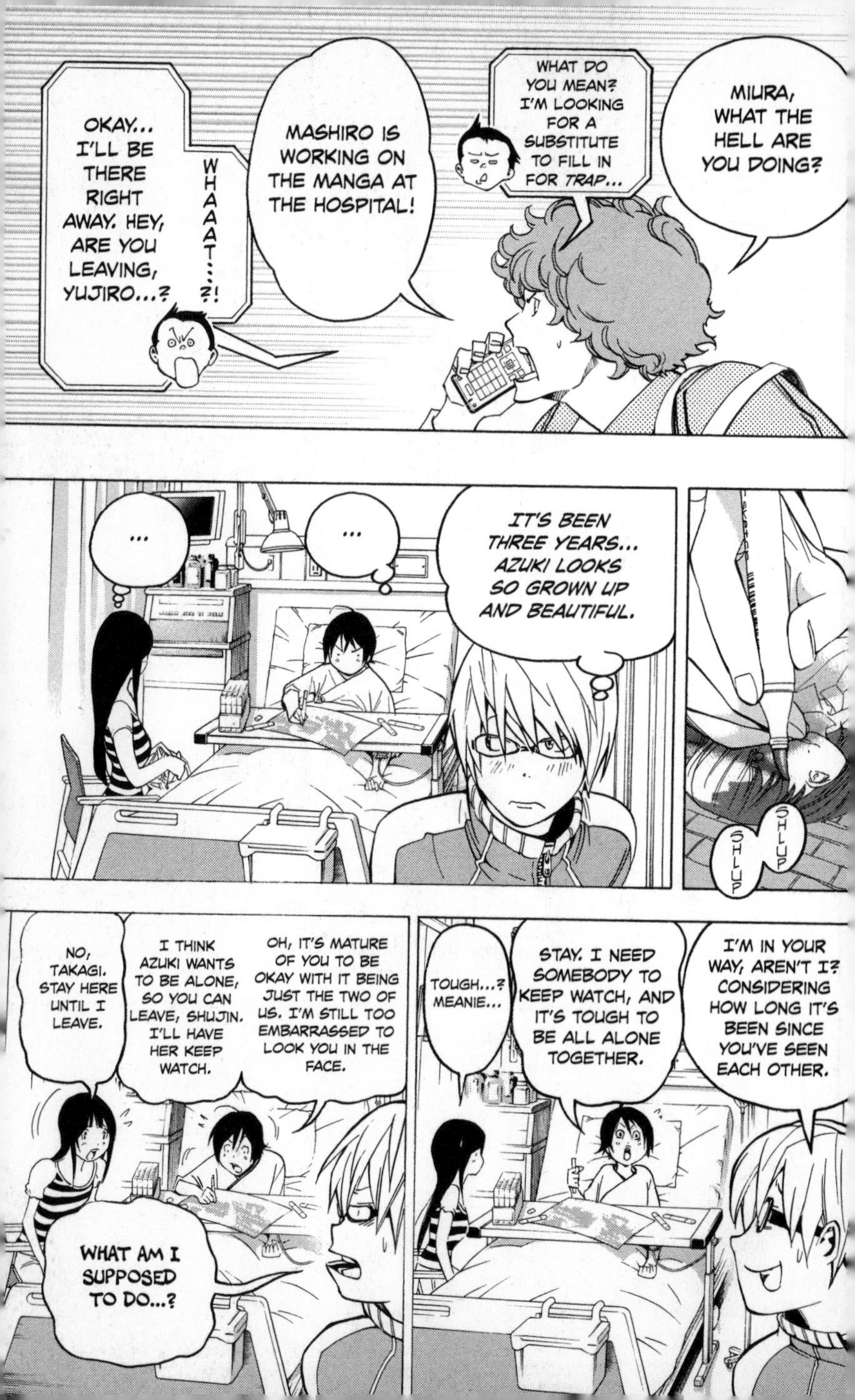
MIURA, WHAT THE HELL ARE YOU DOING?
WHAT DO YOU MEAN? I'M LOOKING FOR A SUBSTITUTE TO FILL IN FOR TRAP...
MASHIRO IS WORKING ON THE MANGA AT THE HOSPITAL!
WHAAAAT...?!
OKAY... I'LL BE THERE RIGHT AWAY. HEY, ARE YOU LEAVING, YUJIRO...?
SHLUP
SHLUP
IT'S BEEN THREE YEARS... AZUKI LOOKS SO GROWN UP AND BEAUTIFUL.
...
...
I'M IN YOUR WAY, AREN'T I? CONSIDERING HOW LONG IT'S BEEN SINCE YOU'VE SEEN EACH OTHER.
STAY. I NEED SOMEBODY TO KEEP WATCH, AND IT'S TOUGH TO BE ALL ALONE TOGETHER.
TOUGH...? MEANIE...
OH, IT'S MATURE OF YOU TO BE OKAY WITH IT BEING JUST THE TWO OF US. I'M STILL TOO EMBARRASSED TO LOOK YOU IN THE FACE.
I THINK AZUKI WANTS TO BE ALONE, SO YOU CAN LEAVE, SHUJIN. I'LL HAVE HER KEEP WATCH.
NO, TAKAGI. STAY HERE UNTIL I LEAVE.
WHAT AM I SUPPOSED TO DO...?

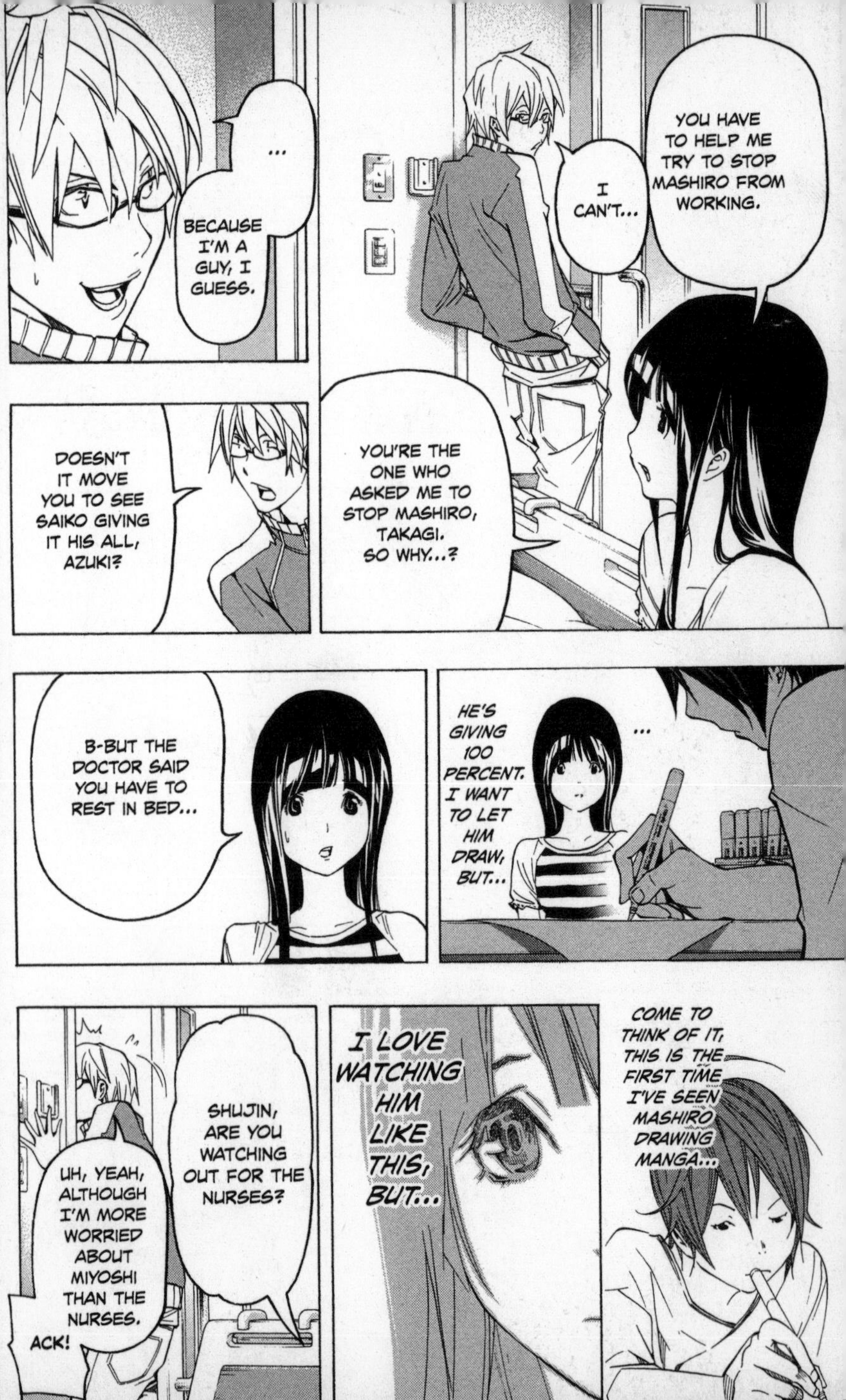
YOU HAVE TO HELP ME TRY TO STOP MASHIRO FROM WORKING.
I CAN'T...
YOU'RE THE ONE WHO ASKED ME TO STOP MASHIRO, TAKAGI. SO WHY...?
...
BECAUSE I'M A GUY, I GUESS.
DOESN'T IT MOVE YOU TO SEE SAIKO GIVING IT HIS ALL, AZUKI?
...
HE'S GIVING 100 PERCENT. I WANT TO LET HIM DRAW, BUT...
B-BUT THE DOCTOR SAID YOU HAVE TO REST IN BED...
COME TO THINK OF IT, THIS IS THE FIRST TIME I'VE SEEN MASHIRO DRAWING MANGA...
I LOVE WATCHING HIM LIKE THIS, BUT...
SHUJIN, ARE YOU WATCHING OUT FOR THE NURSES?
UH, YEAH, ALTHOUGH I'M MORE WORRIED ABOUT MIYOSHI THAN THE NURSES.
ACK!

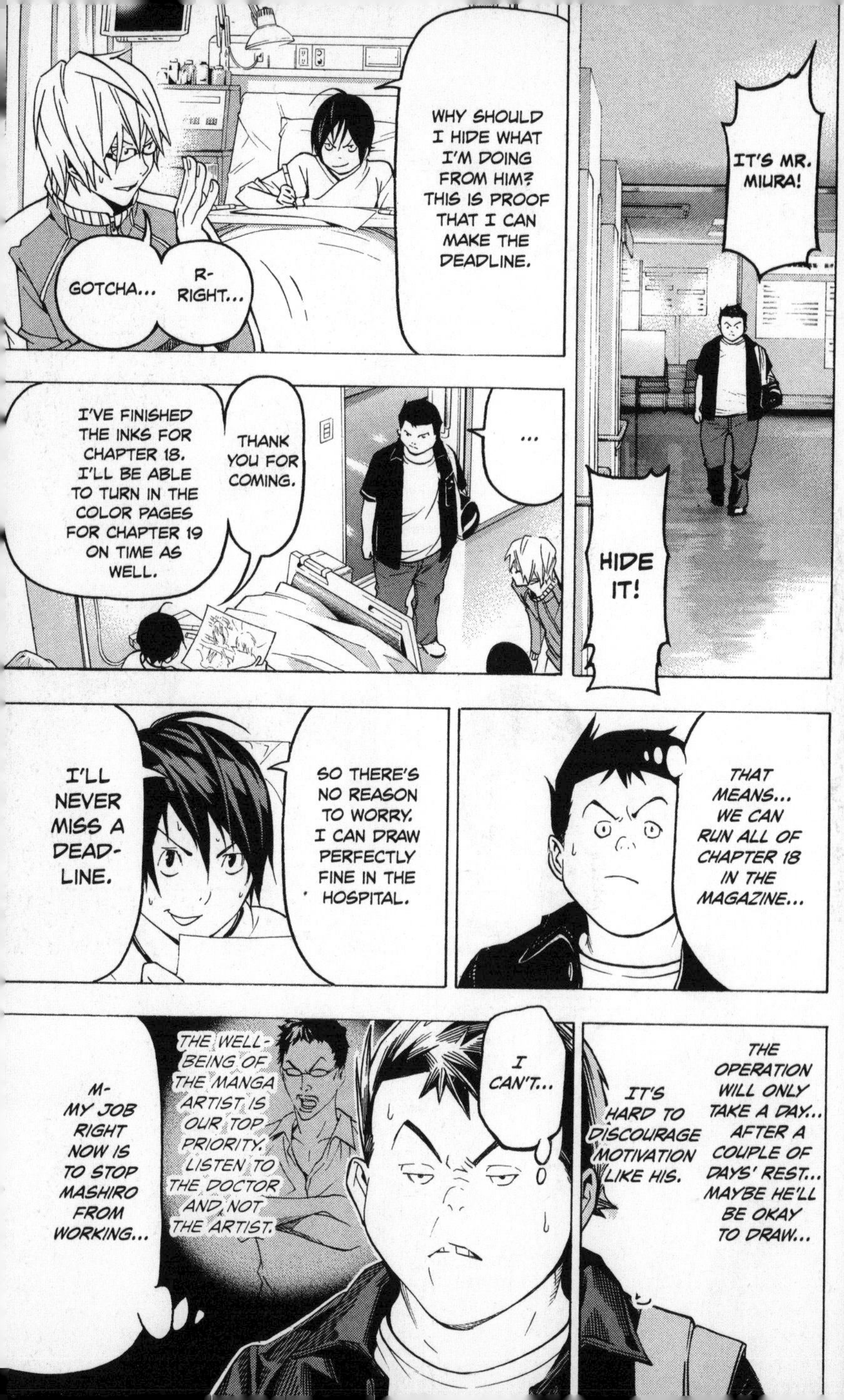
IT'S MR. MIURA!
HIDE IT!
WHY SHOULD I HIDE WHAT I'M DOING FROM HIM? THIS IS PROOF THAT I CAN MAKE THE DEADLINE.
R-RIGHT...
GOTCHA...
...
THANK YOU FOR COMING.
I'VE FINISHED THE INKS FOR CHAPTER 18. I'LL BE ABLE TO TURN IN THE COLOR PAGES FOR CHAPTER 19 ON TIME AS WELL.
THAT MEANS... WE CAN RUN ALL OF CHAPTER 18 IN THE MAGAZINE...
SO THERE'S NO REASON TO WORRY. I CAN DRAW PERFECTLY FINE IN THE HOSPITAL.
I'LL NEVER MISS A DEAD-LINE.
THE OPERATION WILL ONLY TAKE A DAY... AFTER A COUPLE OF DAYS' REST... MAYBE HE'LL BE OKAY TO DRAW...
IT'S HARD TO DISCOURAGE MOTIVATION LIKE HIS.
I CAN'T...
THE WELL-BEING OF THE MANGA ARTIST IS OUR TOP PRIORITY. LISTEN TO THE DOCTOR AND NOT THE ARTIST.
M-MY JOB RIGHT NOW IS TO STOP MASHIRO FROM WORKING...

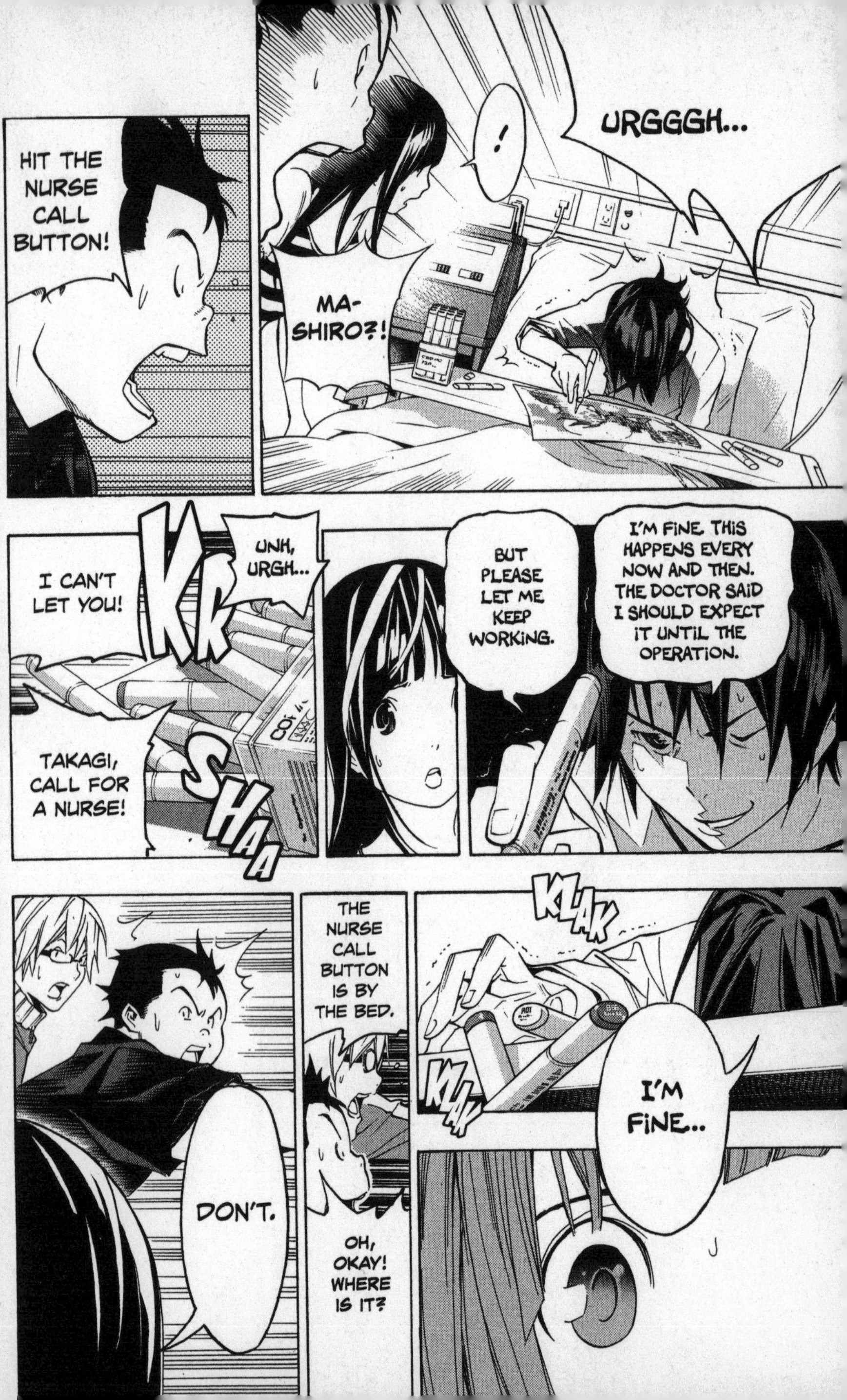
URGGGH...
!
MA-SHIRO?!
HIT THE NURSE CALL BUTTON!
I'M FINE THIS HAPPENS EVERY NOW AND THEN. THE DOCTOR SAID I SHOULD EXPECT IT UNTIL THE OPERATION.
BUT PLEASE LET ME KEEP WORKING.
UNH, URGH...
KK
I CAN'T LET YOU!
SHAA
TAKAGI, CALL FOR A NURSE!
KLAK
KLAK
I'M FINE...
THE NURSE CALL BUTTON IS BY THE BED.
OH, OKAY! WHERE IS IT?
DON'T.

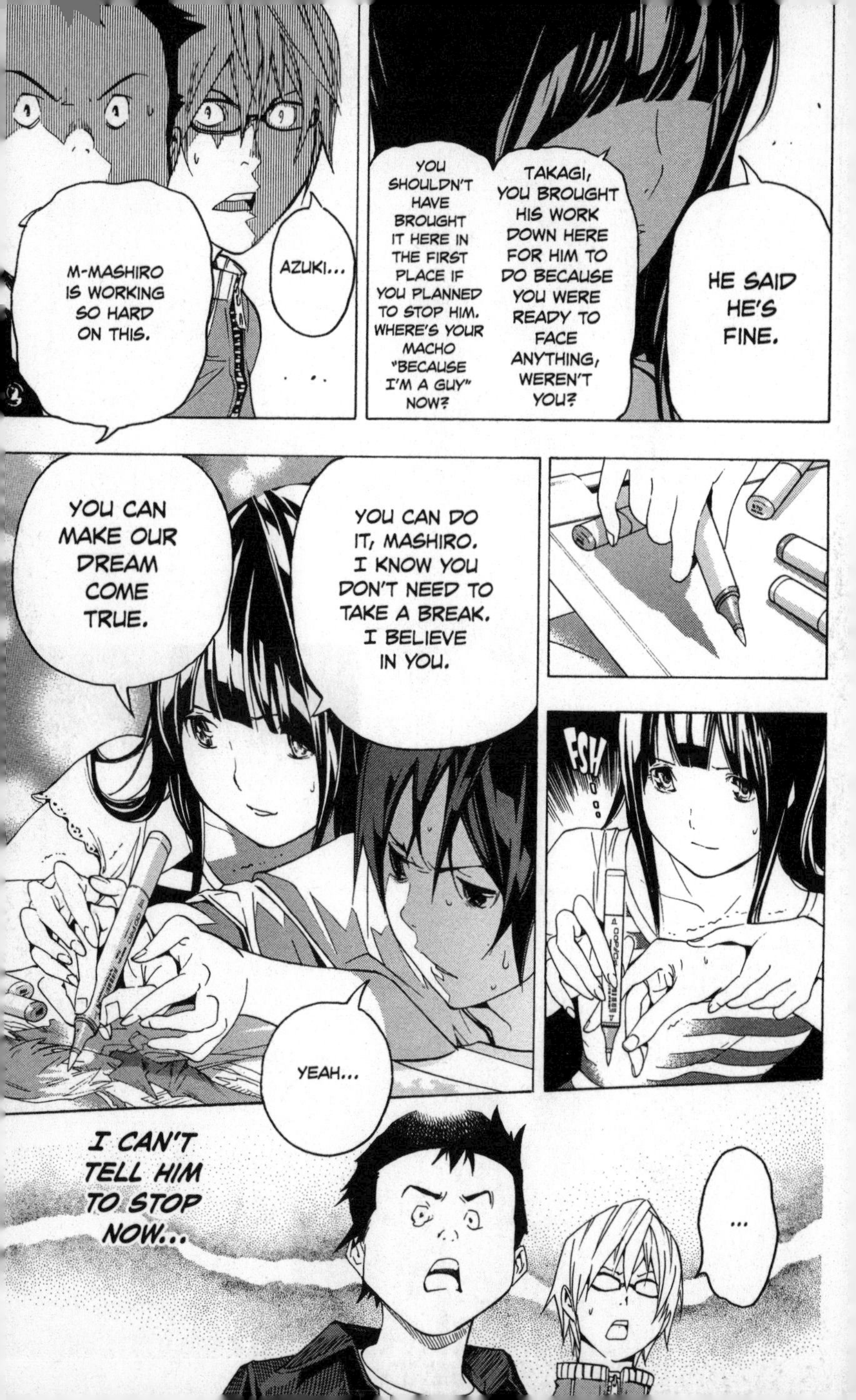

HE SAID HE'S FINE.
TAKAGI, YOU BROUGHT HIS WORK DOWN HERE FOR HIM TO DO BECAUSE YOU WERE READY TO FACE ANYTHING, WEREN'T YOU?
YOU SHOULDN'T HAVE BROUGHT IT HERE IN THE FIRST PLACE IF YOU PLANNED TO STOP HIM. WHERE'S YOUR MACHO "BECAUSE I'M A GUY" NOW?
AZUKI...
M-MASHIRO IS WORKING SO HARD ON THIS.
FSH
YOU CAN DO IT, MASHIRO. I KNOW YOU DON'T NEED TO TAKE A BREAK. I BELIEVE IN YOU.
YOU CAN MAKE OUR DREAM COME TRUE.
YEAH...
...
I CAN'T TELL HIM TO STOP NOW...

OHBA'S STORYBOARD

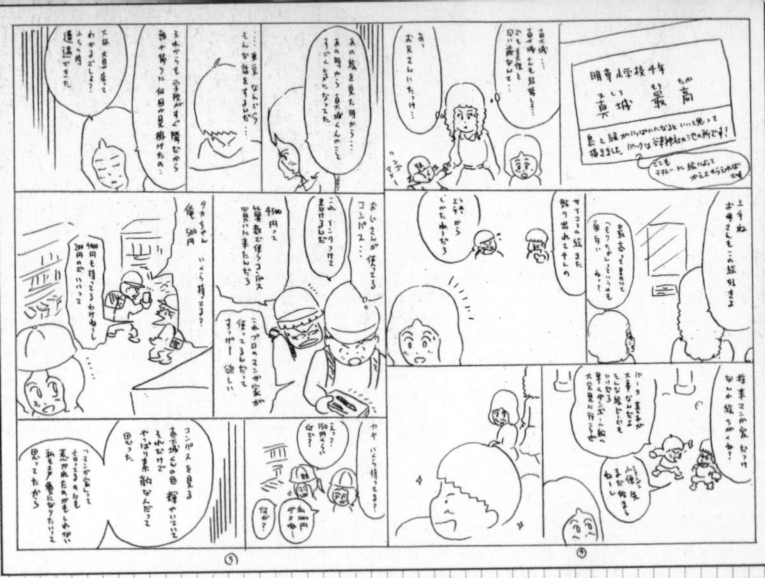
明草小学校4年
真城最高

OBATA'S STORYBOARD

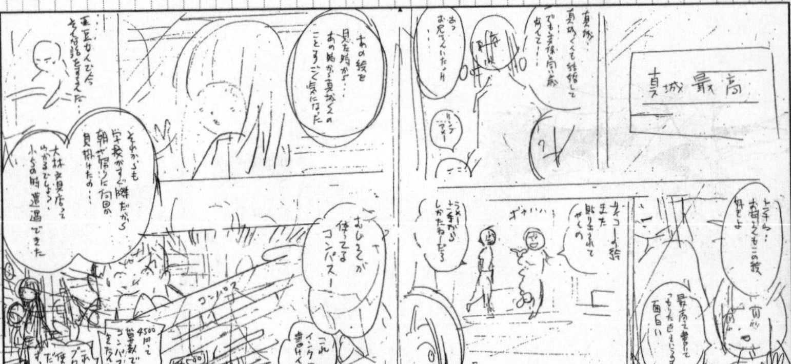
真城最高

COMPLETE!

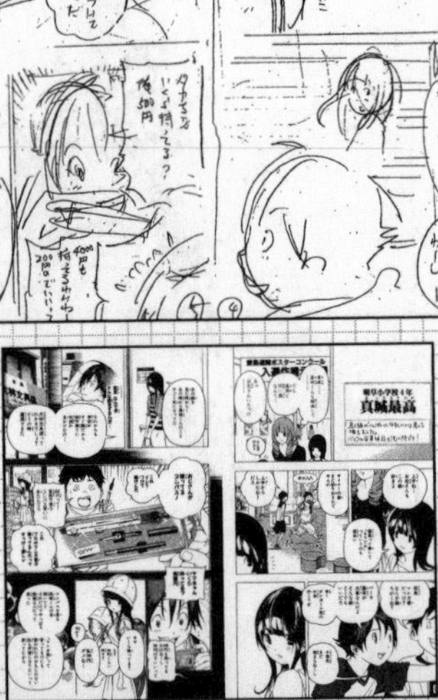

※CREATOR STORYBOARDS AND FINISHED PAGES IN JAPANESE

BAKUMAN。 vol.6

"Until the Final Draft Is Complete"

Chapter 46, pp. 50-51

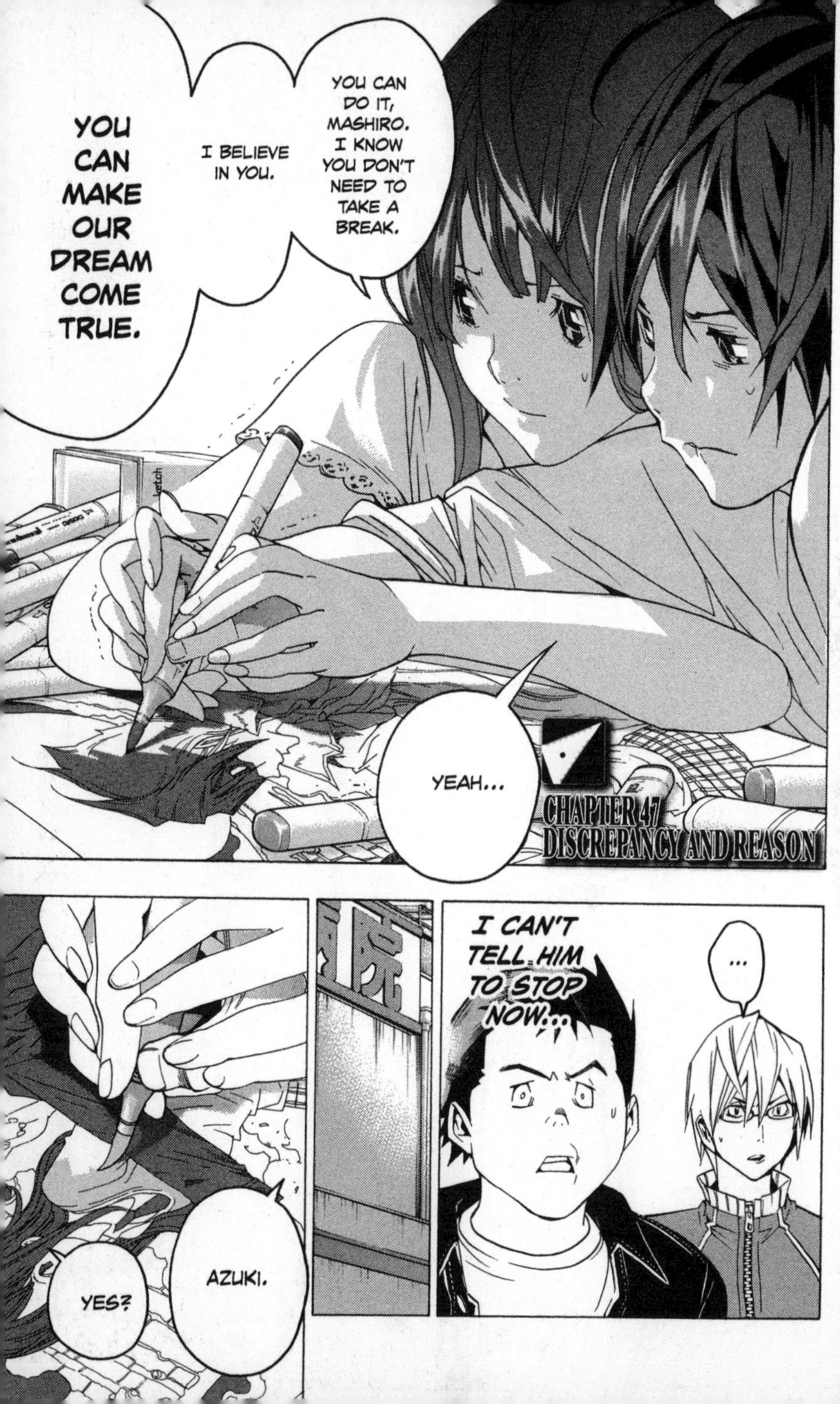
YOU CAN DO IT, MASHIRO. I KNOW YOU DON'T NEED TO TAKE A BREAK.
I BELIEVE IN YOU.
YOU CAN MAKE OUR DREAM COME TRUE.
YEAH...
CHAPTER 47
DISCREPANCY AND REASON
...
I CAN'T TELL HIM TO STOP NOW...
AZUKI.
YES?

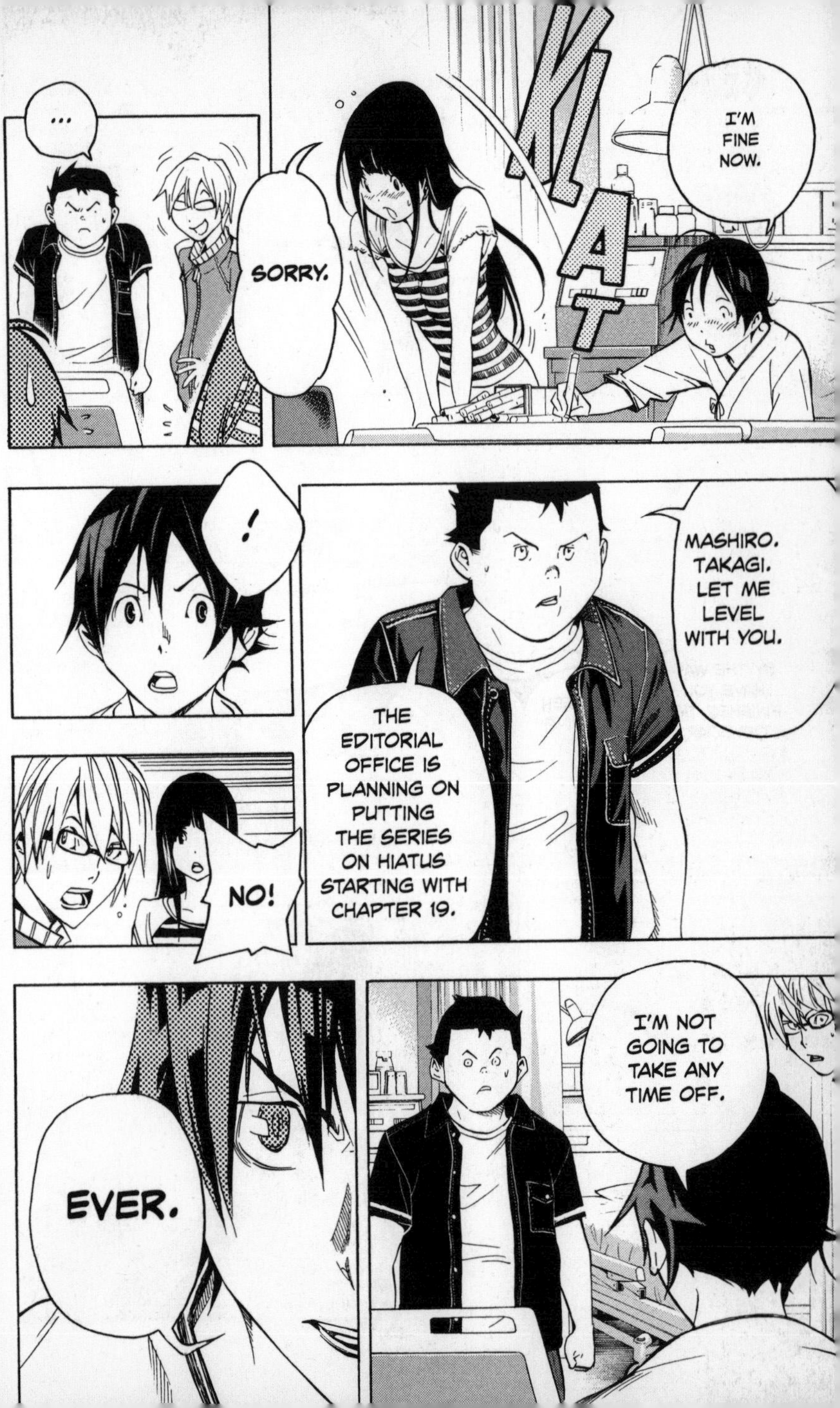
I'M FINE NOW.
KLAT
SORRY.
...
MASHIRO. TAKAGI. LET ME LEVEL WITH YOU.
THE EDITORIAL OFFICE IS PLANNING ON PUTTING THE SERIES ON HIATUS STARTING WITH CHAPTER 19.
!
NO!
I'M NOT GOING TO TAKE ANY TIME OFF.
EVER.

READ THIS WAY

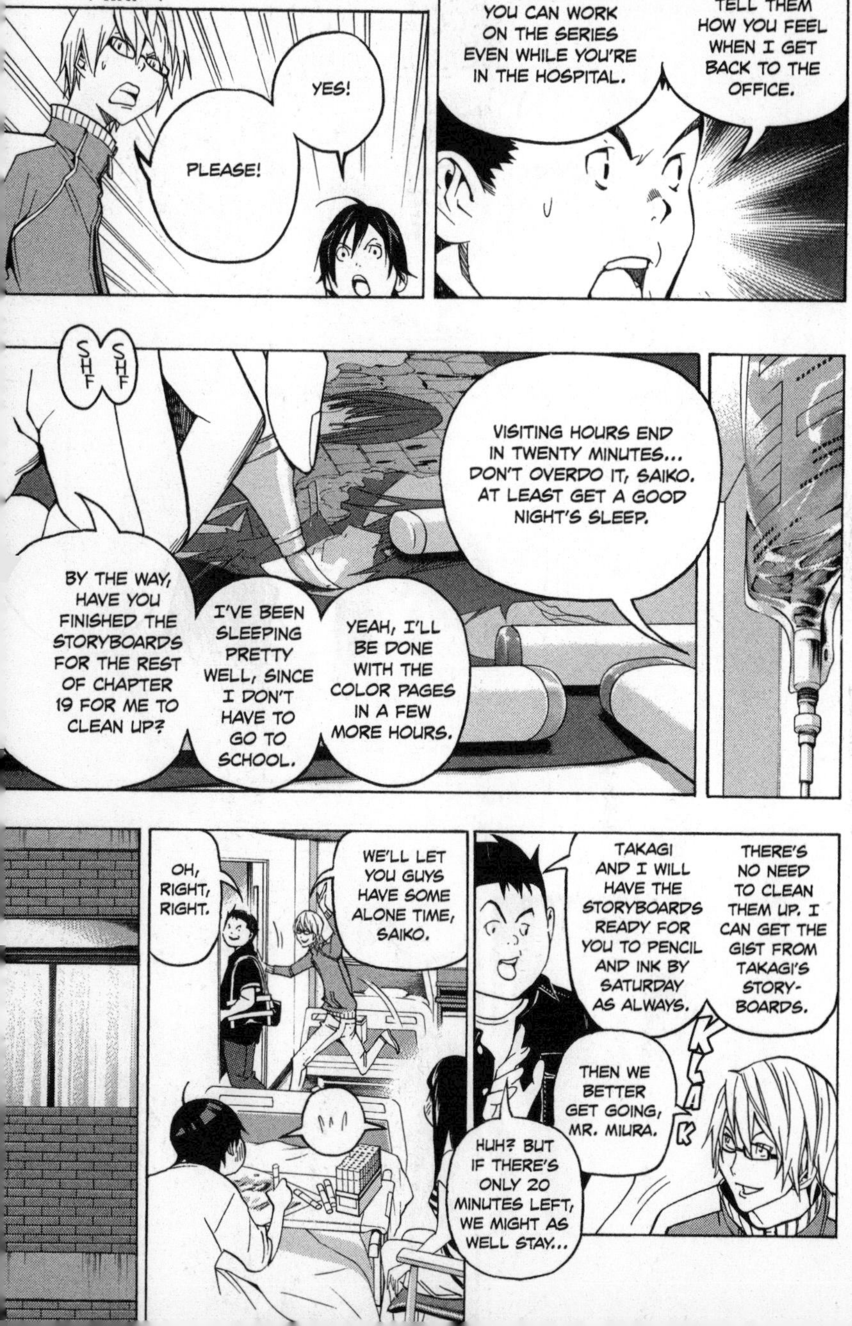
OKAY. I'LL TELL THEM HOW YOU FEEL WHEN I GET BACK TO THE OFFICE.
I BELIEVE THAT YOU CAN WORK ON THE SERIES EVEN WHILE YOU'RE IN THE HOSPITAL.
YES!
PLEASE!
VISITING HOURS END IN TWENTY MINUTES... DON'T OVERDO IT, SAIKO. AT LEAST GET A GOOD NIGHT'S SLEEP.
YEAH, I'LL BE DONE WITH THE COLOR PAGES IN A FEW MORE HOURS.
I'VE BEEN SLEEPING PRETTY WELL, SINCE I DON'T HAVE TO GO TO SCHOOL.
BY THE WAY, HAVE YOU FINISHED THE STORYBOARDS FOR THE REST OF CHAPTER 19 FOR ME TO CLEAN UP?
SHF SHF
THERE'S NO NEED TO CLEAN THEM UP. I CAN GET THE GIST FROM TAKAGI'S STORY-BOARDS.
TAKAGI AND I WILL HAVE THE STORYBOARDS READY FOR YOU TO PENCIL AND INK BY SATURDAY AS ALWAYS.
KAK
THEN WE BETTER GET GOING, MR. MIURA.
HUH? BUT IF THERE'S ONLY 20 MINUTES LEFT, WE MIGHT AS WELL STAY...
WE'LL LET YOU GUYS HAVE SOME ALONE TIME, SAIKO.
OH, RIGHT, RIGHT.

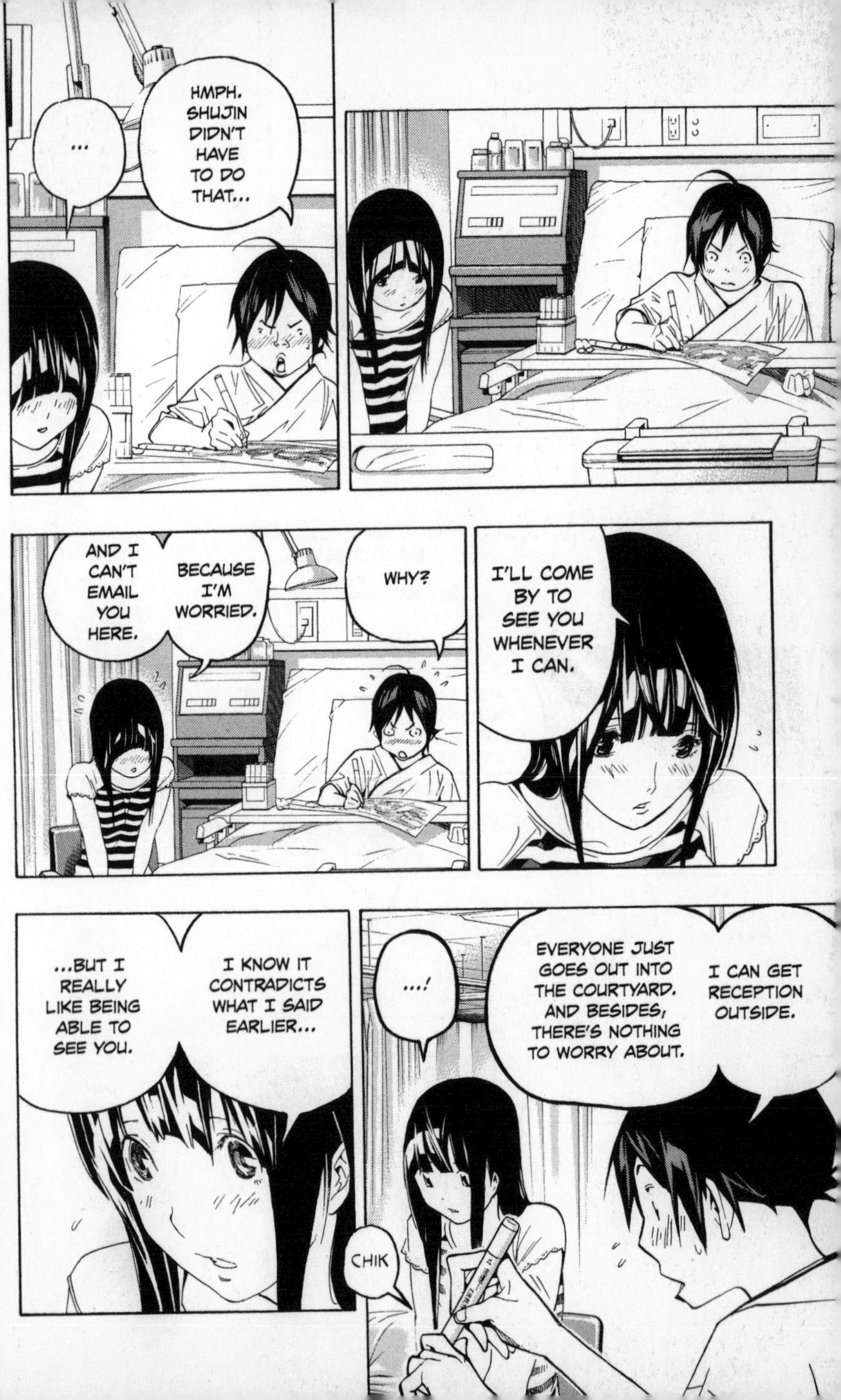
HMPH. SHUJIN DIDN'T HAVE TO DO THAT...
...
I'LL COME BY TO SEE YOU WHENEVER I CAN.
WHY?
BECAUSE I'M WORRIED.
AND I CAN'T EMAIL YOU HERE.
I CAN GET RECEPTION OUTSIDE.
EVERYONE JUST GOES OUT INTO THE COURTYARD. AND BESIDES, THERE'S NOTHING TO WORRY ABOUT.
...!
CHIK
I KNOW IT CONTRADICTS WHAT I SAID EARLIER...
...BUT I REALLY LIKE BEING ABLE TO SEE YOU.

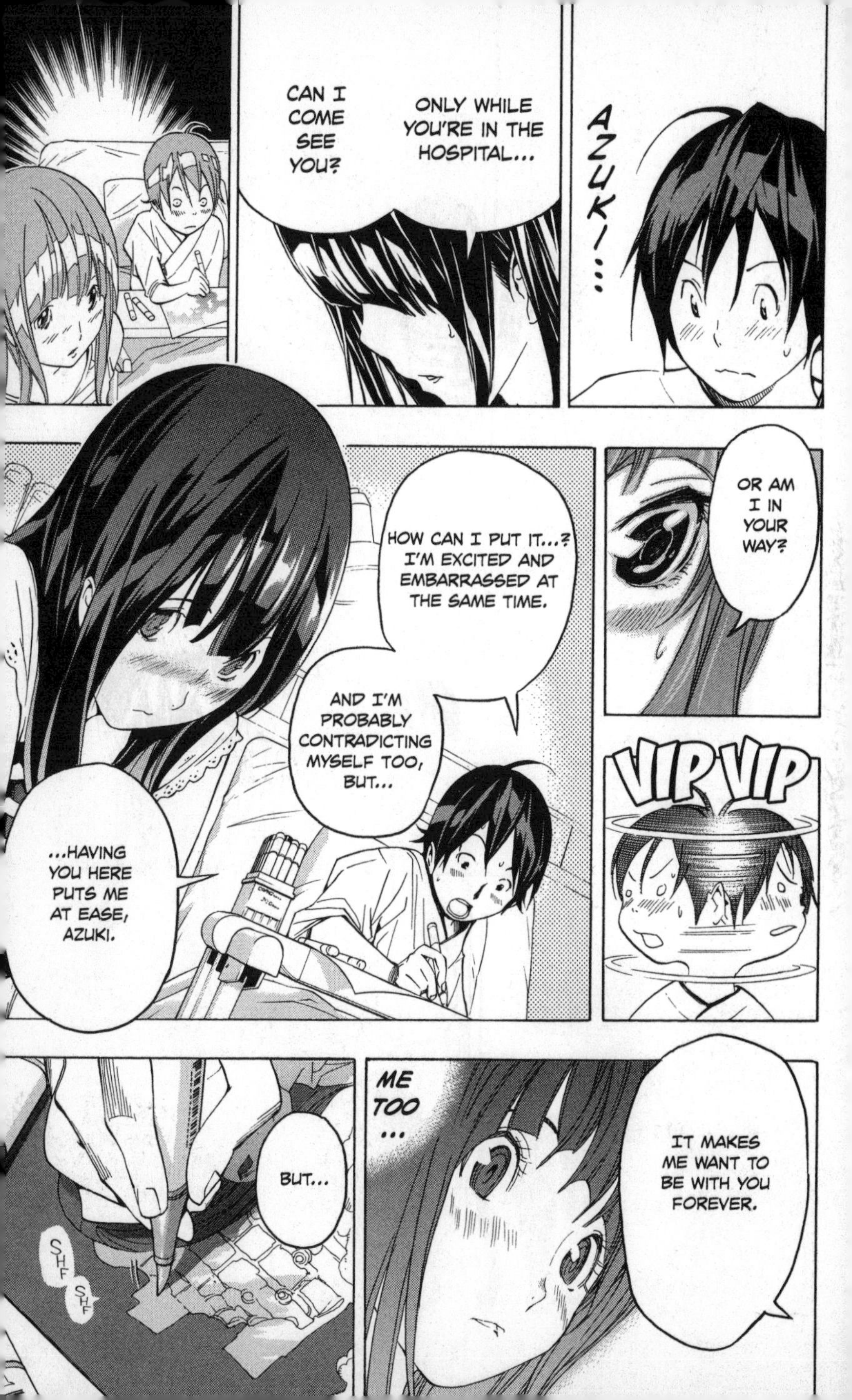
AZUKI...
ONLY WHILE YOU'RE IN THE HOSPITAL...
CAN I COME SEE YOU?
OR AM I IN YOUR WAY?
VIP VIP
HOW CAN I PUT IT...? I'M EXCITED AND EMBARRASSED AT THE SAME TIME.
AND I'M PROBABLY CONTRADICTING MYSELF TOO, BUT...
...HAVING YOU HERE PUTS ME AT EASE, AZUKI.
IT MAKES ME WANT TO BE WITH YOU FOREVER.
ME TOO...
BUT...
SHF SHF

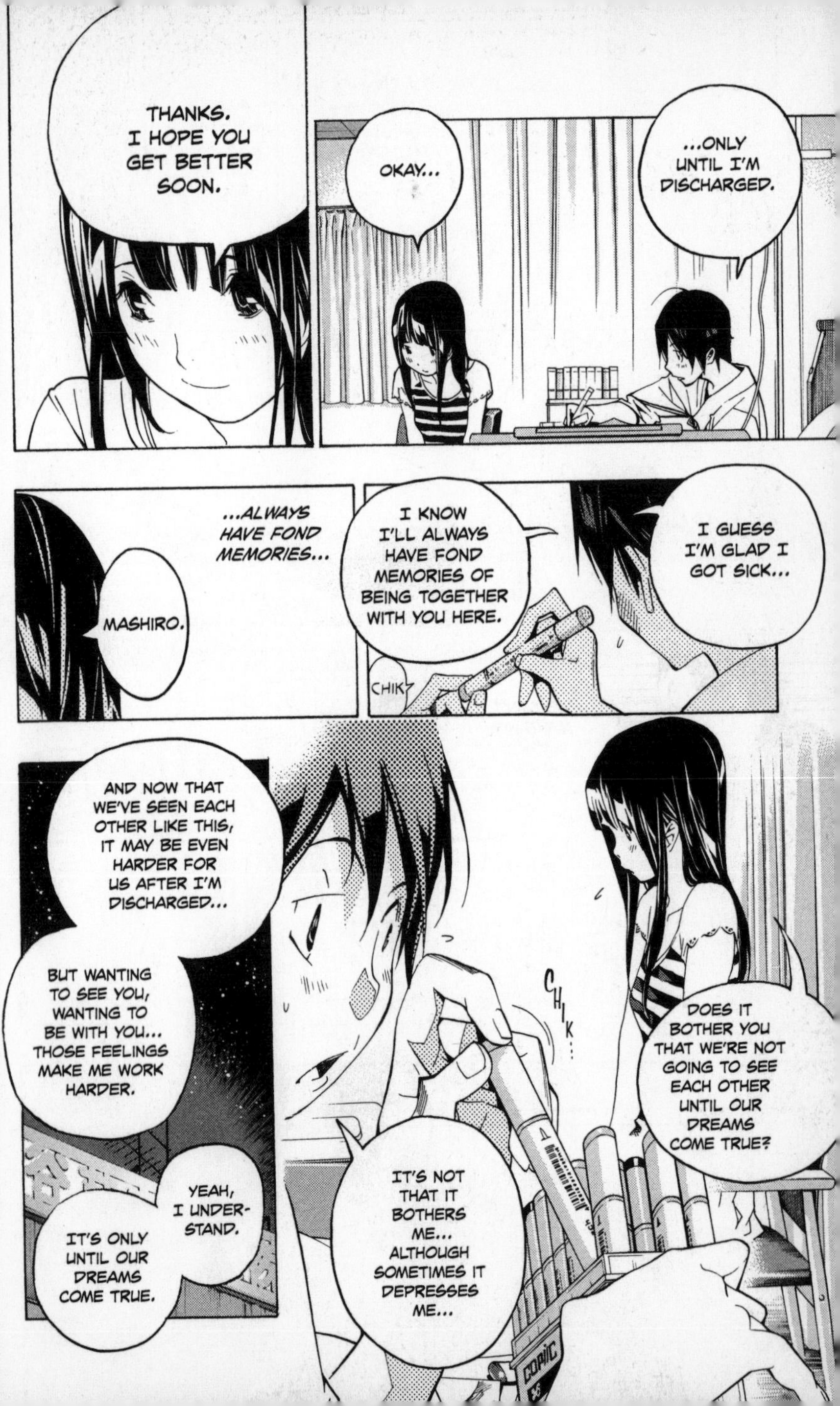
...ONLY UNTIL I'M DISCHARGED.
OKAY...
THANKS. I HOPE YOU GET BETTER SOON.
I GUESS I'M GLAD I GOT SICK...
I KNOW I'LL ALWAYS HAVE FOND MEMORIES OF BEING TOGETHER WITH YOU HERE.
CHIK
...ALWAYS HAVE FOND MEMORIES...
MASHIRO.
DOES IT BOTHER YOU THAT WE'RE NOT GOING TO SEE EACH OTHER UNTIL OUR DREAMS COME TRUE?
CHIK...
IT'S NOT THAT IT BOTHERS ME... ALTHOUGH SOMETIMES IT DEPRESSES ME...
COPIC
AND NOW THAT WE'VE SEEN EACH OTHER LIKE THIS, IT MAY BE EVEN HARDER FOR US AFTER I'M DISCHARGED...
BUT WANTING TO SEE YOU, WANTING TO BE WITH YOU... THOSE FEELINGS MAKE ME WORK HARDER.
YEAH, I UNDER-STAND.
IT'S ONLY UNTIL OUR DREAMS COME TRUE.

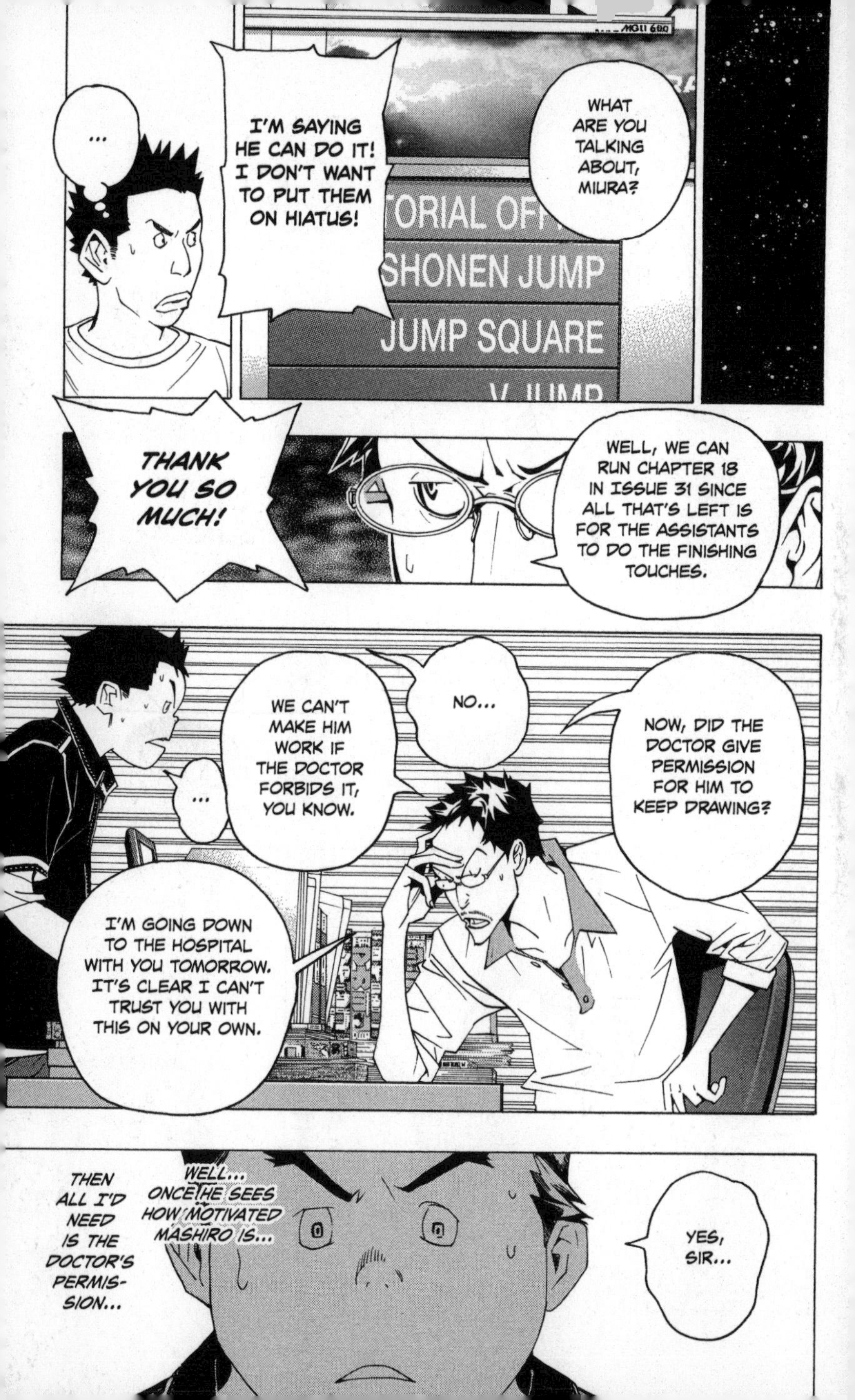
WHAT ARE YOU TALKING ABOUT, MIURA?
TORIAL OFF
SHONEN JUMP
JUMP SQUARE
I'M SAYING HE CAN DO IT! I DON'T WANT TO PUT THEM ON HIATUS!
...
WELL, WE CAN RUN CHAPTER 18 IN ISSUE 31 SINCE ALL THAT'S LEFT IS FOR THE ASSISTANTS TO DO THE FINISHING TOUCHES.
THANK YOU SO MUCH!
NOW, DID THE DOCTOR GIVE PERMISSION FOR HIM TO KEEP DRAWING?
NO...
WE CAN'T MAKE HIM WORK IF THE DOCTOR FORBIDS IT, YOU KNOW.
...
I'M GOING DOWN TO THE HOSPITAL WITH YOU TOMORROW. IT'S CLEAR I CAN'T TRUST YOU WITH THIS ON YOUR OWN.
YES, SIR...
WELL... ONCE HE SEES HOW MOTIVATED MASHIRO IS...
THEN ALL I'D NEED IS THE DOCTOR'S PERMISSION...

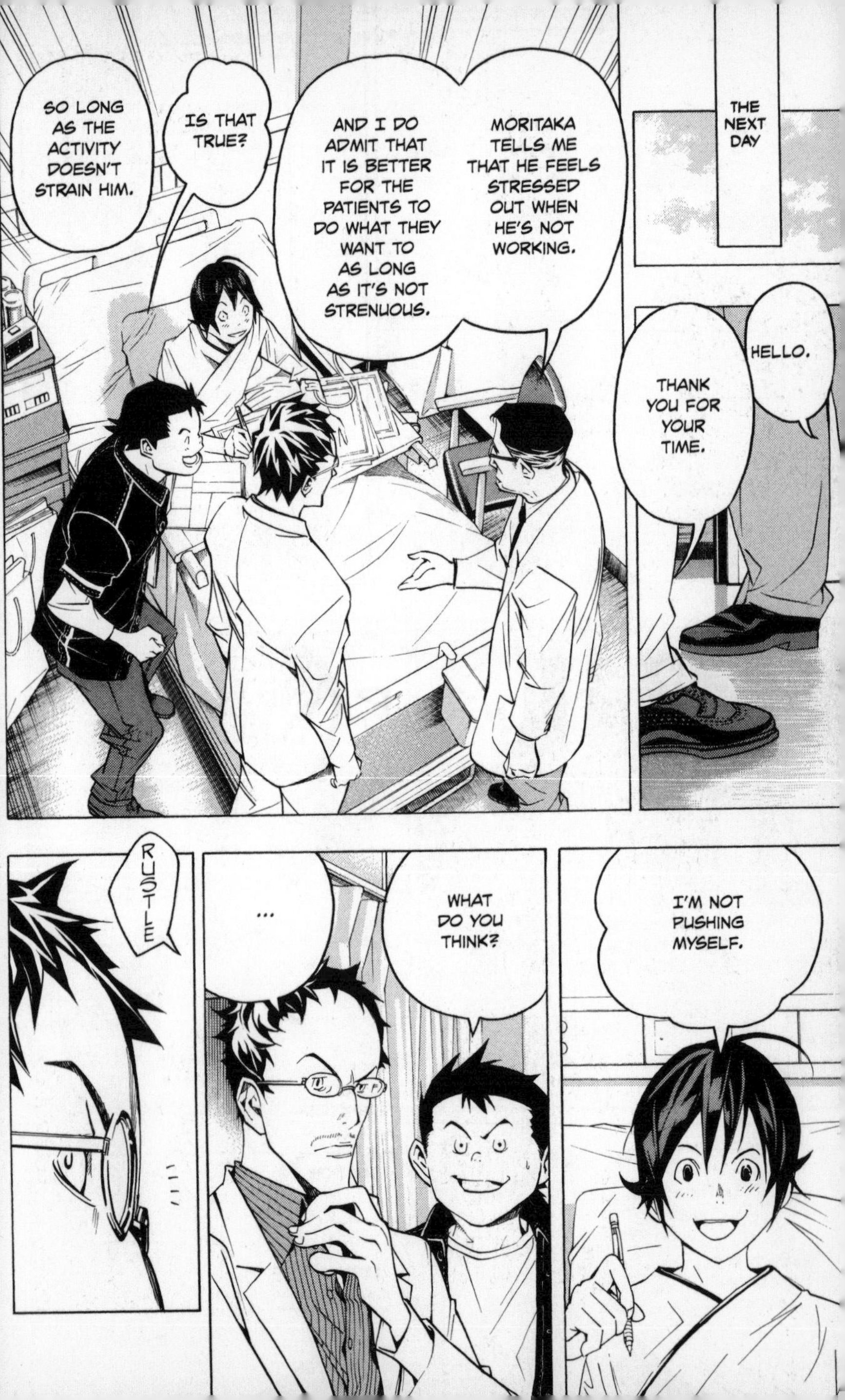
THE NEXT DAY
HELLO.
THANK YOU FOR YOUR TIME.
MORITAKA TELLS ME THAT HE FEELS STRESSED OUT WHEN HE'S NOT WORKING.
AND I DO ADMIT THAT IT IS BETTER FOR THE PATIENTS TO DO WHAT THEY WANT TO AS LONG AS IT'S NOT STRENUOUS.
IS THAT TRUE?
SO LONG AS THE ACTIVITY DOESN'T STRAIN HIM.
I'M NOT PUSHING MYSELF.
WHAT DO YOU THINK?
...
RUSTLE

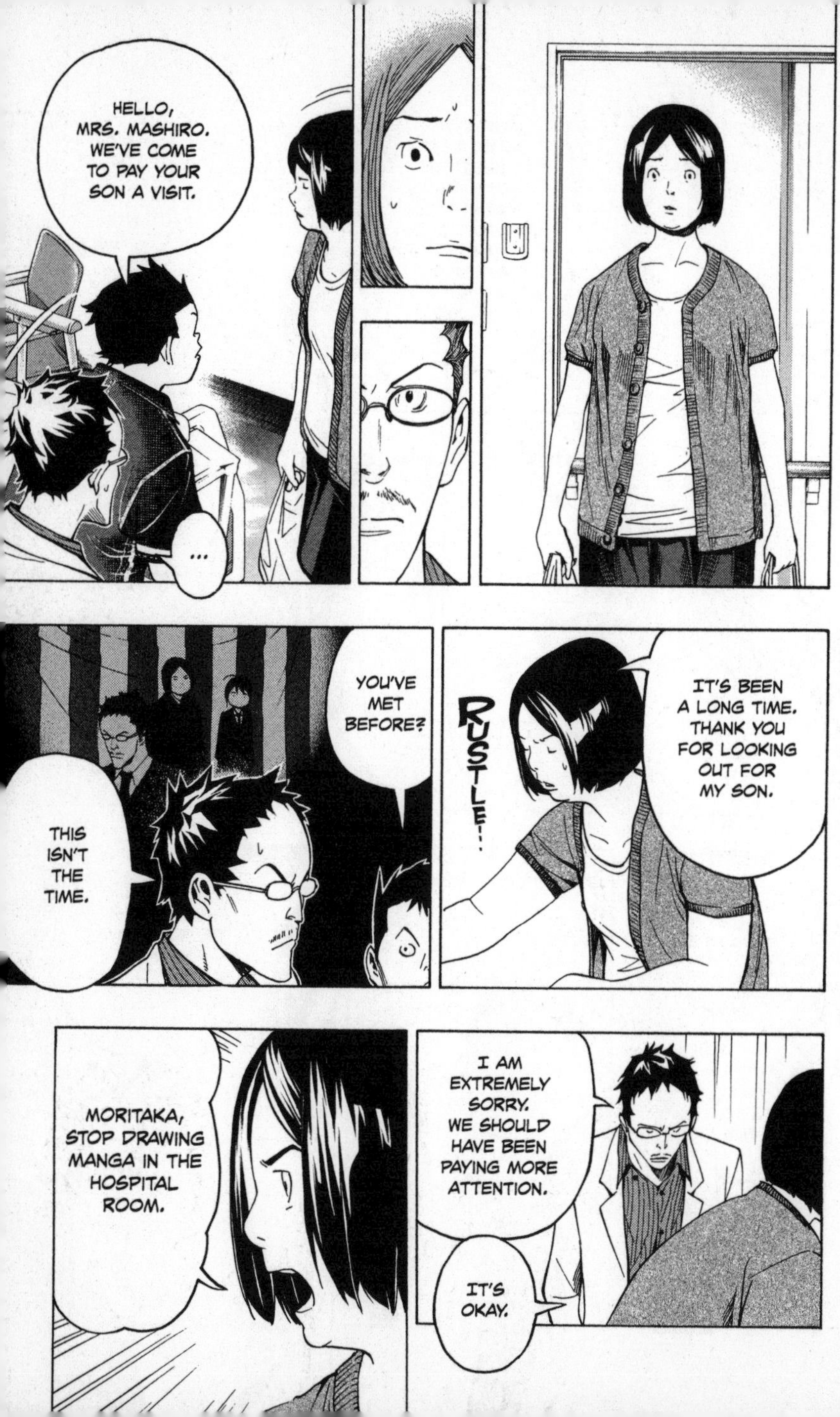
HELLO, MRS. MASHIRO. WE'VE COME TO PAY YOUR SON A VISIT.
...
IT'S BEEN A LONG TIME. THANK YOU FOR LOOKING OUT FOR MY SON.
RUSTLE
YOU'VE MET BEFORE?
THIS ISN'T THE TIME.
I AM EXTREMELY SORRY. WE SHOULD HAVE BEEN PAYING MORE ATTENTION.
IT'S OKAY.
MORITAKA, STOP DRAWING MANGA IN THE HOSPITAL ROOM.

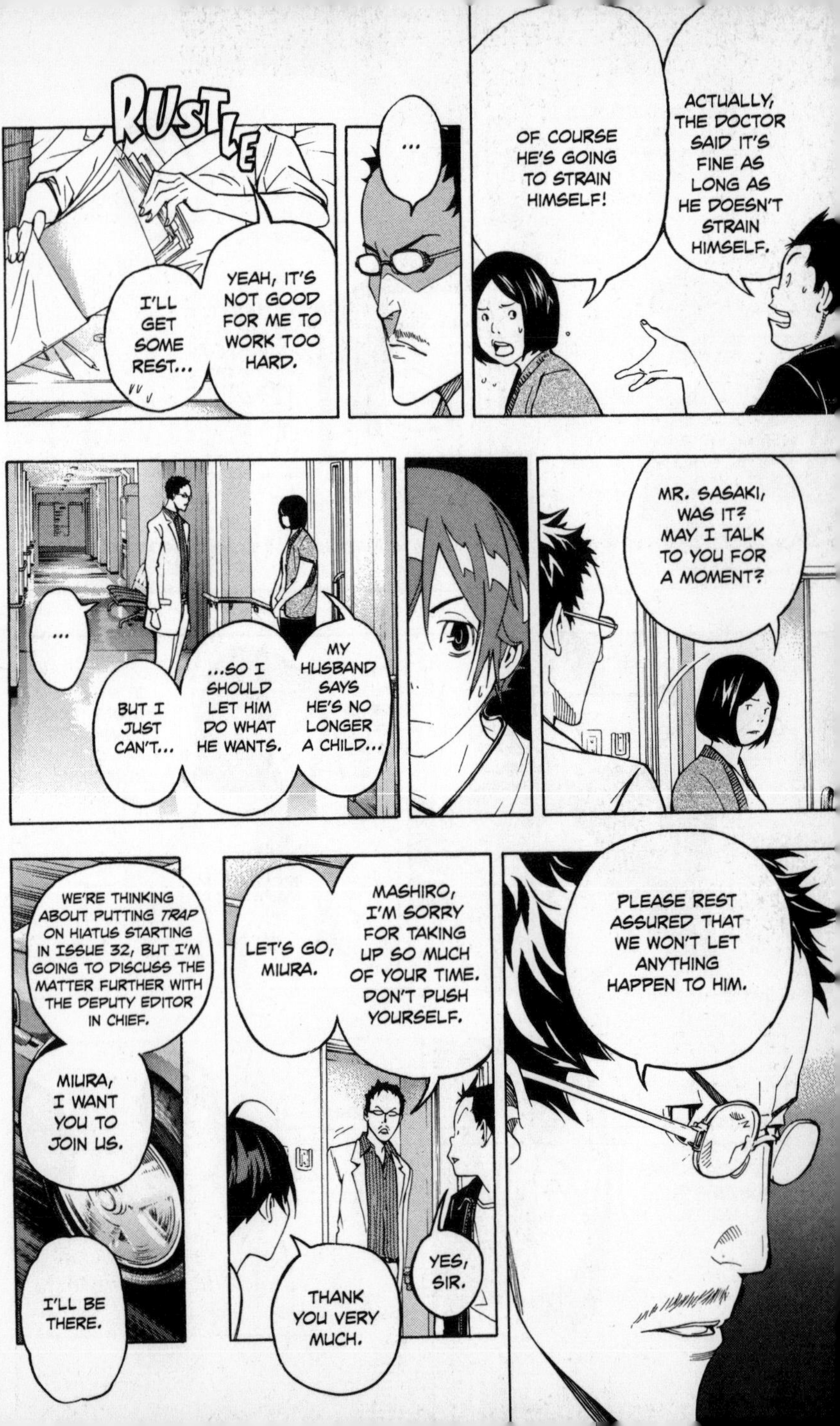
ACTUALLY, THE DOCTOR SAID IT'S FINE AS LONG AS HE DOESN'T STRAIN HIMSELF.
OF COURSE HE'S GOING TO STRAIN HIMSELF!
...
RUSTLE
YEAH, IT'S NOT GOOD FOR ME TO WORK TOO HARD.
I'LL GET SOME REST...
MR. SASAKI, WAS IT? MAY I TALK TO YOU FOR A MOMENT?
MY HUSBAND SAYS HE'S NO LONGER A CHILD...
...SO I SHOULD LET HIM DO WHAT HE WANTS.
BUT I JUST CAN'T...
...
PLEASE REST ASSURED THAT WE WON'T LET ANYTHING HAPPEN TO HIM.
MASHIRO, I'M SORRY FOR TAKING UP SO MUCH OF YOUR TIME. DON'T PUSH YOURSELF.
LET'S GO, MIURA.
YES, SIR.
THANK YOU VERY MUCH.
WE'RE THINKING ABOUT PUTTING *TRAP* ON HIATUS STARTING IN ISSUE 32, BUT I'M GOING TO DISCUSS THE MATTER FURTHER WITH THE DEPUTY EDITOR IN CHIEF.
MIURA, I WANT YOU TO JOIN US.
I'LL BE THERE.

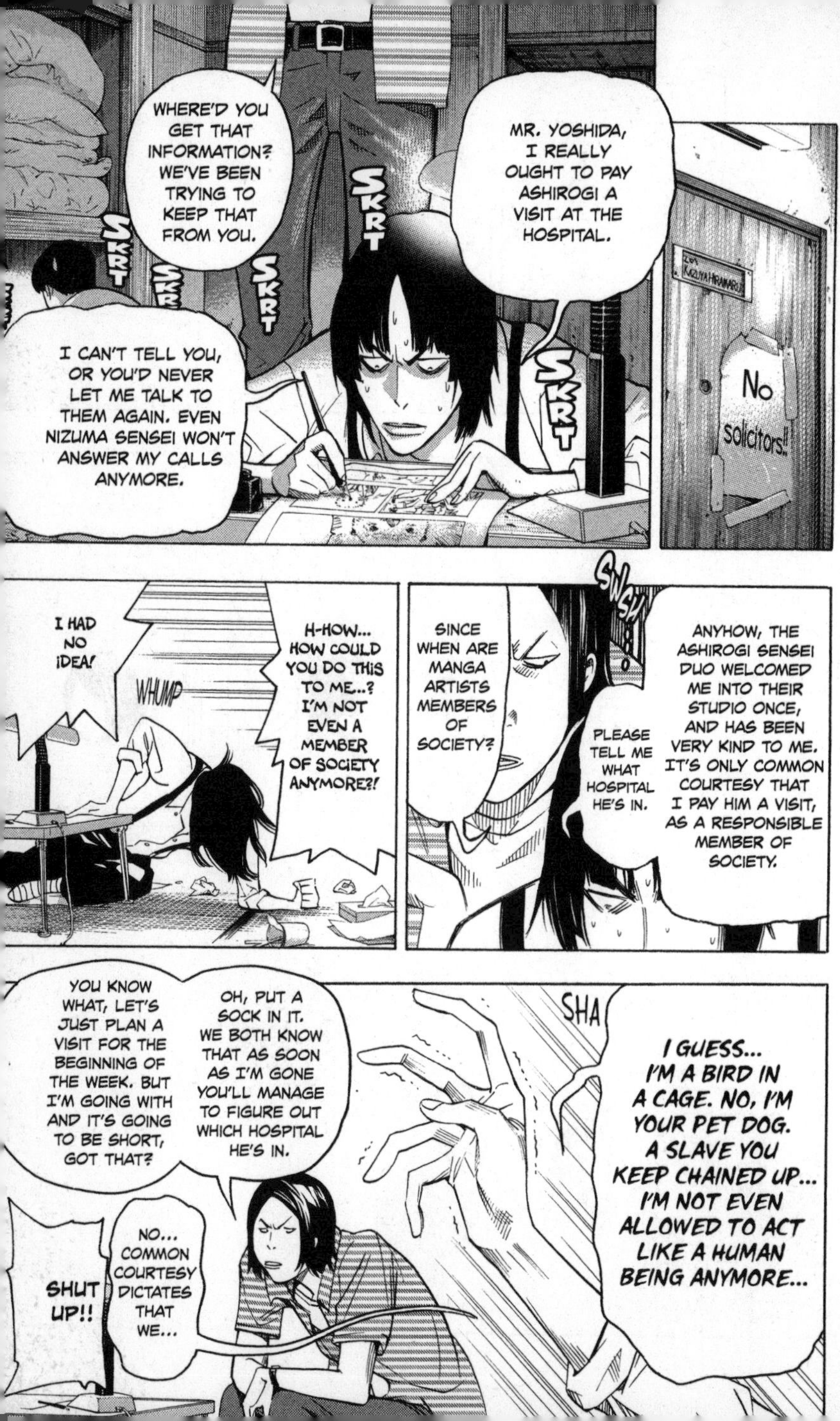
No solicitors!!
MR. YOSHIDA, I REALLY OUGHT TO PAY ASHIROGI A VISIT AT THE HOSPITAL.
SKRT
SKRT
WHERE'D YOU GET THAT INFORMATION? WE'VE BEEN TRYING TO KEEP THAT FROM YOU.
SKRT
SKRT
SKRT
I CAN'T TELL YOU, OR YOU'D NEVER LET ME TALK TO THEM AGAIN. EVEN NIZUMA SENSEI WON'T ANSWER MY CALLS ANYMORE.
SWSH
ANYHOW, THE ASHIROGI SENSEI DUO WELCOMED ME INTO THEIR STUDIO ONCE, AND HAS BEEN VERY KIND TO ME. IT'S ONLY COMMON COURTESY THAT I PAY HIM A VISIT, AS A RESPONSIBLE MEMBER OF SOCIETY.
PLEASE TELL ME WHAT HOSPITAL HE'S IN.
SINCE WHEN ARE MANGA ARTISTS MEMBERS OF SOCIETY?
H-HOW... HOW COULD YOU DO THIS TO ME...? I'M NOT EVEN A MEMBER OF SOCIETY ANYMORE?!
WHUMP
I HAD NO IDEA!
SHA
I GUESS... I'M A BIRD IN A CAGE. NO, I'M YOUR PET DOG. A SLAVE YOU KEEP CHAINED UP... I'M NOT EVEN ALLOWED TO ACT LIKE A HUMAN BEING ANYMORE...
OH, PUT A SOCK IN IT. WE BOTH KNOW THAT AS SOON AS I'M GONE YOU'LL MANAGE TO FIGURE OUT WHICH HOSPITAL HE'S IN.
YOU KNOW WHAT, LET'S JUST PLAN A VISIT FOR THE BEGINNING OF THE WEEK. BUT I'M GOING WITH AND IT'S GOING TO BE SHORT, GOT THAT?
NO... COMMON COURTESY DICTATES THAT WE...
SHUT UP!!

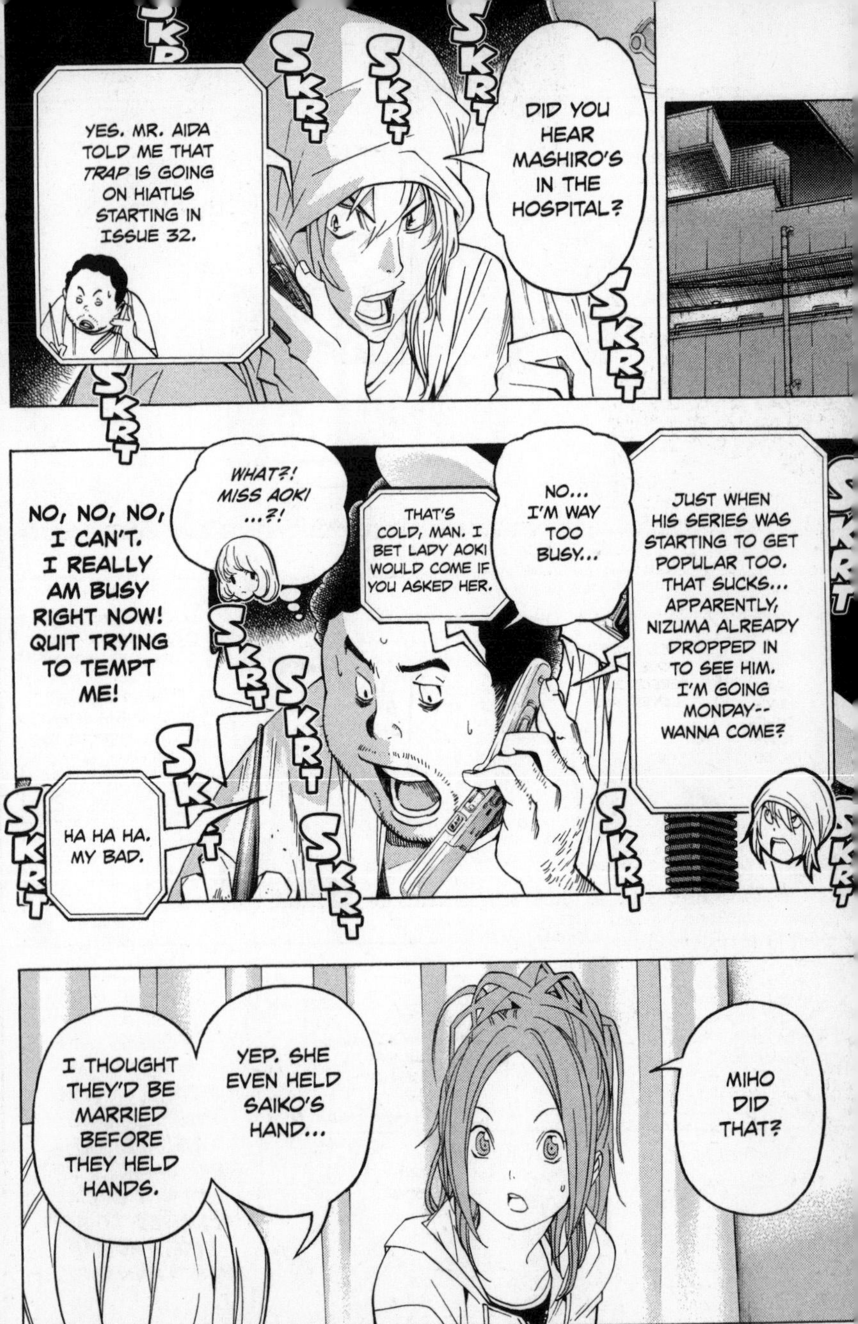
SKRT SKRT SKRT
DID YOU HEAR MASHIRO'S IN THE HOSPITAL?
YES. MR. AIDA TOLD ME THAT *TRAP* IS GOING ON HIATUS STARTING IN ISSUE 32.
SKRT
JUST WHEN HIS SERIES WAS STARTING TO GET POPULAR TOO. THAT SUCKS... APPARENTLY, NIZUMA ALREADY DROPPED IN TO SEE HIM. I'M GOING MONDAY-- WANNA COME?
NO... I'M WAY TOO BUSY...
THAT'S COLD, MAN. I BET LADY AOKI WOULD COME IF YOU ASKED HER.
WHAT?! MISS AOKI ...?!
NO, NO, NO, I CAN'T. I REALLY AM BUSY RIGHT NOW! QUIT TRYING TO TEMPT ME!
HA HA HA. MY BAD.
SKRT SKRT SKRT
MIHO DID THAT?
YEP. SHE EVEN HELD SAIKO'S HAND...
I THOUGHT THEY'D BE MARRIED BEFORE THEY HELD HANDS.

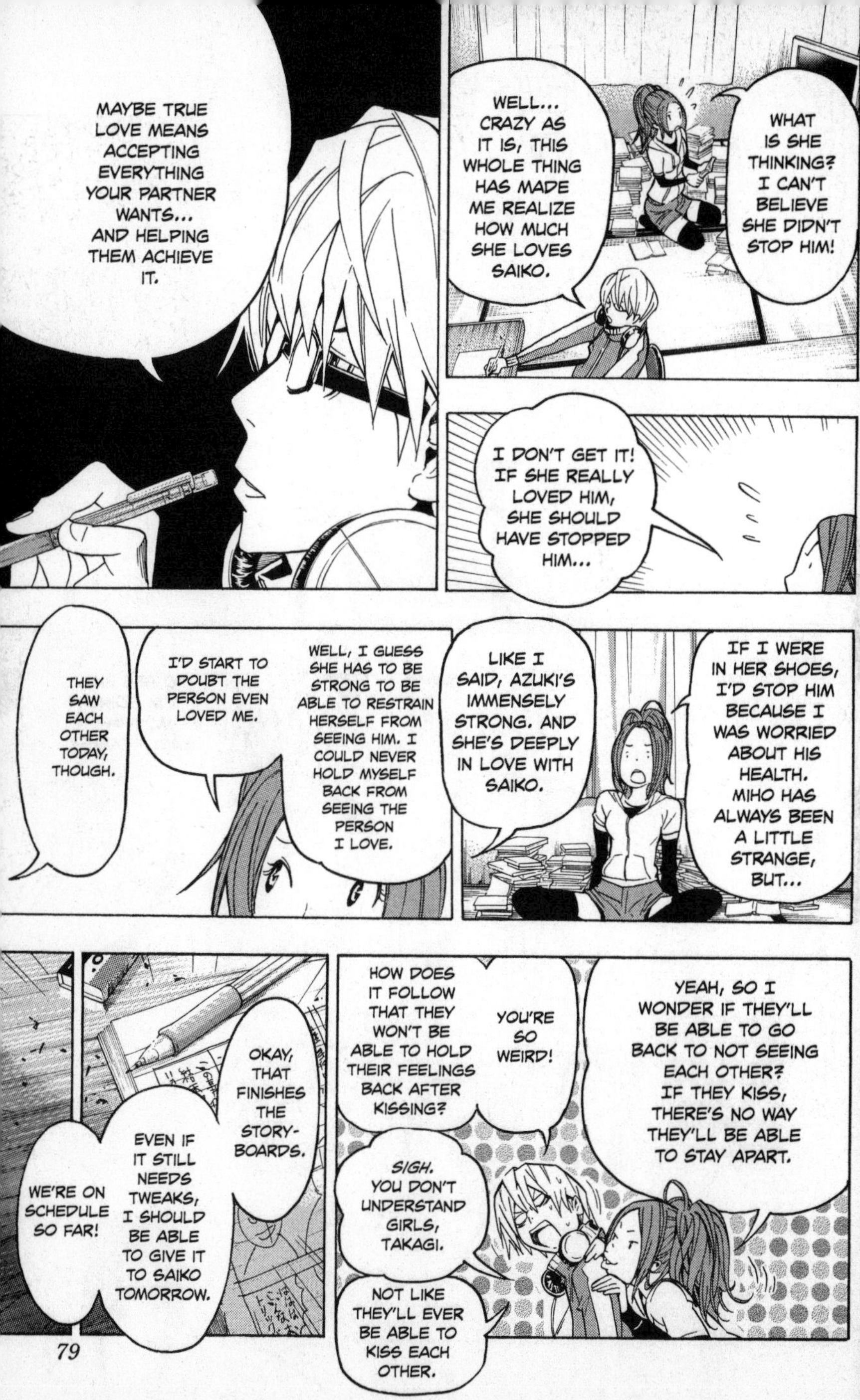
WHAT IS SHE THINKING? I CAN'T BELIEVE SHE DIDN'T STOP HIM!
WELL... CRAZY AS IT IS, THIS WHOLE THING HAS MADE ME REALIZE HOW MUCH SHE LOVES SAIKO.
I DON'T GET IT! IF SHE REALLY LOVED HIM, SHE SHOULD HAVE STOPPED HIM...
MAYBE TRUE LOVE MEANS ACCEPTING EVERYTHING YOUR PARTNER WANTS... AND HELPING THEM ACHIEVE IT.
IF I WERE IN HER SHOES, I'D STOP HIM BECAUSE I WAS WORRIED ABOUT HIS HEALTH. MIHO HAS ALWAYS BEEN A LITTLE STRANGE, BUT...
LIKE I SAID, AZUKI'S IMMENSELY STRONG. AND SHE'S DEEPLY IN LOVE WITH SAIKO.
WELL, I GUESS SHE HAS TO BE STRONG TO BE ABLE TO RESTRAIN HERSELF FROM SEEING HIM. I COULD NEVER HOLD MYSELF BACK FROM SEEING THE PERSON I LOVE.
I'D START TO DOUBT THE PERSON EVEN LOVED ME.
THEY SAW EACH OTHER TODAY, THOUGH.
YEAH, SO I WONDER IF THEY'LL BE ABLE TO GO BACK TO NOT SEEING EACH OTHER? IF THEY KISS, THERE'S NO WAY THEY'LL BE ABLE TO STAY APART.
YOU'RE SO WEIRD!
HOW DOES IT FOLLOW THAT THEY WON'T BE ABLE TO HOLD THEIR FEELINGS BACK AFTER KISSING?
SIGH. YOU DON'T UNDERSTAND GIRLS, TAKAGI.
NOT LIKE THEY'LL EVER BE ABLE TO KISS EACH OTHER.
OKAY, THAT FINISHES THE STORY-BOARDS.
EVEN IF IT STILL NEEDS TWEAKS, I SHOULD BE ABLE TO GIVE IT TO SAIKO TOMORROW.
WE'RE ON SCHEDULE SO FAR!

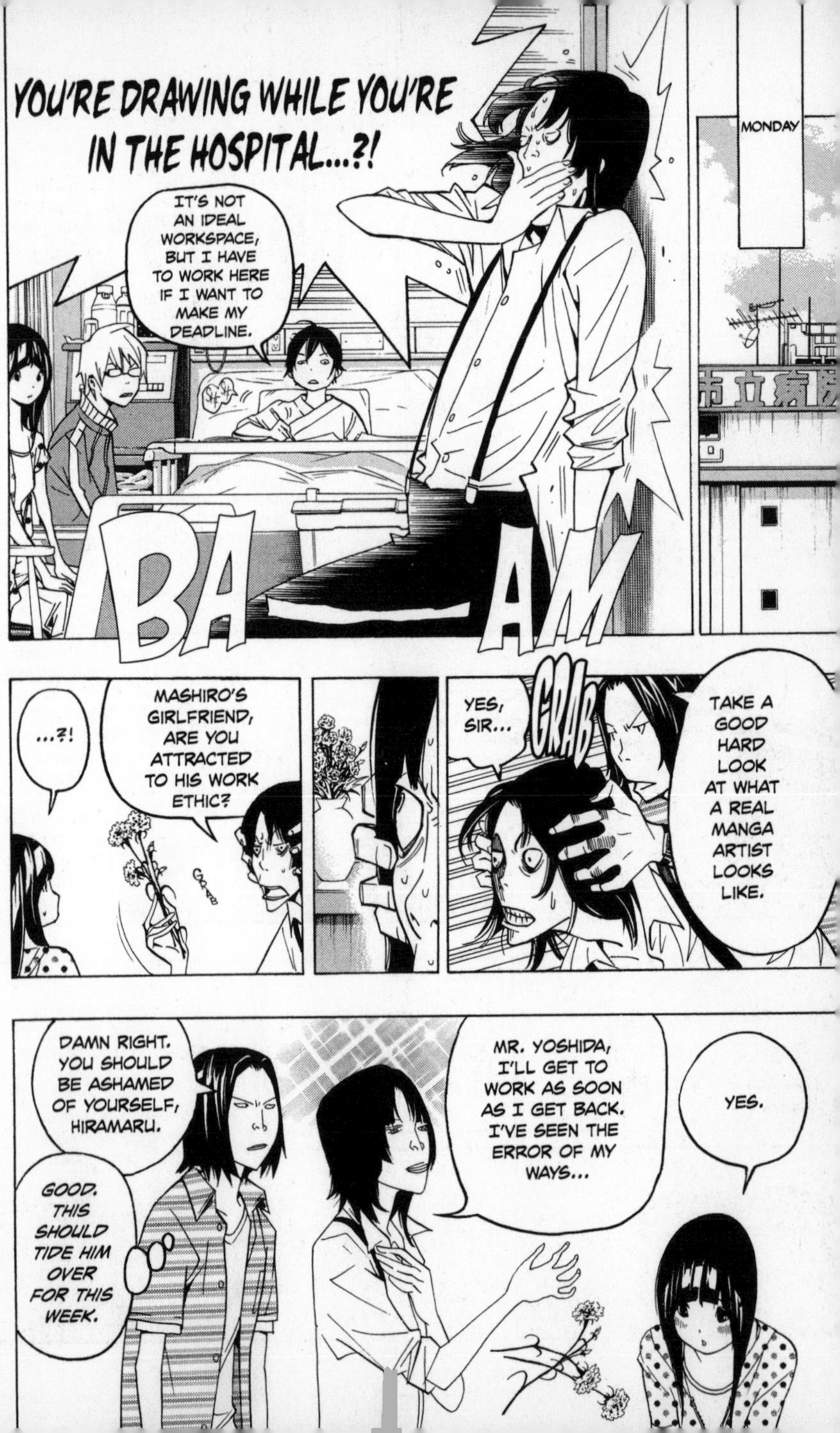
MONDAY
YOU'RE DRAWING WHILE YOU'RE IN THE HOSPITAL...?!
IT'S NOT AN IDEAL WORKSPACE, BUT I HAVE TO WORK HERE IF I WANT TO MAKE MY DEADLINE.
BA
AM
TAKE A GOOD HARD LOOK AT WHAT A REAL MANGA ARTIST LOOKS LIKE.
GRAB
YES, SIR...
MASHIRO'S GIRLFRIEND, ARE YOU ATTRACTED TO HIS WORK ETHIC?
GRAB
...?!
YES.
MR. YOSHIDA, I'LL GET TO WORK AS SOON AS I GET BACK. I'VE SEEN THE ERROR OF MY WAYS...
DAMN RIGHT. YOU SHOULD BE ASHAMED OF YOURSELF, HIRAMARU.
GOOD. THIS SHOULD TIDE HIM OVER FOR THIS WEEK.

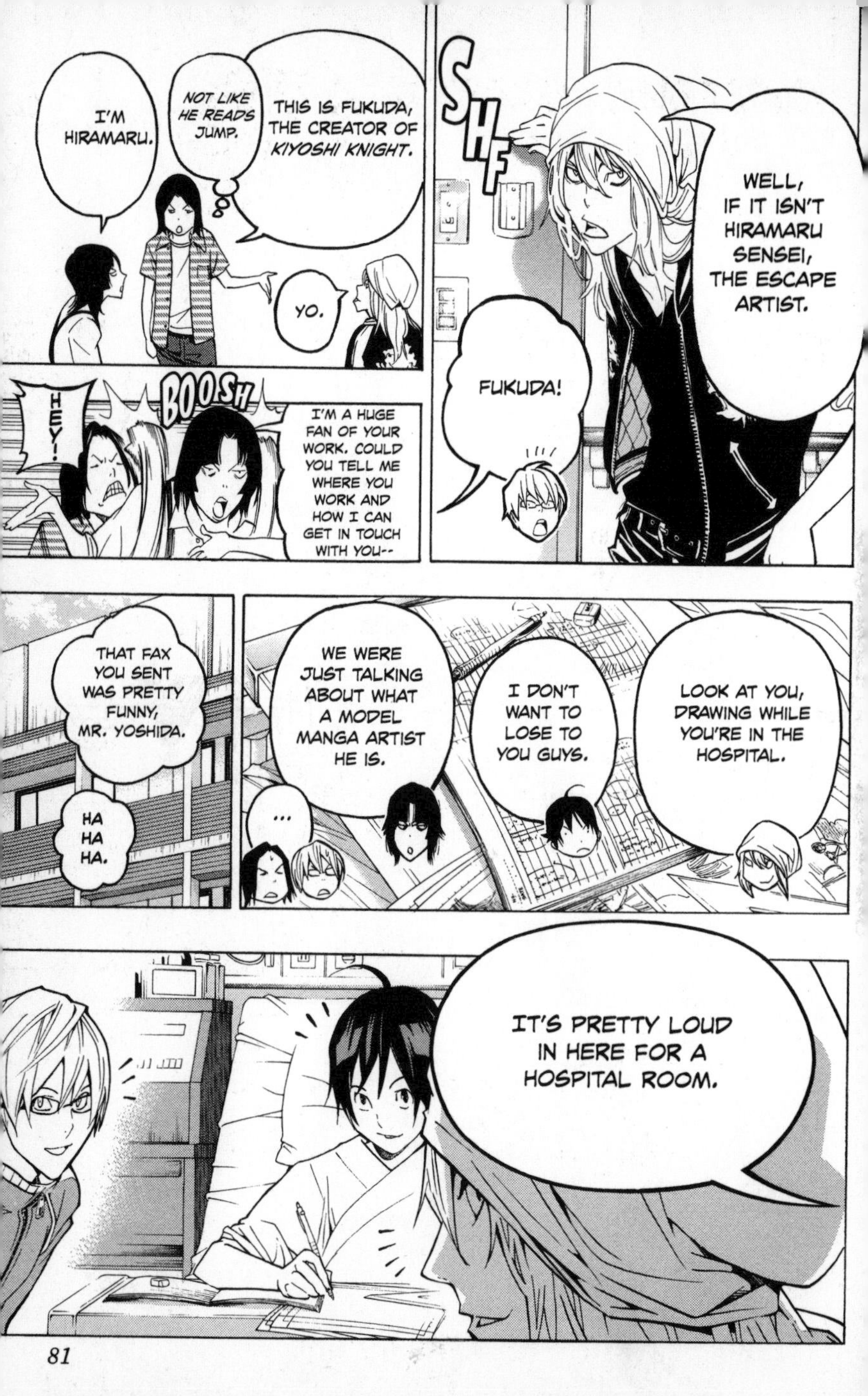
SHF
WELL, IF IT ISN'T HIRAMARU SENSEI, THE ESCAPE ARTIST.
FUKUDA!
THIS IS FUKUDA, THE CREATOR OF *KIYOSHI KNIGHT*.
NOT LIKE HE READS JUMP.
I'M HIRAMARU.
YO.
BOOSH
I'M A HUGE FAN OF YOUR WORK. COULD YOU TELL ME WHERE YOU WORK AND HOW I CAN GET IN TOUCH WITH YOU--
HEY!
LOOK AT YOU, DRAWING WHILE YOU'RE IN THE HOSPITAL.
I DON'T WANT TO LOSE TO YOU GUYS.
WE WERE JUST TALKING ABOUT WHAT A MODEL MANGA ARTIST HE IS.
...
THAT FAX YOU SENT WAS PRETTY FUNNY, MR. YOSHIDA.
HA HA HA.
IT'S PRETTY LOUD IN HERE FOR A HOSPITAL ROOM.

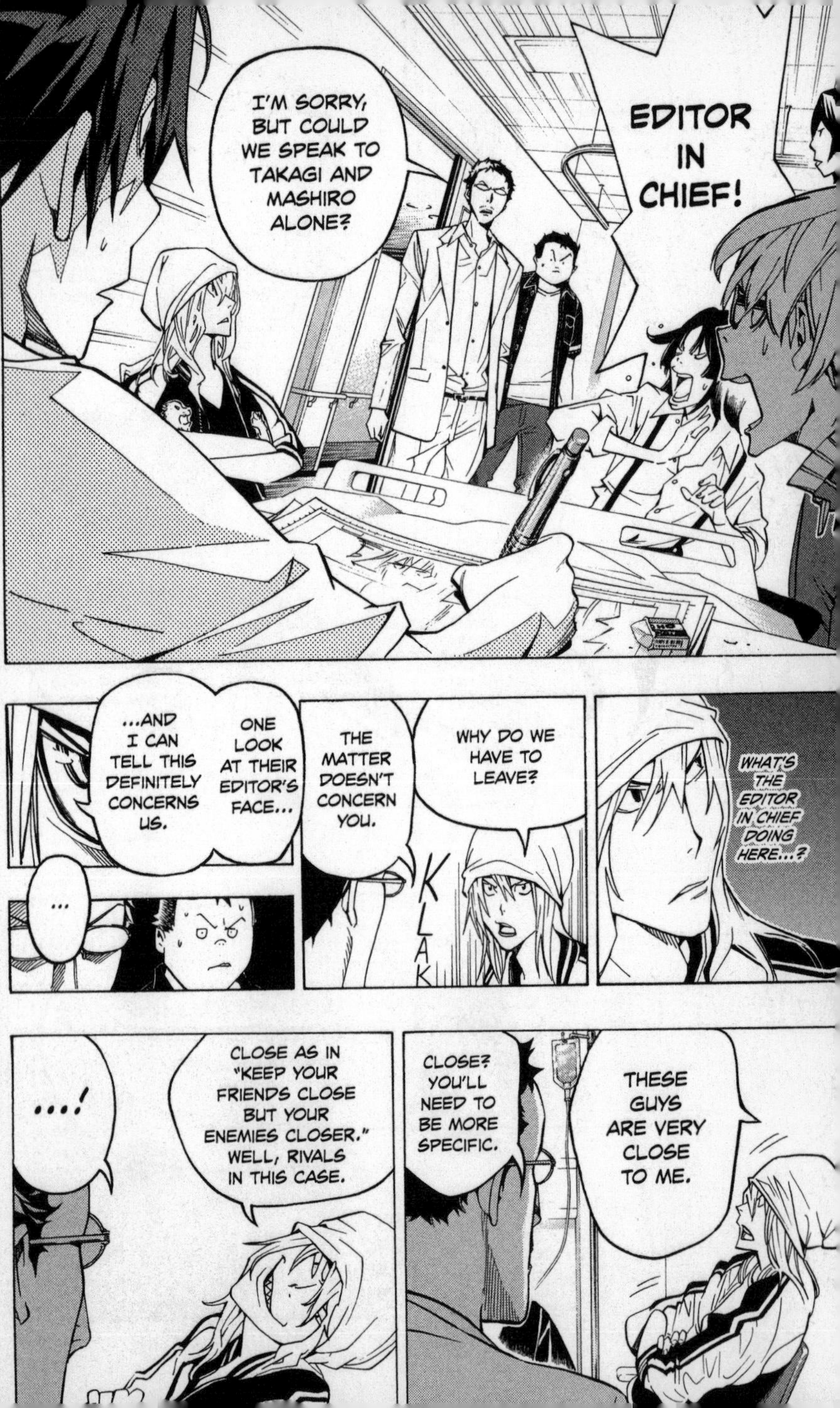
EDITOR IN CHIEF!
I'M SORRY, BUT COULD WE SPEAK TO TAKAGI AND MASHIRO ALONE?
WHAT'S THE EDITOR IN CHIEF DOING HERE...?
WHY DO WE HAVE TO LEAVE?
KLAK
THE MATTER DOESN'T CONCERN YOU.
ONE LOOK AT THEIR EDITOR'S FACE...
...AND I CAN TELL THIS DEFINITELY CONCERNS US.
...
THESE GUYS ARE VERY CLOSE TO ME.
CLOSE? YOU'LL NEED TO BE MORE SPECIFIC.
CLOSE AS IN "KEEP YOUR FRIENDS CLOSE BUT YOUR ENEMIES CLOSER." WELL, RIVALS IN THIS CASE.
...!

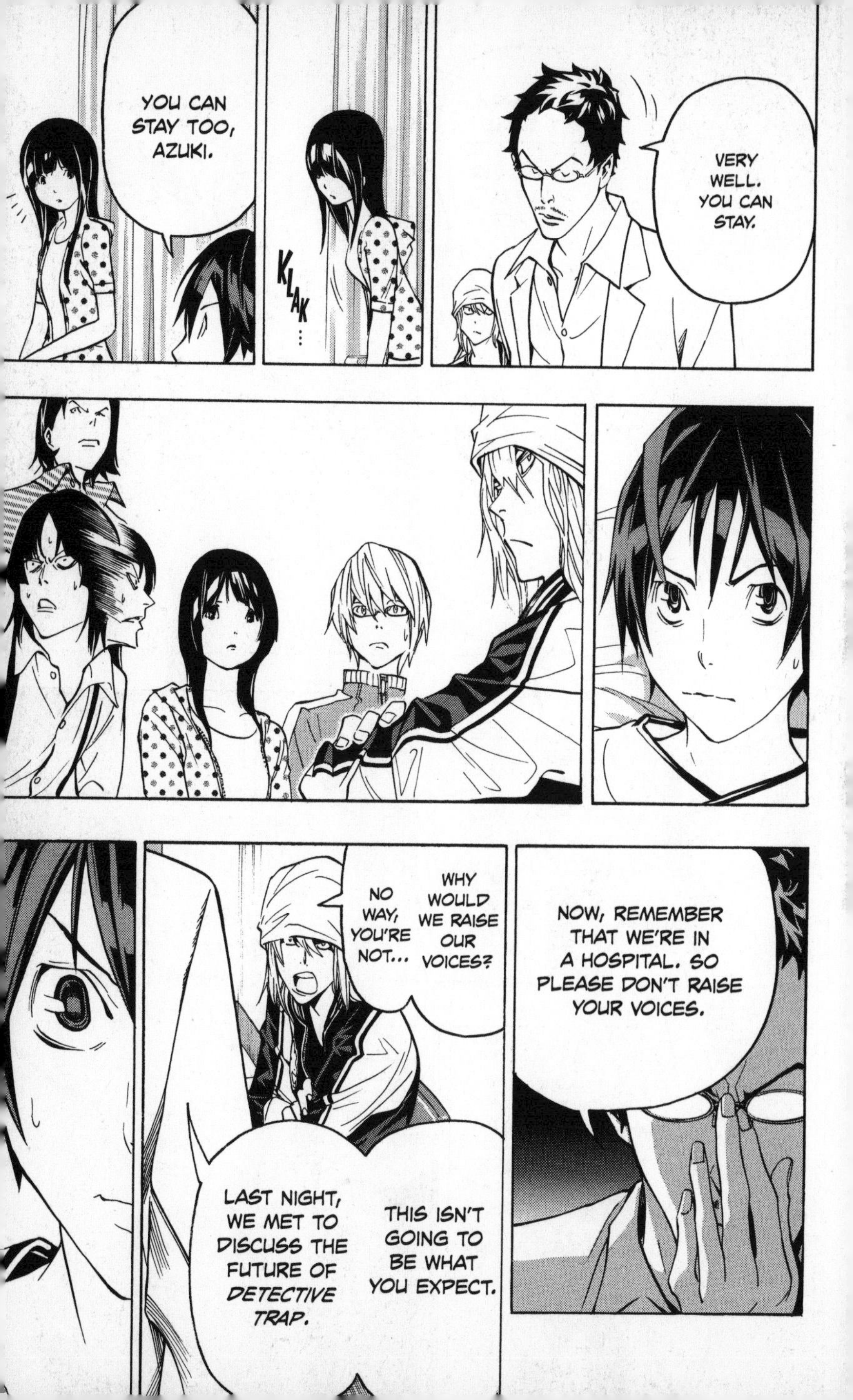
VERY WELL. YOU CAN STAY.
KLAK...
YOU CAN STAY TOO, AZUKI.
NOW, REMEMBER THAT WE'RE IN A HOSPITAL. SO PLEASE DON'T RAISE YOUR VOICES.
WHY WOULD WE RAISE OUR VOICES?
NO WAY, YOU'RE NOT...
THIS ISN'T GOING TO BE WHAT YOU EXPECT.
LAST NIGHT, WE MET TO DISCUSS THE FUTURE OF *DETECTIVE TRAP*.

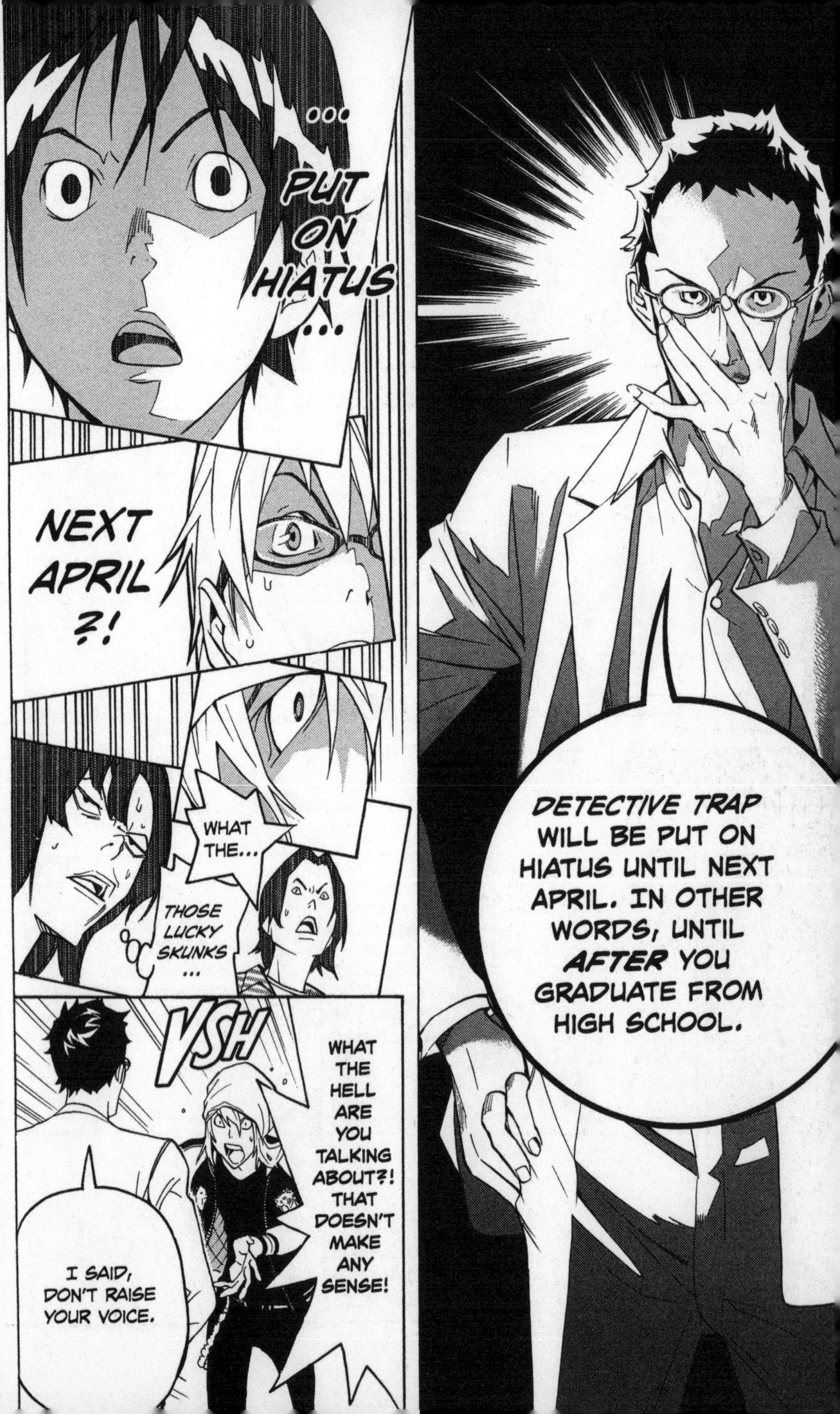
DETECTIVE TRAP WILL BE PUT ON HIATUS UNTIL NEXT APRIL. IN OTHER WORDS, UNTIL AFTER YOU GRADUATE FROM HIGH SCHOOL.
...PUT ON HIATUS...
NEXT APRIL ?!
WHAT THE...
THOSE LUCKY SKUNKS...
VSH
WHAT THE HELL ARE YOU TALKING ABOUT?! THAT DOESN'T MAKE ANY SENSE!
I SAID, DON'T RAISE YOUR VOICE.

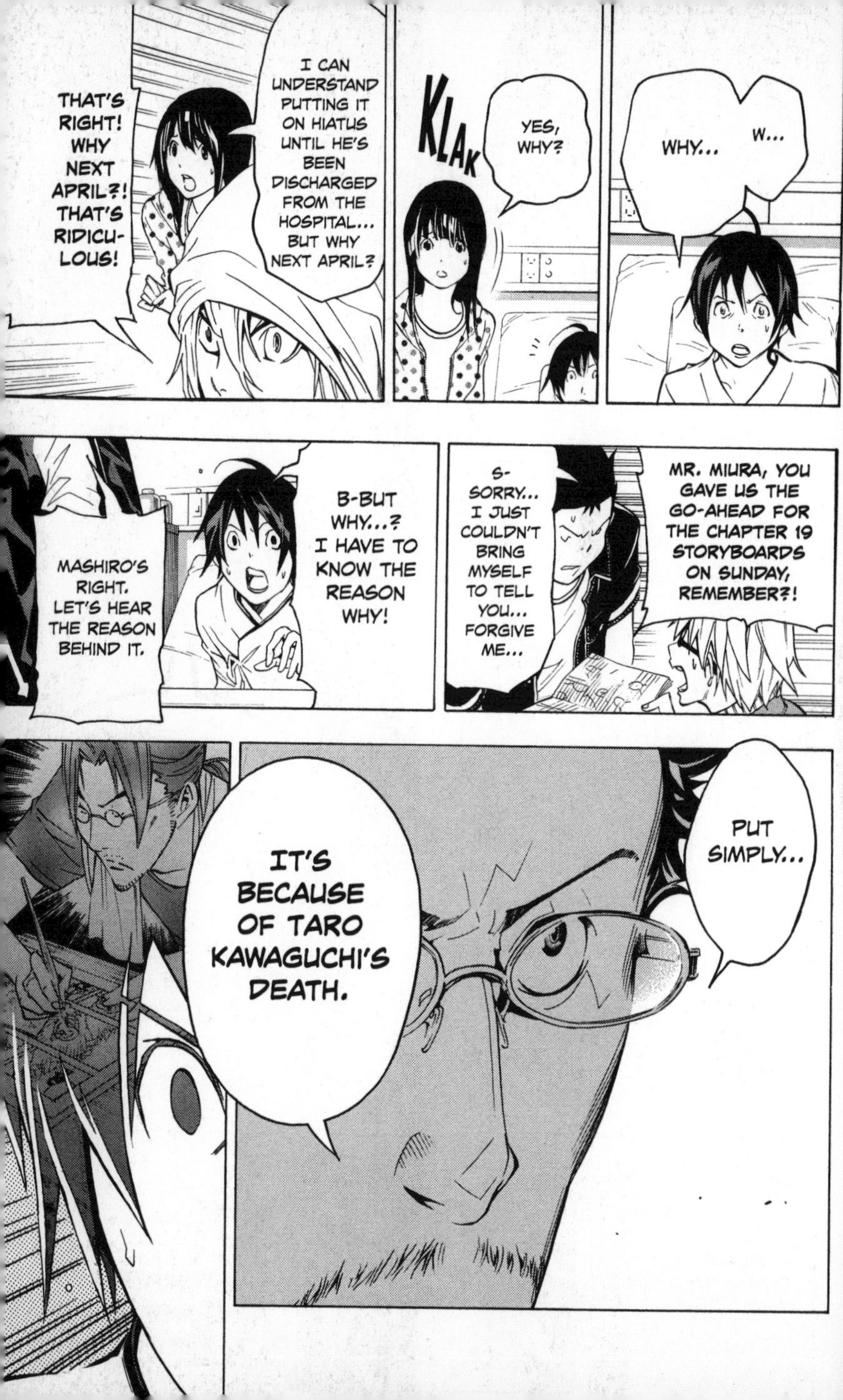
WHY... W...
KLAK
YES, WHY?
I CAN UNDERSTAND PUTTING IT ON HIATUS UNTIL HE'S BEEN DISCHARGED FROM THE HOSPITAL... BUT WHY NEXT APRIL?
THAT'S RIGHT! WHY NEXT APRIL?! THAT'S RIDICULOUS!
MR. MIURA, YOU GAVE US THE GO-AHEAD FOR THE CHAPTER 19 STORYBOARDS ON SUNDAY, REMEMBER?!
S-SORRY... I JUST COULDN'T BRING MYSELF TO TELL YOU... FORGIVE ME...
B-BUT WHY...? I HAVE TO KNOW THE REASON WHY!
MASHIRO'S RIGHT. LET'S HEAR THE REASON BEHIND IT.
PUT SIMPLY...
IT'S BECAUSE OF TARO KAWAGUCHI'S DEATH.

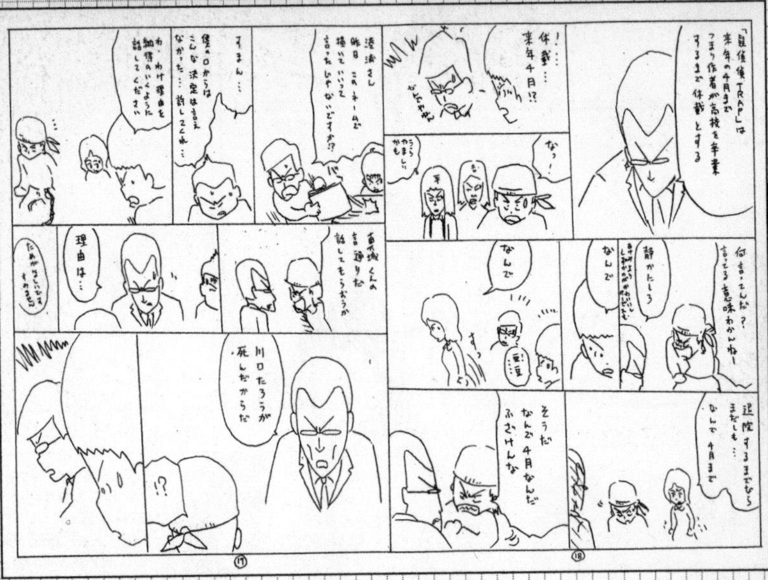
「疑探偵TRAP」は来年の4月まで つまり作者が高校を卒業するまで休載とする
！… 休載… 来年4月!?
なっ！
何言ってんな？ 言ってる意味わかんねー
静かにしろ
なんで
なんで
退院するまでならまだしも… なんで4月まで
そうだ なんで4月なんだ ふざけんな
浅浦さん 昨日このネームで描いていいって言ったじゃないですか!?
すまん… 僕の口からはこんな決定は言えなかった… 許してくれ…
わ・わけ理由を納得のいくように話してください
話してもらおうか
理由は…
川口たろうが死んだからだ
!?
17
18

OHBA'S STORYBOARD

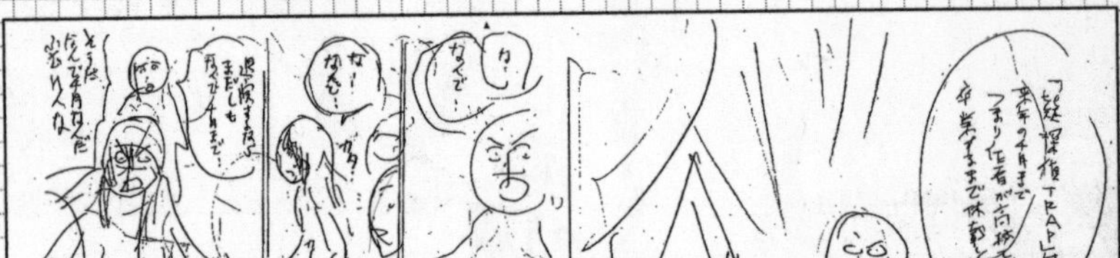
川口たろうが死んだからだ
理由は
18

OBATA'S STORYBOARD

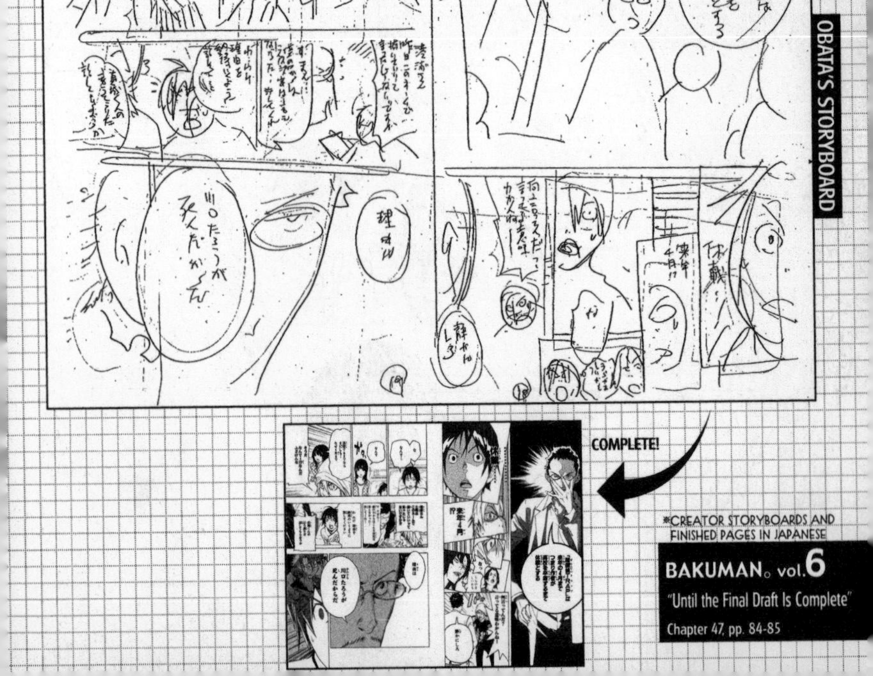

COMPLETE!

※CREATOR STORYBOARDS AND FINISHED PAGES IN JAPANESE

BAKUMAN。 vol.6

"Until the Final Draft Is Complete"

Chapter 47, pp. 84-85

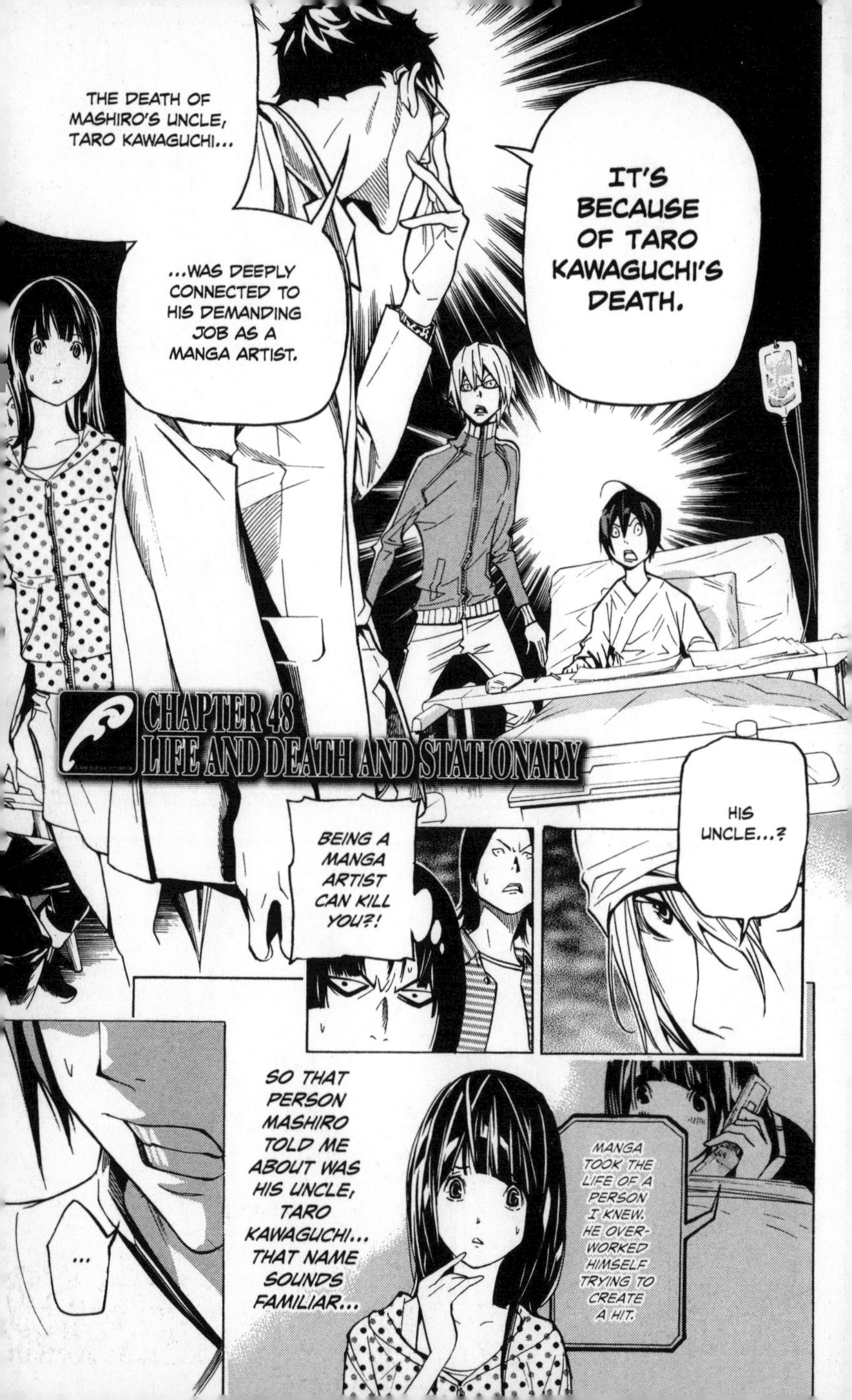
IT'S BECAUSE OF TARO KAWAGUCHI'S DEATH.
THE DEATH OF MASHIRO'S UNCLE, TARO KAWAGUCHI...
...WAS DEEPLY CONNECTED TO HIS DEMANDING JOB AS A MANGA ARTIST.
CHAPTER 48
LIFE AND DEATH AND STATIONARY
HIS UNCLE...?
BEING A MANGA ARTIST CAN KILL YOU?!
MANGA TOOK THE LIFE OF A PERSON I KNEW. HE OVER-WORKED HIMSELF TRYING TO CREATE A HIT.
SO THAT PERSON MASHIRO TOLD ME ABOUT WAS HIS UNCLE, TARO KAWAGUCHI... THAT NAME SOUNDS FAMILIAR...
...

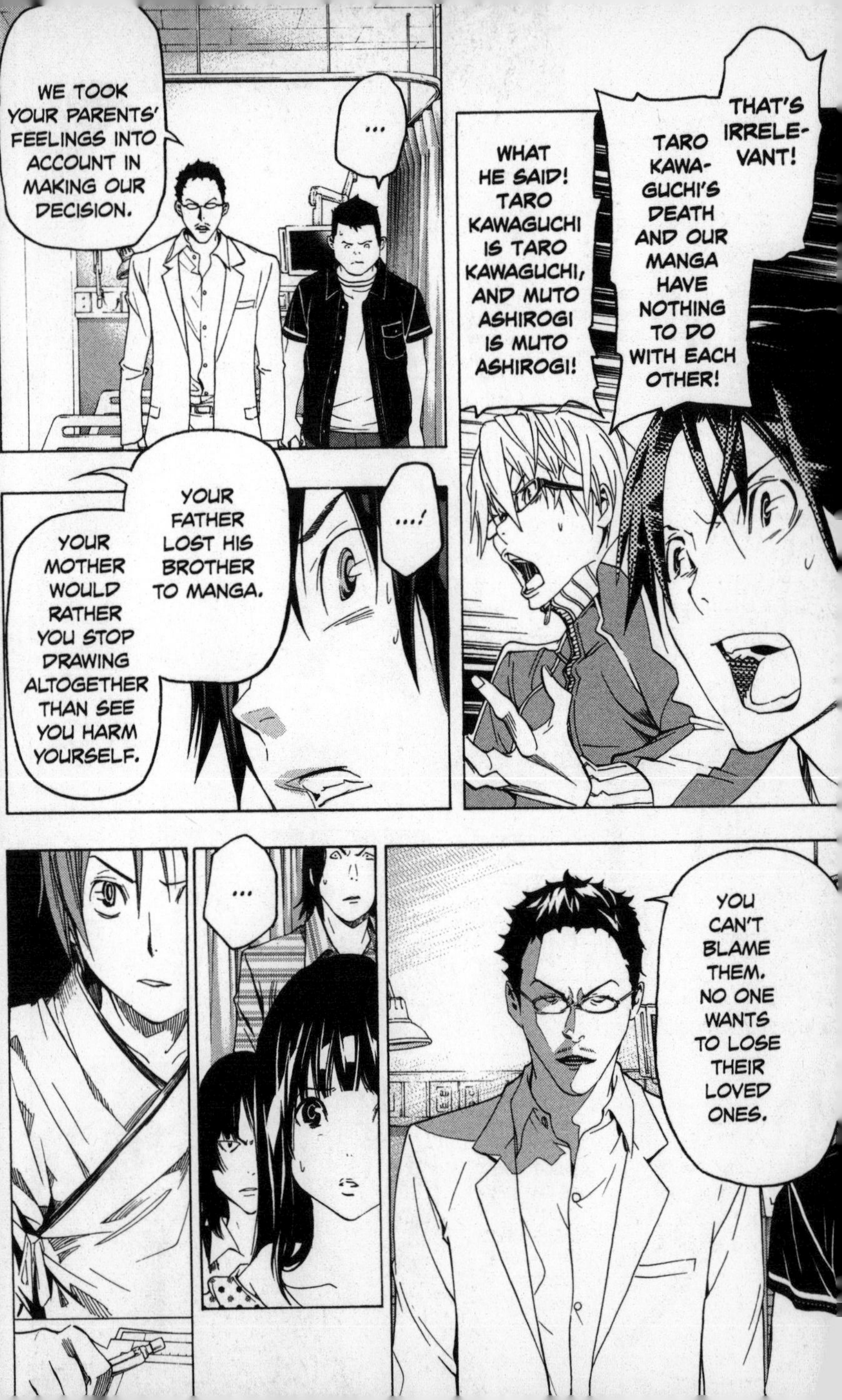
WE TOOK YOUR PARENTS' FEELINGS INTO ACCOUNT IN MAKING OUR DECISION.
...
THAT'S IRRELEVANT!
TARO KAWAGUCHI'S DEATH AND OUR MANGA HAVE NOTHING TO DO WITH EACH OTHER!
WHAT HE SAID! TARO KAWAGUCHI IS TARO KAWAGUCHI, AND MUTO ASHIROGI IS MUTO ASHIROGI!
YOUR FATHER LOST HIS BROTHER TO MANGA.
YOUR MOTHER WOULD RATHER YOU STOP DRAWING ALTOGETHER THAN SEE YOU HARM YOURSELF.
...!
YOU CAN'T BLAME THEM. NO ONE WANTS TO LOSE THEIR LOVED ONES.
...

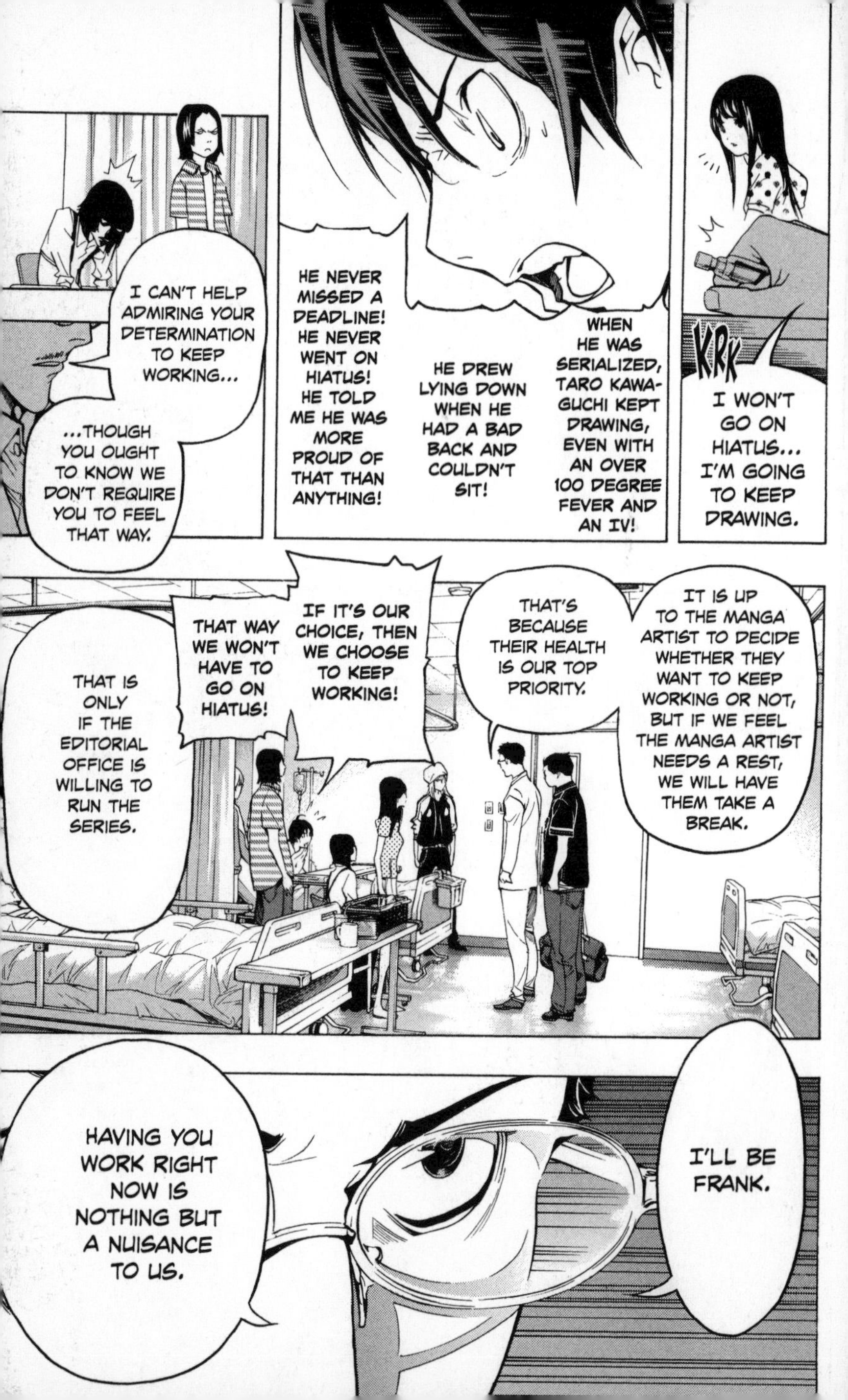
KRK
I WON'T GO ON HIATUS... I'M GOING TO KEEP DRAWING.
WHEN HE WAS SERIALIZED, TARO KAWAGUCHI KEPT DRAWING, EVEN WITH AN OVER 100 DEGREE FEVER AND AN IV!
HE DREW LYING DOWN WHEN HE HAD A BAD BACK AND COULDN'T SIT!
HE NEVER MISSED A DEADLINE! HE NEVER WENT ON HIATUS! HE TOLD ME HE WAS MORE PROUD OF THAT THAN ANYTHING!
I CAN'T HELP ADMIRING YOUR DETERMINATION TO KEEP WORKING...
...THOUGH YOU OUGHT TO KNOW WE DON'T REQUIRE YOU TO FEEL THAT WAY.
IT IS UP TO THE MANGA ARTIST TO DECIDE WHETHER THEY WANT TO KEEP WORKING OR NOT, BUT IF WE FEEL THE MANGA ARTIST NEEDS A REST, WE WILL HAVE THEM TAKE A BREAK.
THAT'S BECAUSE THEIR HEALTH IS OUR TOP PRIORITY.
IF IT'S OUR CHOICE, THEN WE CHOOSE TO KEEP WORKING!
THAT WAY WE WON'T HAVE TO GO ON HIATUS!
THAT IS ONLY IF THE EDITORIAL OFFICE IS WILLING TO RUN THE SERIES.
I'LL BE FRANK.
HAVING YOU WORK RIGHT NOW IS NOTHING BUT A NUISANCE TO US.

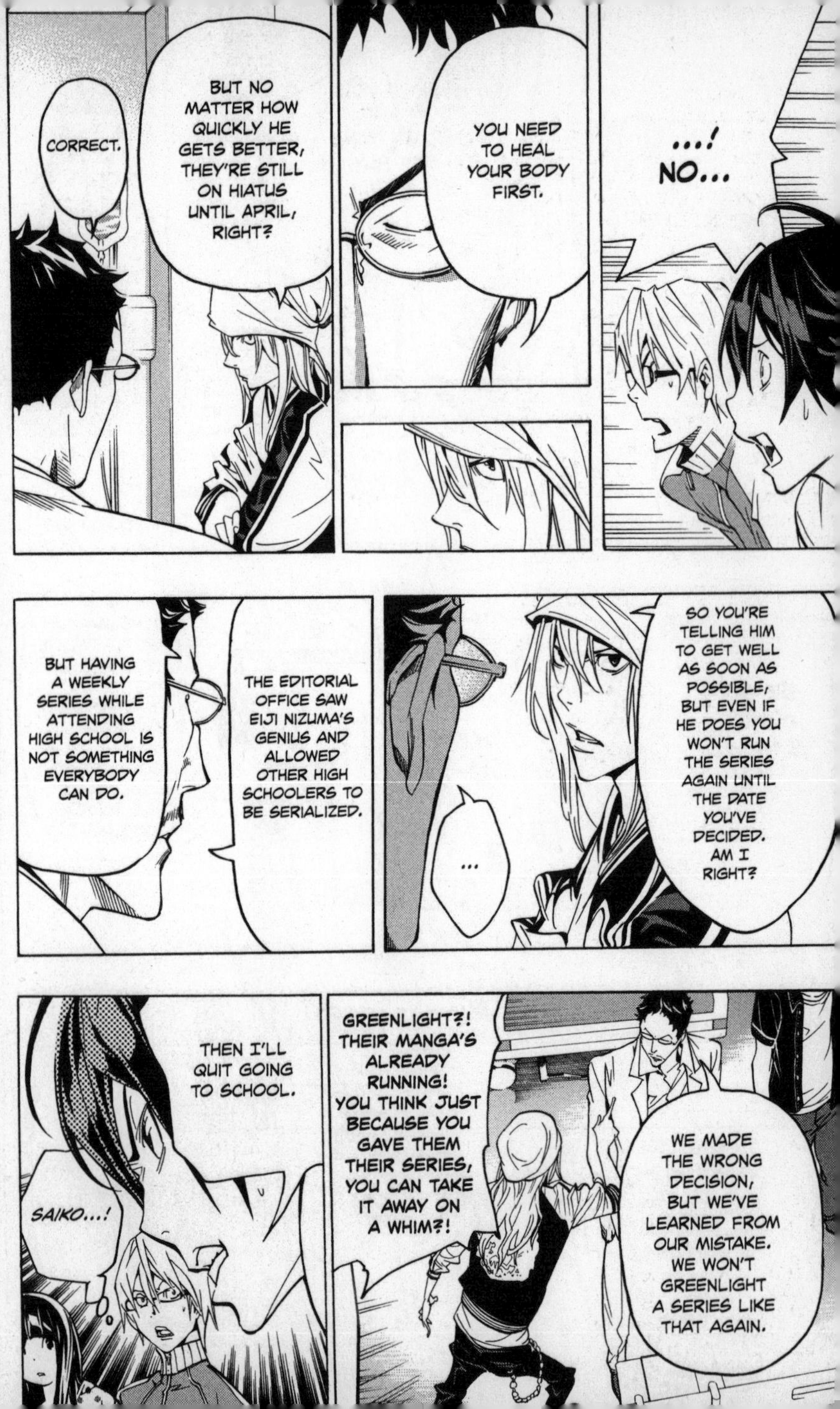
...! NO...
YOU NEED TO HEAL YOUR BODY FIRST.
BUT NO MATTER HOW QUICKLY HE GETS BETTER, THEY'RE STILL ON HIATUS UNTIL APRIL, RIGHT?
CORRECT.
SO YOU'RE TELLING HIM TO GET WELL AS SOON AS POSSIBLE, BUT EVEN IF HE DOES YOU WON'T RUN THE SERIES AGAIN UNTIL THE DATE YOU'VE DECIDED. AM I RIGHT?
...
THE EDITORIAL OFFICE SAW EIJI NIZUMA'S GENIUS AND ALLOWED OTHER HIGH SCHOOLERS TO BE SERIALIZED.
BUT HAVING A WEEKLY SERIES WHILE ATTENDING HIGH SCHOOL IS NOT SOMETHING EVERYBODY CAN DO.
WE MADE THE WRONG DECISION, BUT WE'VE LEARNED FROM OUR MISTAKE. WE WON'T GREENLIGHT A SERIES LIKE THAT AGAIN.
GREENLIGHT?! THEIR MANGA'S ALREADY RUNNING! YOU THINK JUST BECAUSE YOU GAVE THEM THEIR SERIES, YOU CAN TAKE IT AWAY ON A WHIM?!
THEN I'LL QUIT GOING TO SCHOOL.
SAIKO...!

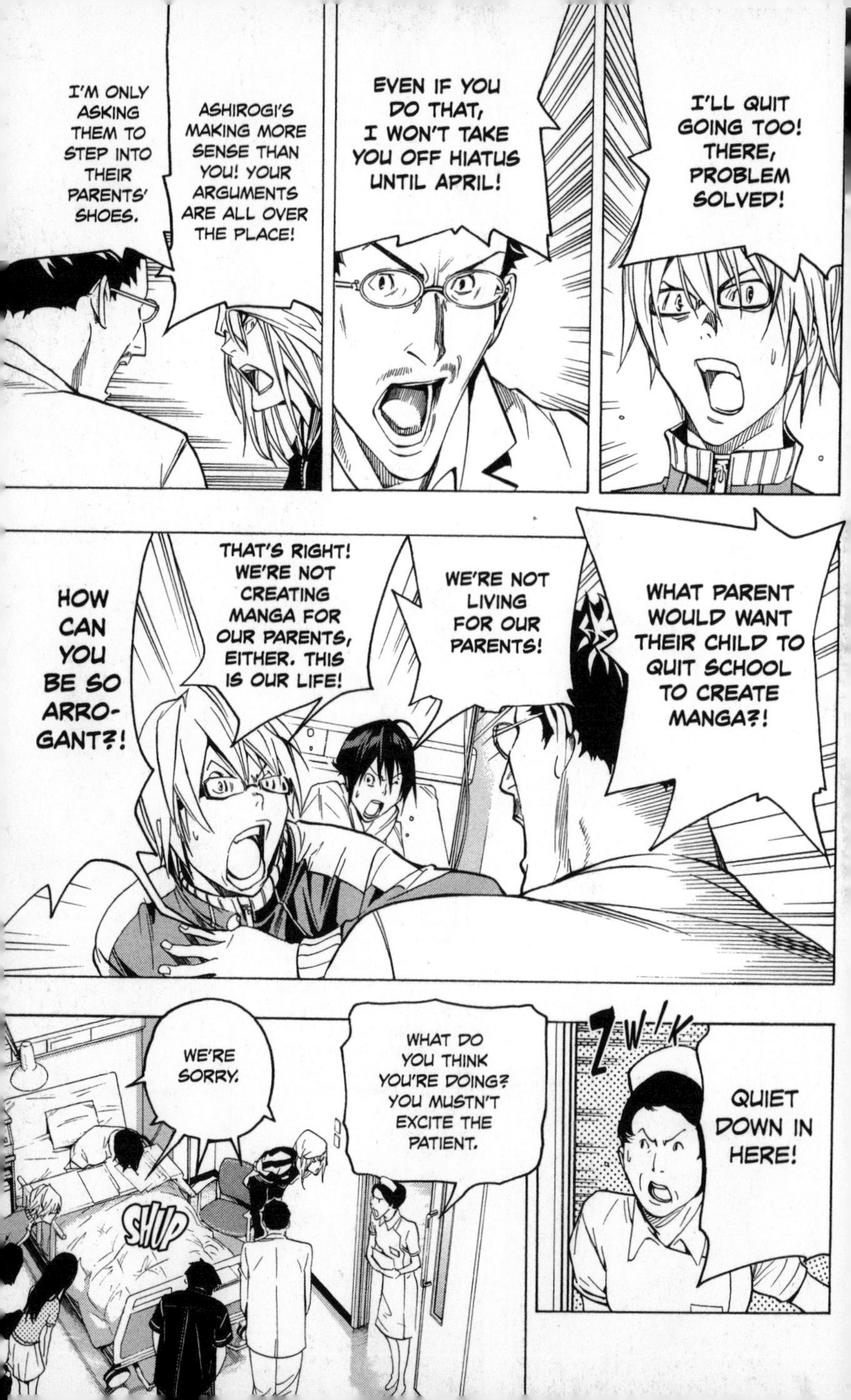
I'LL QUIT GOING TOO! THERE, PROBLEM SOLVED!
EVEN IF YOU DO THAT, I WON'T TAKE YOU OFF HIATUS UNTIL APRIL!
ASHIROGI'S MAKING MORE SENSE THAN YOU! YOUR ARGUMENTS ARE ALL OVER THE PLACE!
I'M ONLY ASKING THEM TO STEP INTO THEIR PARENTS' SHOES.
WHAT PARENT WOULD WANT THEIR CHILD TO QUIT SCHOOL TO CREATE MANGA?!
WE'RE NOT LIVING FOR OUR PARENTS!
THAT'S RIGHT! WE'RE NOT CREATING MANGA FOR OUR PARENTS, EITHER. THIS IS OUR LIFE!
HOW CAN YOU BE SO ARRO-GANT?!
ZWIK
QUIET DOWN IN HERE!
WHAT DO YOU THINK YOU'RE DOING? YOU MUSTN'T EXCITE THE PATIENT.
WE'RE SORRY.
SHUP

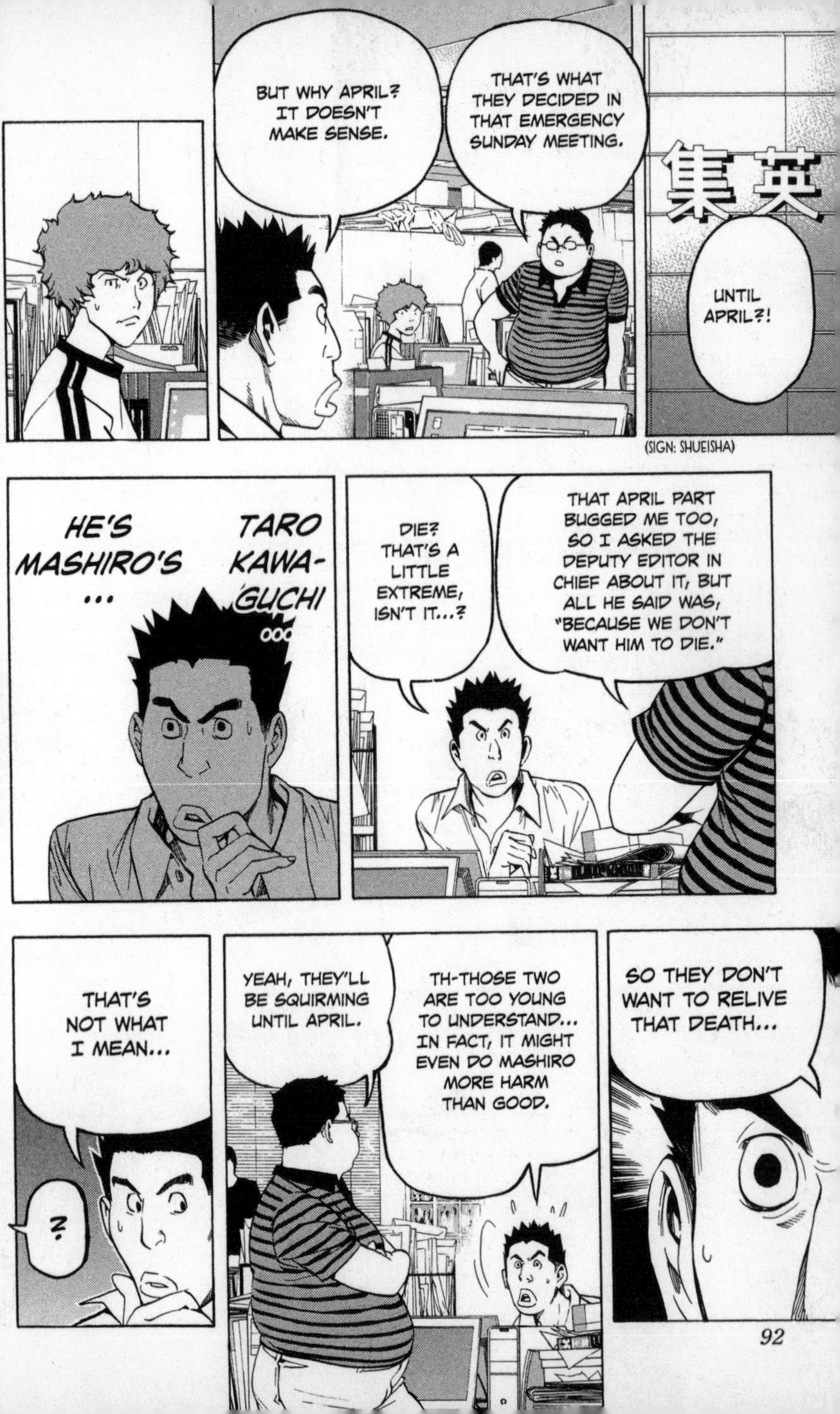
集英
(SIGN: SHUEISHA)
UNTIL APRIL?!
THAT'S WHAT THEY DECIDED IN THAT EMERGENCY SUNDAY MEETING.
BUT WHY APRIL? IT DOESN'T MAKE SENSE.
THAT APRIL PART BUGGED ME TOO, SO I ASKED THE DEPUTY EDITOR IN CHIEF ABOUT IT, BUT ALL HE SAID WAS, "BECAUSE WE DON'T WANT HIM TO DIE."
DIE? THAT'S A LITTLE EXTREME, ISN'T IT...?
TARO KAWAGUCHI
HE'S MASHIRO'S ...
SO THEY DON'T WANT TO RELIVE THAT DEATH...
TH-THOSE TWO ARE TOO YOUNG TO UNDERSTAND... IN FACT, IT MIGHT EVEN DO MASHIRO MORE HARM THAN GOOD.
YEAH, THEY'LL BE SQUIRMING UNTIL APRIL.
THAT'S NOT WHAT I MEAN...
?

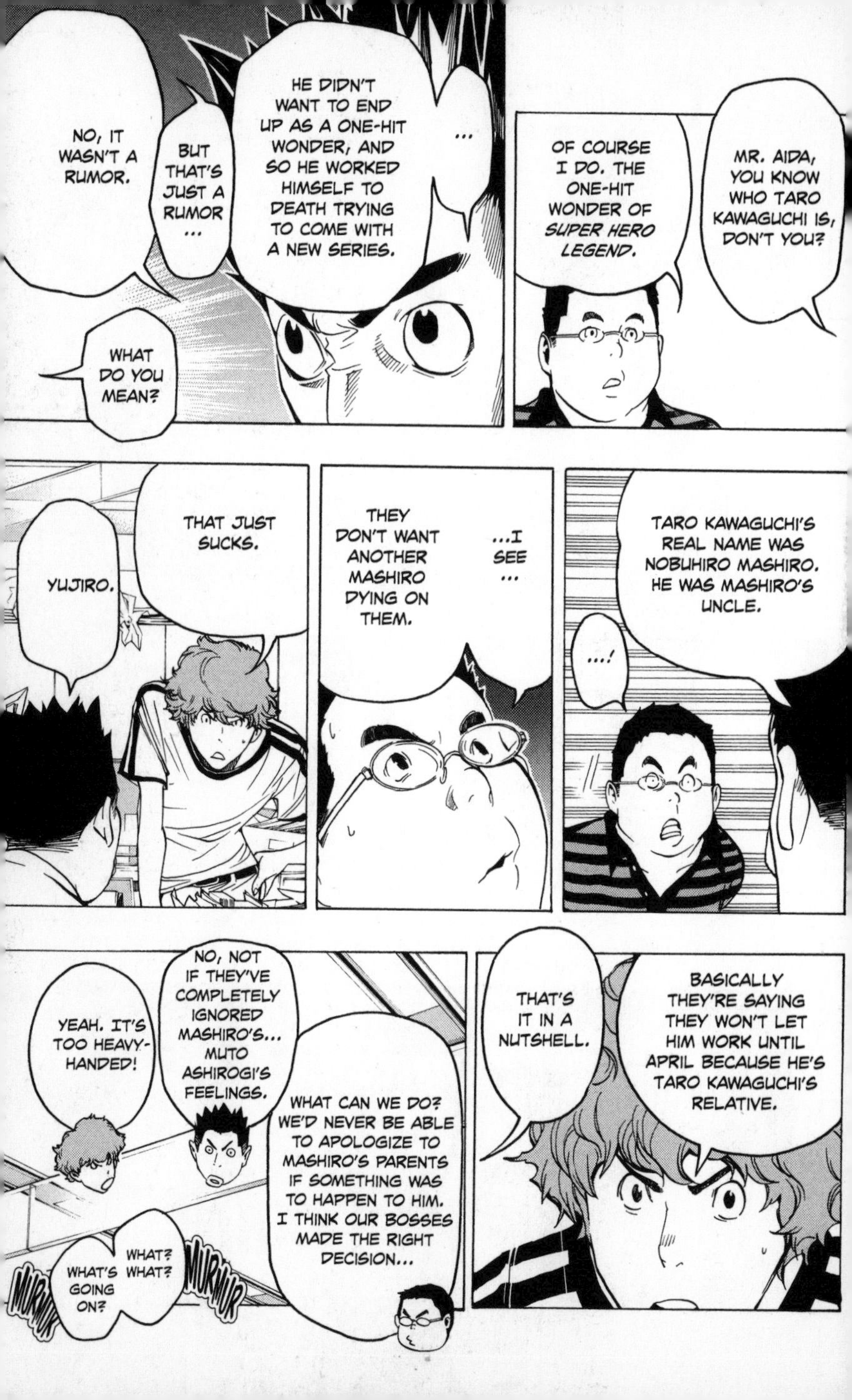
MR. AIDA, YOU KNOW WHO TARO KAWAGUCHI IS, DON'T YOU?
OF COURSE I DO. THE ONE-HIT WONDER OF *SUPER HERO LEGEND*.
...
HE DIDN'T WANT TO END UP AS A ONE-HIT WONDER, AND SO HE WORKED HIMSELF TO DEATH TRYING TO COME WITH A NEW SERIES.
BUT THAT'S JUST A RUMOR...
NO, IT WASN'T A RUMOR.
WHAT DO YOU MEAN?
TARO KAWAGUCHI'S REAL NAME WAS NOBUHIRO MASHIRO. HE WAS MASHIRO'S UNCLE.
....!
...I SEE...
THEY DON'T WANT ANOTHER MASHIRO DYING ON THEM.
THAT JUST SUCKS.
YUJIRO.
BASICALLY THEY'RE SAYING THEY WON'T LET HIM WORK UNTIL APRIL BECAUSE HE'S TARO KAWAGUCHI'S RELATIVE.
THAT'S IT IN A NUTSHELL.
WHAT CAN WE DO? WE'D NEVER BE ABLE TO APOLOGIZE TO MASHIRO'S PARENTS IF SOMETHING WAS TO HAPPEN TO HIM. I THINK OUR BOSSES MADE THE RIGHT DECISION...
NO, NOT IF THEY'VE COMPLETELY IGNORED MASHIRO'S... MUTO ASHIROGI'S FEELINGS.
YEAH. IT'S TOO HEAVY-HANDED!
MURMUR
WHAT? WHAT?
WHAT'S GOING ON?
MURMUR

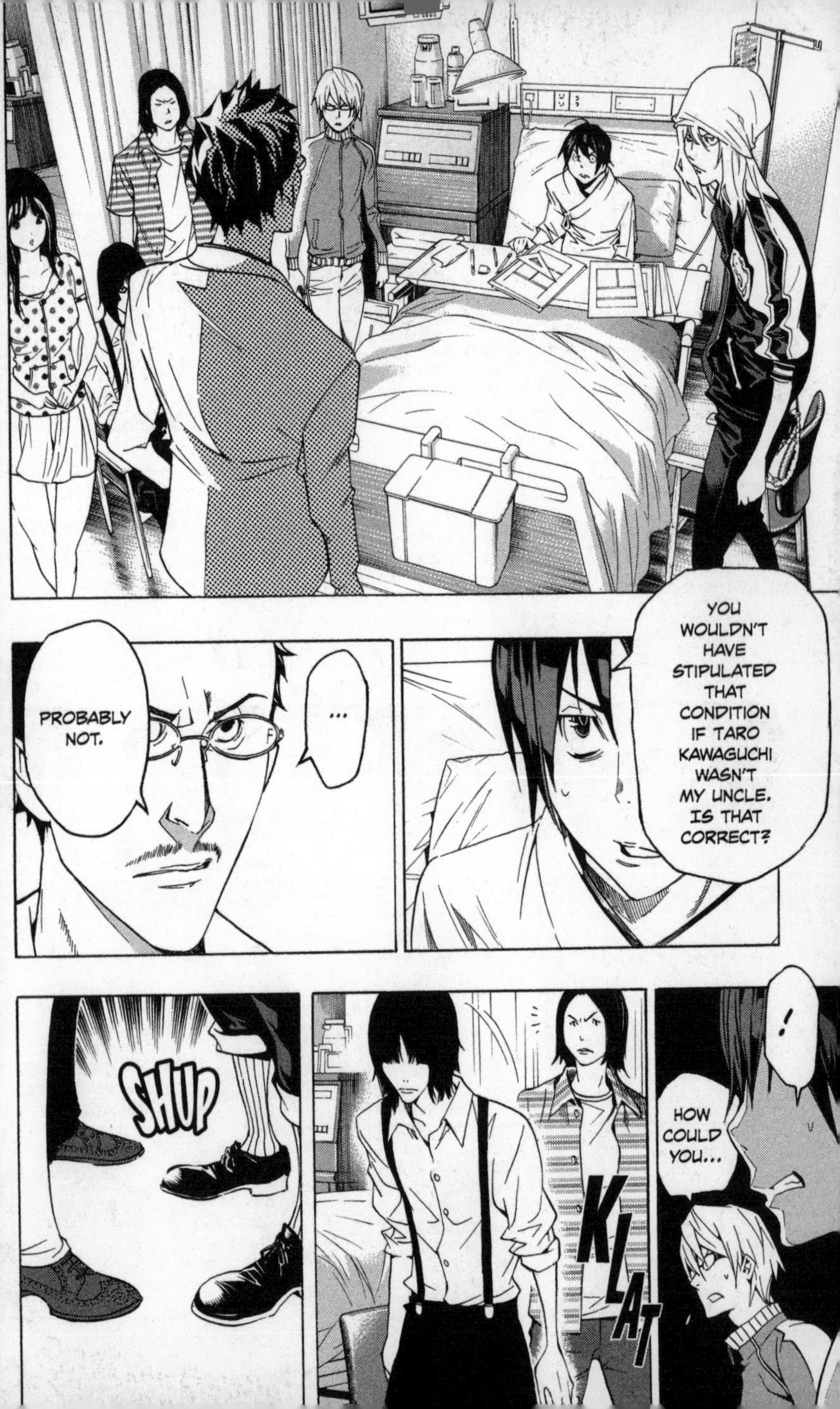
YOU WOULDN'T HAVE STIPULATED THAT CONDITION IF TARO KAWAGUCHI WASN'T MY UNCLE. IS THAT CORRECT?
...
PROBABLY NOT.
!
HOW COULD YOU...
KLAT
SHUP

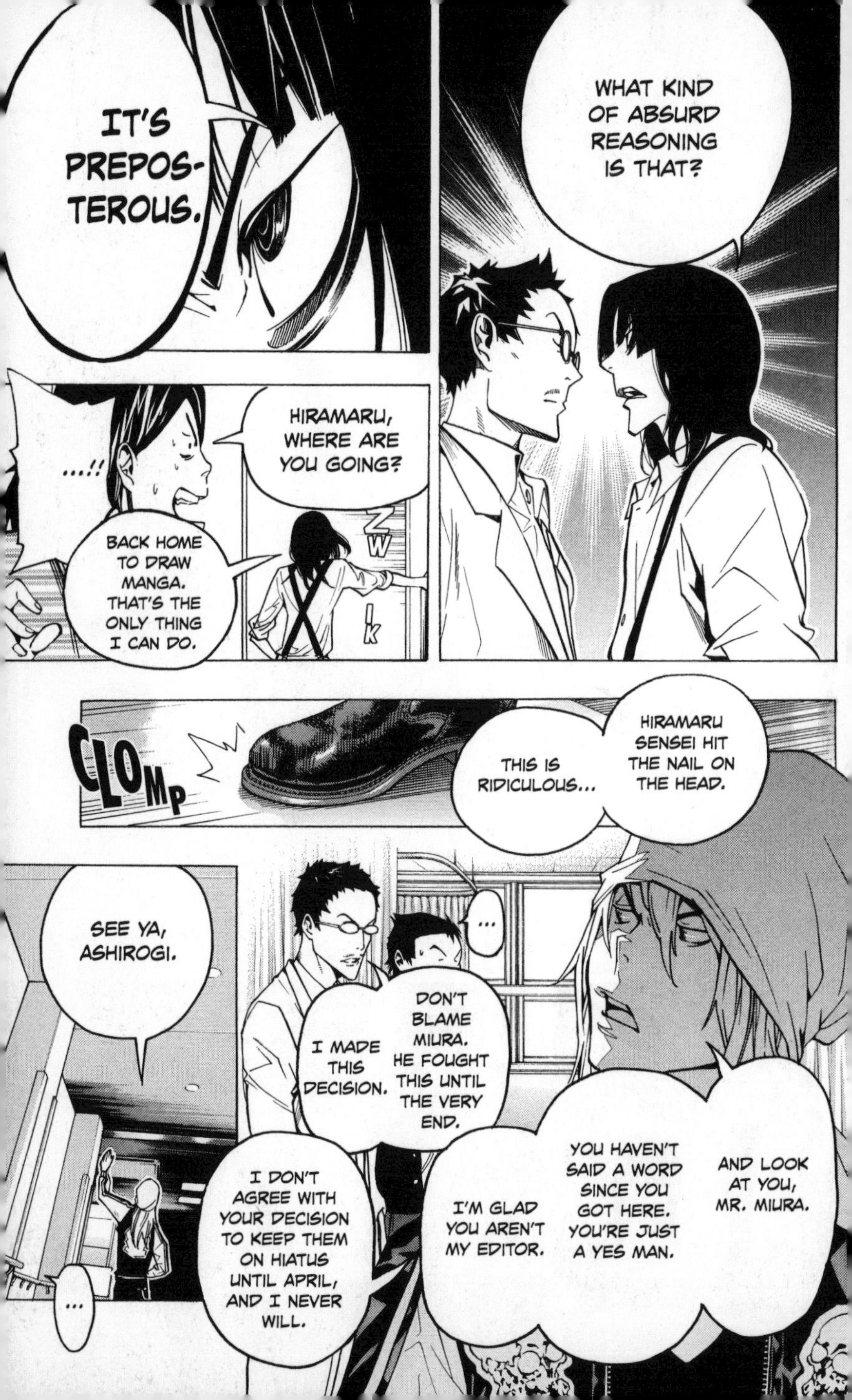
WHAT KIND OF ABSURD REASONING IS THAT?
IT'S PREPOSTEROUS.
HIRAMARU, WHERE ARE YOU GOING?
...!!
BACK HOME TO DRAW MANGA. THAT'S THE ONLY THING I CAN DO.
ZWIK
CLOMP
HIRAMARU SENSEI HIT THE NAIL ON THE HEAD.
THIS IS RIDICULOUS...
...
AND LOOK AT YOU, MR. MIURA.
YOU HAVEN'T SAID A WORD SINCE YOU GOT HERE. YOU'RE JUST A YES MAN.
I'M GLAD YOU AREN'T MY EDITOR.
DON'T BLAME MIURA. HE FOUGHT THIS UNTIL THE VERY END.
I MADE THIS DECISION.
I DON'T AGREE WITH YOUR DECISION TO KEEP THEM ON HIATUS UNTIL APRIL, AND I NEVER WILL.
SEE YA, ASHIROGI.
...

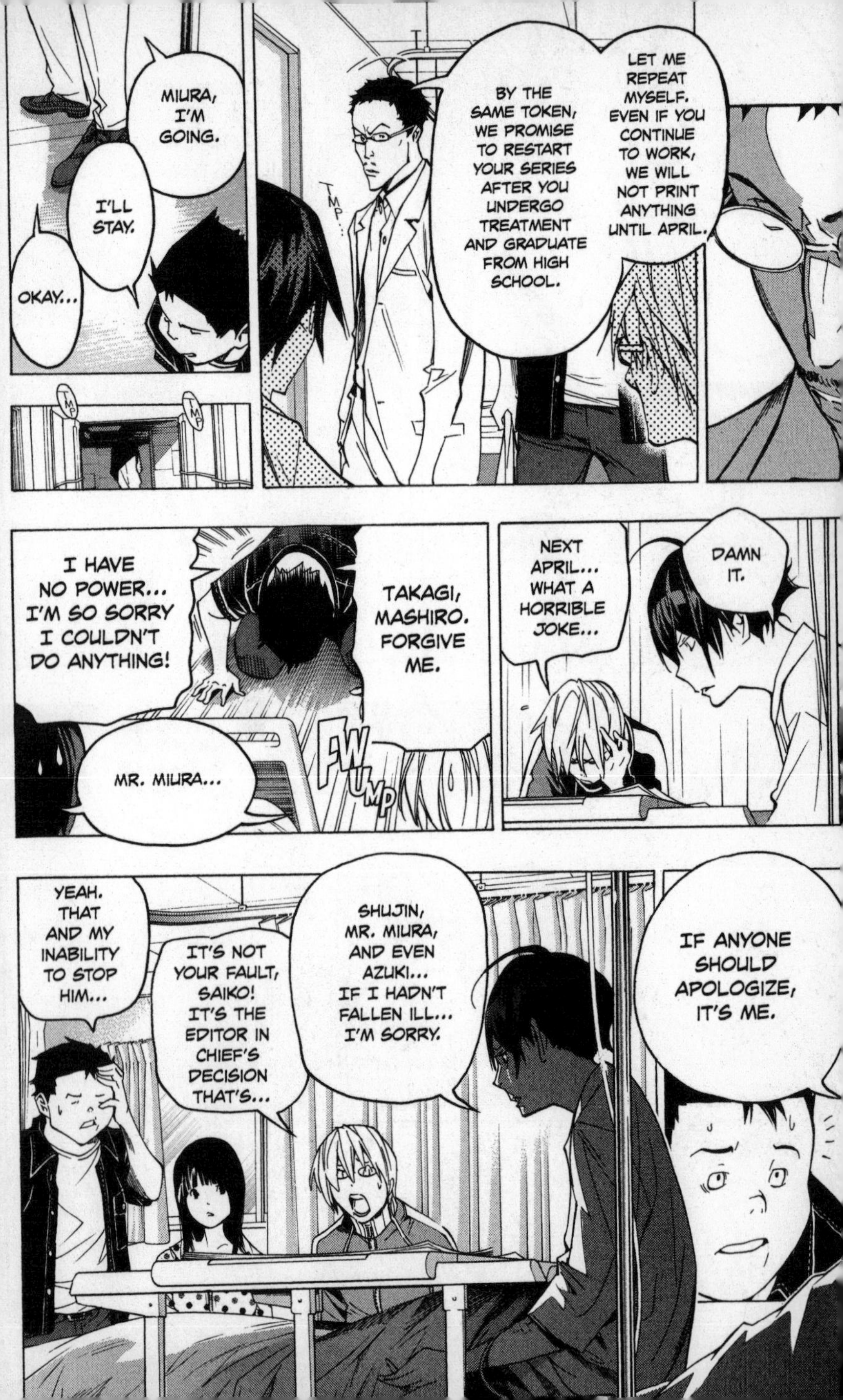
LET ME REPEAT MYSELF. EVEN IF YOU CONTINUE TO WORK, WE WILL NOT PRINT ANYTHING UNTIL APRIL.
BY THE SAME TOKEN, WE PROMISE TO RESTART YOUR SERIES AFTER YOU UNDERGO TREATMENT AND GRADUATE FROM HIGH SCHOOL.
TMP...
MIURA, I'M GOING.
I'LL STAY.
OKAY...
TMP
TMP
DAMN IT.
NEXT APRIL... WHAT A HORRIBLE JOKE...
TAKAGI, MASHIRO. FORGIVE ME.
I HAVE NO POWER... I'M SO SORRY I COULDN'T DO ANYTHING!
FWUMP
MR. MIURA...
IF ANYONE SHOULD APOLOGIZE, IT'S ME.
SHUJIN, MR. MIURA, AND EVEN AZUKI... IF I HADN'T FALLEN ILL... I'M SORRY.
IT'S NOT YOUR FAULT, SAIKO! IT'S THE EDITOR IN CHIEF'S DECISION THAT'S...
YEAH. THAT AND MY INABILITY TO STOP HIM...

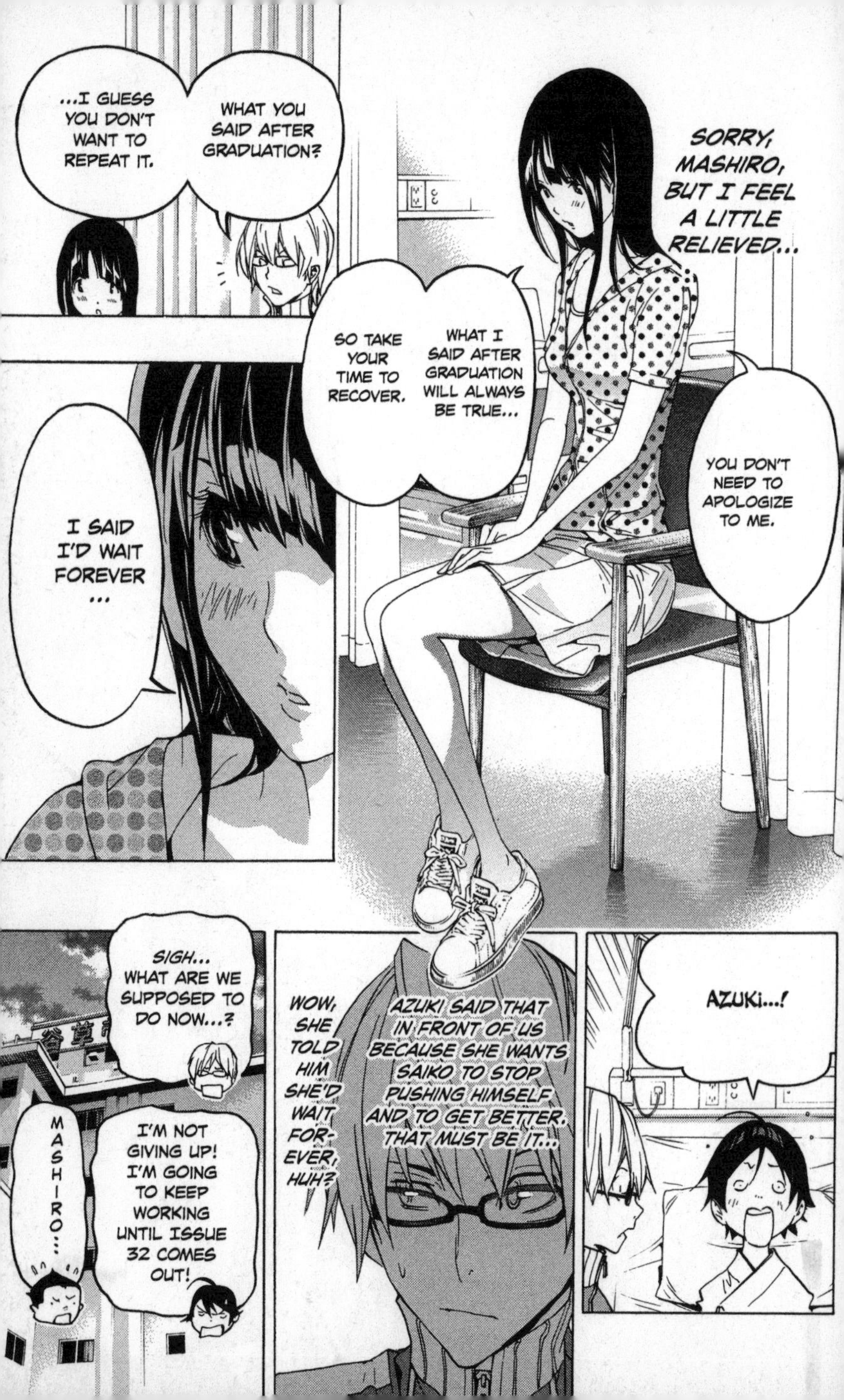
SORRY, MASHIRO, BUT I FEEL A LITTLE RELIEVED...
YOU DON'T NEED TO APOLOGIZE TO ME.
WHAT I SAID AFTER GRADUATION WILL ALWAYS BE TRUE...
SO TAKE YOUR TIME TO RECOVER.
WHAT YOU SAID AFTER GRADUATION?
...I GUESS YOU DON'T WANT TO REPEAT IT.
I SAID I'D WAIT FOREVER ...
AZUKi...!
AZUKI SAID THAT IN FRONT OF US BECAUSE SHE WANTS SAIKO TO STOP PUSHING HIMSELF AND TO GET BETTER. THAT MUST BE IT...
WOW, SHE TOLD HIM SHE'D WAIT FOR-EVER, HUH?
SIGH... WHAT ARE WE SUPPOSED TO DO NOW...?
I'M NOT GIVING UP! I'M GOING TO KEEP WORKING UNTIL ISSUE 32 COMES OUT!
MASHIRO...

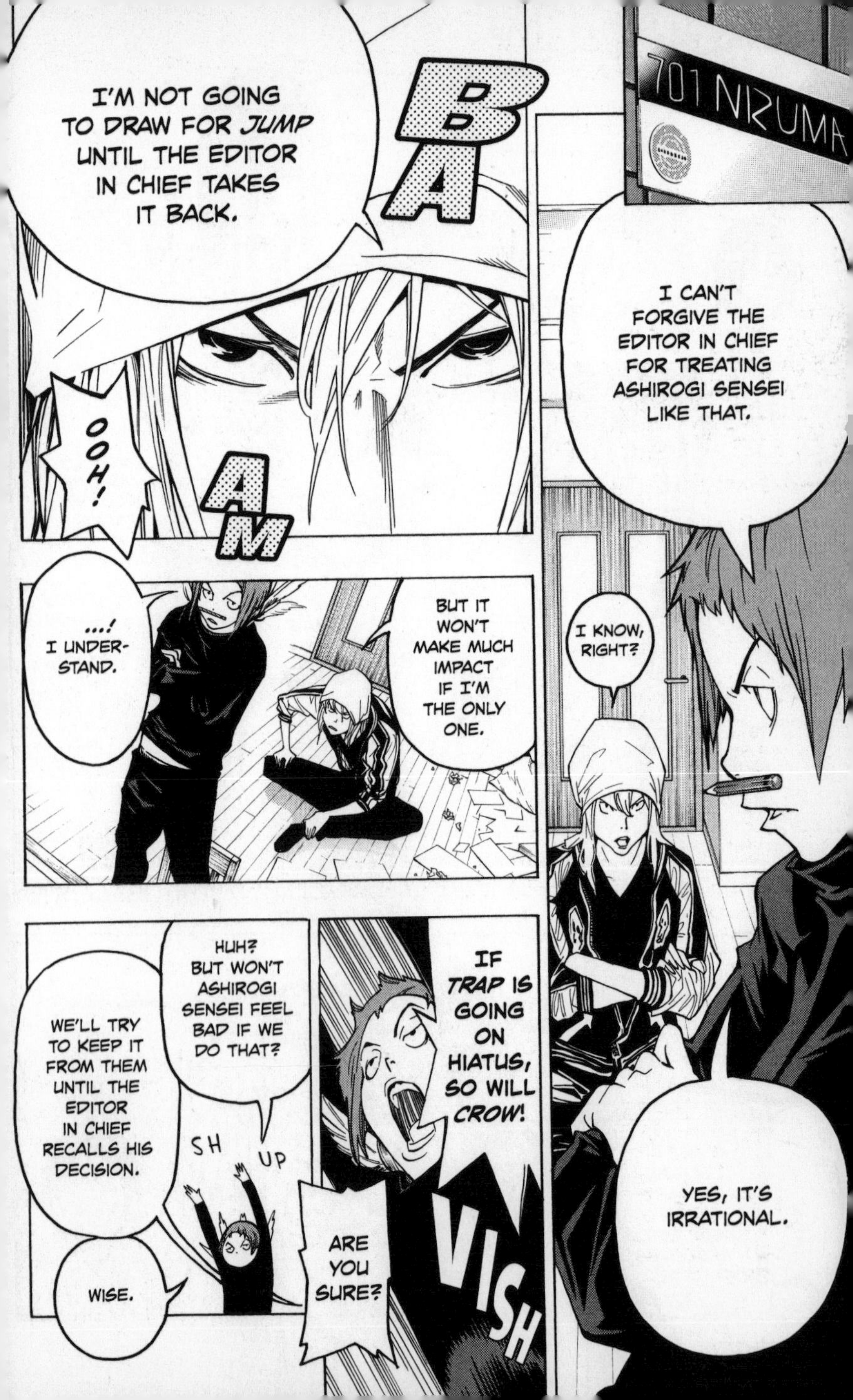
701 NIZUMA
I CAN'T FORGIVE THE EDITOR IN CHIEF FOR TREATING ASHIROGI SENSEI LIKE THAT.
I KNOW, RIGHT?
YES, IT'S IRRATIONAL.
I'M NOT GOING TO DRAW FOR *JUMP* UNTIL THE EDITOR IN CHIEF TAKES IT BACK.
BA
AM
OOH!
BUT IT WON'T MAKE MUCH IMPACT IF I'M THE ONLY ONE.
...! I UNDER-STAND.
IF *TRAP* IS GOING ON HIATUS, SO WILL *CROW*!
VISH
ARE YOU SURE?
HUH? BUT WON'T ASHIROGI SENSEI FEEL BAD IF WE DO THAT?
WE'LL TRY TO KEEP IT FROM THEM UNTIL THE EDITOR IN CHIEF RECALLS HIS DECISION.
SH UP
WISE.

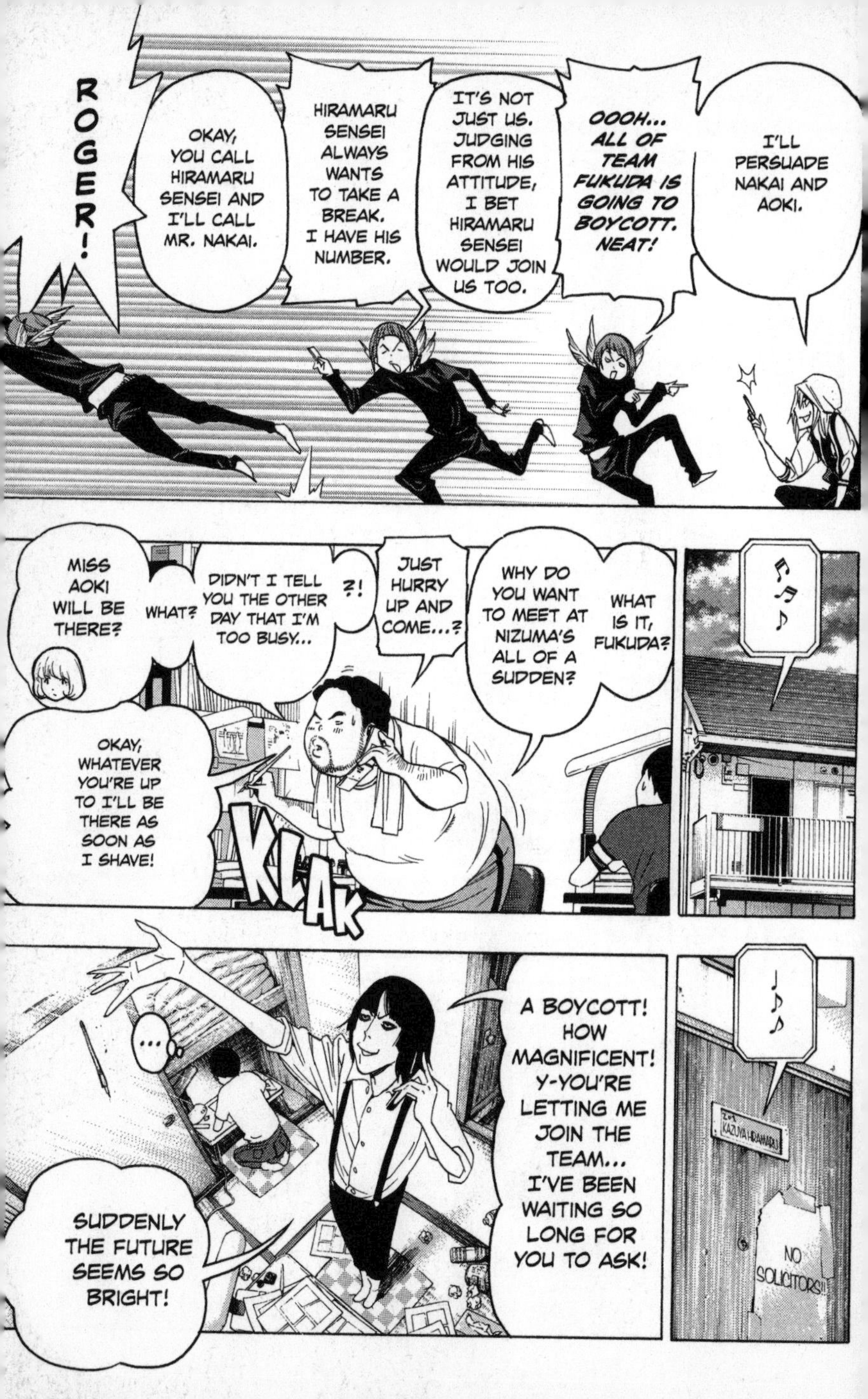
I'LL PERSUADE NAKAI AND AOKI.
OOOH... ALL OF TEAM FUKUDA IS GOING TO BOYCOTT. NEAT!
IT'S NOT JUST US. JUDGING FROM HIS ATTITUDE, I BET HIRAMARU SENSEI WOULD JOIN US TOO.
HIRAMARU SENSEI ALWAYS WANTS TO TAKE A BREAK. I HAVE HIS NUMBER.
OKAY, YOU CALL HIRAMARU SENSEI AND I'LL CALL MR. NAKAI.
ROGER!
WHAT IS IT, FUKUDA?
WHY DO YOU WANT TO MEET AT NIZUMA'S ALL OF A SUDDEN?
JUST HURRY UP AND COME...?
?!
DIDN'T I TELL YOU THE OTHER DAY THAT I'M TOO BUSY...
WHAT?
MISS AOKI WILL BE THERE?
OKAY, WHATEVER YOU'RE UP TO I'LL BE THERE AS SOON AS I SHAVE!
KLAK
KAZUYA HIRAMARU
NO SOLICITORS!!
A BOYCOTT! HOW MAGNIFICENT! Y-YOU'RE LETTING ME JOIN THE TEAM... I'VE BEEN WAITING SO LONG FOR YOU TO ASK!
...
SUDDENLY THE FUTURE SEEMS SO BRIGHT!

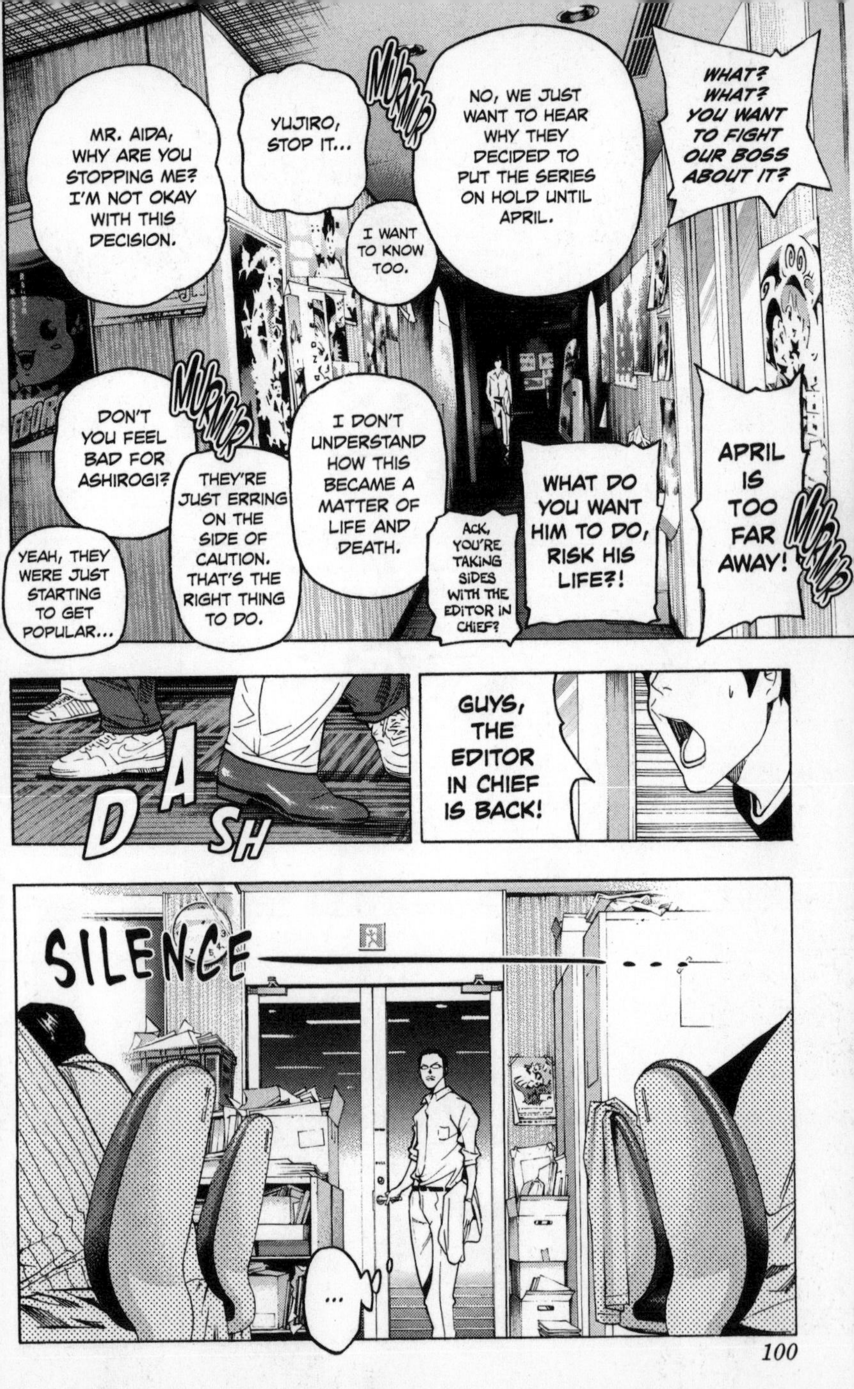
WHAT? WHAT? YOU WANT TO FIGHT OUR BOSS ABOUT IT?
NO, WE JUST WANT TO HEAR WHY THEY DECIDED TO PUT THE SERIES ON HOLD UNTIL APRIL.
MURMUR
YUJIRO, STOP IT...
MR. AIDA, WHY ARE YOU STOPPING ME? I'M NOT OKAY WITH THIS DECISION.
I WANT TO KNOW TOO.
MURMUR
APRIL IS TOO FAR AWAY!
WHAT DO YOU WANT HIM TO DO, RISK HIS LIFE?!
ACK, YOU'RE TAKING SIDES WITH THE EDITOR IN CHIEF?
I DON'T UNDERSTAND HOW THIS BECAME A MATTER OF LIFE AND DEATH.
THEY'RE JUST ERRING ON THE SIDE OF CAUTION. THAT'S THE RIGHT THING TO DO.
MURMUR
DON'T YOU FEEL BAD FOR ASHIROGI?
YEAH, THEY WERE JUST STARTING TO GET POPULAR...
GUYS, THE EDITOR IN CHIEF IS BACK!
DASH
SILENCE
...

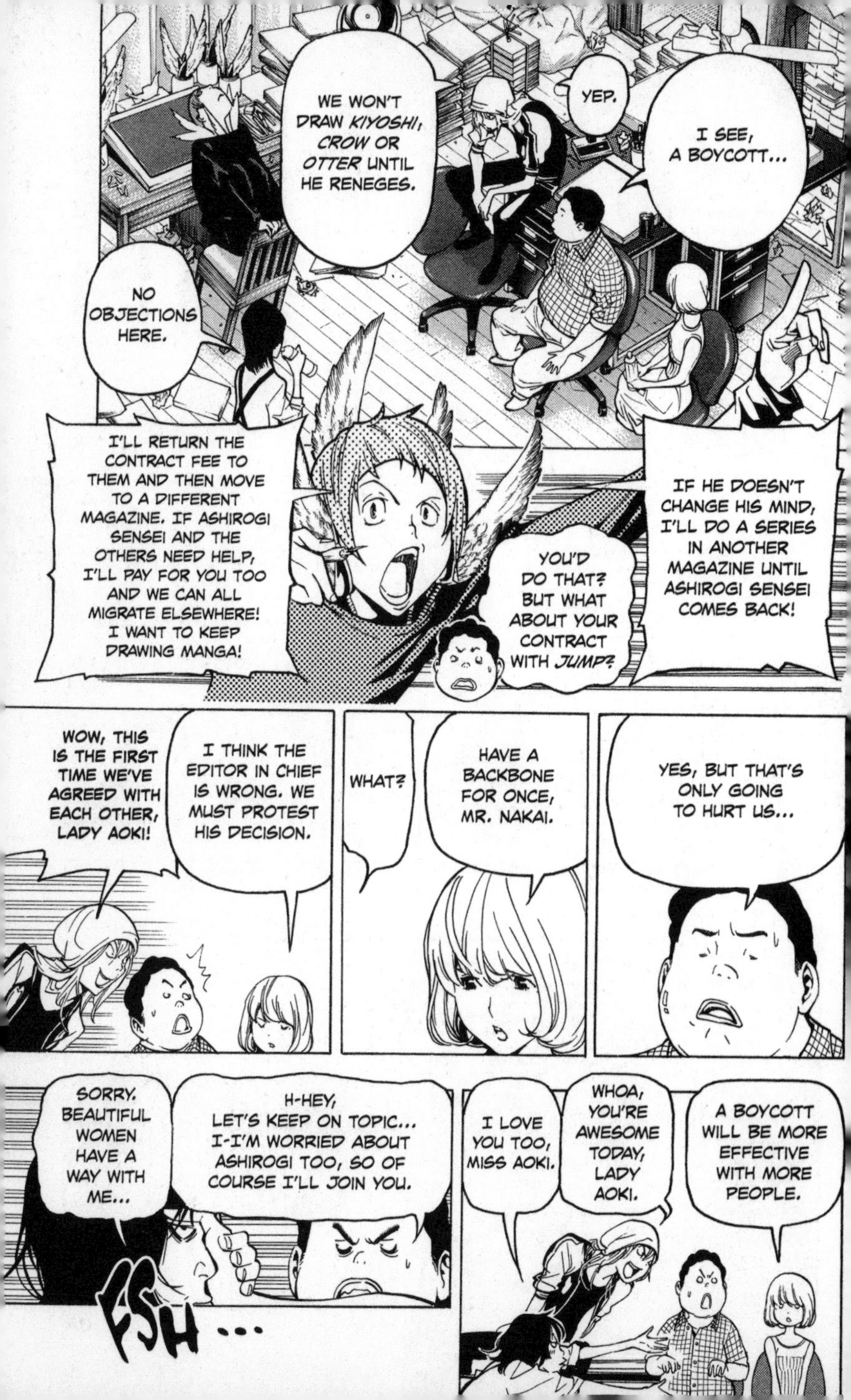
I SEE, A BOYCOTT...
YEP.
WE WON'T DRAW *KIYOSHI*, *CROW* OR *OTTER* UNTIL HE RENEGES.
NO OBJECTIONS HERE.
IF HE DOESN'T CHANGE HIS MIND, I'LL DO A SERIES IN ANOTHER MAGAZINE UNTIL ASHIROGI SENSEI COMES BACK!
YOU'D DO THAT? BUT WHAT ABOUT YOUR CONTRACT WITH *JUMP*?
I'LL RETURN THE CONTRACT FEE TO THEM AND THEN MOVE TO A DIFFERENT MAGAZINE. IF ASHIROGI SENSEI AND THE OTHERS NEED HELP, I'LL PAY FOR YOU TOO AND WE CAN ALL MIGRATE ELSEWHERE! I WANT TO KEEP DRAWING MANGA!
YES, BUT THAT'S ONLY GOING TO HURT US...
HAVE A BACKBONE FOR ONCE, MR. NAKAI.
WHAT?
I THINK THE EDITOR IN CHIEF IS WRONG. WE MUST PROTEST HIS DECISION.
WOW, THIS IS THE FIRST TIME WE'VE AGREED WITH EACH OTHER, LADY AOKI!
A BOYCOTT WILL BE MORE EFFECTIVE WITH MORE PEOPLE.
WHOA, YOU'RE AWESOME TODAY, LADY AOKI.
I LOVE YOU TOO, MISS AOKI.
H-HEY, LET'S KEEP ON TOPIC... I-I'M WORRIED ABOUT ASHIROGI TOO, SO OF COURSE I'LL JOIN YOU.
SORRY. BEAUTIFUL WOMEN HAVE A WAY WITH ME...
FSH...

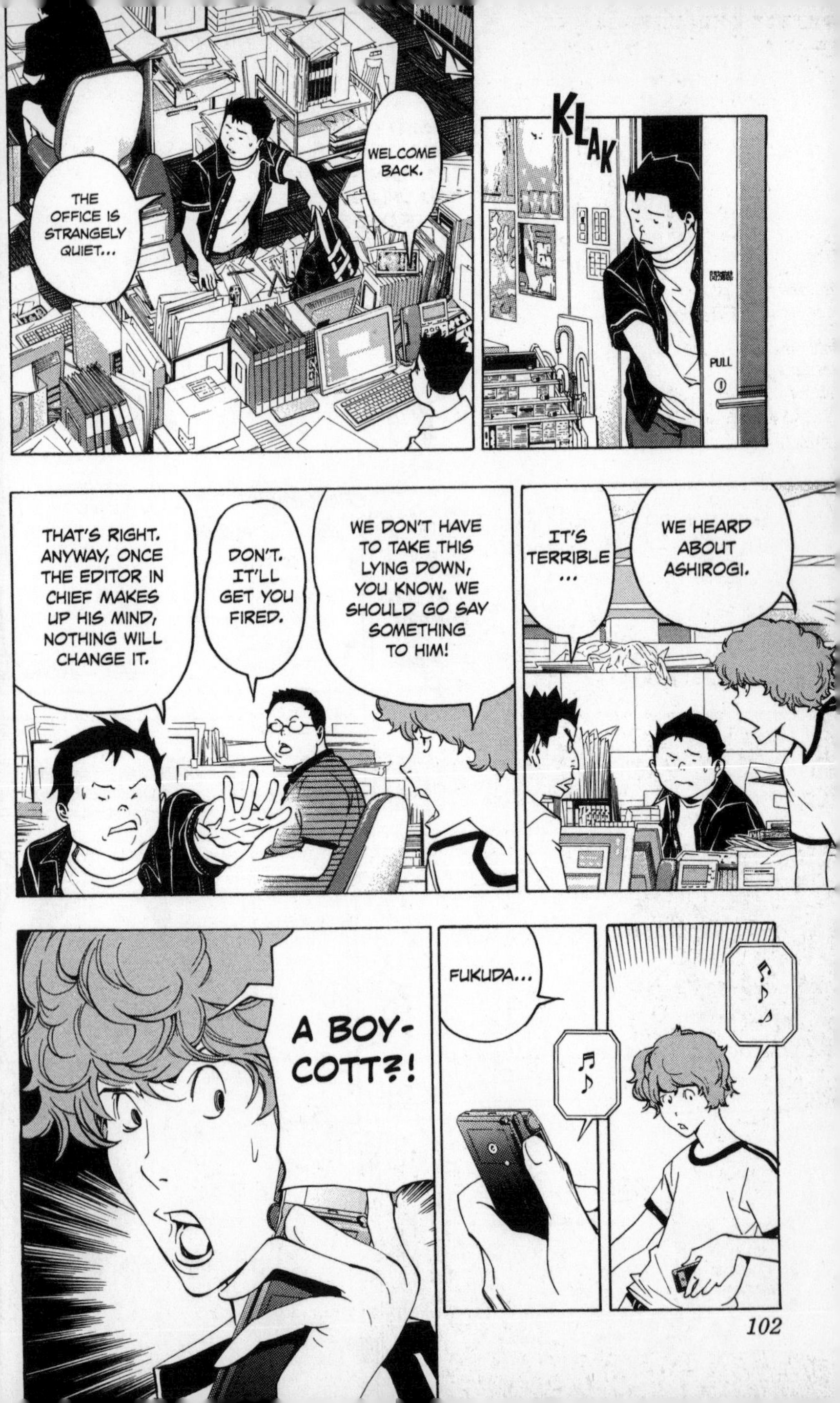
KLAK
PULL
WELCOME BACK.
THE OFFICE IS STRANGELY QUIET...
WE HEARD ABOUT ASHIROGI.
IT'S TERRIBLE...
WE DON'T HAVE TO TAKE THIS LYING DOWN, YOU KNOW. WE SHOULD GO SAY SOMETHING TO HIM!
DON'T. IT'LL GET YOU FIRED.
THAT'S RIGHT. ANYWAY, ONCE THE EDITOR IN CHIEF MAKES UP HIS MIND, NOTHING WILL CHANGE IT.
♪♪♪
FUKUDA...
♪♪
A BOY-COTT?!

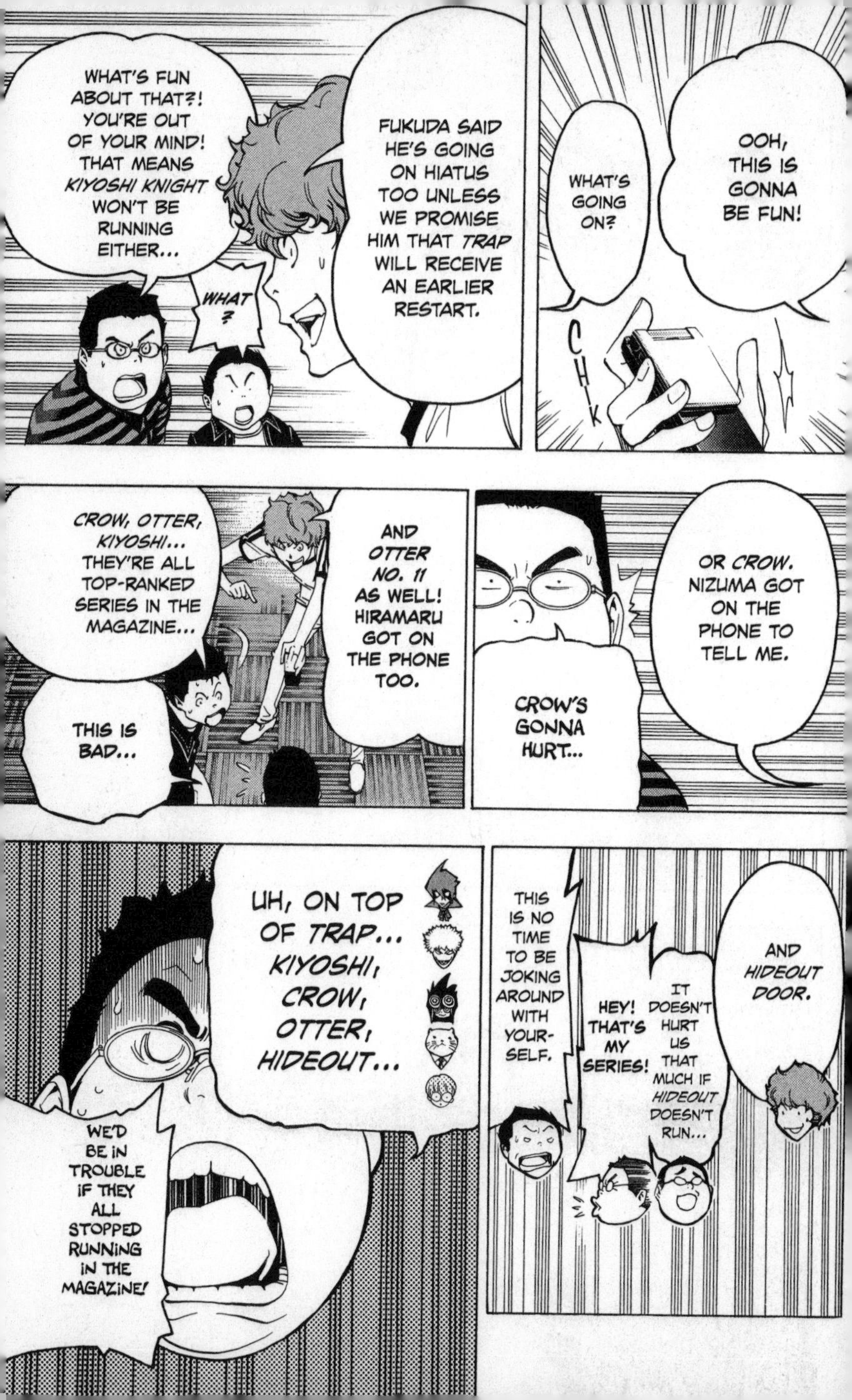
OOH, THIS IS GONNA BE FUN!
WHAT'S GOING ON?
CHIK
FUKUDA SAID HE'S GOING ON HIATUS TOO UNLESS WE PROMISE HIM THAT *TRAP* WILL RECEIVE AN EARLIER RESTART.
WHAT?
WHAT'S FUN ABOUT THAT?! YOU'RE OUT OF YOUR MIND! THAT MEANS *KIYOSHI KNIGHT* WON'T BE RUNNING EITHER...
OR *CROW*. NIZUMA GOT ON THE PHONE TO TELL ME.
CROW'S GONNA HURT...
AND *OTTER NO. 11* AS WELL! HIRAMARU GOT ON THE PHONE TOO.
CROW, OTTER, KIYOSHI... THEY'RE ALL TOP-RANKED SERIES IN THE MAGAZINE...
THIS IS BAD...
AND *HIDEOUT DOOR*.
IT DOESN'T HURT US THAT MUCH IF *HIDEOUT* DOESN'T RUN...
HEY! THAT'S MY SERIES!
THIS IS NO TIME TO BE JOKING AROUND WITH YOURSELF.
UH, ON TOP OF *TRAP*... *KIYOSHI, CROW, OTTER, HIDEOUT*...
WE'D BE IN TROUBLE IF THEY ALL STOPPED RUNNING IN THE MAGAZINE!

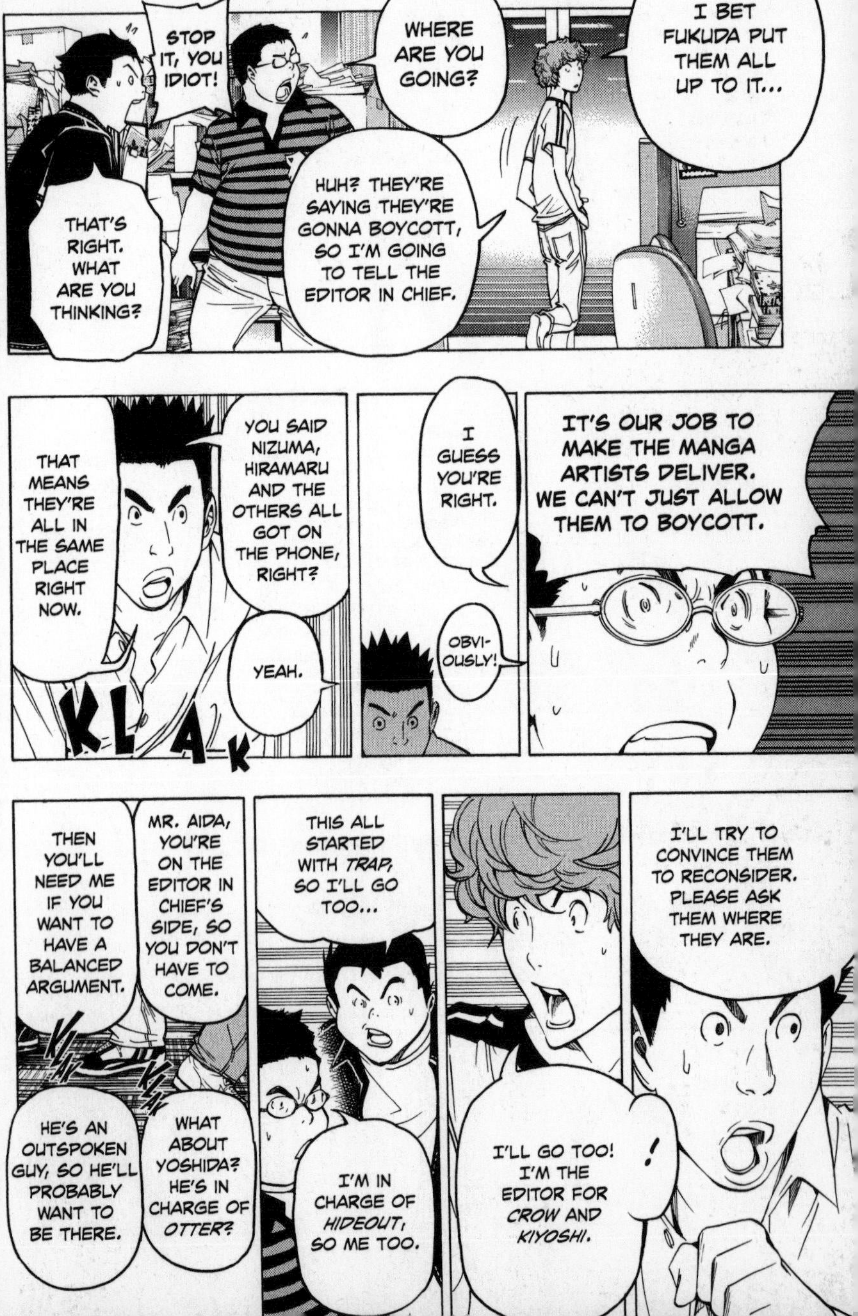
I BET FUKUDA PUT THEM ALL UP TO IT...
WHERE ARE YOU GOING?
HUH? THEY'RE SAYING THEY'RE GONNA BOYCOTT, SO I'M GOING TO TELL THE EDITOR IN CHIEF.
STOP IT, YOU IDIOT!
THAT'S RIGHT. WHAT ARE YOU THINKING?
IT'S OUR JOB TO MAKE THE MANGA ARTISTS DELIVER. WE CAN'T JUST ALLOW THEM TO BOYCOTT.
I GUESS YOU'RE RIGHT.
OBVI- OUSLY!
YOU SAID NIZUMA, HIRAMARU AND THE OTHERS ALL GOT ON THE PHONE, RIGHT?
THAT MEANS THEY'RE ALL IN THE SAME PLACE RIGHT NOW.
YEAH.
KLAK
I'LL TRY TO CONVINCE THEM TO RECONSIDER. PLEASE ASK THEM WHERE THEY ARE.
I'LL GO TOO! I'M THE EDITOR FOR *CROW* AND *KIYOSHI*.
THIS ALL STARTED WITH *TRAP*, SO I'LL GO TOO...
I'M IN CHARGE OF *HIDEOUT*, SO ME TOO.
MR. AIDA, YOU'RE ON THE EDITOR IN CHIEF'S SIDE, SO YOU DON'T HAVE TO COME.
THEN YOU'LL NEED ME IF YOU WANT TO HAVE A BALANCED ARGUMENT.
WHAT ABOUT YOSHIDA? HE'S IN CHARGE OF *OTTER*?
HE'S AN OUTSPOKEN GUY, SO HE'LL PROBABLY WANT TO BE THERE.

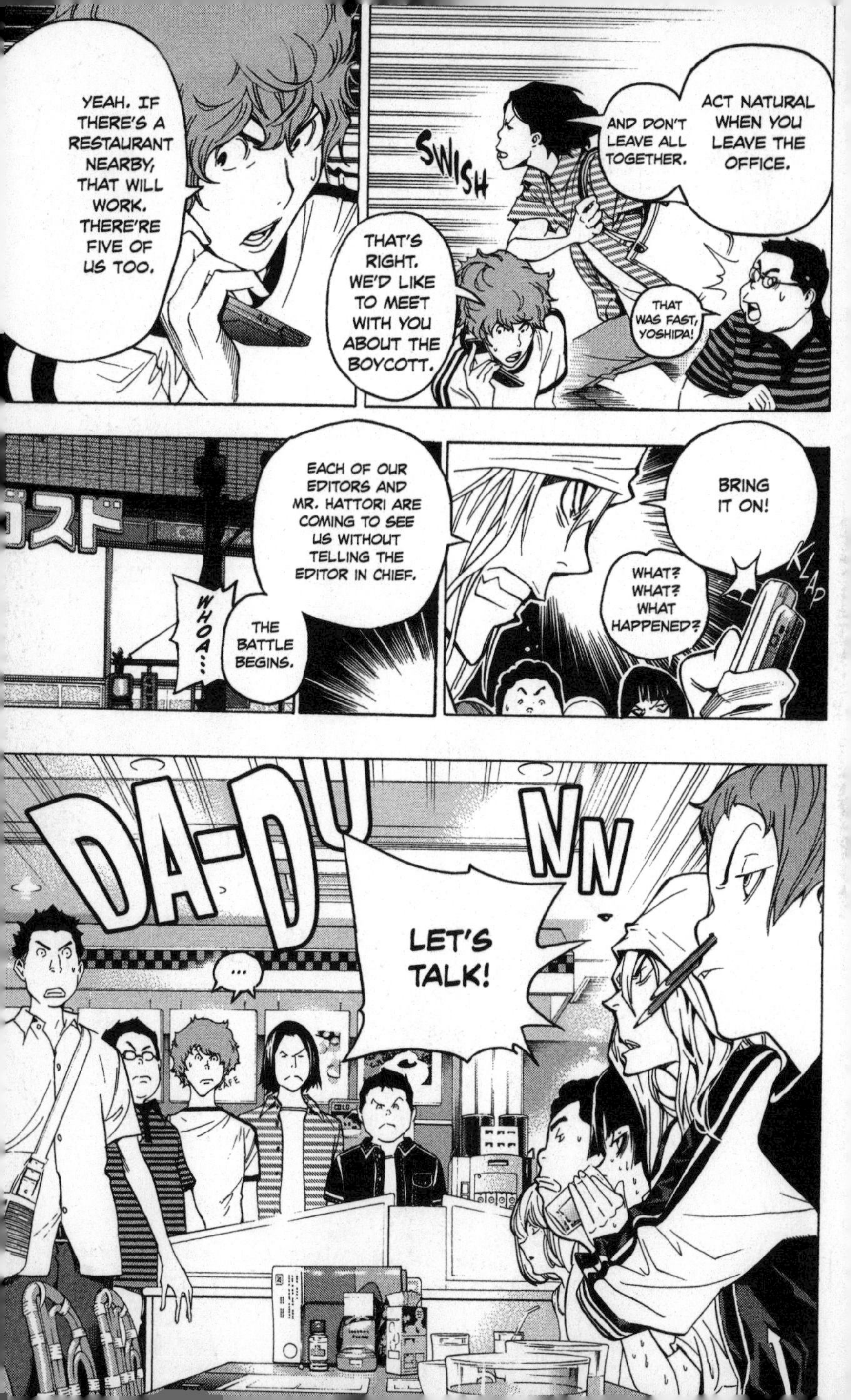
ACT NATURAL WHEN YOU LEAVE THE OFFICE.
AND DON'T LEAVE ALL TOGETHER.
SWISH
THAT WAS FAST, YOSHIDA!
THAT'S RIGHT. WE'D LIKE TO MEET WITH YOU ABOUT THE BOYCOTT.
YEAH. IF THERE'S A RESTAURANT NEARBY, THAT WILL WORK. THERE'RE FIVE OF US TOO.
BRING IT ON!
KLAP
WHAT? WHAT? WHAT HAPPENED?
EACH OF OUR EDITORS AND MR. HATTORI ARE COMING TO SEE US WITHOUT TELLING THE EDITOR IN CHIEF.
THE BATTLE BEGINS.
WHOA...
DA-DUNN
LET'S TALK!
...

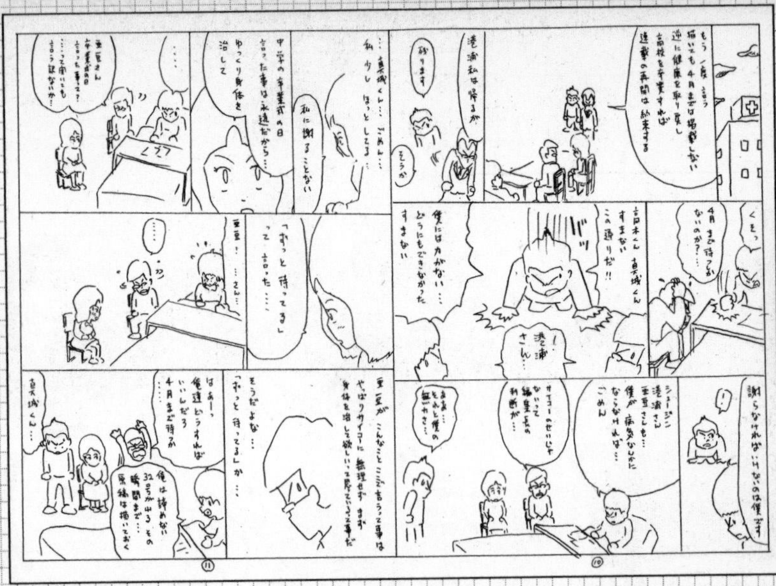
もう一度 描いても4月までは掲載しない
逆に健康を取り戻し 高校を卒業すれば 連載の再開は約束する
港浦 私は帰るか
戻ります
そうか
くそっ
4月まで待つしかないのか?…
ダッ
高木くん 真城くん すまない この通りだ!!
港浦さん…
僕には力がない… どうにもできなかった すまない
謝らなければいけないのは僕です
!
シュージン 港浦さん 亜豆さんも… 僕が病気なんかにならなければ… ごめん
サイコーのせいじゃないって 編集長の判断が…
まあ…もとは僕の無茶が…
…真城くん… ごめん… 私少しほっとしてる…
私に謝ることない
中学の卒業式の日 言った事は永遠だから… ゆっくり身体を治して
……
亜豆さん 卒業式の日 言った事って?
…って聞いても言う訳ないか…
亜豆!…さん…
「ずっと待ってる」って言った…
……
亜豆がこんなところで言うって事は やはりサイコーに無理せず まず身体を治して欲しいと思ってる事だ
そうだよな… 「ずっと待ってる」か…
はぁー、俺達どうすれば いいんだろ 4月まで待つか
俺は諦めない 32号が出るその瞬間まで… 原稿は描いておく
真城くん…

OHBA'S STORYBOARD

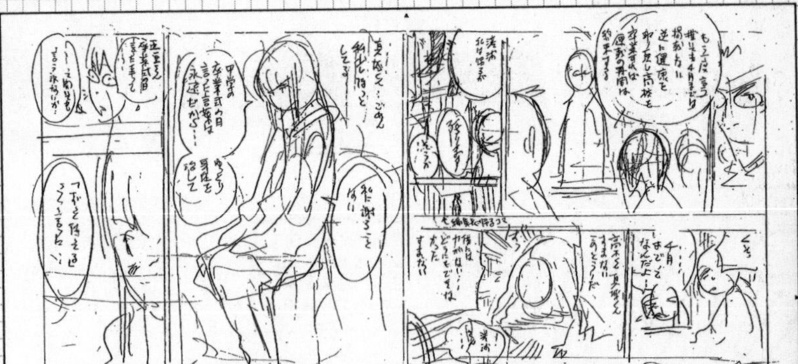

OBATA'S STORYBOARD

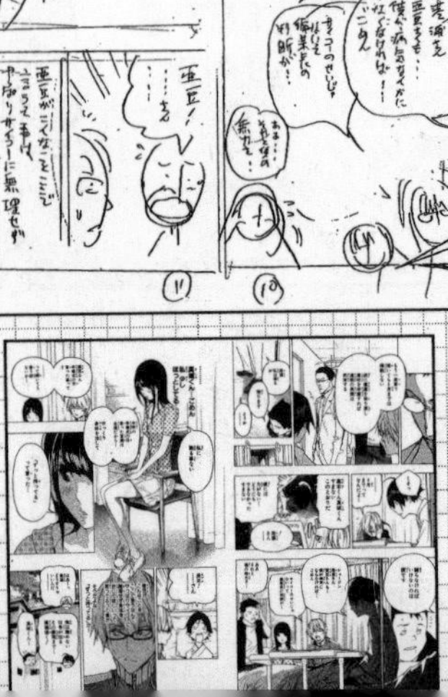

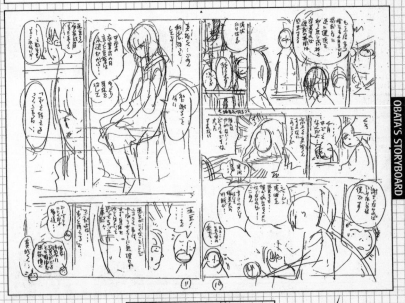

COMPLETE!

※CREATOR STORYBOARDS AND FINISHED PAGES IN JAPANESE

BAKUMAN。 vol. 6

"Until the Final Draft Is Complete"

Chapter 48, pp. 96-97

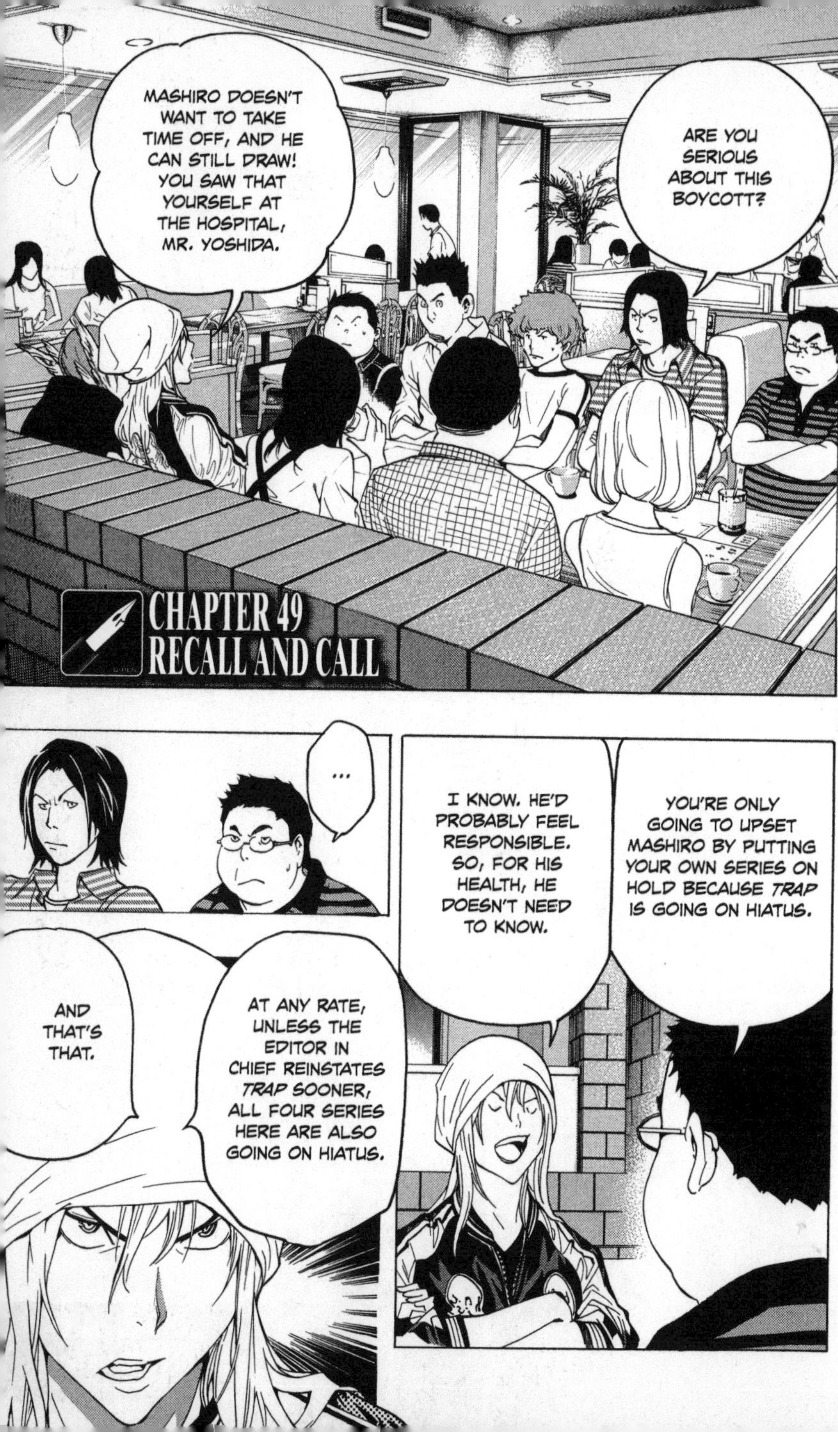
ARE YOU SERIOUS ABOUT THIS BOYCOTT?
MASHIRO DOESN'T WANT TO TAKE TIME OFF, AND HE CAN STILL DRAW! YOU SAW THAT YOURSELF AT THE HOSPITAL, MR. YOSHIDA.
CHAPTER 49
RECALL AND CALL
YOU'RE ONLY GOING TO UPSET MASHIRO BY PUTTING YOUR OWN SERIES ON HOLD BECAUSE *TRAP* IS GOING ON HIATUS.
I KNOW. HE'D PROBABLY FEEL RESPONSIBLE. SO, FOR HIS HEALTH, HE DOESN'T NEED TO KNOW.
...
AT ANY RATE, UNLESS THE EDITOR IN CHIEF REINSTATES *TRAP* SOONER, ALL FOUR SERIES HERE ARE ALSO GOING ON HIATUS.
AND THAT'S THAT.

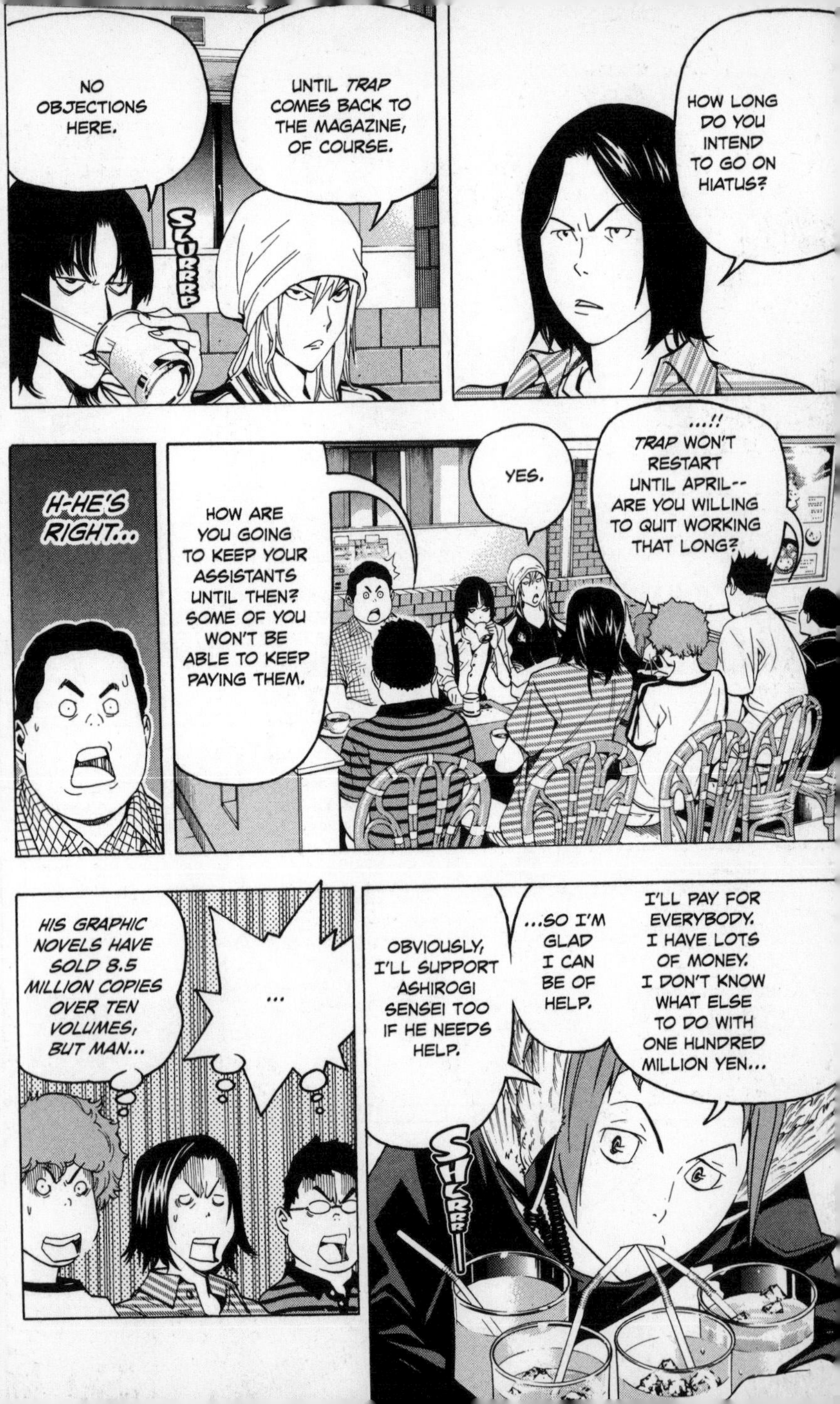
HOW LONG DO YOU INTEND TO GO ON HIATUS?
UNTIL TRAP COMES BACK TO THE MAGAZINE, OF COURSE.
NO OBJECTIONS HERE.
SLURRRP
...!! TRAP WON'T RESTART UNTIL APRIL-- ARE YOU WILLING TO QUIT WORKING THAT LONG?
YES.
HOW ARE YOU GOING TO KEEP YOUR ASSISTANTS UNTIL THEN? SOME OF YOU WON'T BE ABLE TO KEEP PAYING THEM.
H-HE'S RIGHT...
I'LL PAY FOR EVERYBODY. I HAVE LOTS OF MONEY. I DON'T KNOW WHAT ELSE TO DO WITH ONE HUNDRED MILLION YEN...
...SO I'M GLAD I CAN BE OF HELP.
OBVIOUSLY, I'LL SUPPORT ASHIROGI SENSEI TOO IF HE NEEDS HELP.
SHLRRR
HIS GRAPHIC NOVELS HAVE SOLD 8.5 MILLION COPIES OVER TEN VOLUMES, BUT MAN...
...

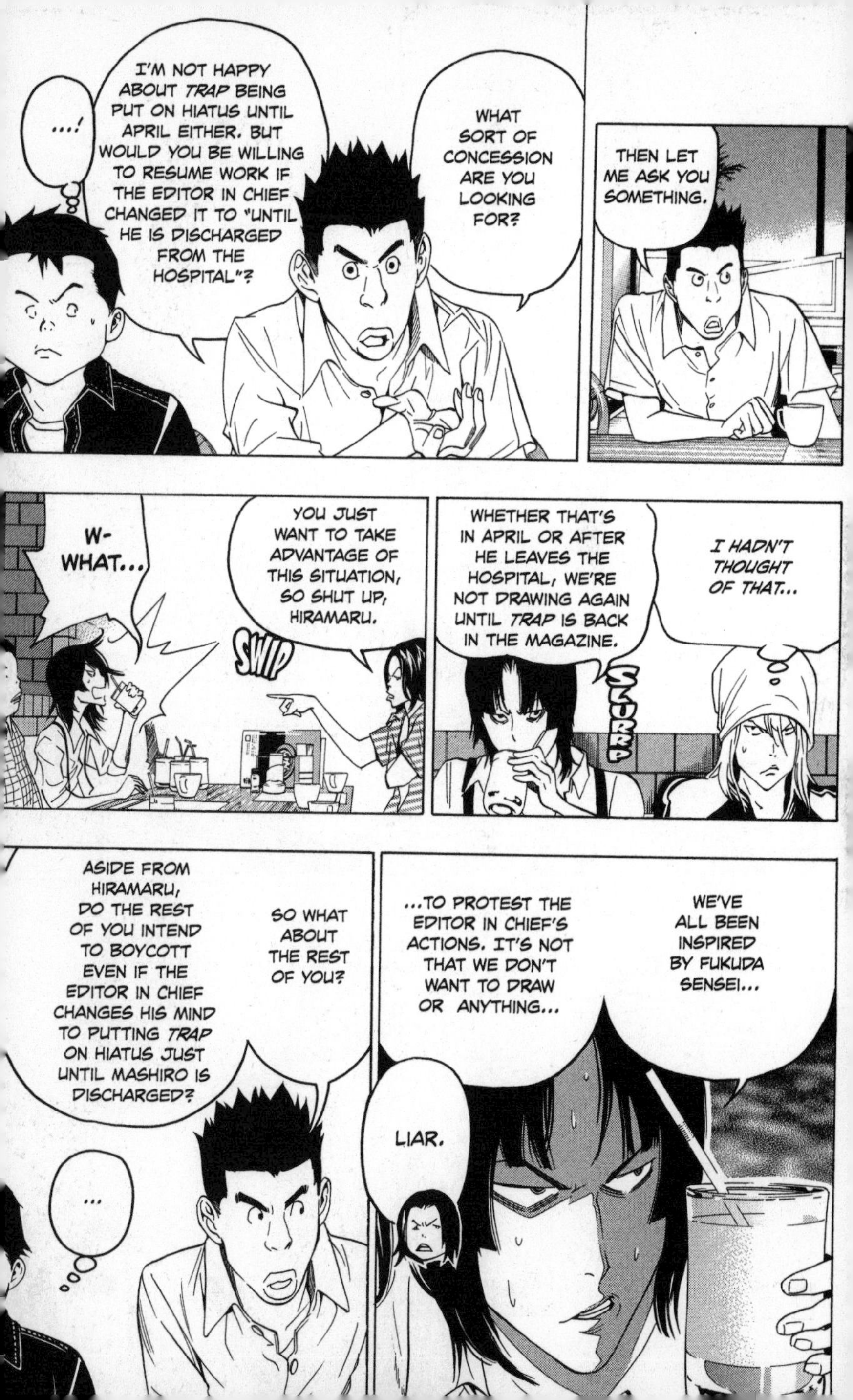
THEN LET ME ASK YOU SOMETHING.
WHAT SORT OF CONCESSION ARE YOU LOOKING FOR?
I'M NOT HAPPY ABOUT *TRAP* BEING PUT ON HIATUS UNTIL APRIL EITHER. BUT WOULD YOU BE WILLING TO RESUME WORK IF THE EDITOR IN CHIEF CHANGED IT TO "UNTIL HE IS DISCHARGED FROM THE HOSPITAL"?
...!
WHETHER THAT'S IN APRIL OR AFTER HE LEAVES THE HOSPITAL, WE'RE NOT DRAWING AGAIN UNTIL *TRAP* IS BACK IN THE MAGAZINE.
SLURRP
I HADN'T THOUGHT OF THAT...
YOU JUST WANT TO TAKE ADVANTAGE OF THIS SITUATION, SO SHUT UP, HIRAMARU.
SWIP
W-WHAT...
WE'VE ALL BEEN INSPIRED BY FUKUDA SENSEI...
...TO PROTEST THE EDITOR IN CHIEF'S ACTIONS. IT'S NOT THAT WE DON'T WANT TO DRAW OR ANYTHING...
LIAR.
SO WHAT ABOUT THE REST OF YOU?
ASIDE FROM HIRAMARU, DO THE REST OF YOU INTEND TO BOYCOTT EVEN IF THE EDITOR IN CHIEF CHANGES HIS MIND TO PUTTING *TRAP* ON HIATUS JUST UNTIL MASHIRO IS DISCHARGED?
...

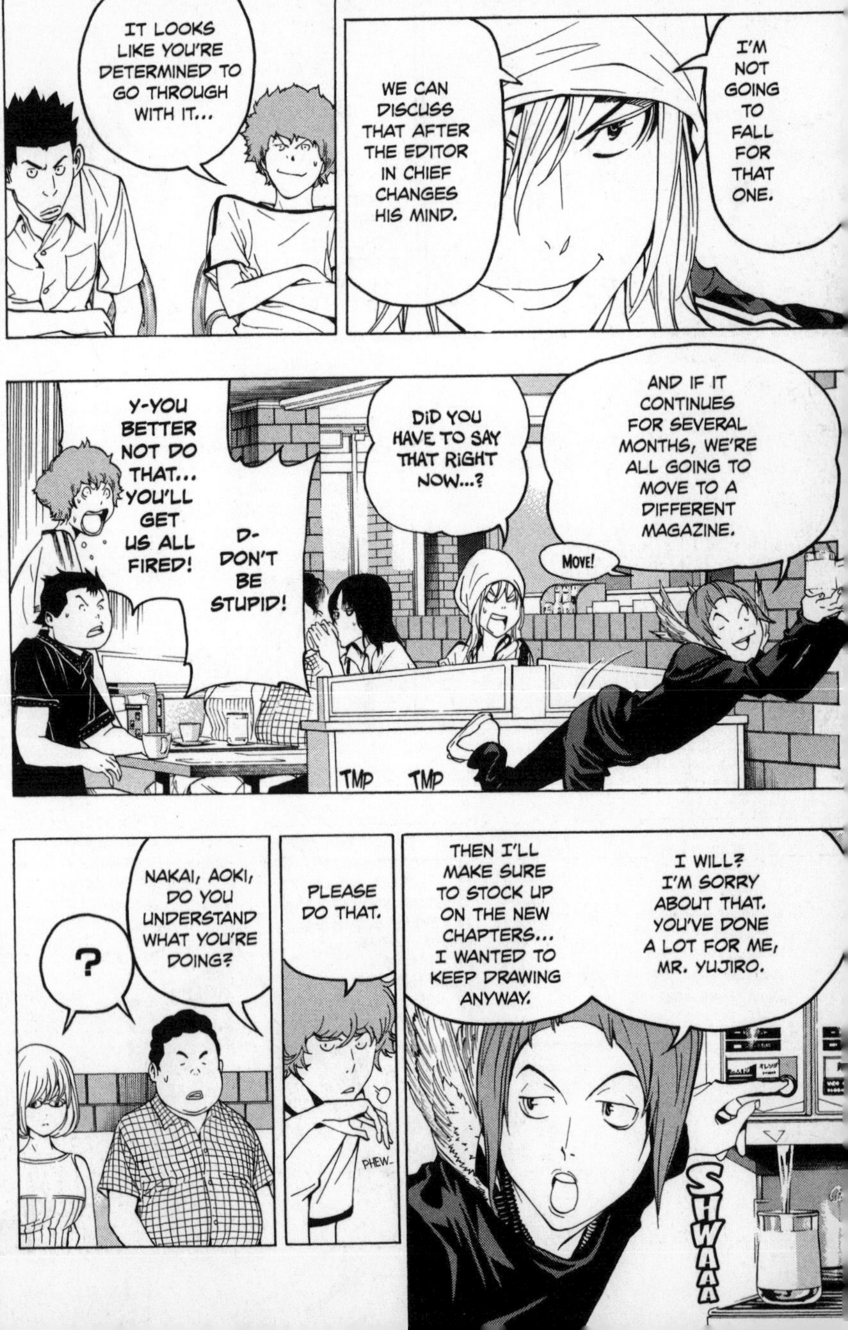
I'M NOT GOING TO FALL FOR THAT ONE.
WE CAN DISCUSS THAT AFTER THE EDITOR IN CHIEF CHANGES HIS MIND.
IT LOOKS LIKE YOU'RE DETERMINED TO GO THROUGH WITH IT...
AND IF IT CONTINUES FOR SEVERAL MONTHS, WE'RE ALL GOING TO MOVE TO A DIFFERENT MAGAZINE.
DID YOU HAVE TO SAY THAT RIGHT NOW...?
MOVE!
Y-YOU BETTER NOT DO THAT... YOU'LL GET US ALL FIRED!
D-DON'T BE STUPID!
TMP
TMP
I WILL? I'M SORRY ABOUT THAT. YOU'VE DONE A LOT FOR ME, MR. YUJIRO.
THEN I'LL MAKE SURE TO STOCK UP ON THE NEW CHAPTERS... I WANTED TO KEEP DRAWING ANYWAY.
SHWAAA
PLEASE DO THAT.
PHEW...
NAKAI, AOKI, DO YOU UNDERSTAND WHAT YOU'RE DOING?
?

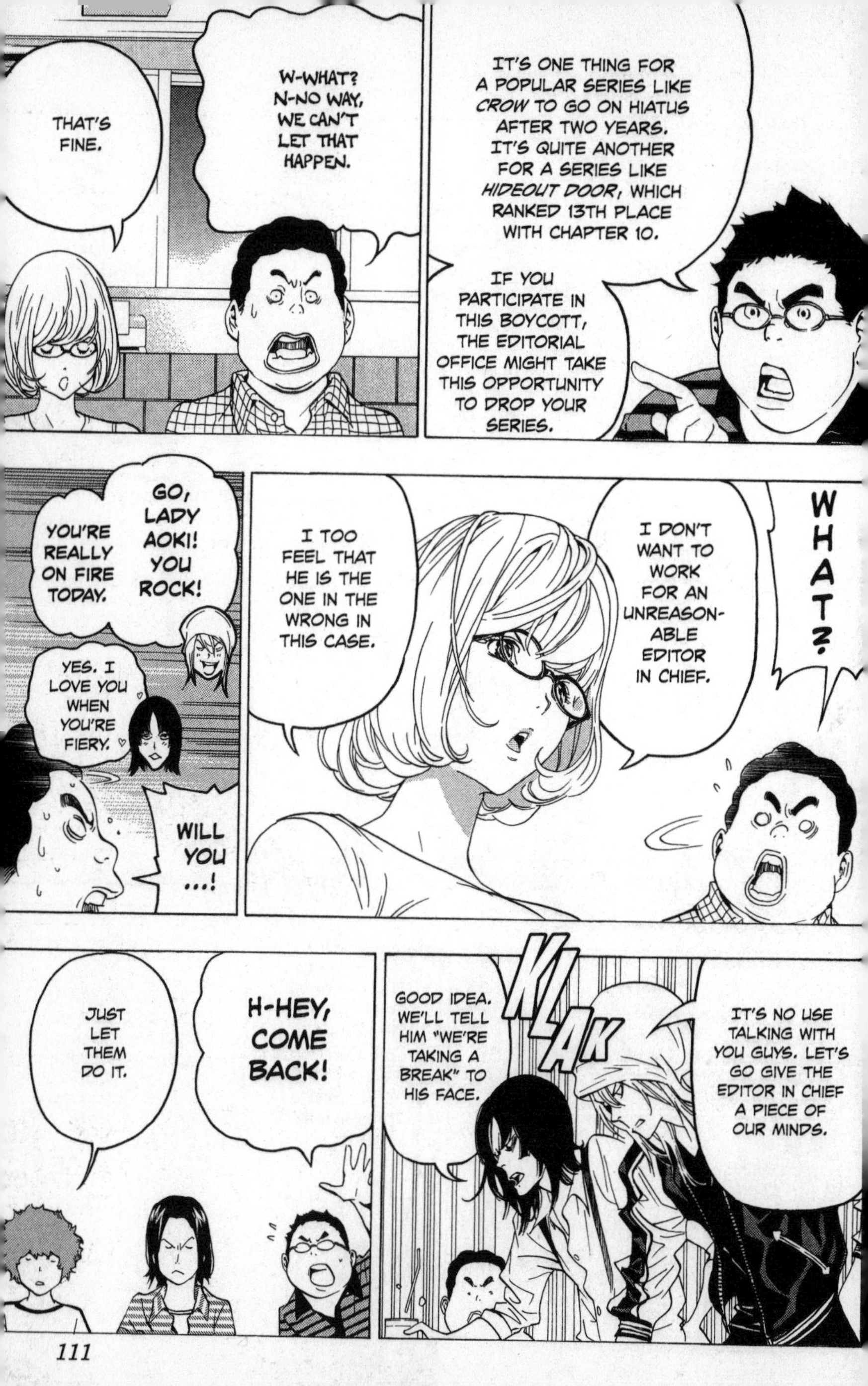
IT'S ONE THING FOR A POPULAR SERIES LIKE *CROW* TO GO ON HIATUS AFTER TWO YEARS. IT'S QUITE ANOTHER FOR A SERIES LIKE *HIDEOUT DOOR*, WHICH RANKED 13TH PLACE WITH CHAPTER 10.
IF YOU PARTICIPATE IN THIS BOYCOTT, THE EDITORIAL OFFICE MIGHT TAKE THIS OPPORTUNITY TO DROP YOUR SERIES.
W-WHAT? N-NO WAY, WE CAN'T LET THAT HAPPEN.
THAT'S FINE.
WHAT?
I DON'T WANT TO WORK FOR AN UNREASON-ABLE EDITOR IN CHIEF.
I TOO FEEL THAT HE IS THE ONE IN THE WRONG IN THIS CASE.
GO, LADY AOKI! YOU ROCK!
YOU'RE REALLY ON FIRE TODAY.
YES. I LOVE YOU WHEN YOU'RE FIERY.
WILL YOU ...!
IT'S NO USE TALKING WITH YOU GUYS. LET'S GO GIVE THE EDITOR IN CHIEF A PIECE OF OUR MINDS.
KLAK
GOOD IDEA. WE'LL TELL HIM "WE'RE TAKING A BREAK" TO HIS FACE.
H-HEY, COME BACK!
JUST LET THEM DO IT.

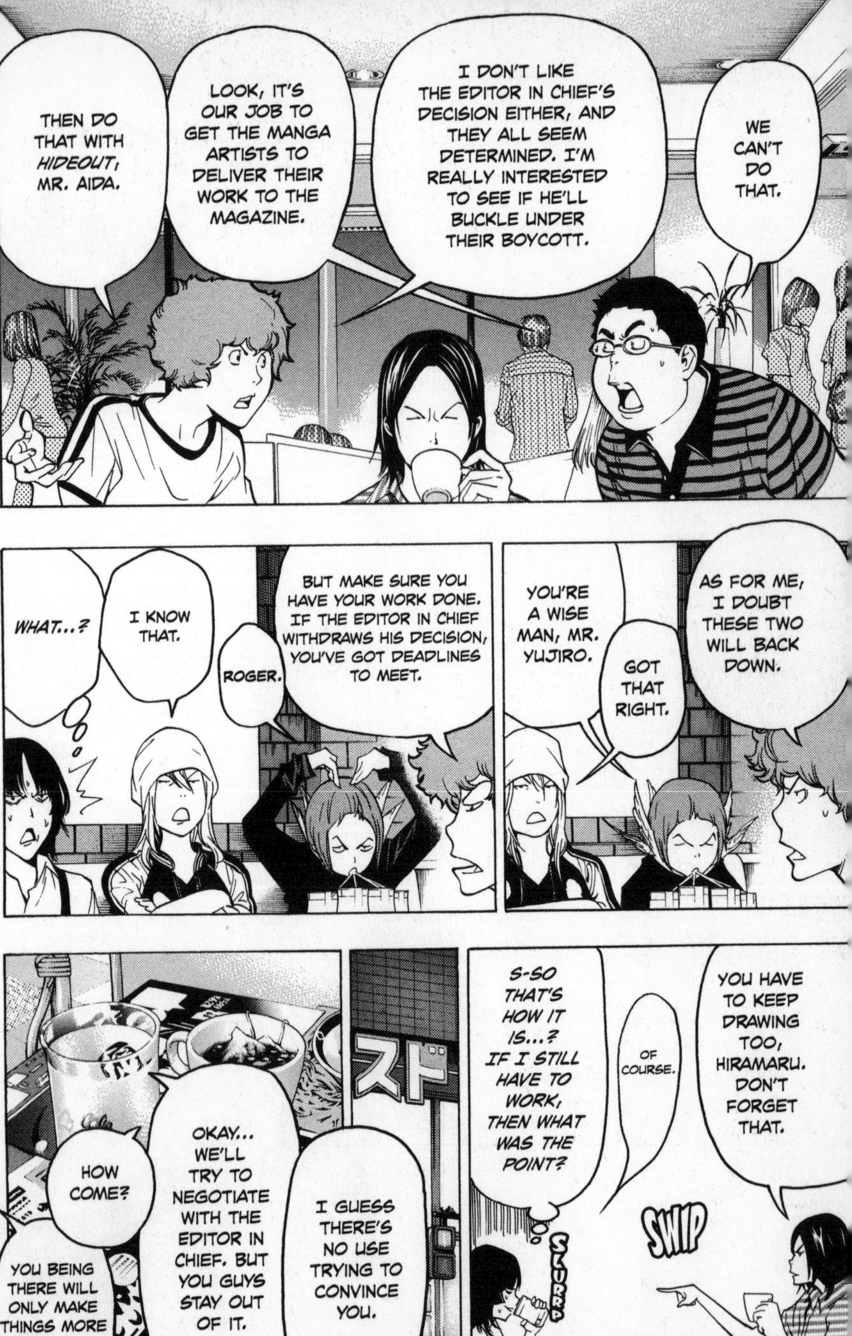
WE CAN'T DO THAT.
I DON'T LIKE THE EDITOR IN CHIEF'S DECISION EITHER, AND THEY ALL SEEM DETERMINED. I'M REALLY INTERESTED TO SEE IF HE'LL BUCKLE UNDER THEIR BOYCOTT.
LOOK, IT'S OUR JOB TO GET THE MANGA ARTISTS TO DELIVER THEIR WORK TO THE MAGAZINE.
THEN DO THAT WITH *HIDEOUT*, MR. AIDA.
AS FOR ME, I DOUBT THESE TWO WILL BACK DOWN.
YOU'RE A WISE MAN, MR. YUJIRO.
GOT THAT RIGHT.
BUT MAKE SURE YOU HAVE YOUR WORK DONE. IF THE EDITOR IN CHIEF WITHDRAWS HIS DECISION, YOU'VE GOT DEADLINES TO MEET.
ROGER.
I KNOW THAT.
WHAT...?
YOU HAVE TO KEEP DRAWING TOO, HIRAMARU. DON'T FORGET THAT.
OF COURSE.
S-SO THAT'S HOW IT IS...? IF I STILL HAVE TO WORK, THEN WHAT WAS THE POINT?
SWIP
SLURRP
I GUESS THERE'S NO USE TRYING TO CONVINCE YOU.
OKAY... WE'LL TRY TO NEGOTIATE WITH THE EDITOR IN CHIEF. BUT YOU GUYS STAY OUT OF IT.
HOW COME?
YOU BEING THERE WILL ONLY MAKE THINGS MORE DIFFICULT.

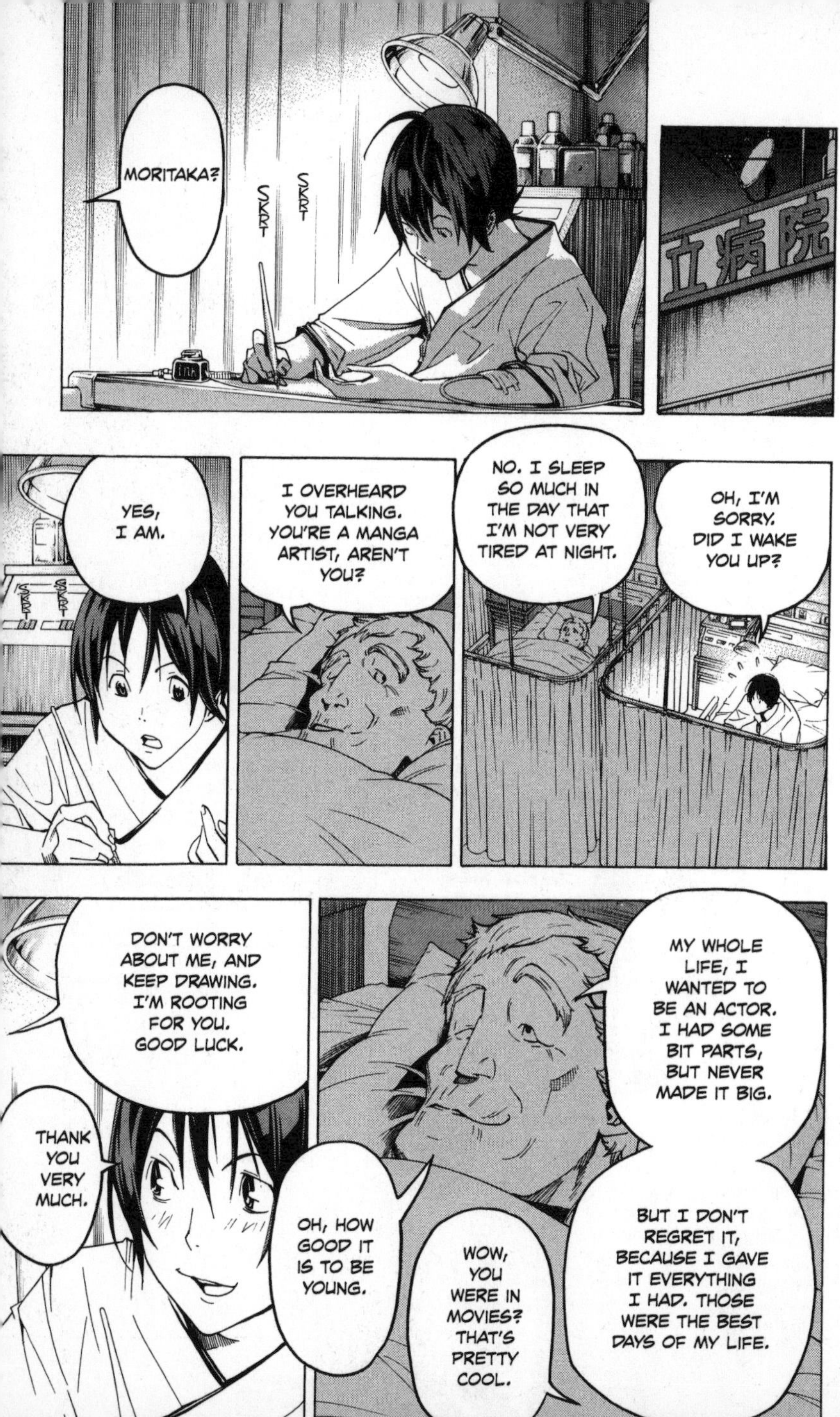
立病院
SKRT
SKRT
MORITAKA?
OH, I'M SORRY. DID I WAKE YOU UP?
NO. I SLEEP SO MUCH IN THE DAY THAT I'M NOT VERY TIRED AT NIGHT.
I OVERHEARD YOU TALKING. YOU'RE A MANGA ARTIST, AREN'T YOU?
YES, I AM.
SKRT
SKRT
MY WHOLE LIFE, I WANTED TO BE AN ACTOR. I HAD SOME BIT PARTS, BUT NEVER MADE IT BIG.
BUT I DON'T REGRET IT, BECAUSE I GAVE IT EVERYTHING I HAD. THOSE WERE THE BEST DAYS OF MY LIFE.
WOW, YOU WERE IN MOVIES? THAT'S PRETTY COOL.
OH, HOW GOOD IT IS TO BE YOUNG.
DON'T WORRY ABOUT ME, AND KEEP DRAWING. I'M ROOTING FOR YOU. GOOD LUCK.
THANK YOU VERY MUCH.

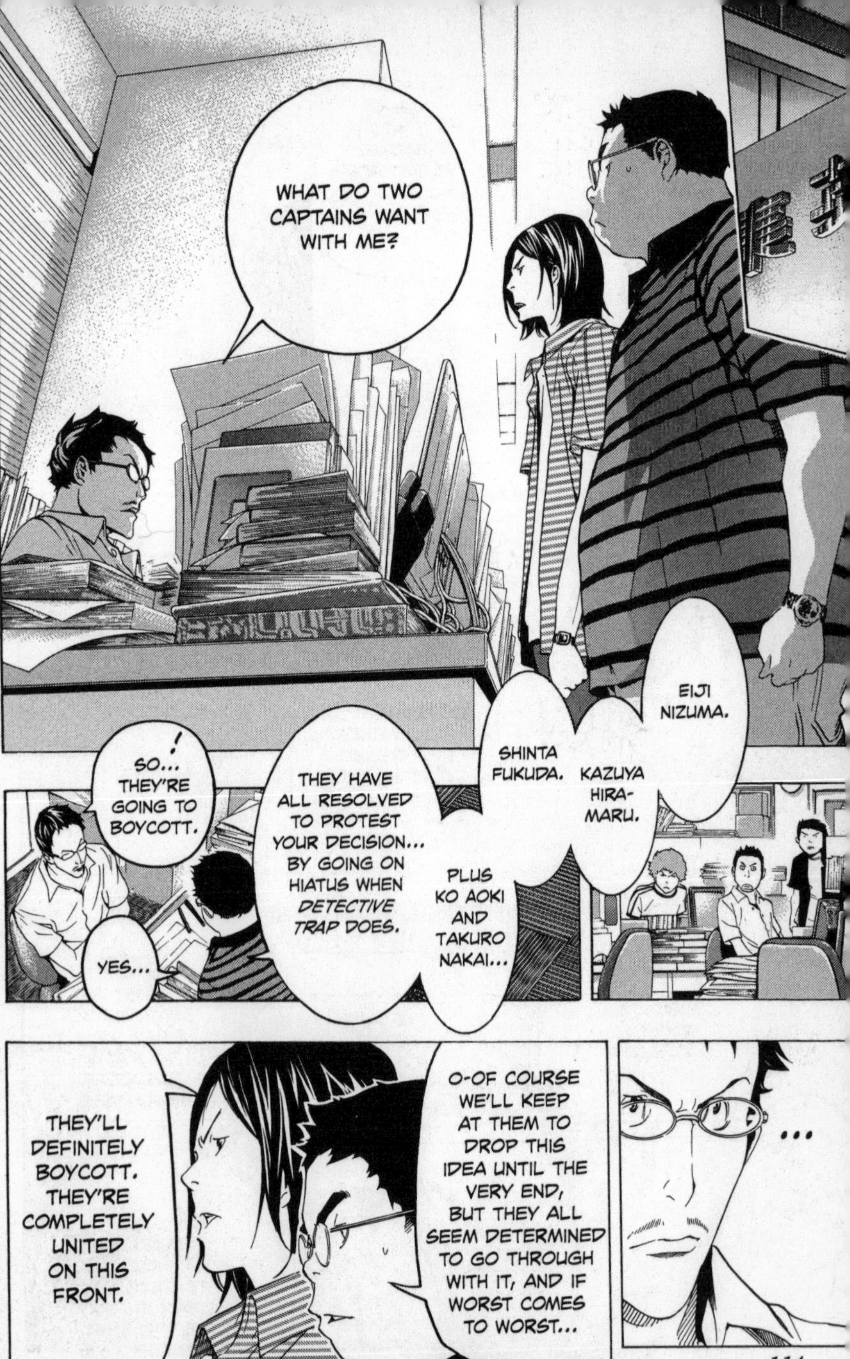
WHAT DO TWO CAPTAINS WANT WITH ME?
EIJI NIZUMA.
KAZUYA HIRA-MARU.
SHINTA FUKUDA.
PLUS KO AOKI AND TAKURO NAKAI...
THEY HAVE ALL RESOLVED TO PROTEST YOUR DECISION... BY GOING ON HIATUS WHEN *DETECTIVE TRAP* DOES.
SO... THEY'RE GOING TO BOYCOTT.
YES...
...
O-OF COURSE WE'LL KEEP AT THEM TO DROP THIS IDEA UNTIL THE VERY END, BUT THEY ALL SEEM DETERMINED TO GO THROUGH WITH IT, AND IF WORST COMES TO WORST...
THEY'LL DEFINITELY BOYCOTT. THEY'RE COMPLETELY UNITED ON THIS FRONT.

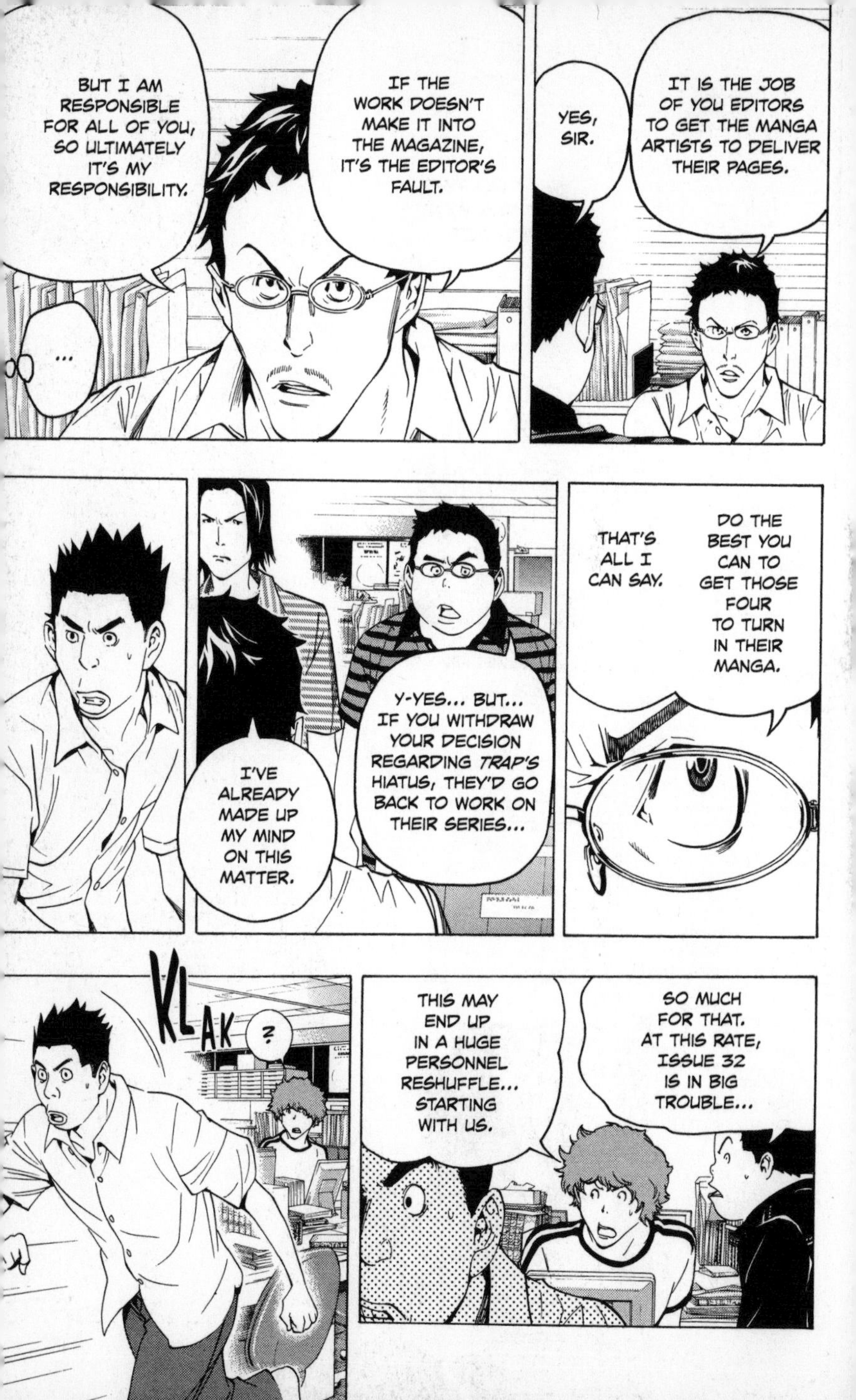
IT IS THE JOB OF YOU EDITORS TO GET THE MANGA ARTISTS TO DELIVER THEIR PAGES.
YES, SIR.
IF THE WORK DOESN'T MAKE IT INTO THE MAGAZINE, IT'S THE EDITOR'S FAULT.
BUT I AM RESPONSIBLE FOR ALL OF YOU, SO ULTIMATELY IT'S MY RESPONSIBILITY.
...
DO THE BEST YOU CAN TO GET THOSE FOUR TO TURN IN THEIR MANGA.
THAT'S ALL I CAN SAY.
Y-YES... BUT... IF YOU WITHDRAW YOUR DECISION REGARDING *TRAP'S* HIATUS, THEY'D GO BACK TO WORK ON THEIR SERIES...
I'VE ALREADY MADE UP MY MIND ON THIS MATTER.
SO MUCH FOR THAT. AT THIS RATE, ISSUE 32 IS IN BIG TROUBLE...
THIS MAY END UP IN A HUGE PERSONNEL RESHUFFLE... STARTING WITH US.
KLAK
?

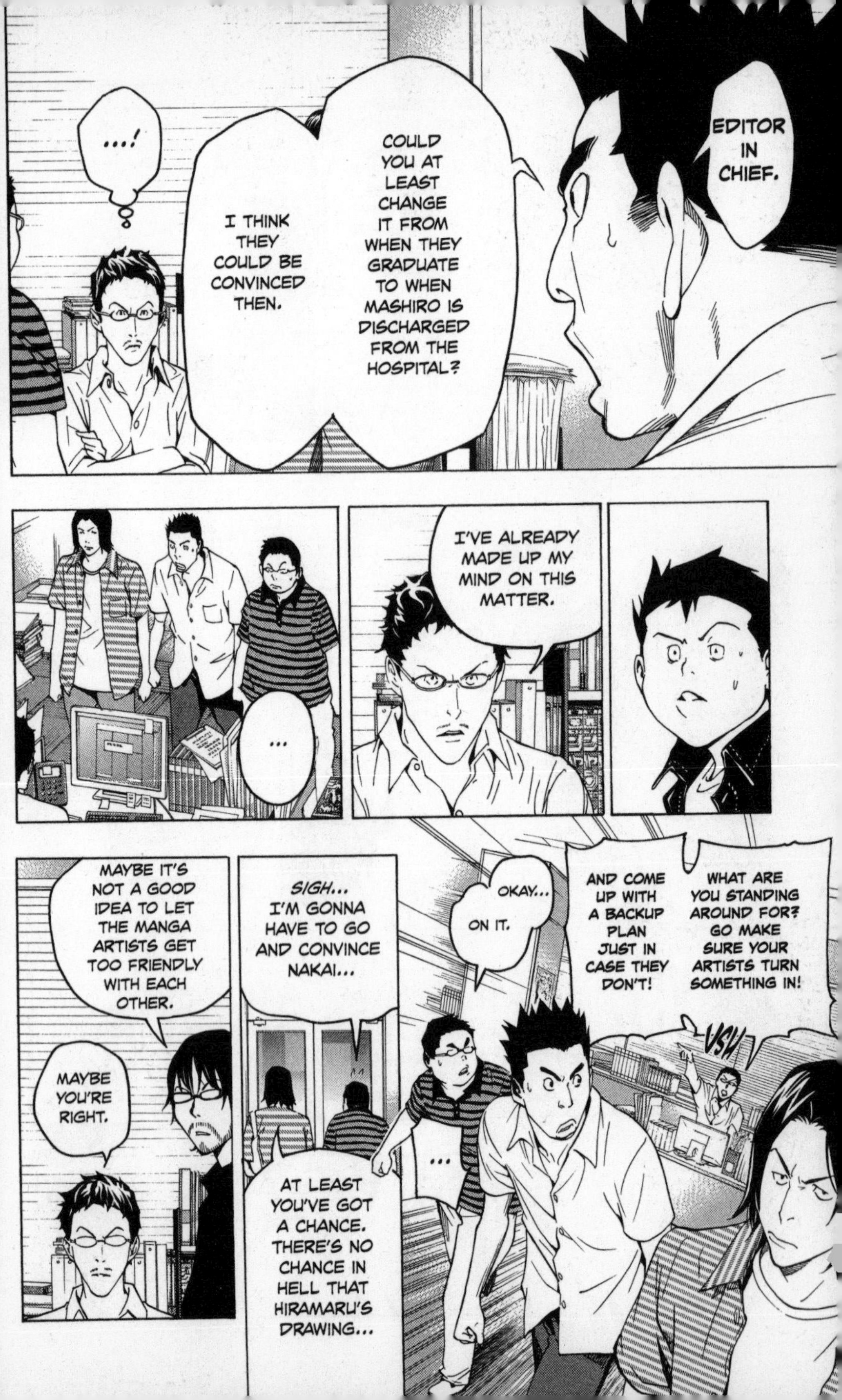
EDITOR IN CHIEF.
COULD YOU AT LEAST CHANGE IT FROM WHEN THEY GRADUATE TO WHEN MASHIRO IS DISCHARGED FROM THE HOSPITAL?
I THINK THEY COULD BE CONVINCED THEN.
....!
I'VE ALREADY MADE UP MY MIND ON THIS MATTER.
...
WHAT ARE YOU STANDING AROUND FOR? GO MAKE SURE YOUR ARTISTS TURN SOMETHING IN!
AND COME UP WITH A BACKUP PLAN JUST IN CASE THEY DON'T!
VSH
OKAY... ON IT.
...
SIGH... I'M GONNA HAVE TO GO AND CONVINCE NAKAI...
AT LEAST YOU'VE GOT A CHANCE. THERE'S NO CHANCE IN HELL THAT HIRAMARU'S DRAWING...
MAYBE IT'S NOT A GOOD IDEA TO LET THE MANGA ARTISTS GET TOO FRIENDLY WITH EACH OTHER.
MAYBE YOU'RE RIGHT.

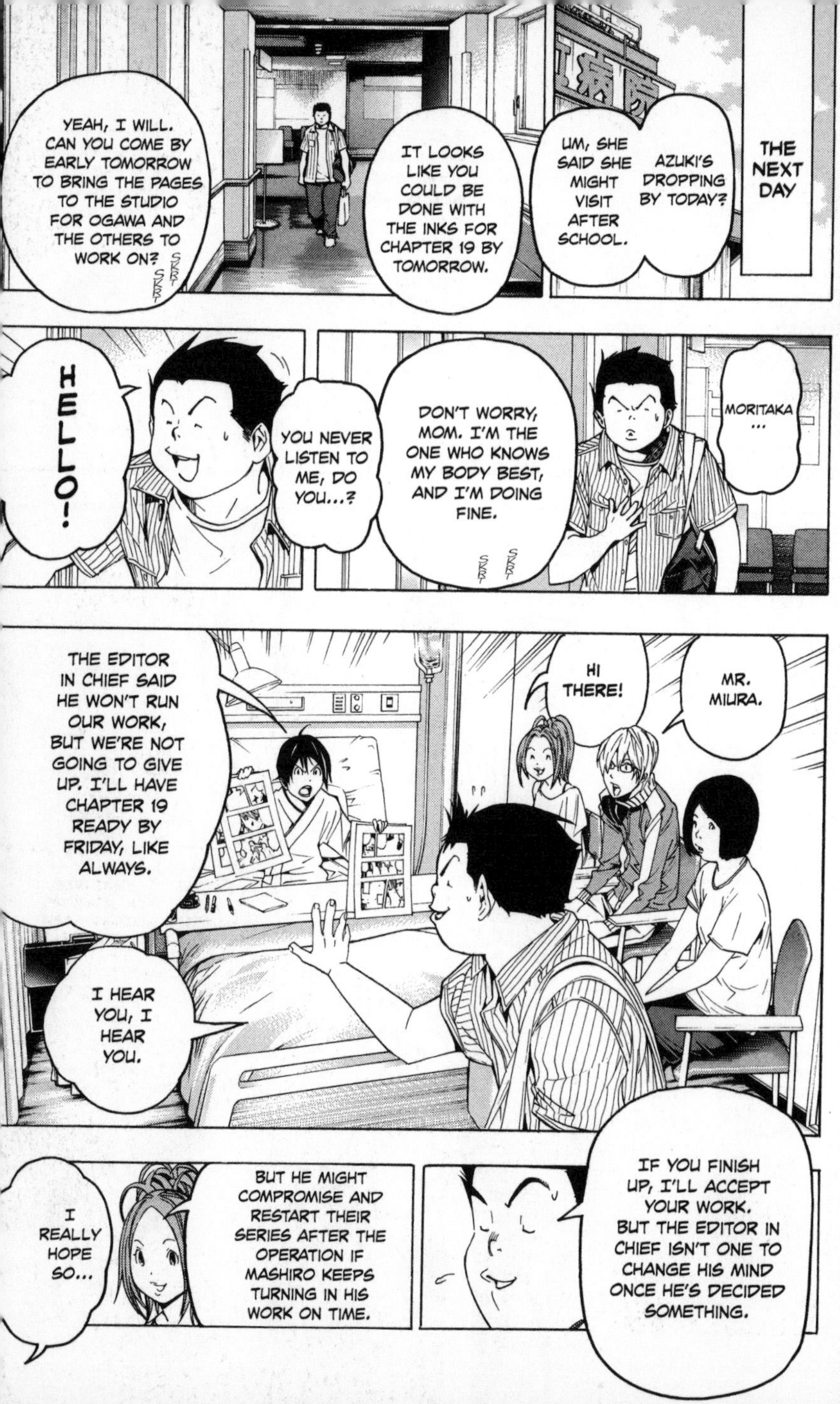
THE NEXT DAY
AZUKI'S DROPPING BY TODAY?
UM, SHE SAID SHE MIGHT VISIT AFTER SCHOOL.
IT LOOKS LIKE YOU COULD BE DONE WITH THE INKS FOR CHAPTER 19 BY TOMORROW.
YEAH, I WILL. CAN YOU COME BY EARLY TOMORROW TO BRING THE PAGES TO THE STUDIO FOR OGAWA AND THE OTHERS TO WORK ON?
SKRT SKRT
MORITAKA...
DON'T WORRY, MOM. I'M THE ONE WHO KNOWS MY BODY BEST, AND I'M DOING FINE.
SKRT SKRT
YOU NEVER LISTEN TO ME, DO YOU...?
HELLO!
MR. MIURA.
HI THERE!
THE EDITOR IN CHIEF SAID HE WON'T RUN OUR WORK, BUT WE'RE NOT GOING TO GIVE UP. I'LL HAVE CHAPTER 19 READY BY FRIDAY, LIKE ALWAYS.
I HEAR YOU, I HEAR YOU.
IF YOU FINISH UP, I'LL ACCEPT YOUR WORK. BUT THE EDITOR IN CHIEF ISN'T ONE TO CHANGE HIS MIND ONCE HE'S DECIDED SOMETHING.
BUT HE MIGHT COMPROMISE AND RESTART THEIR SERIES AFTER THE OPERATION IF MASHIRO KEEPS TURNING IN HIS WORK ON TIME.
I REALLY HOPE SO...

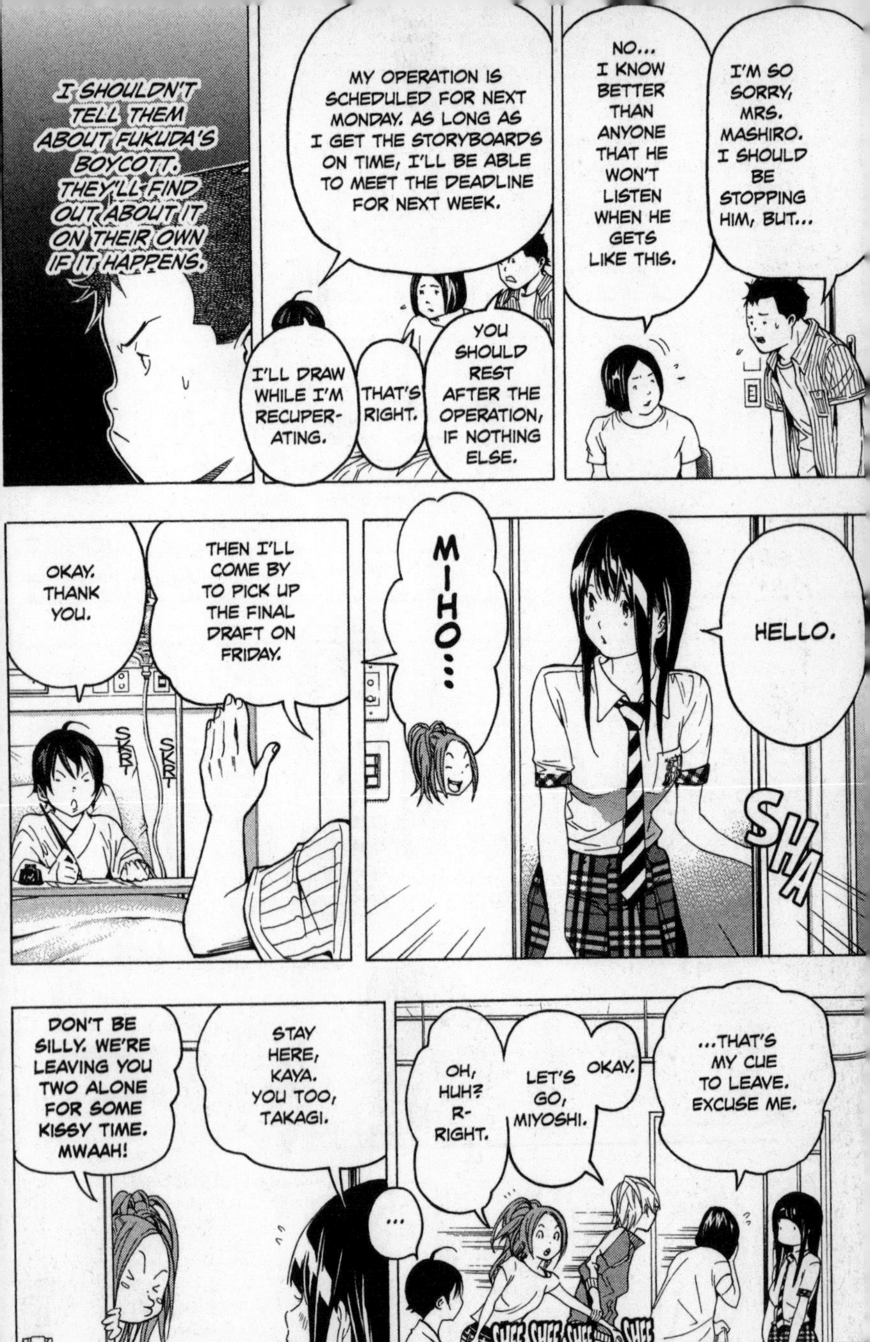
I'M SO SORRY, MRS. MASHIRO. I SHOULD BE STOPPING HIM, BUT...
NO... I KNOW BETTER THAN ANYONE THAT HE WON'T LISTEN WHEN HE GETS LIKE THIS.
MY OPERATION IS SCHEDULED FOR NEXT MONDAY. AS LONG AS I GET THE STORYBOARDS ON TIME, I'LL BE ABLE TO MEET THE DEADLINE FOR NEXT WEEK.
YOU SHOULD REST AFTER THE OPERATION, IF NOTHING ELSE.
THAT'S RIGHT.
I'LL DRAW WHILE I'M RECUPERATING.
I SHOULDN'T TELL THEM ABOUT FUKUDA'S BOYCOTT. THEY'LL FIND OUT ABOUT IT ON THEIR OWN IF IT HAPPENS.
HELLO.
SHA
MIHO...
THEN I'LL COME BY TO PICK UP THE FINAL DRAFT ON FRIDAY.
OKAY. THANK YOU.
SKRT
SKRT
...THAT'S MY CUE TO LEAVE. EXCUSE ME.
OKAY.
LET'S GO, MIYOSHI.
OH, HUH? R-RIGHT.
...
SHFF SHFF SHFF SHFF
STAY HERE, KAYA. YOU TOO, TAKAGI.
DON'T BE SILLY. WE'RE LEAVING YOU TWO ALONE FOR SOME KISSY TIME. MWAAH!

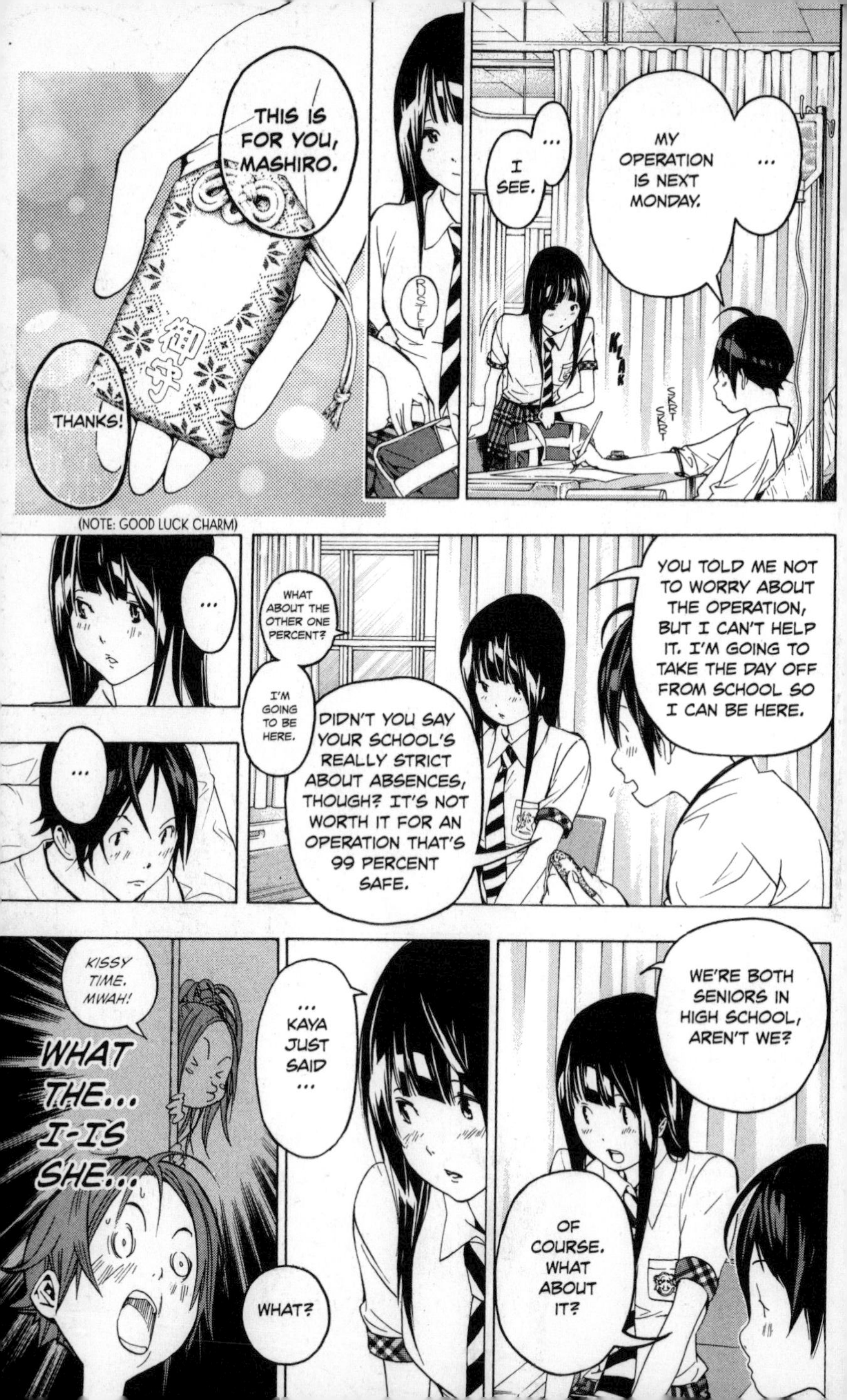
...
MY OPERATION IS NEXT MONDAY.
KLAK
SKRT SKRT
... I SEE.
RUSTLE
THIS IS FOR YOU, MASHIRO.
御守
THANKS!
YOU TOLD ME NOT TO WORRY ABOUT THE OPERATION, BUT I CAN'T HELP IT. I'M GOING TO TAKE THE DAY OFF FROM SCHOOL SO I CAN BE HERE.
DIDN'T YOU SAY YOUR SCHOOL'S REALLY STRICT ABOUT ABSENCES, THOUGH? IT'S NOT WORTH IT FOR AN OPERATION THAT'S 99 PERCENT SAFE.
WHAT ABOUT THE OTHER ONE PERCENT?
I'M GOING TO BE HERE.
...
...
WE'RE BOTH SENIORS IN HIGH SCHOOL, AREN'T WE?
OF COURSE. WHAT ABOUT IT?
... KAYA JUST SAID ...
WHAT?
KISSY TIME. MWAH!
WHAT THE... I-IS SHE...
(NOTE: GOOD LUCK CHARM)

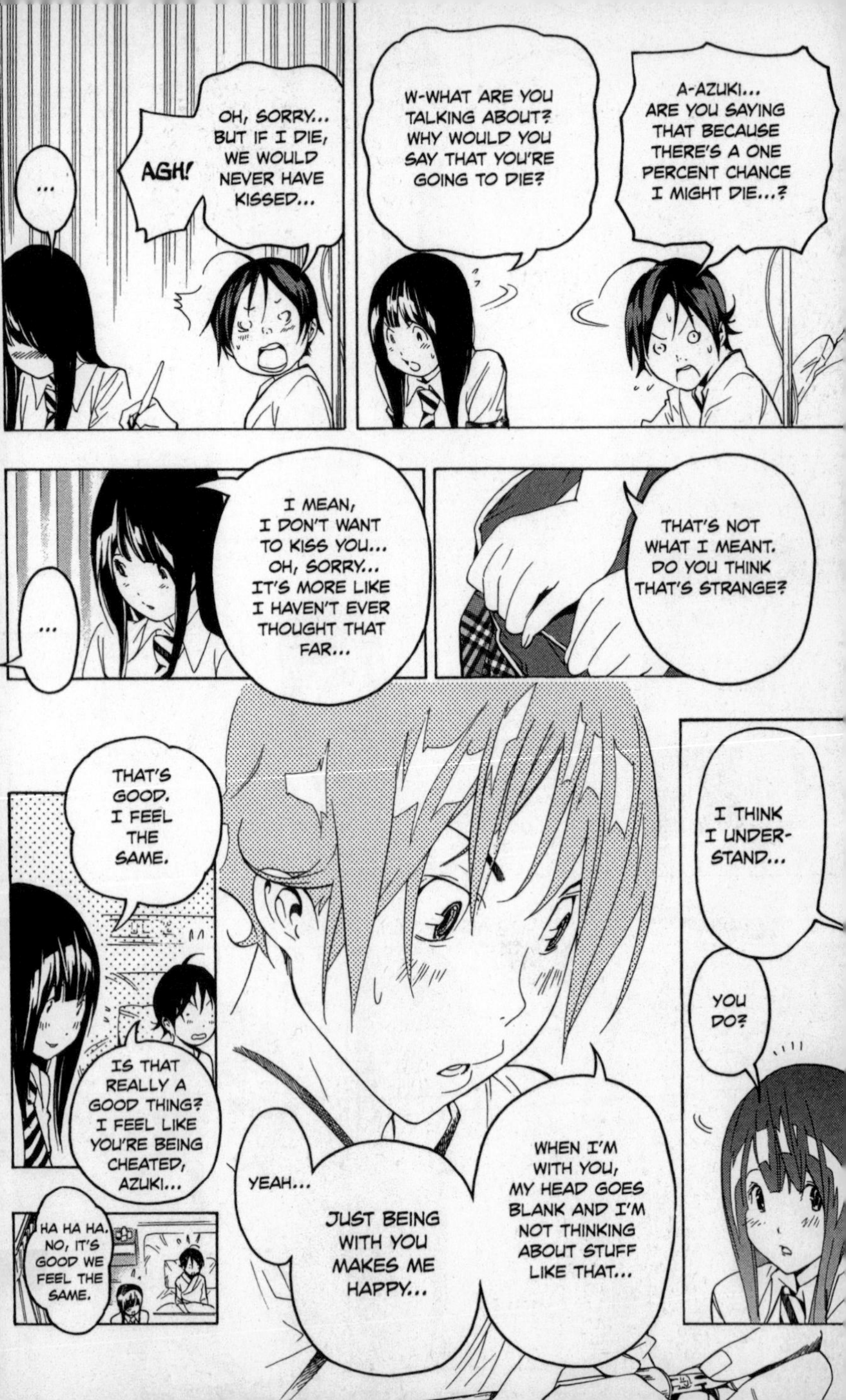
A-AZUKI... ARE YOU SAYING THAT BECAUSE THERE'S A ONE PERCENT CHANCE I MIGHT DIE...?
W-WHAT ARE YOU TALKING ABOUT? WHY WOULD YOU SAY THAT YOU'RE GOING TO DIE?
OH, SORRY... BUT IF I DIE, WE WOULD NEVER HAVE KISSED...
AGH!
...
THAT'S NOT WHAT I MEANT. DO YOU THINK THAT'S STRANGE?
I MEAN, I DON'T WANT TO KISS YOU... OH, SORRY... IT'S MORE LIKE I HAVEN'T EVER THOUGHT THAT FAR...
...
I THINK I UNDER-STAND...
YOU DO?
WHEN I'M WITH YOU, MY HEAD GOES BLANK AND I'M NOT THINKING ABOUT STUFF LIKE THAT...
YEAH...
JUST BEING WITH YOU MAKES ME HAPPY...
THAT'S GOOD. I FEEL THE SAME.
IS THAT REALLY A GOOD THING? I FEEL LIKE YOU'RE BEING CHEATED, AZUKI...
HA HA HA. NO, IT'S GOOD WE FEEL THE SAME.

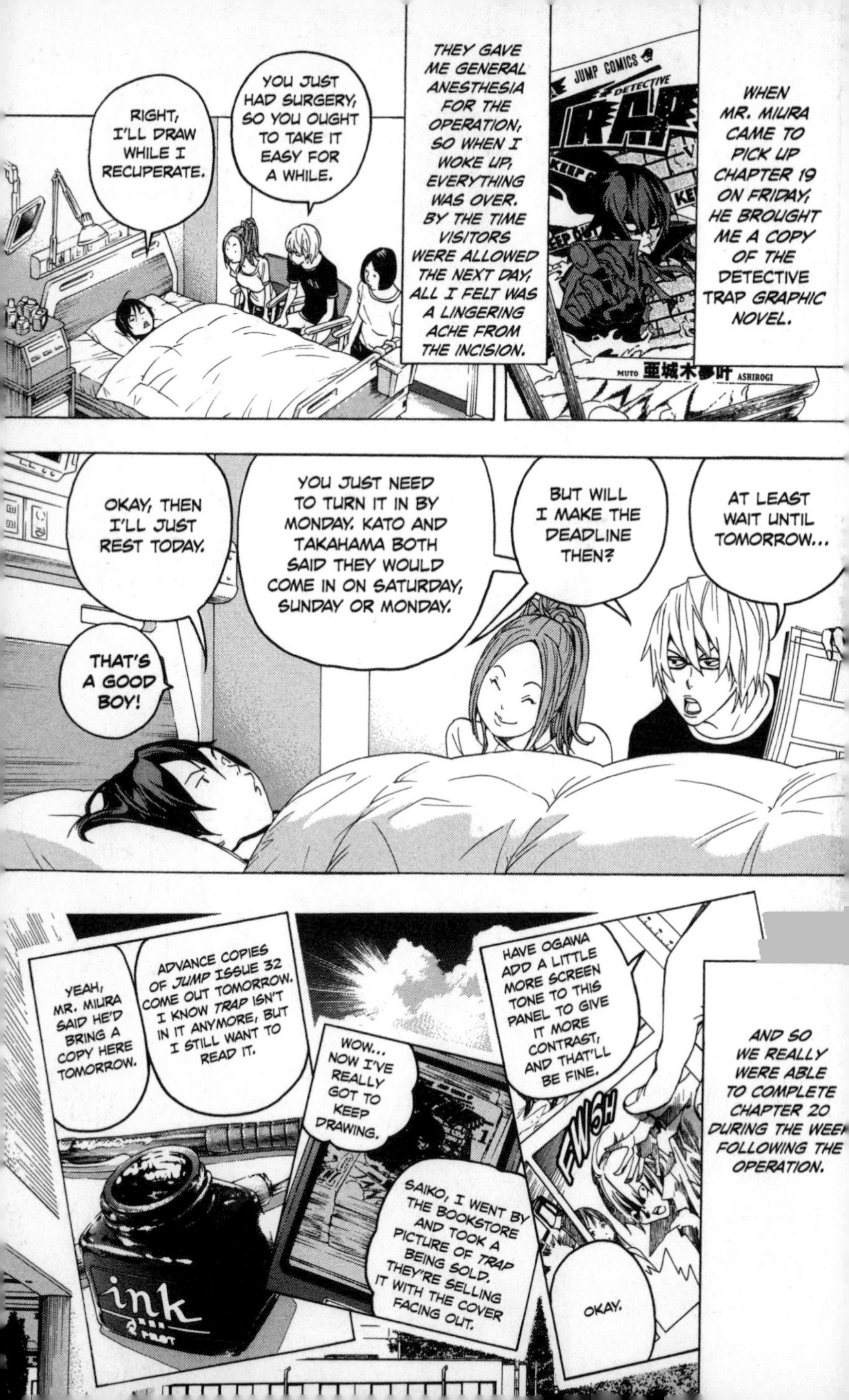
WHEN MR. MIURA CAME TO PICK UP CHAPTER 19 ON FRIDAY, HE BROUGHT ME A COPY OF THE DETECTIVE TRAP GRAPHIC NOVEL.
JUMP COMICS
DETECTIVE TRAP
KEEP OUT
MUTO 亜城木夢叶 ASHIROGI
THEY GAVE ME GENERAL ANESTHESIA FOR THE OPERATION, SO WHEN I WOKE UP, EVERYTHING WAS OVER. BY THE TIME VISITORS WERE ALLOWED THE NEXT DAY, ALL I FELT WAS A LINGERING ACHE FROM THE INCISION.
YOU JUST HAD SURGERY, SO YOU OUGHT TO TAKE IT EASY FOR A WHILE.
RIGHT, I'LL DRAW WHILE I RECUPERATE.
AT LEAST WAIT UNTIL TOMORROW...
BUT WILL I MAKE THE DEADLINE THEN?
YOU JUST NEED TO TURN IT IN BY MONDAY. KATO AND TAKAHAMA BOTH SAID THEY WOULD COME IN ON SATURDAY, SUNDAY OR MONDAY.
OKAY, THEN I'LL JUST REST TODAY.
THAT'S A GOOD BOY!
AND SO WE REALLY WERE ABLE TO COMPLETE CHAPTER 20 DURING THE WEE FOLLOWING THE OPERATION.
HAVE OGAWA ADD A LITTLE MORE SCREEN TONE TO THIS PANEL TO GIVE IT MORE CONTRAST, AND THAT'LL BE FINE.
FWSH
OKAY.
WOW... NOW I'VE REALLY GOT TO KEEP DRAWING.
SAIKO, I WENT BY THE BOOKSTORE AND TOOK A PICTURE OF *TRAP* BEING SOLD. THEY'RE SELLING IT WITH THE COVER FACING OUT.
ADVANCE COPIES OF *JUMP* ISSUE 32 COME OUT TOMORROW. I KNOW *TRAP* ISN'T IN IT ANYMORE, BUT I STILL WANT TO READ IT.
YEAH, MR. MIURA SAID HE'D BRING A COPY HERE TOMORROW.
ink

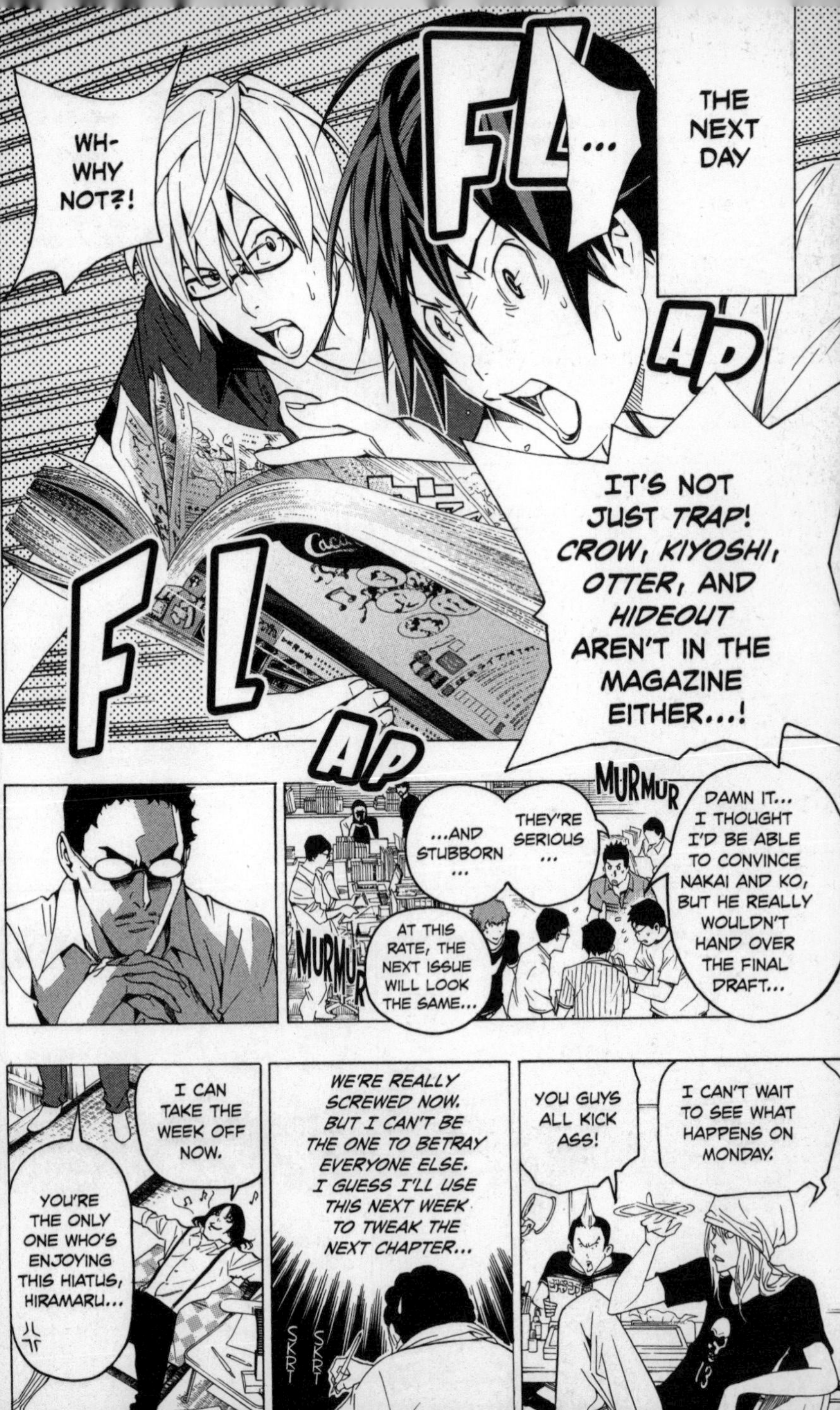
THE NEXT DAY
FL... AP
WH- WHY NOT?!
IT'S NOT JUST TRAP! CROW, KIYOSHI, OTTER, AND HIDEOUT AREN'T IN THE MAGAZINE EITHER...!
FL AP
DAMN IT... I THOUGHT I'D BE ABLE TO CONVINCE NAKAI AND KO, BUT HE REALLY WOULDN'T HAND OVER THE FINAL DRAFT...
MURMUR
THEY'RE SERIOUS...
...AND STUBBORN...
AT THIS RATE, THE NEXT ISSUE WILL LOOK THE SAME...
MURMUR
I CAN'T WAIT TO SEE WHAT HAPPENS ON MONDAY.
YOU GUYS ALL KICK ASS!
WE'RE REALLY SCREWED NOW. BUT I CAN'T BE THE ONE TO BETRAY EVERYONE ELSE. I GUESS I'LL USE THIS NEXT WEEK TO TWEAK THE NEXT CHAPTER...
SKRT SKRT
I CAN TAKE THE WEEK OFF NOW.
YOU'RE THE ONLY ONE WHO'S ENJOYING THIS HIATUS, HIRAMARU...

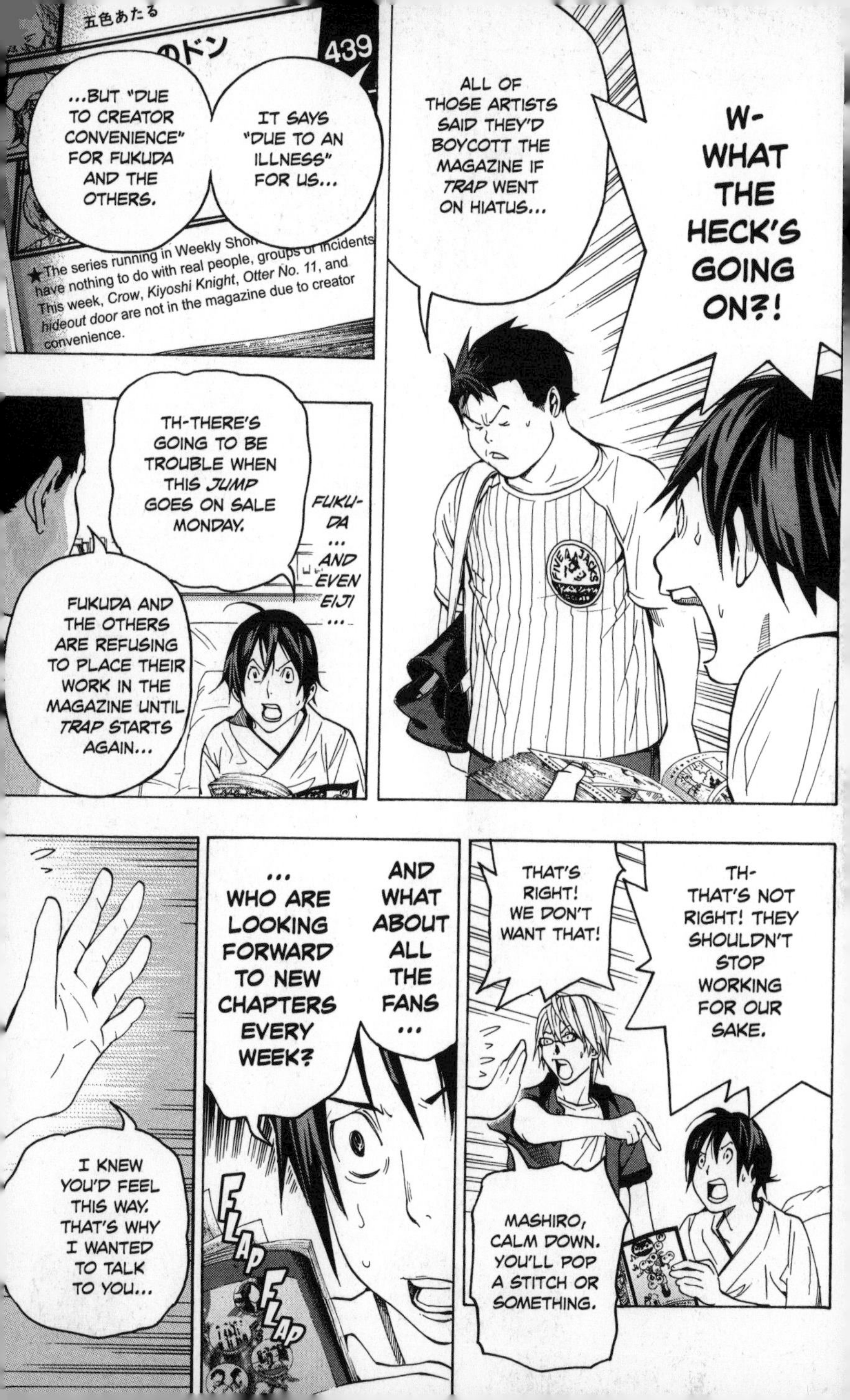
W- WHAT THE HECK'S GOING ON?!
ALL OF THOSE ARTISTS SAID THEY'D BOYCOTT THE MAGAZINE IF *TRAP* WENT ON HIATUS...
五色あたる
のドン
439
IT SAYS "DUE TO AN ILLNESS" FOR US...
...BUT "DUE TO CREATOR CONVENIENCE" FOR FUKUDA AND THE OTHERS.
★The series running in Weekly Shon
have nothing to do with real people, groups or incidents
This week, *Crow*, *Kiyoshi Knight*, *Otter No. 11*, and
hideout door are not in the magazine due to creator
convenience.
FUKUDA ... AND EVEN EIJI ...
TH-THERE'S GOING TO BE TROUBLE WHEN THIS *JUMP* GOES ON SALE MONDAY.
FUKUDA AND THE OTHERS ARE REFUSING TO PLACE THEIR WORK IN THE MAGAZINE UNTIL *TRAP* STARTS AGAIN...
TH- THAT'S NOT RIGHT! THEY SHOULDN'T STOP WORKING FOR OUR SAKE.
THAT'S RIGHT! WE DON'T WANT THAT!
MASHIRO, CALM DOWN. YOU'LL POP A STITCH OR SOMETHING.
AND WHAT ABOUT ALL THE FANS ...
... WHO ARE LOOKING FORWARD TO NEW CHAPTERS EVERY WEEK?
FLAP FLAP
I KNEW YOU'D FEEL THIS WAY. THAT'S WHY I WANTED TO TALK TO YOU...

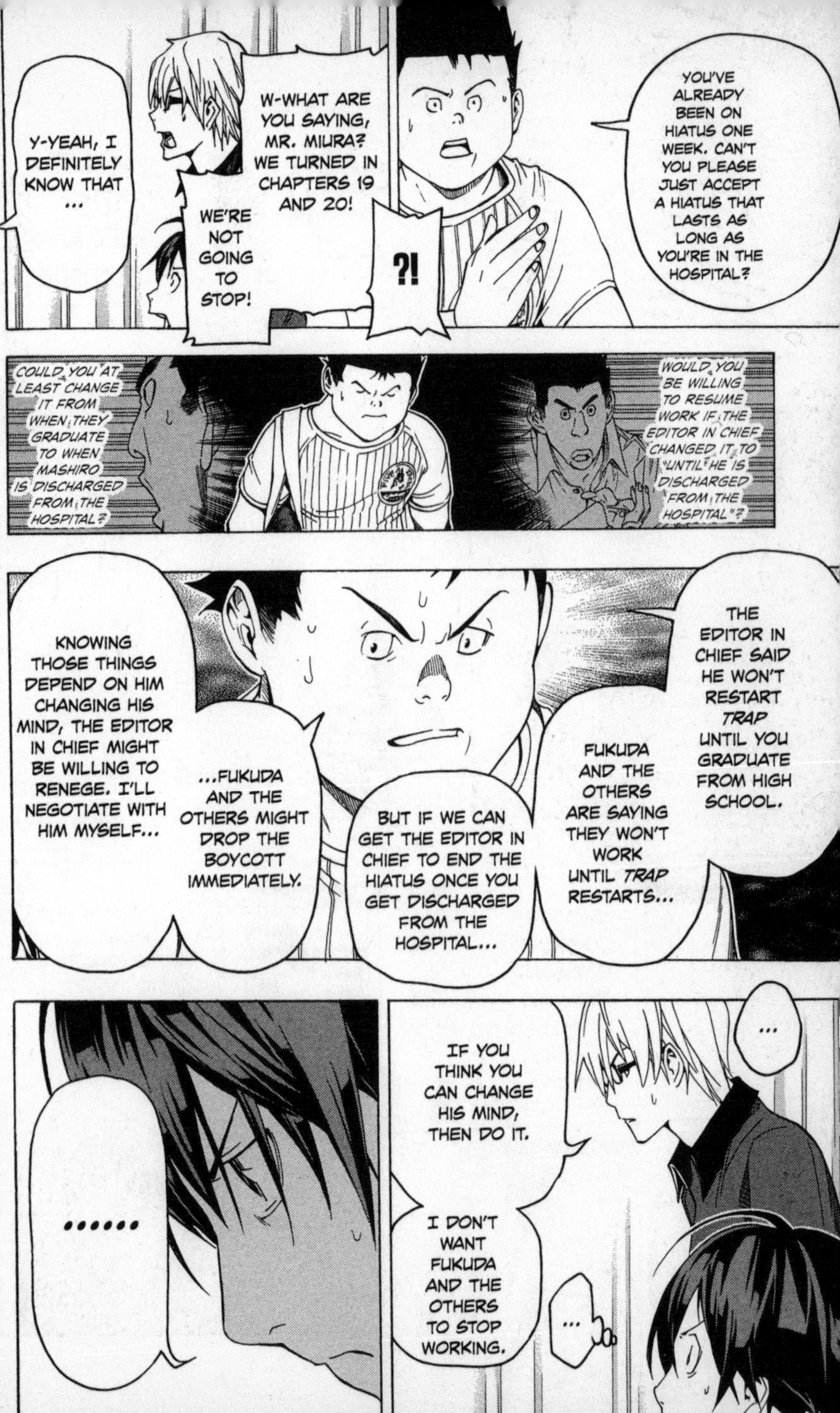
YOU'VE ALREADY BEEN ON HIATUS ONE WEEK. CAN'T YOU PLEASE JUST ACCEPT A HIATUS THAT LASTS AS LONG AS YOU'RE IN THE HOSPITAL?
?!
W-WHAT ARE YOU SAYING, MR. MIURA? WE TURNED IN CHAPTERS 19 AND 20!
WE'RE NOT GOING TO STOP!
Y-YEAH, I DEFINITELY KNOW THAT...
WOULD YOU BE WILLING TO RESUME WORK IF THE EDITOR IN CHIEF CHANGED IT TO "UNTIL HE IS DISCHARGED FROM THE HOSPITAL"?
COULD YOU AT LEAST CHANGE IT FROM WHEN THEY GRADUATE TO WHEN MASHIRO IS DISCHARGED FROM THE HOSPITAL?
THE EDITOR IN CHIEF SAID HE WON'T RESTART *TRAP* UNTIL YOU GRADUATE FROM HIGH SCHOOL.
FUKUDA AND THE OTHERS ARE SAYING THEY WON'T WORK UNTIL *TRAP* RESTARTS...
BUT IF WE CAN GET THE EDITOR IN CHIEF TO END THE HIATUS ONCE YOU GET DISCHARGED FROM THE HOSPITAL...
...FUKUDA AND THE OTHERS MIGHT DROP THE BOYCOTT IMMEDIATELY.
KNOWING THOSE THINGS DEPEND ON HIM CHANGING HIS MIND, THE EDITOR IN CHIEF MIGHT BE WILLING TO RENEGE. I'LL NEGOTIATE WITH HIM MYSELF...
...
IF YOU THINK YOU CAN CHANGE HIS MIND, THEN DO IT.
I DON'T WANT FUKUDA AND THE OTHERS TO STOP WORKING.
...
......

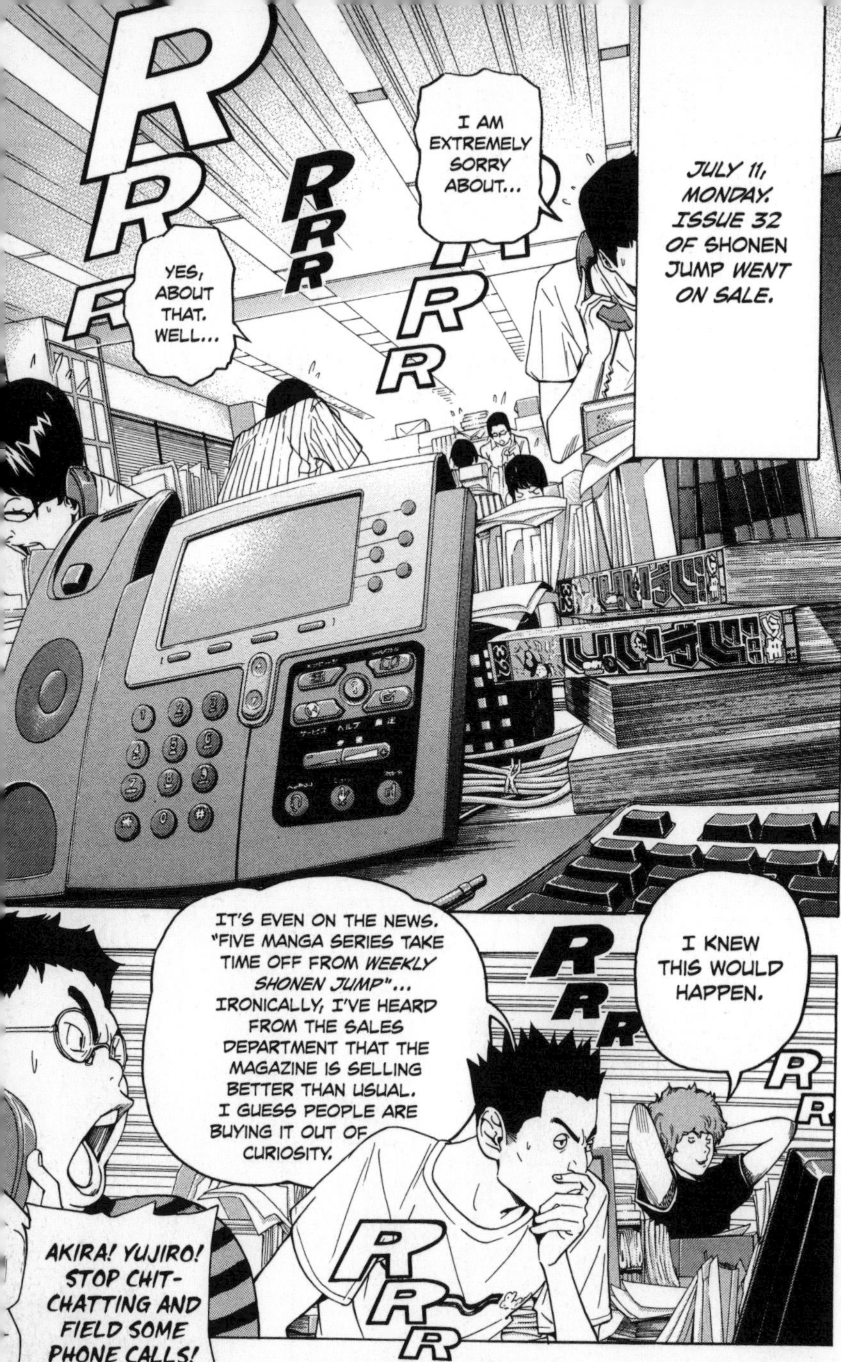
JULY 11, MONDAY. ISSUE 32 OF SHONEN JUMP WENT ON SALE.
I AM EXTREMELY SORRY ABOUT...
RRRR
RRRR
YES, ABOUT THAT. WELL...
I KNEW THIS WOULD HAPPEN.
RR
RRR
IT'S EVEN ON THE NEWS. "FIVE MANGA SERIES TAKE TIME OFF FROM *WEEKLY SHONEN JUMP*"... IRONICALLY, I'VE HEARD FROM THE SALES DEPARTMENT THAT THE MAGAZINE IS SELLING BETTER THAN USUAL. I GUESS PEOPLE ARE BUYING IT OUT OF CURIOSITY.
RRR
AKIRA! YUJIRO! STOP CHIT-CHATTING AND FIELD SOME PHONE CALLS!

OHBA'S STORYBOARD

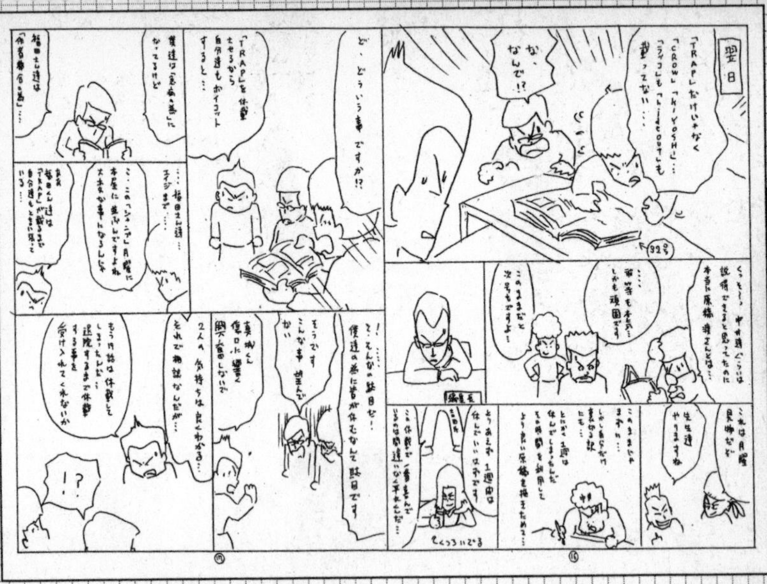

OBATA'S STORYBOARD

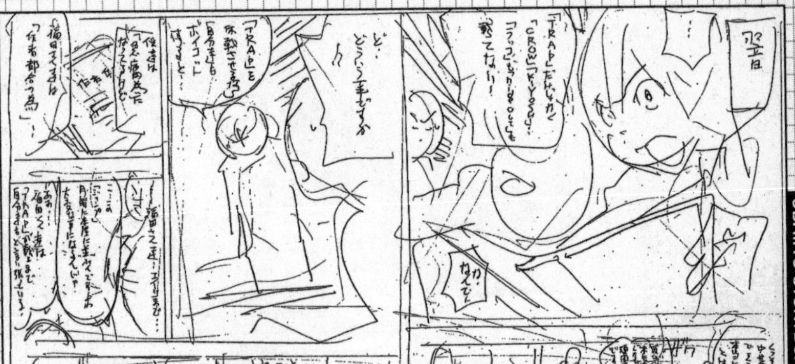

COMPLETE!

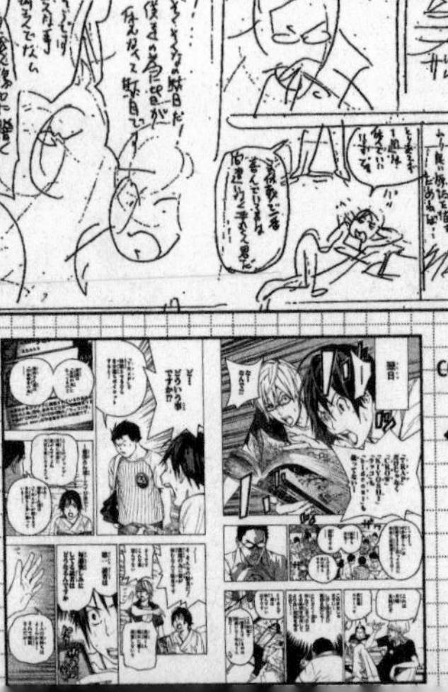

*CREATOR STORYBOARDS AND FINISHED PAGES IN JAPANESE

BAKUMAN。 vol.6

"Until the Final Draft Is Complete"

Chapter 49, pp. 122-123

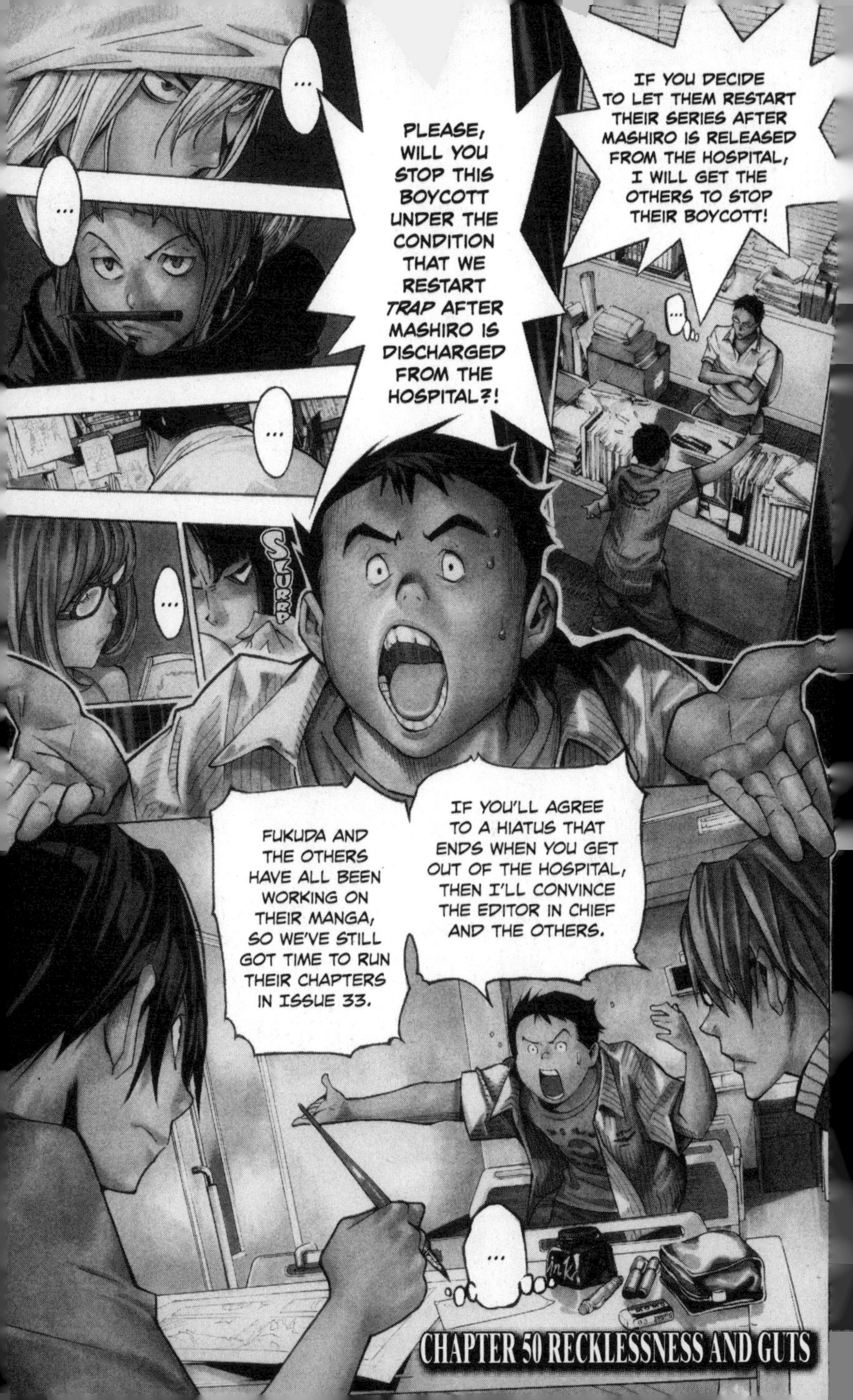
IF YOU DECIDE TO LET THEM RESTART THEIR SERIES AFTER MASHIRO IS RELEASED FROM THE HOSPITAL, I WILL GET THE OTHERS TO STOP THEIR BOYCOTT!
...
PLEASE, WILL YOU STOP THIS BOYCOTT UNDER THE CONDITION THAT WE RESTART *TRAP* AFTER MASHIRO IS DISCHARGED FROM THE HOSPITAL?!
...
...
...
...
SLURRP
IF YOU'LL AGREE TO A HIATUS THAT ENDS WHEN YOU GET OUT OF THE HOSPITAL, THEN I'LL CONVINCE THE EDITOR IN CHIEF AND THE OTHERS.
FUKUDA AND THE OTHERS HAVE ALL BEEN WORKING ON THEIR MANGA, SO WE'VE STILL GOT TIME TO RUN THEIR CHAPTERS IN ISSUE 33.
...
ink

CHAPTER 50 RECKLESSNESS AND GUTS

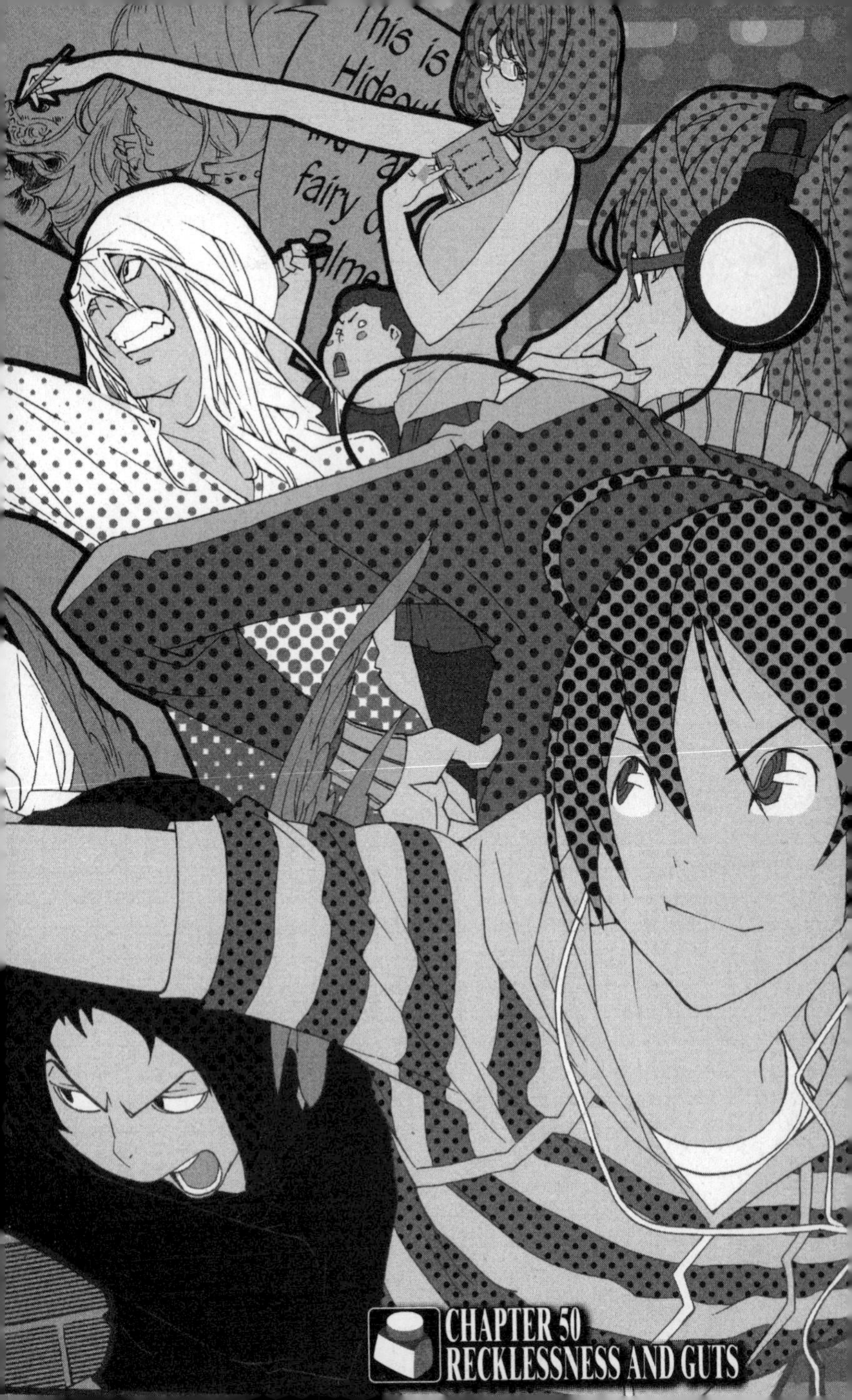
This is
Hideout
fairy

CHAPTER 50
RECKLESSNESS AND GUTS

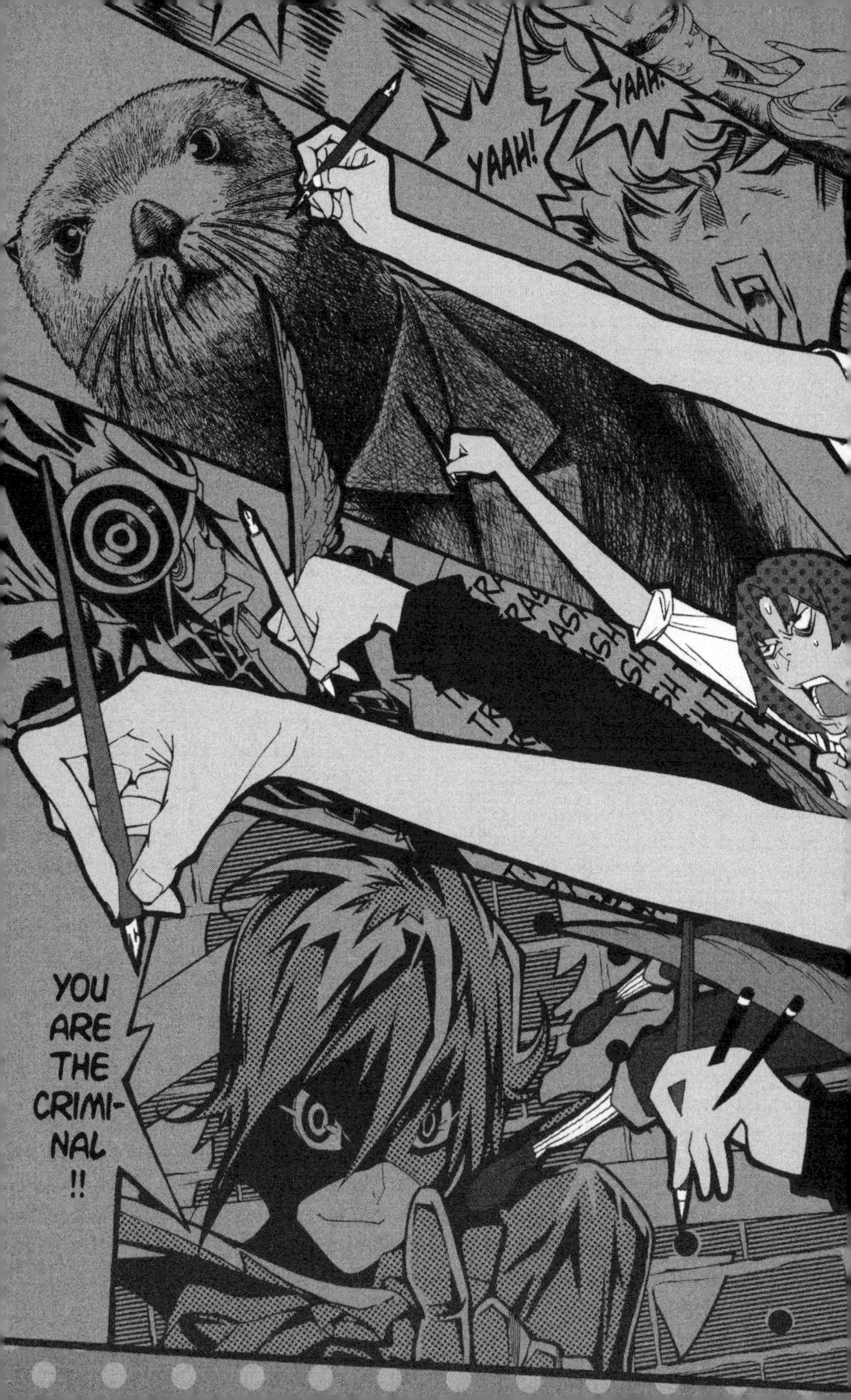
YAAH!
YAAH!
YOU ARE THE CRIMI-NAL !!

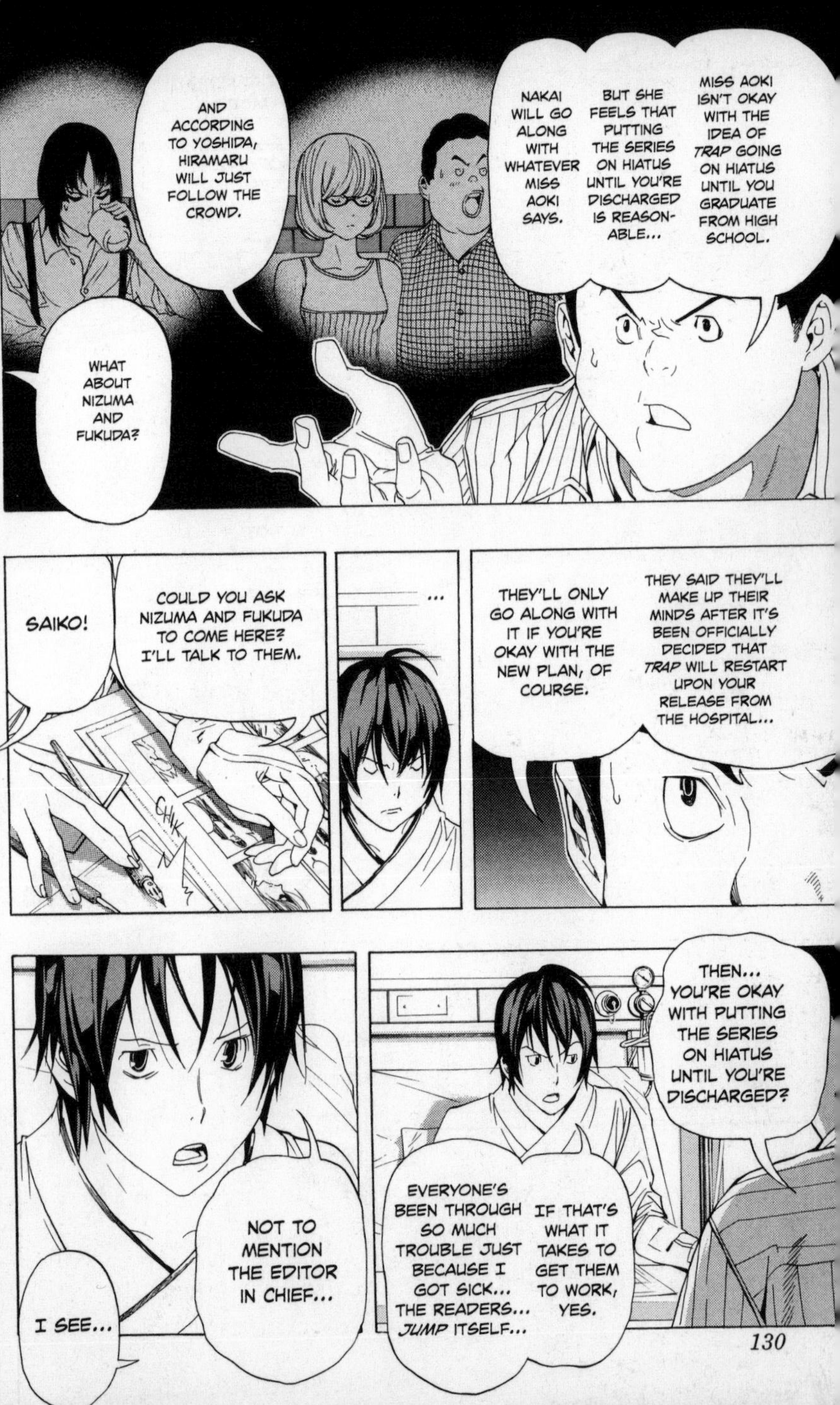
MISS AOKI ISN'T OKAY WITH THE IDEA OF *TRAP* GOING ON HIATUS UNTIL YOU GRADUATE FROM HIGH SCHOOL.
BUT SHE FEELS THAT PUTTING THE SERIES ON HIATUS UNTIL YOU'RE DISCHARGED IS REASONABLE...
NAKAI WILL GO ALONG WITH WHATEVER MISS AOKI SAYS.
AND ACCORDING TO YOSHIDA, HIRAMARU WILL JUST FOLLOW THE CROWD.
WHAT ABOUT NIZUMA AND FUKUDA?
THEY SAID THEY'LL MAKE UP THEIR MINDS AFTER IT'S BEEN OFFICIALLY DECIDED THAT *TRAP* WILL RESTART UPON YOUR RELEASE FROM THE HOSPITAL...
THEY'LL ONLY GO ALONG WITH IT IF YOU'RE OKAY WITH THE NEW PLAN, OF COURSE.
...
COULD YOU ASK NIZUMA AND FUKUDA TO COME HERE? I'LL TALK TO THEM.
SAIKO!
CHIK
THEN... YOU'RE OKAY WITH PUTTING THE SERIES ON HIATUS UNTIL YOU'RE DISCHARGED?
IF THAT'S WHAT IT TAKES TO GET THEM TO WORK, YES.
EVERYONE'S BEEN THROUGH SO MUCH TROUBLE JUST BECAUSE I GOT SICK... THE READERS... *JUMP* ITSELF...
NOT TO MENTION THE EDITOR IN CHIEF...
I SEE...

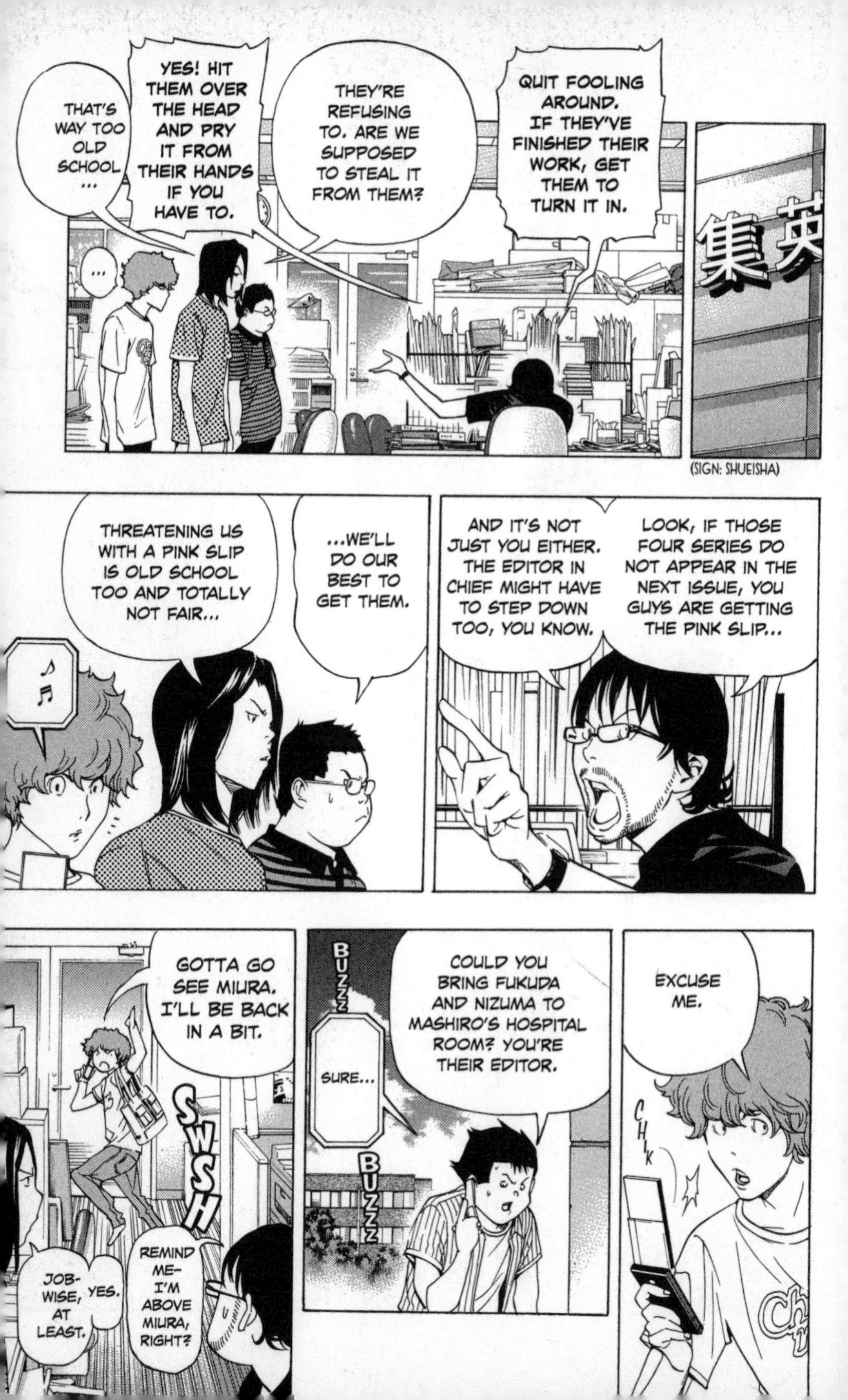
(SIGN: SHUEISHA)
QUIT FOOLING AROUND. IF THEY'VE FINISHED THEIR WORK, GET THEM TO TURN IT IN.
THEY'RE REFUSING TO. ARE WE SUPPOSED TO STEAL IT FROM THEM?
YES! HIT THEM OVER THE HEAD AND PRY IT FROM THEIR HANDS IF YOU HAVE TO.
THAT'S WAY TOO OLD SCHOOL...
...
LOOK, IF THOSE FOUR SERIES DO NOT APPEAR IN THE NEXT ISSUE, YOU GUYS ARE GETTING THE PINK SLIP...
AND IT'S NOT JUST YOU EITHER. THE EDITOR IN CHIEF MIGHT HAVE TO STEP DOWN TOO, YOU KNOW.
...WE'LL DO OUR BEST TO GET THEM.
THREATENING US WITH A PINK SLIP IS OLD SCHOOL TOO AND TOTALLY NOT FAIR...
♪ ♬
EXCUSE ME.
CHIK
COULD YOU BRING FUKUDA AND NIZUMA TO MASHIRO'S HOSPITAL ROOM? YOU'RE THEIR EDITOR.
BUZZZ
SURE...
BUZZZ
GOTTA GO SEE MIURA. I'LL BE BACK IN A BIT.
SWSH
REMIND ME- I'M ABOVE MIURA, RIGHT?
YES.
JOB-WISE, AT LEAST.

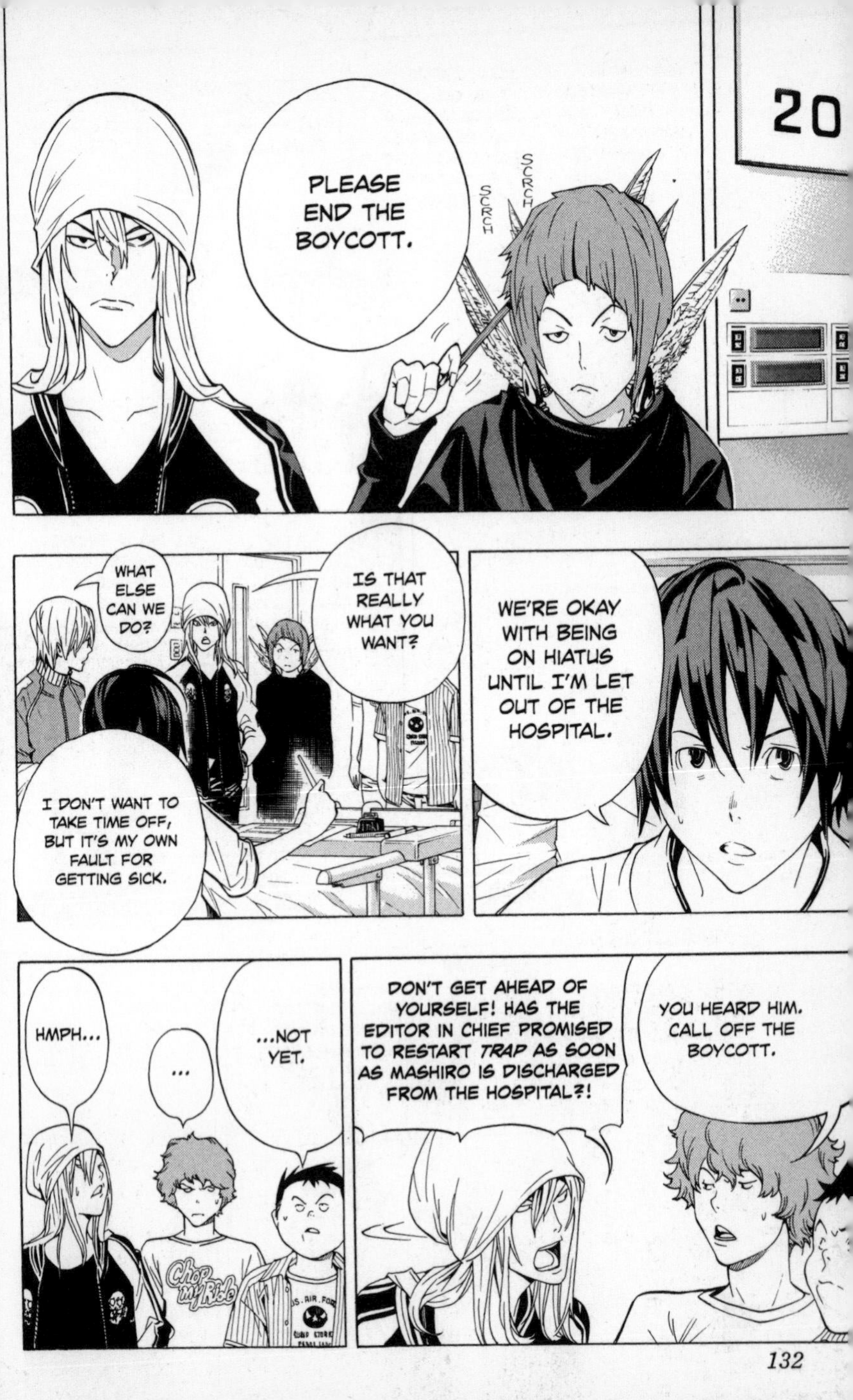
20
SCRCH
SCRCH
PLEASE END THE BOYCOTT.
WE'RE OKAY WITH BEING ON HIATUS UNTIL I'M LET OUT OF THE HOSPITAL.
IS THAT REALLY WHAT YOU WANT?
WHAT ELSE CAN WE DO?
I DON'T WANT TO TAKE TIME OFF, BUT IT'S MY OWN FAULT FOR GETTING SICK.
YOU HEARD HIM. CALL OFF THE BOYCOTT.
DON'T GET AHEAD OF YOURSELF! HAS THE EDITOR IN CHIEF PROMISED TO RESTART *TRAP* AS SOON AS MASHIRO IS DISCHARGED FROM THE HOSPITAL?!
...NOT YET.
...
HMPH...

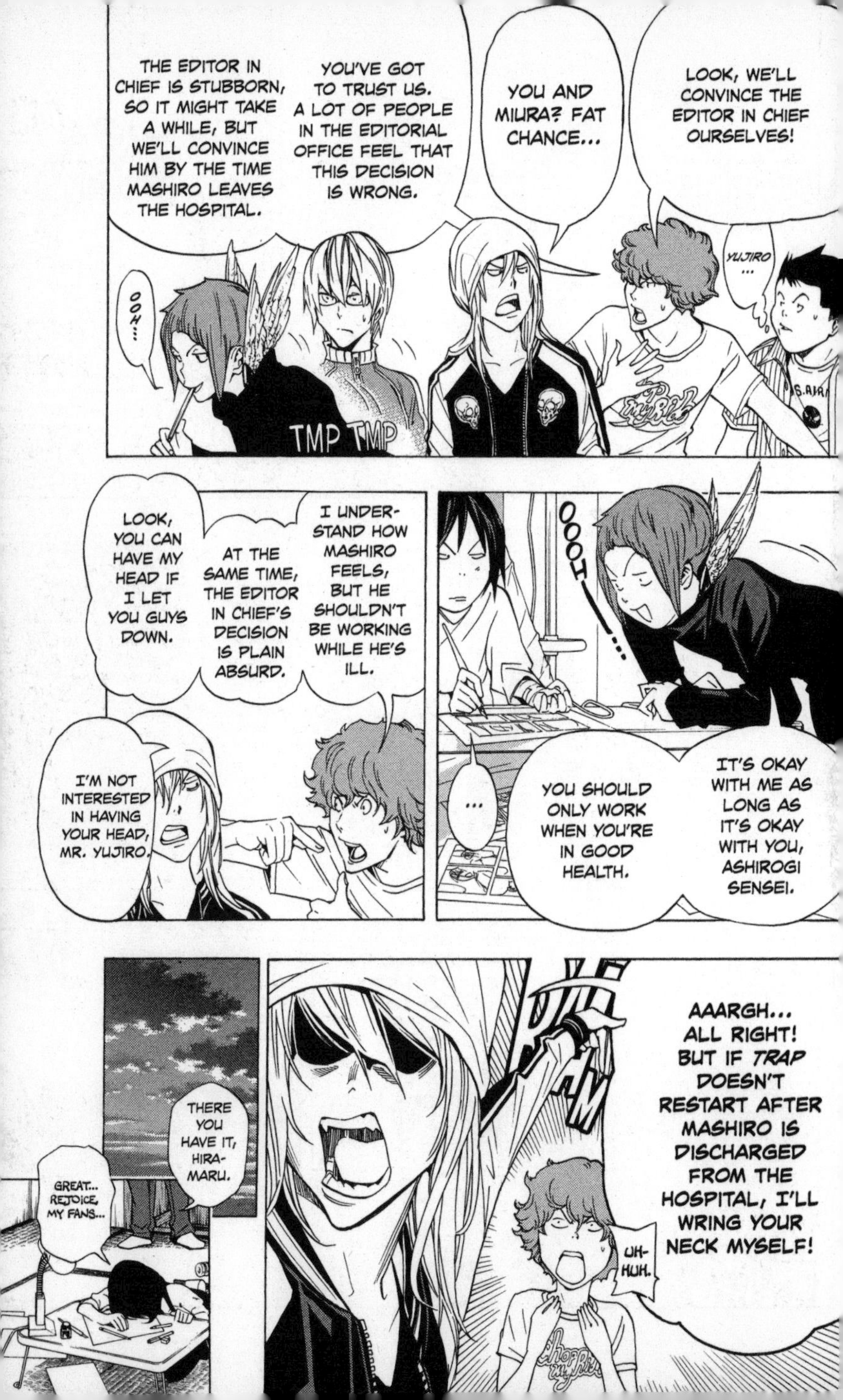
LOOK, WE'LL CONVINCE THE EDITOR IN CHIEF OURSELVES!
YUJIRO...
YOU AND MIURA? FAT CHANCE...
YOU'VE GOT TO TRUST US. A LOT OF PEOPLE IN THE EDITORIAL OFFICE FEEL THAT THIS DECISION IS WRONG.
THE EDITOR IN CHIEF IS STUBBORN, SO IT MIGHT TAKE A WHILE, BUT WE'LL CONVINCE HIM BY THE TIME MASHIRO LEAVES THE HOSPITAL.
OOH...
TMP TMP
OOOH...
IT'S OKAY WITH ME AS LONG AS IT'S OKAY WITH YOU, ASHIROGI SENSEI.
YOU SHOULD ONLY WORK WHEN YOU'RE IN GOOD HEALTH.
...
I UNDER-STAND HOW MASHIRO FEELS, BUT HE SHOULDN'T BE WORKING WHILE HE'S ILL.
AT THE SAME TIME, THE EDITOR IN CHIEF'S DECISION IS PLAIN ABSURD.
LOOK, YOU CAN HAVE MY HEAD IF I LET YOU GUYS DOWN.
I'M NOT INTERESTED IN HAVING YOUR HEAD, MR. YUJIRO.
AAARGH... ALL RIGHT! BUT IF *TRAP* DOESN'T RESTART AFTER MASHIRO IS DISCHARGED FROM THE HOSPITAL, I'LL WRING YOUR NECK MYSELF!
UH-HUH.
THERE YOU HAVE IT, HIRA-MARU.
GREAT... REJOICE, MY FANS...

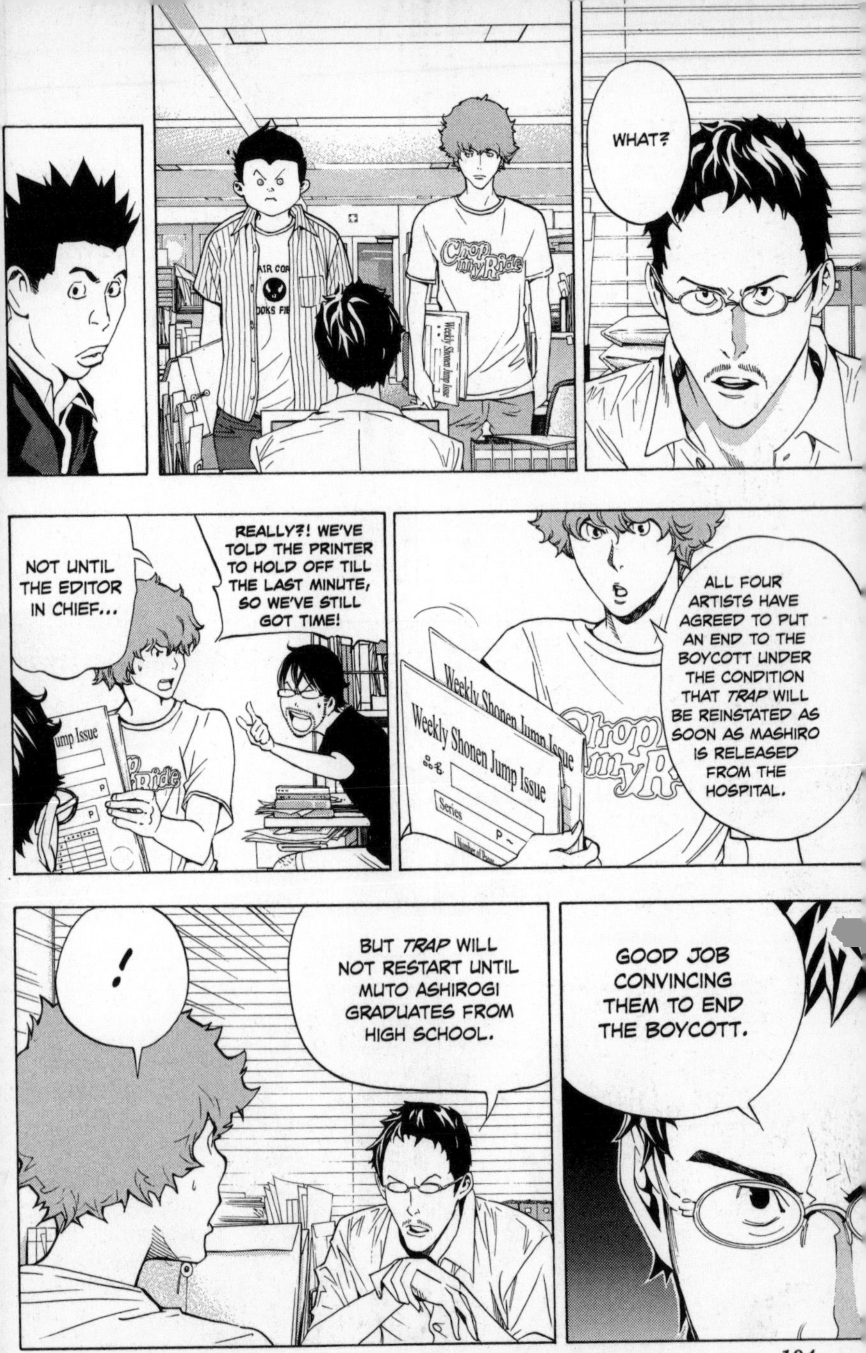
WHAT?
ALL FOUR ARTISTS HAVE AGREED TO PUT AN END TO THE BOYCOTT UNDER THE CONDITION THAT *TRAP* WILL BE REINSTATED AS SOON AS MASHIRO IS RELEASED FROM THE HOSPITAL.
REALLY?! WE'VE TOLD THE PRINTER TO HOLD OFF TILL THE LAST MINUTE, SO WE'VE STILL GOT TIME!
NOT UNTIL THE EDITOR IN CHIEF...
GOOD JOB CONVINCING THEM TO END THE BOYCOTT.
BUT *TRAP* WILL NOT RESTART UNTIL MUTO ASHIROGI GRADUATES FROM HIGH SCHOOL.
!

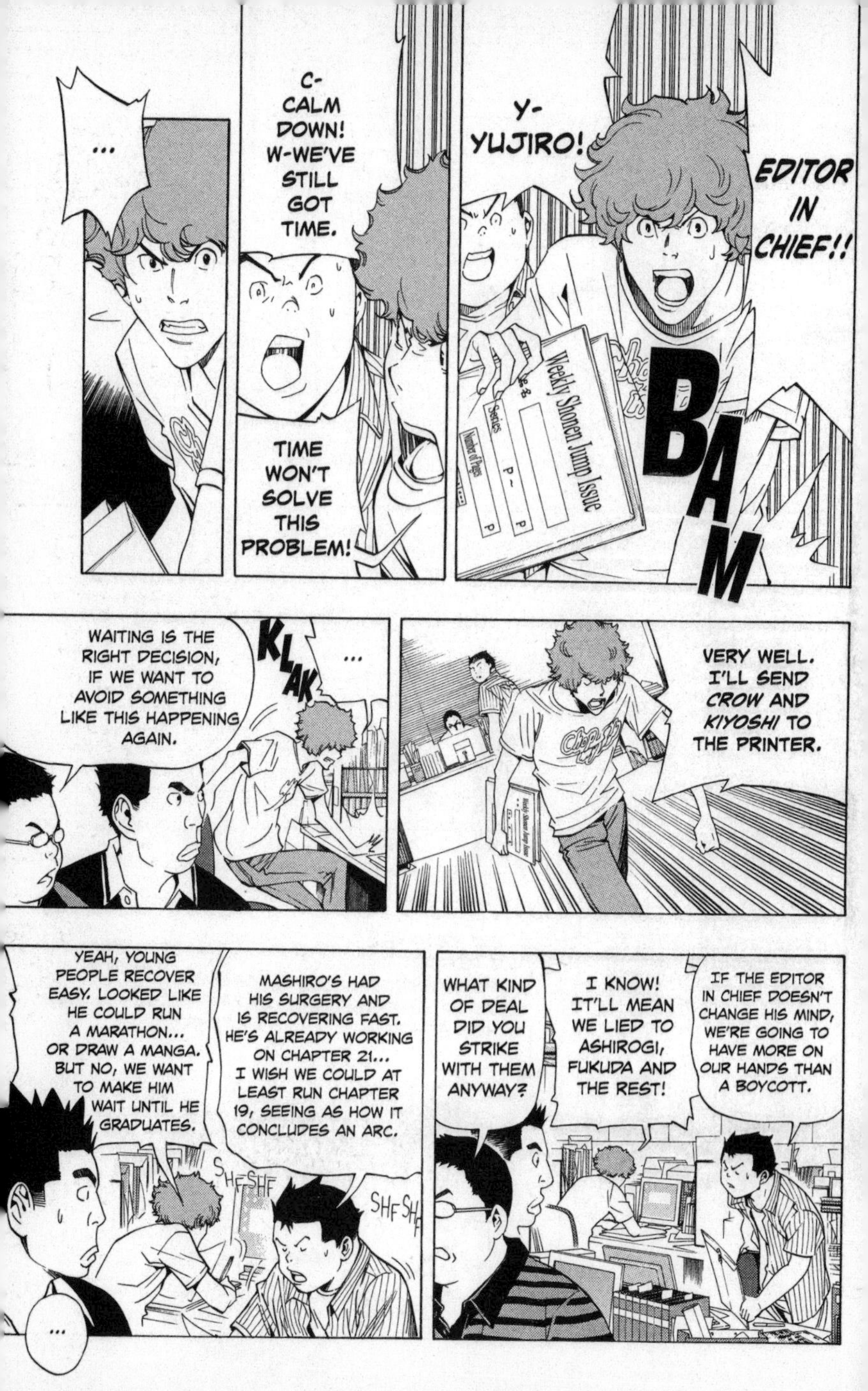
EDITOR IN CHIEF!!
Y- YUJIRO!
BAM
Weekly Shonen Jump Issue
Series
Number of Pages
C- CALM DOWN! W-WE'VE STILL GOT TIME.
TIME WON'T SOLVE THIS PROBLEM!
...
VERY WELL. I'LL SEND CROW AND KIYOSHI TO THE PRINTER.
...
KLAK
WAITING IS THE RIGHT DECISION, IF WE WANT TO AVOID SOMETHING LIKE THIS HAPPENING AGAIN.
IF THE EDITOR IN CHIEF DOESN'T CHANGE HIS MIND, WE'RE GOING TO HAVE MORE ON OUR HANDS THAN A BOYCOTT.
I KNOW! IT'LL MEAN WE LIED TO ASHIROGI, FUKUDA AND THE REST!
WHAT KIND OF DEAL DID YOU STRIKE WITH THEM ANYWAY?
MASHIRO'S HAD HIS SURGERY AND IS RECOVERING FAST. HE'S ALREADY WORKING ON CHAPTER 21... I WISH WE COULD AT LEAST RUN CHAPTER 19, SEEING AS HOW IT CONCLUDES AN ARC.
YEAH, YOUNG PEOPLE RECOVER EASY. LOOKED LIKE HE COULD RUN A MARATHON... OR DRAW A MANGA. BUT NO, WE WANT TO MAKE HIM WAIT UNTIL HE GRADUATES.
SHF SHF
SHF SHF
...

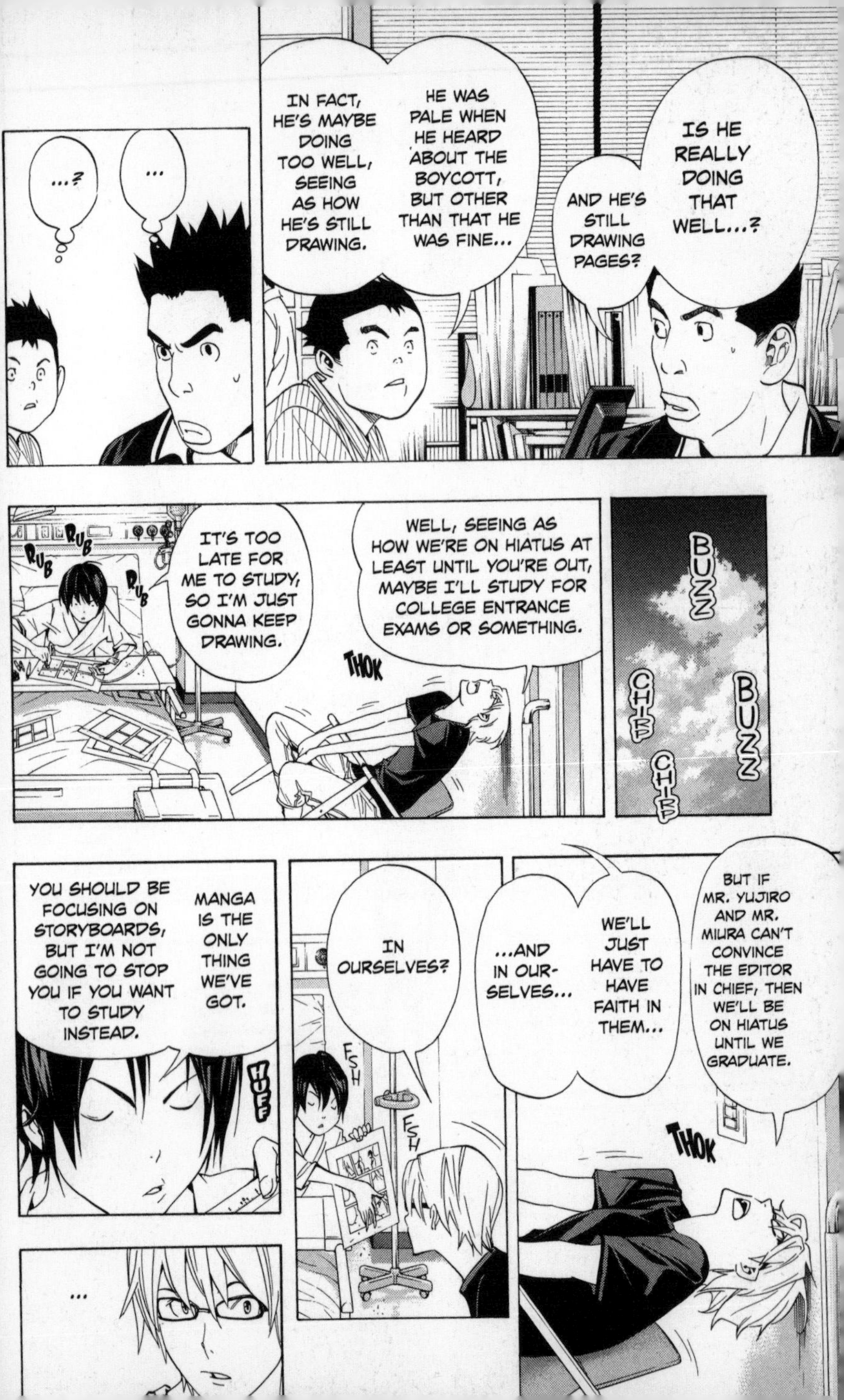
IS HE REALLY DOING THAT WELL...?
AND HE'S STILL DRAWING PAGES?
HE WAS PALE WHEN HE HEARD ABOUT THE BOYCOTT, BUT OTHER THAN THAT HE WAS FINE...
IN FACT, HE'S MAYBE DOING TOO WELL, SEEING AS HOW HE'S STILL DRAWING.
...
...?
BUZZ
CHIP
BUZZ
CHIP
WELL, SEEING AS HOW WE'RE ON HIATUS AT LEAST UNTIL YOU'RE OUT, MAYBE I'LL STUDY FOR COLLEGE ENTRANCE EXAMS OR SOMETHING.
THOK
IT'S TOO LATE FOR ME TO STUDY, SO I'M JUST GONNA KEEP DRAWING.
RUB
RUB
RUB
BUT IF MR. YUJIRO AND MR. MIURA CAN'T CONVINCE THE EDITOR IN CHIEF, THEN WE'LL BE ON HIATUS UNTIL WE GRADUATE.
WE'LL JUST HAVE TO HAVE FAITH IN THEM...
...AND IN OUR-SELVES...
THOK
IN OURSELVES?
FSH
FSH
MANGA IS THE ONLY THING WE'VE GOT.
YOU SHOULD BE FOCUSING ON STORYBOARDS, BUT I'M NOT GOING TO STOP YOU IF YOU WANT TO STUDY INSTEAD.
HUFF
...

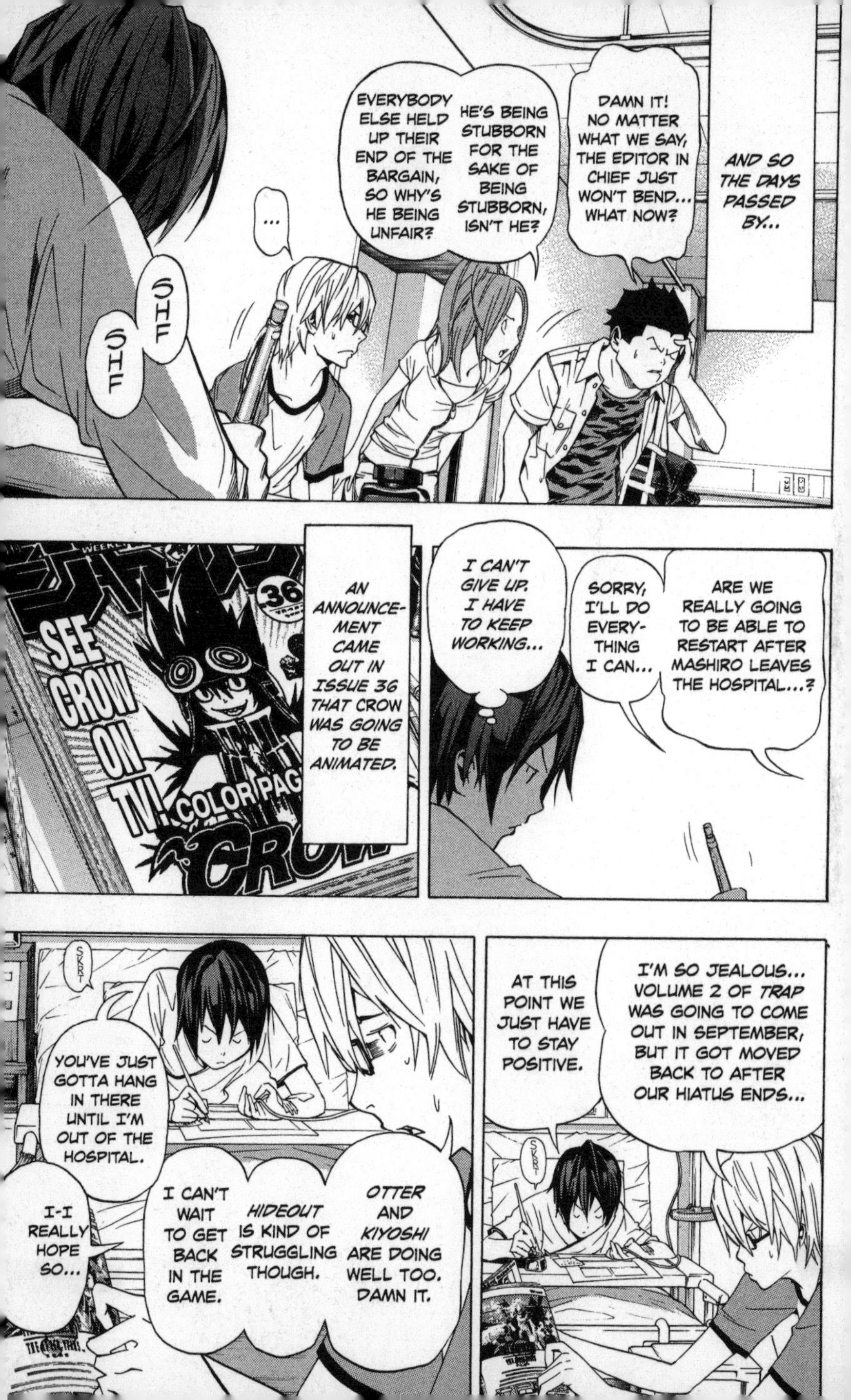
AND SO THE DAYS PASSED BY...
DAMN IT! NO MATTER WHAT WE SAY, THE EDITOR IN CHIEF JUST WON'T BEND... WHAT NOW?
HE'S BEING STUBBORN FOR THE SAKE OF BEING STUBBORN, ISN'T HE?
EVERYBODY ELSE HELD UP THEIR END OF THE BARGAIN, SO WHY'S HE BEING UNFAIR?
...
SHF SHF
ARE WE REALLY GOING TO BE ABLE TO RESTART AFTER MASHIRO LEAVES THE HOSPITAL...?
SORRY, I'LL DO EVERYTHING I CAN...
I CAN'T GIVE UP. I HAVE TO KEEP WORKING...
AN ANNOUNCEMENT CAME OUT IN ISSUE 36 THAT CROW WAS GOING TO BE ANIMATED.
36
SEE CROW ON TV!
COLOR PAG
CROW
I'M SO JEALOUS... VOLUME 2 OF *TRAP* WAS GOING TO COME OUT IN SEPTEMBER, BUT IT GOT MOVED BACK TO AFTER OUR HIATUS ENDS...
AT THIS POINT WE JUST HAVE TO STAY POSITIVE.
SKRT
OTTER AND KIYOSHI ARE DOING WELL TOO. DAMN IT.
HIDEOUT IS KIND OF STRUGGLING THOUGH.
I CAN'T WAIT TO GET BACK IN THE GAME.
YOU'VE JUST GOTTA HANG IN THERE UNTIL I'M OUT OF THE HOSPITAL.
SKRT
I-I REALLY HOPE SO...

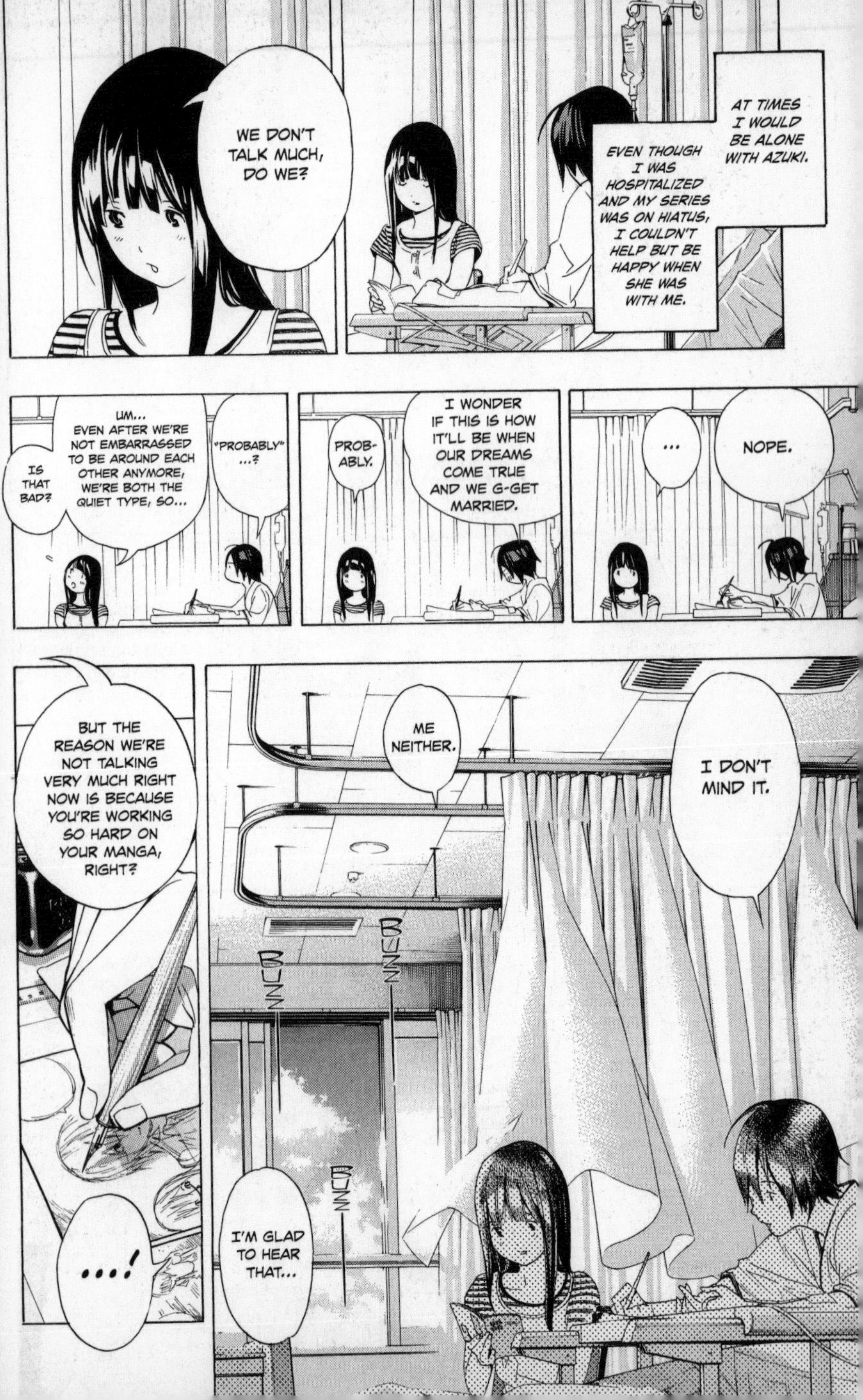
AT TIMES I WOULD BE ALONE WITH AZUKI.
EVEN THOUGH I WAS HOSPITALIZED AND MY SERIES WAS ON HIATUS, I COULDN'T HELP BUT BE HAPPY WHEN SHE WAS WITH ME.
WE DON'T TALK MUCH, DO WE?
NOPE.
...
I WONDER IF THIS IS HOW IT'LL BE WHEN OUR DREAMS COME TRUE AND WE G-GET MARRIED.
PROB-ABLY.
"PROBABLY" ...?
UM... EVEN AFTER WE'RE NOT EMBARRASSED TO BE AROUND EACH OTHER ANYMORE, WE'RE BOTH THE QUIET TYPE, SO...
IS THAT BAD?
I DON'T MIND IT.
ME NEITHER.
BUZZ
BUZZ
BUZZ
I'M GLAD TO HEAR THAT...
BUT THE REASON WE'RE NOT TALKING VERY MUCH RIGHT NOW IS BECAUSE YOU'RE WORKING SO HARD ON YOUR MANGA, RIGHT?
...!

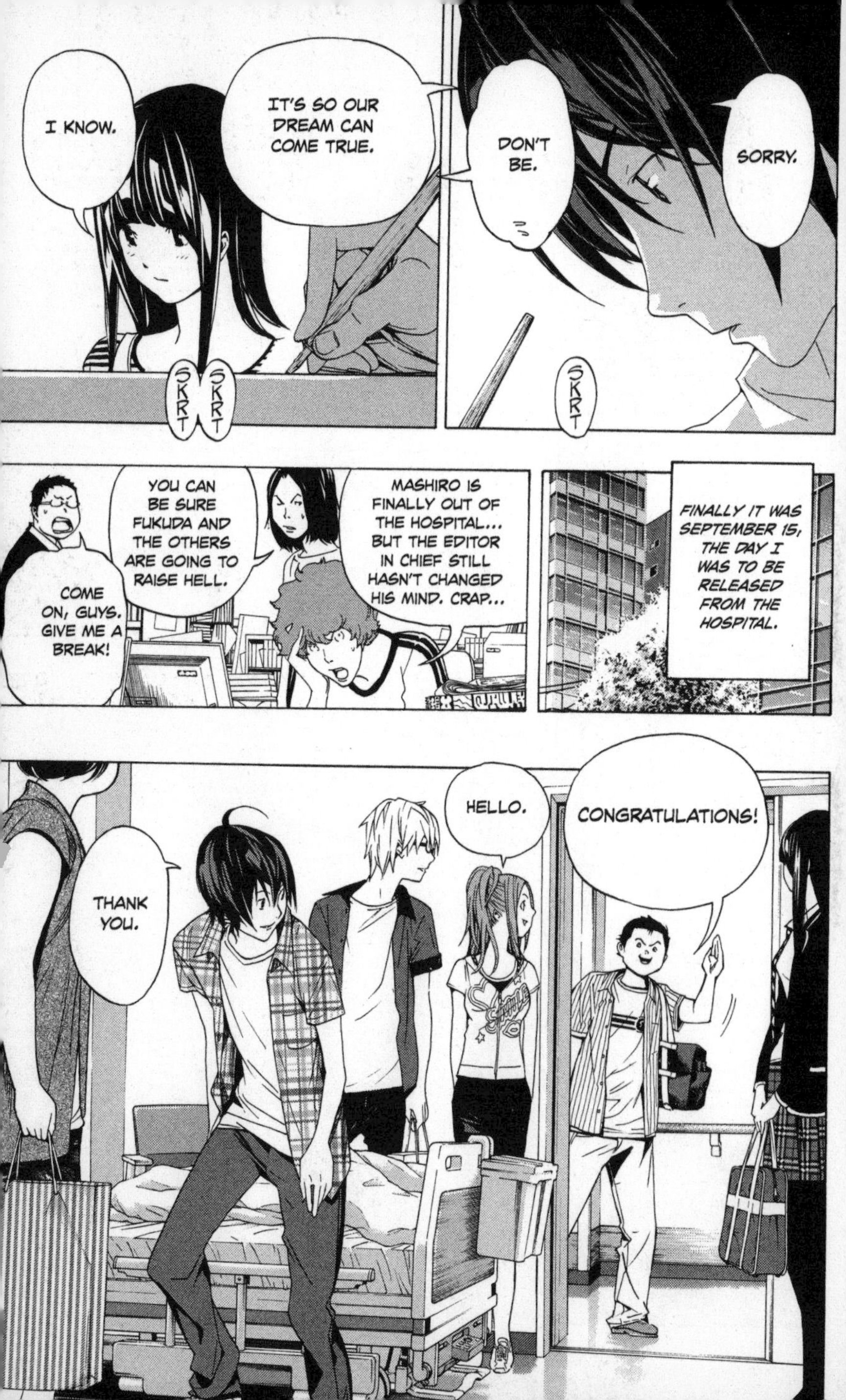
SORRY.
DON'T BE.
SKRT
IT'S SO OUR DREAM CAN COME TRUE.
I KNOW.
SKRT
SKRT
FINALLY IT WAS SEPTEMBER 15, THE DAY I WAS TO BE RELEASED FROM THE HOSPITAL.
MASHIRO IS FINALLY OUT OF THE HOSPITAL... BUT THE EDITOR IN CHIEF STILL HASN'T CHANGED HIS MIND. CRAP...
YOU CAN BE SURE FUKUDA AND THE OTHERS ARE GOING TO RAISE HELL.
COME ON, GUYS. GIVE ME A BREAK!
CONGRATULATIONS!
HELLO.
THANK YOU.

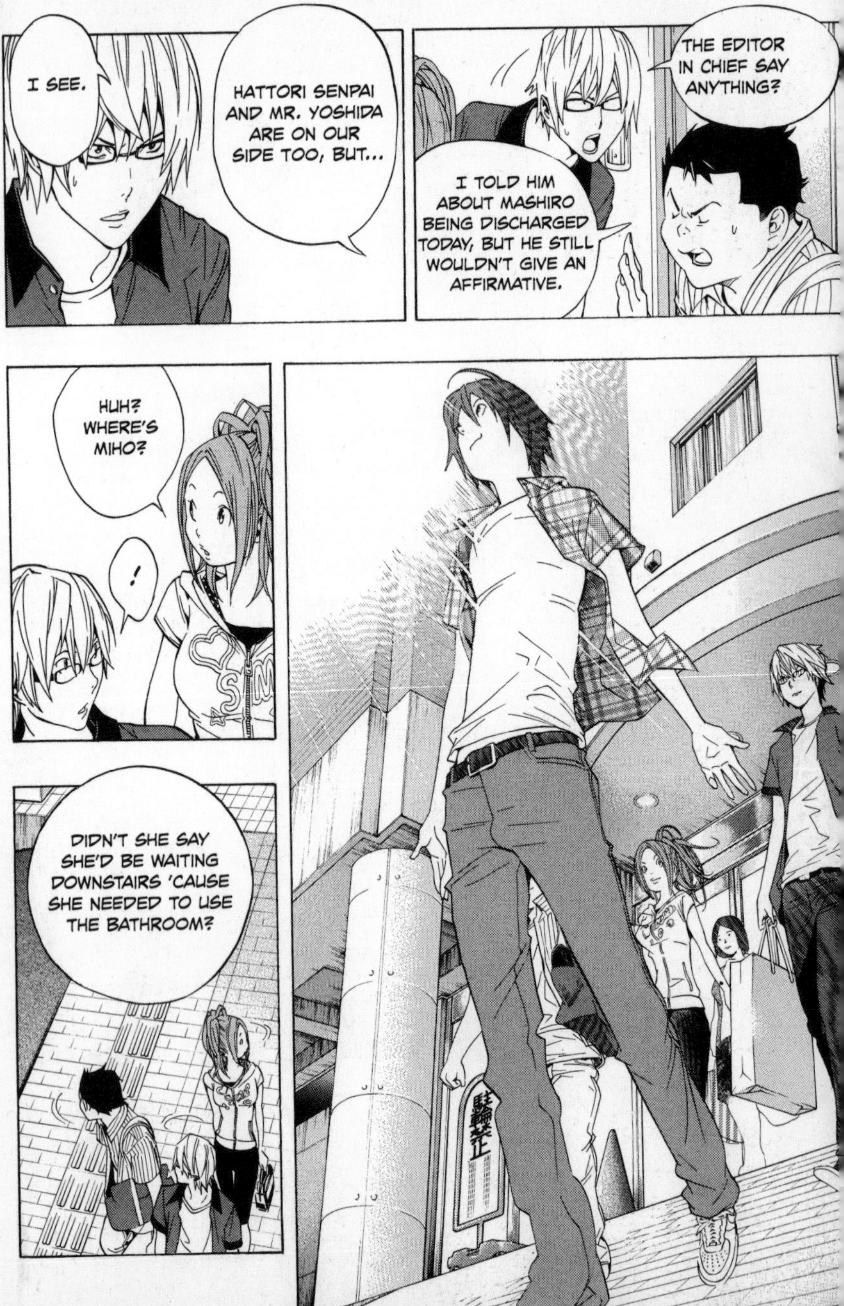
THE EDITOR IN CHIEF SAY ANYTHING?
I TOLD HIM ABOUT MASHIRO BEING DISCHARGED TODAY, BUT HE STILL WOULDN'T GIVE AN AFFIRMATIVE.
HATTORI SENPAI AND MR. YOSHIDA ARE ON OUR SIDE TOO, BUT...
I SEE.
駐輪禁止
HUH? WHERE'S MIHO?
!
DIDN'T SHE SAY SHE'D BE WAITING DOWNSTAIRS 'CAUSE SHE NEEDED TO USE THE BATHROOM?

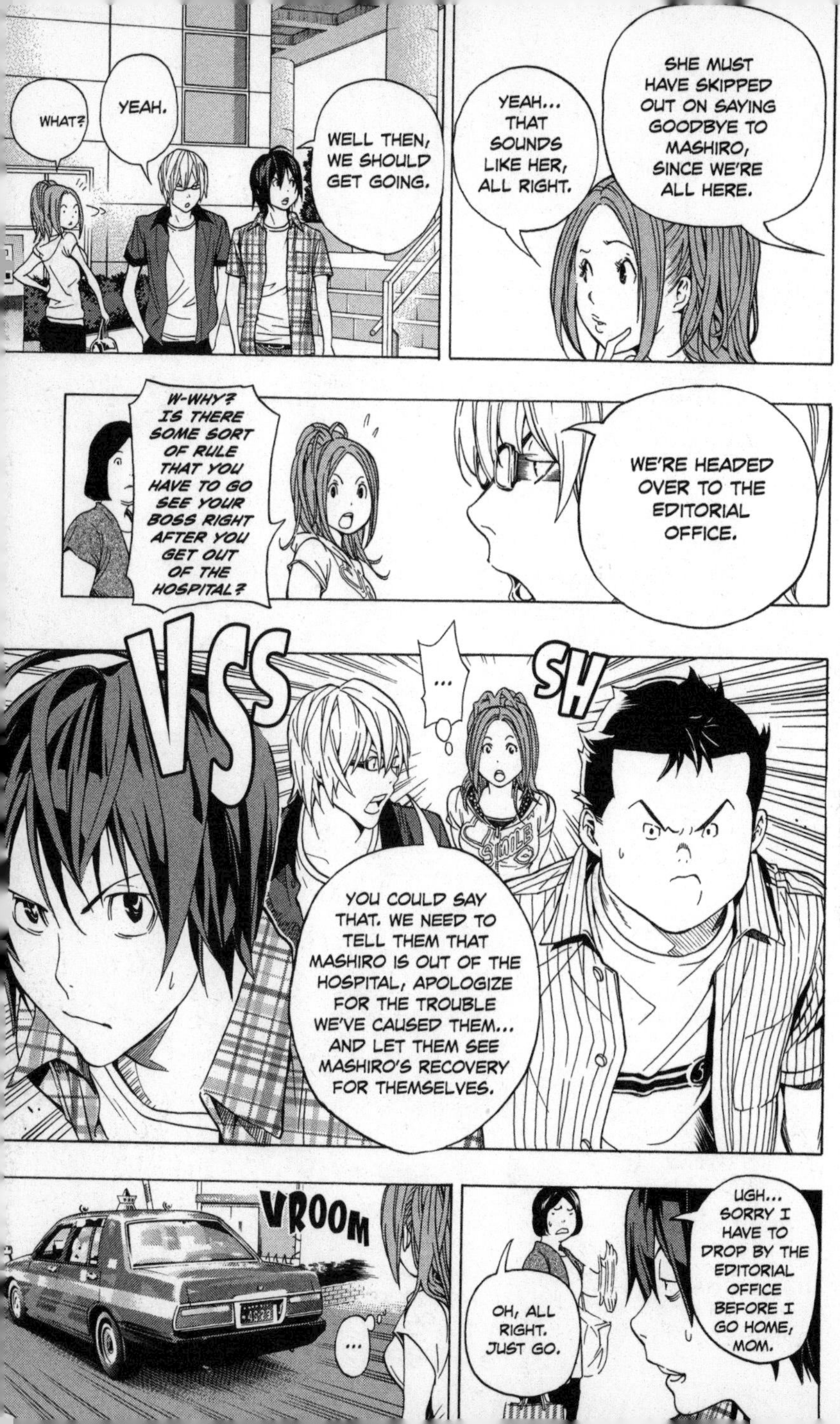
SHE MUST HAVE SKIPPED OUT ON SAYING GOODBYE TO MASHIRO, SINCE WE'RE ALL HERE.
YEAH... THAT SOUNDS LIKE HER, ALL RIGHT.
WELL THEN, WE SHOULD GET GOING.
YEAH.
WHAT?
WE'RE HEADED OVER TO THE EDITORIAL OFFICE.
W-WHY? IS THERE SOME SORT OF RULE THAT YOU HAVE TO GO SEE YOUR BOSS RIGHT AFTER YOU GET OUT OF THE HOSPITAL?
SH
VS
...
YOU COULD SAY THAT. WE NEED TO TELL THEM THAT MASHIRO IS OUT OF THE HOSPITAL, APOLOGIZE FOR THE TROUBLE WE'VE CAUSED THEM... AND LET THEM SEE MASHIRO'S RECOVERY FOR THEMSELVES.
UGH... SORRY I HAVE TO DROP BY THE EDITORIAL OFFICE BEFORE I GO HOME, MOM.
OH, ALL RIGHT. JUST GO.
VROOM
...

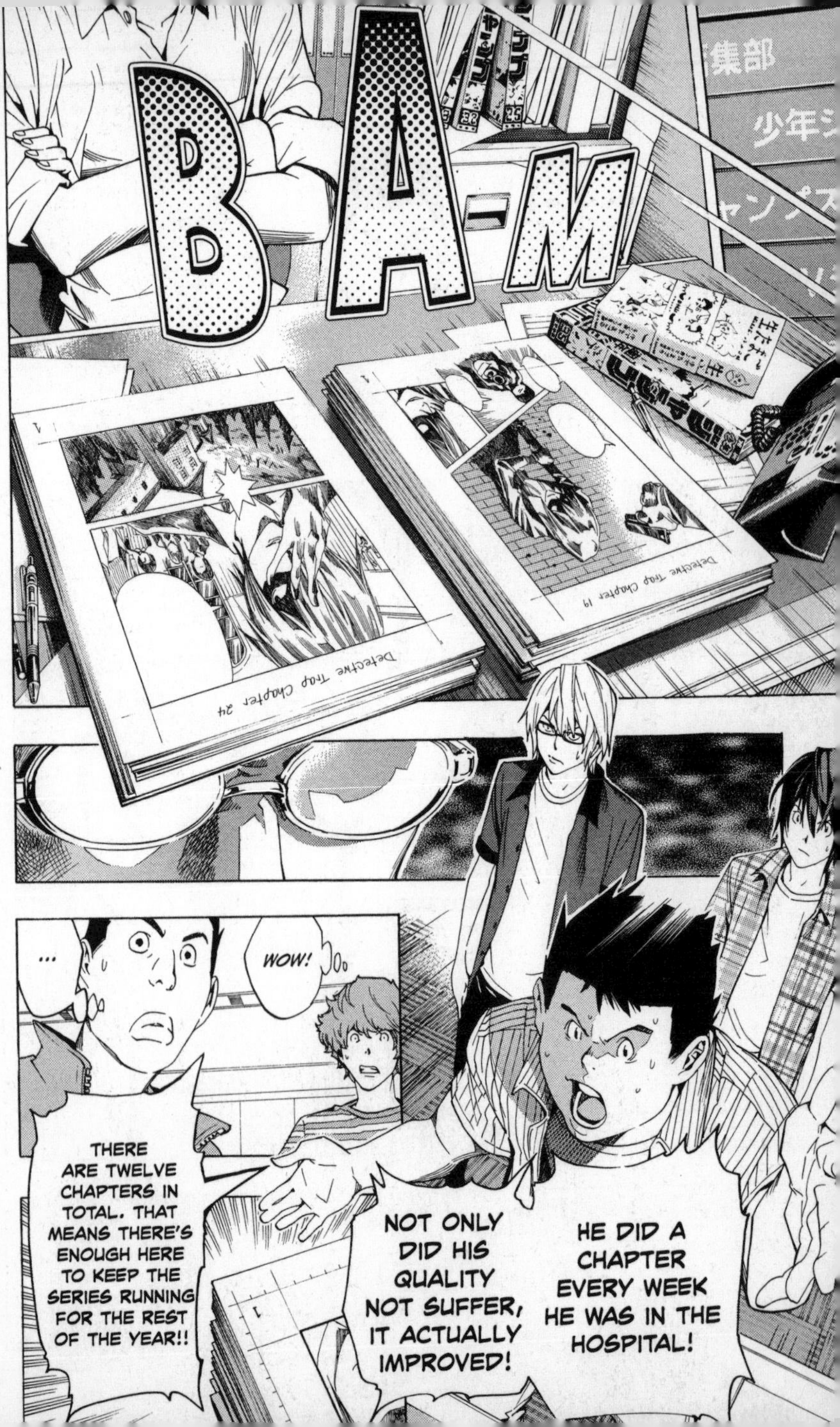
BA-M
Detective Trap Chapter 19
Detective Trap Chapter 24
HE DID A CHAPTER EVERY WEEK HE WAS IN THE HOSPITAL!
NOT ONLY DID HIS QUALITY NOT SUFFER, IT ACTUALLY IMPROVED!
WOW!
...
THERE ARE TWELVE CHAPTERS IN TOTAL. THAT MEANS THERE'S ENOUGH HERE TO KEEP THE SERIES RUNNING FOR THE REST OF THE YEAR!!

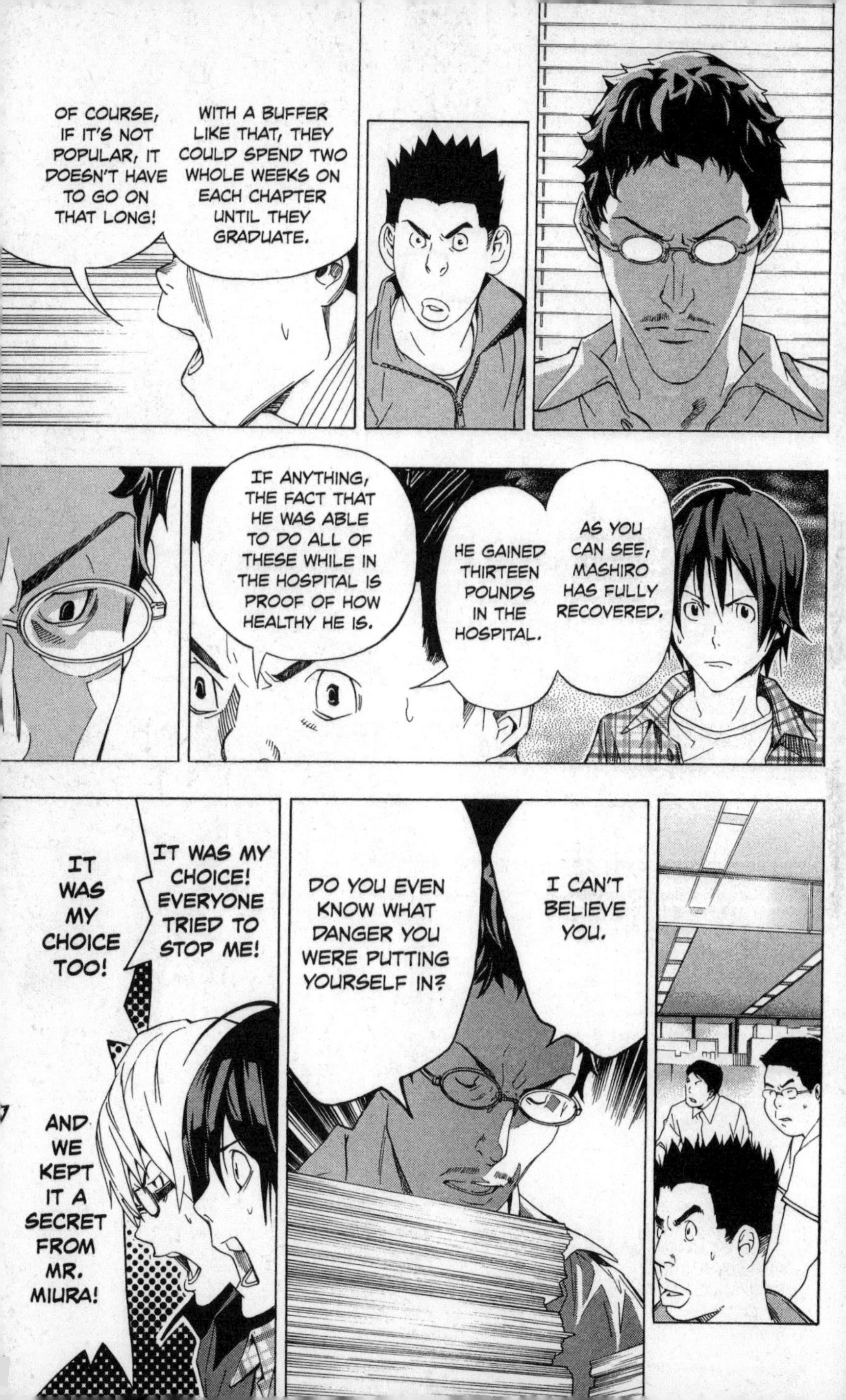
WITH A BUFFER LIKE THAT, THEY COULD SPEND TWO WHOLE WEEKS ON EACH CHAPTER UNTIL THEY GRADUATE.
OF COURSE, IF IT'S NOT POPULAR, IT DOESN'T HAVE TO GO ON THAT LONG!
AS YOU CAN SEE, MASHIRO HAS FULLY RECOVERED.
HE GAINED THIRTEEN POUNDS IN THE HOSPITAL.
IF ANYTHING, THE FACT THAT HE WAS ABLE TO DO ALL OF THESE WHILE IN THE HOSPITAL IS PROOF OF HOW HEALTHY HE IS.
I CAN'T BELIEVE YOU.
DO YOU EVEN KNOW WHAT DANGER YOU WERE PUTTING YOURSELF IN?
IT WAS MY CHOICE! EVERYONE TRIED TO STOP ME!
IT WAS MY CHOICE TOO!
AND WE KEPT IT A SECRET FROM MR. MIURA!

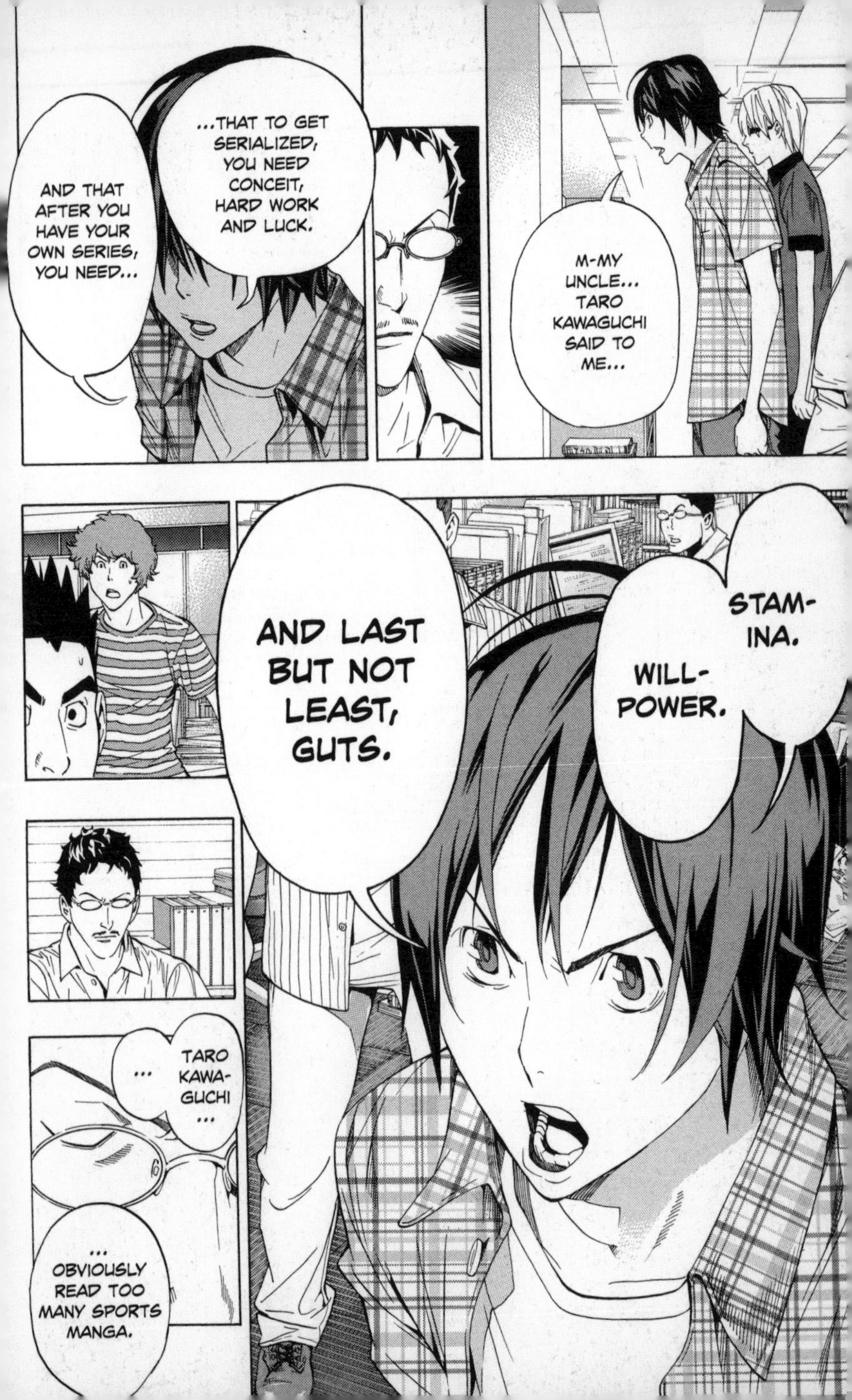

M-MY UNCLE... TARO KAWAGUCHI SAID TO ME...
...THAT TO GET SERIALIZED, YOU NEED CONCEIT, HARD WORK AND LUCK.
AND THAT AFTER YOU HAVE YOUR OWN SERIES, YOU NEED...
STAM-INA.
WILL-POWER.
AND LAST BUT NOT LEAST, GUTS.
...
TARO KAWA-GUCHI ...
... OBVIOUSLY READ TOO MANY SPORTS MANGA.

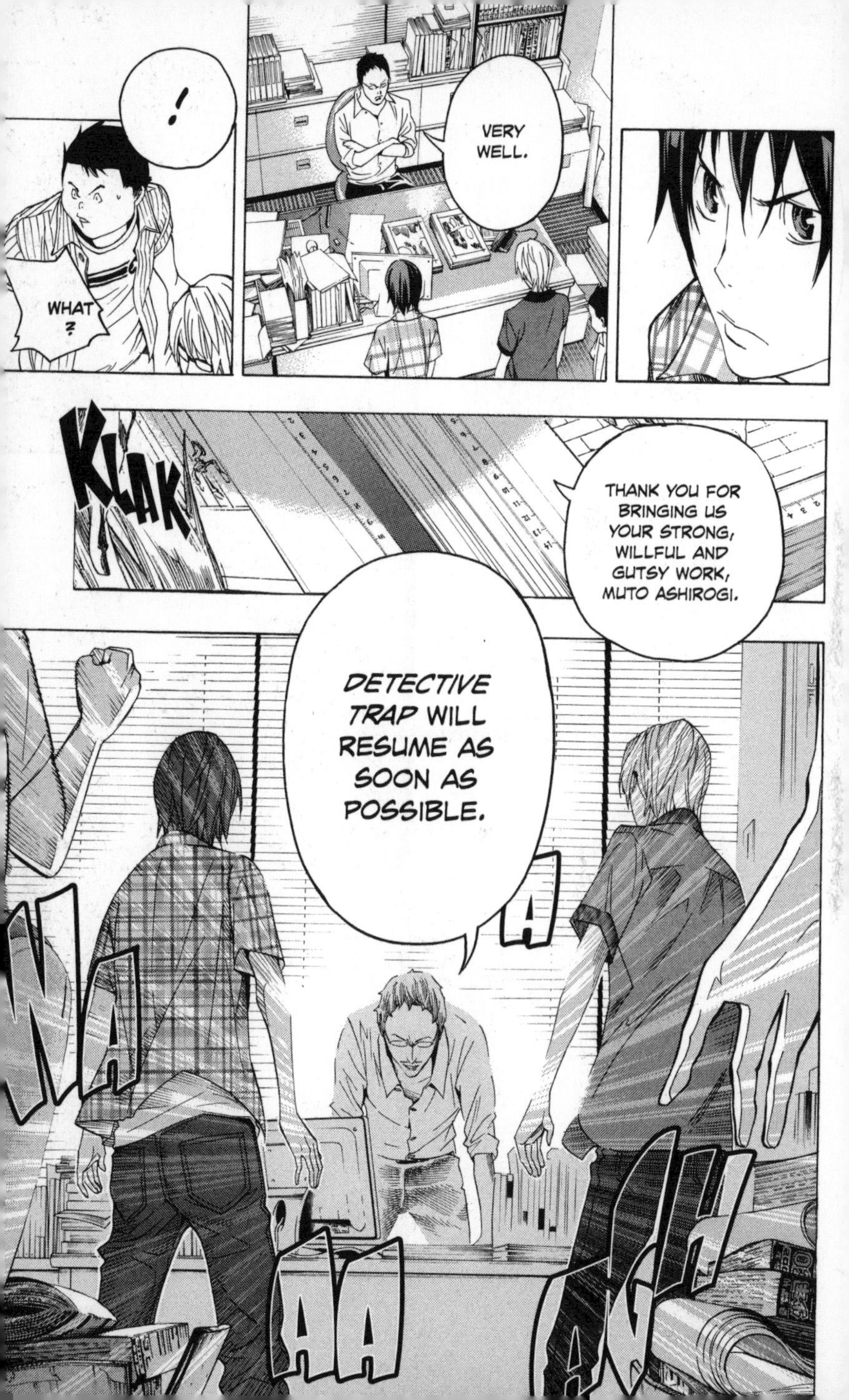
VERY WELL.
!
WHAT ?
THANK YOU FOR BRINGING US YOUR STRONG, WILLFUL AND GUTSY WORK, MUTO ASHIROGI.
KLAK
DETECTIVE TRAP WILL RESUME AS SOON AS POSSIBLE.
WAAAAAGH!

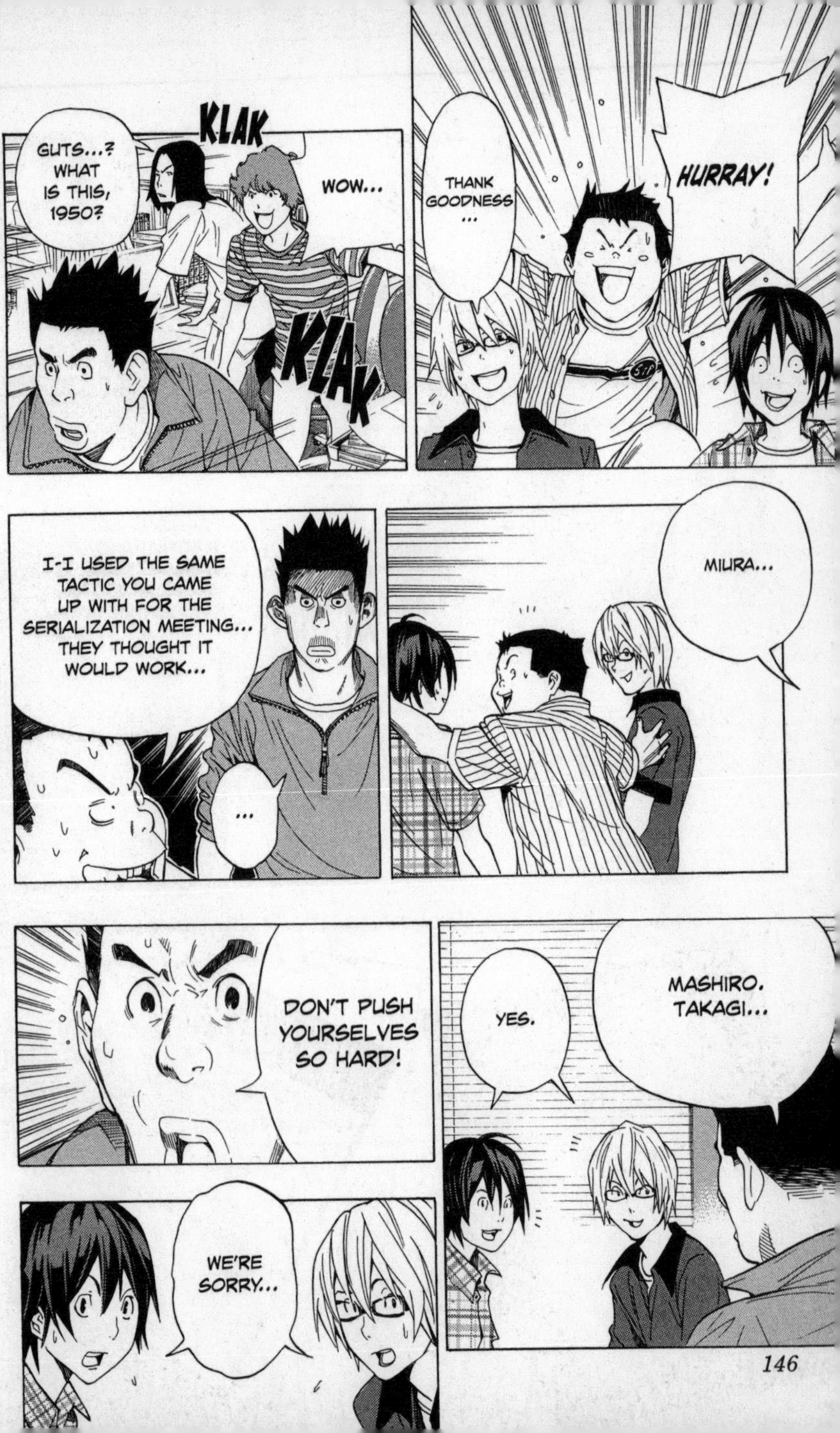
HURRAY!
THANK GOODNESS ...
KLAK
WOW...
GUTS...? WHAT IS THIS, 1950?
KLAK
MIURA...
I-I USED THE SAME TACTIC YOU CAME UP WITH FOR THE SERIALIZATION MEETING... THEY THOUGHT IT WOULD WORK...
...
MASHIRO. TAKAGI...
YES.
DON'T PUSH YOURSELVES SO HARD!
WE'RE SORRY...

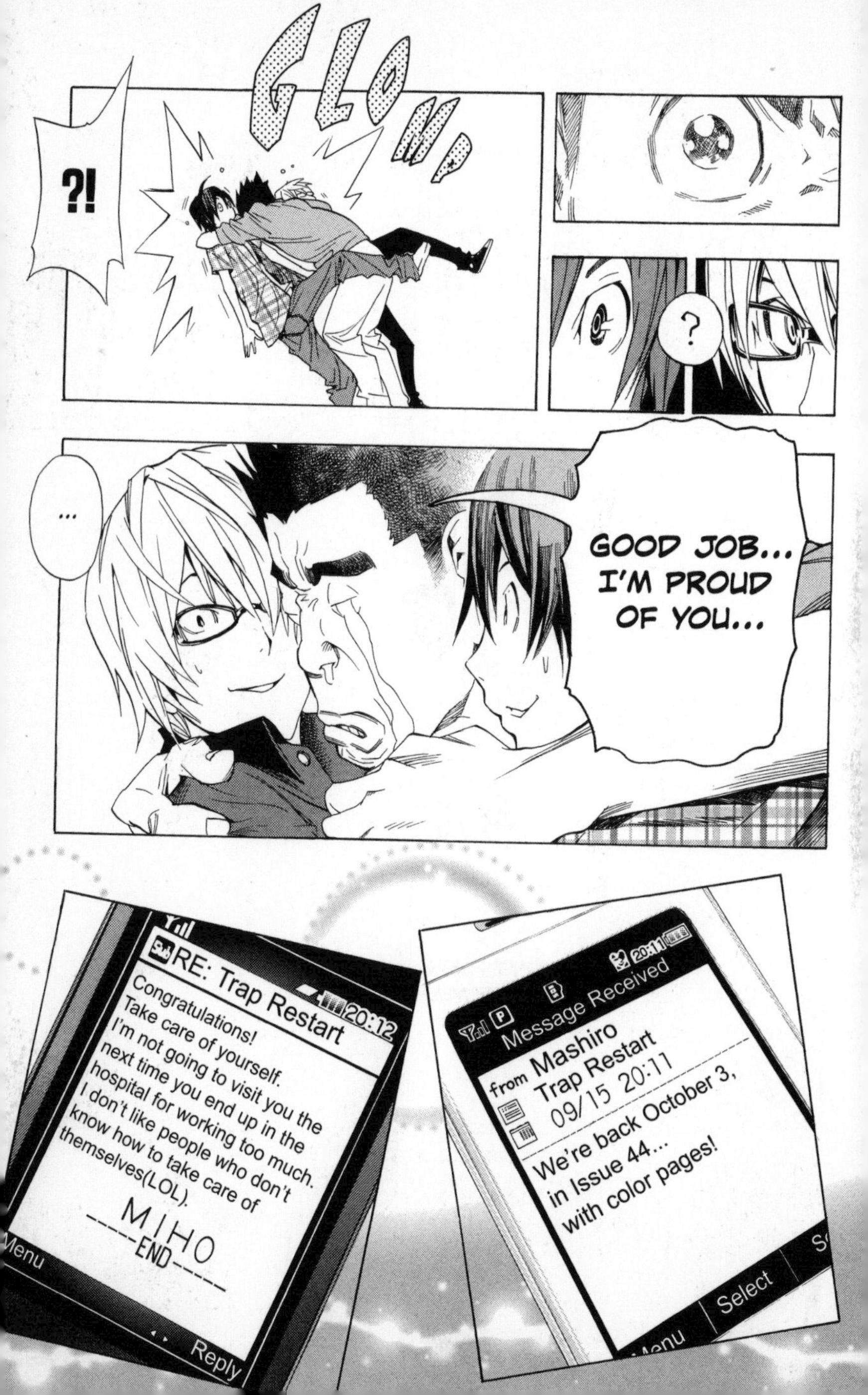
?
GLOMP
?!
GOOD JOB... I'M PROUD OF YOU...
...
20:11
Message Received
from Mashiro
Trap Restart
09/15 20:11
We're back October 3,
in Issue 44...
with color pages!
Select
RE: Trap Restart
20:12
Congratulations!
Take care of yourself.
I'm not going to visit you the
next time you end up in the
hospital for working too much.
I don't like people who don't
know how to take care of
themselves(LOL).
MIHO
END
Menu
Reply

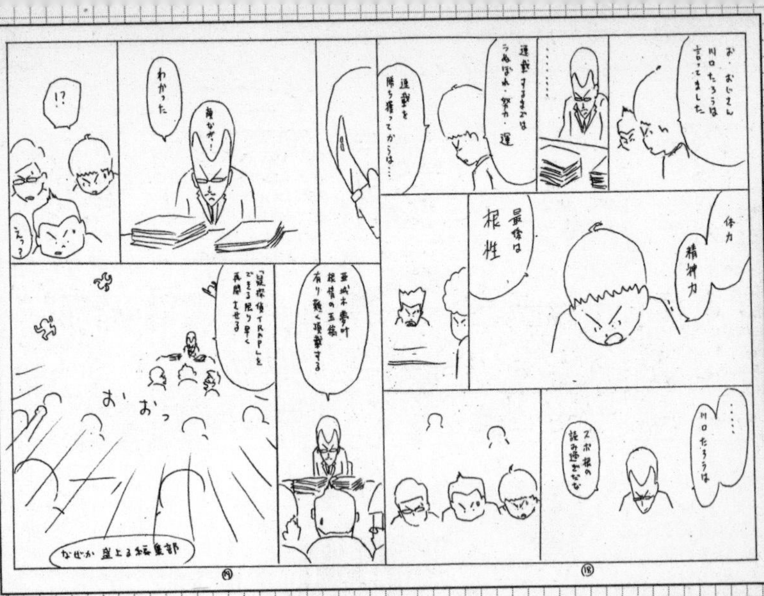
お、おじさん 川口たろうは 言ってました
……
連載するまでは うぬぼれ・努力・運
体力
精神力
最後は 根性
……
川口たろうは
スポ根の 読み過ぎだな
連載を 勝ち獲ってからは…
わかった
!?
えっ？
亜城木夢叶 根性の玉稿 有り難く頂戴する
「疑探偵TRAP」を できる限り早く 再開させる
おおっ
なぜか盛上る編集部
⑱
⑲

OHBA'S STORYBOARD

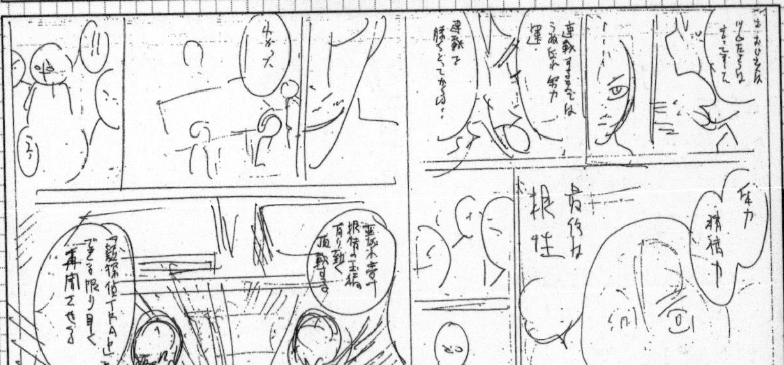

OBATA'S STORYBOARD

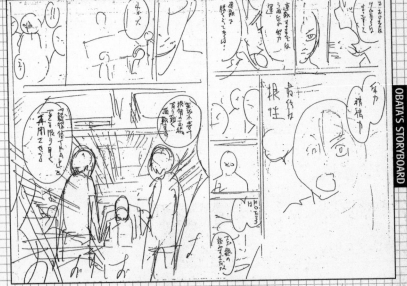

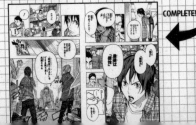

COMPLETE!

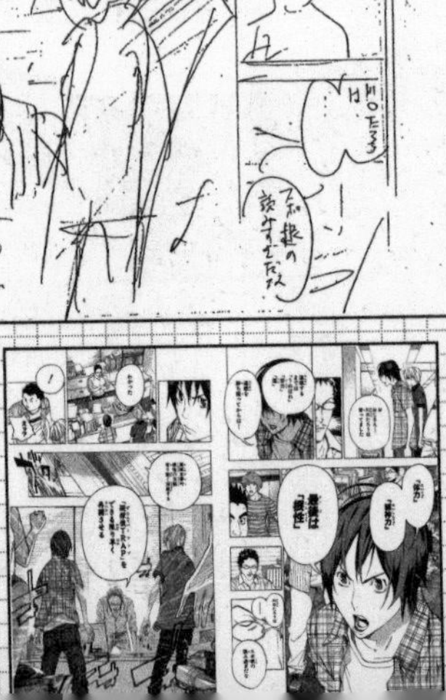

※CREATOR STORYBOARDS AND FINISHED PAGES IN JAPANESE

BAKUMAN。vol.6

"Until the Final Draft Is Complete"

Chapter 50, pp. 144-145

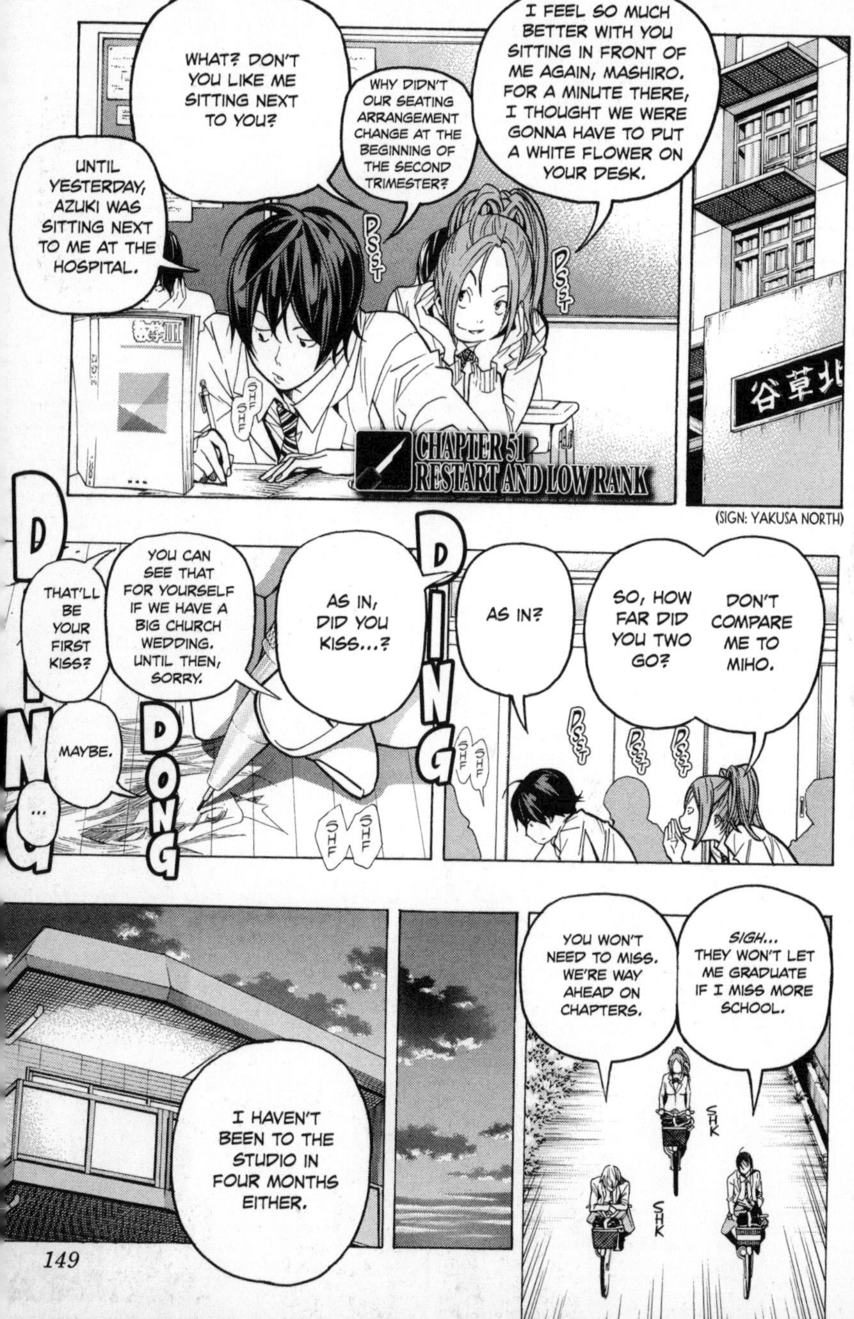
谷草北
I FEEL SO MUCH BETTER WITH YOU SITTING IN FRONT OF ME AGAIN, MASHIRO. FOR A MINUTE THERE, I THOUGHT WE WERE GONNA HAVE TO PUT A WHITE FLOWER ON YOUR DESK.
PSST
WHY DIDN'T OUR SEATING ARRANGEMENT CHANGE AT THE BEGINNING OF THE SECOND TRIMESTER?
PSST
WHAT? DON'T YOU LIKE ME SITTING NEXT TO YOU?
UNTIL YESTERDAY, AZUKI WAS SITTING NEXT TO ME AT THE HOSPITAL.
SHF SHF
...
CHAPTER 51
RESTART AND LOW RANK
(SIGN: YAKUSA NORTH)
DON'T COMPARE ME TO MIHO.
SO, HOW FAR DID YOU TWO GO?
PSST PSST PSST
AS IN?
DING
SHF SHF
AS IN, DID YOU KISS...?
YOU CAN SEE THAT FOR YOURSELF IF WE HAVE A BIG CHURCH WEDDING. UNTIL THEN, SORRY.
THAT'LL BE YOUR FIRST KISS?
MAYBE.
...
SHF SHF
DONG
DING
DONG
SIGH... THEY WON'T LET ME GRADUATE IF I MISS MORE SCHOOL.
YOU WON'T NEED TO MISS. WE'RE WAY AHEAD ON CHAPTERS.
SHK
SHK
I HAVEN'T BEEN TO THE STUDIO IN FOUR MONTHS EITHER.

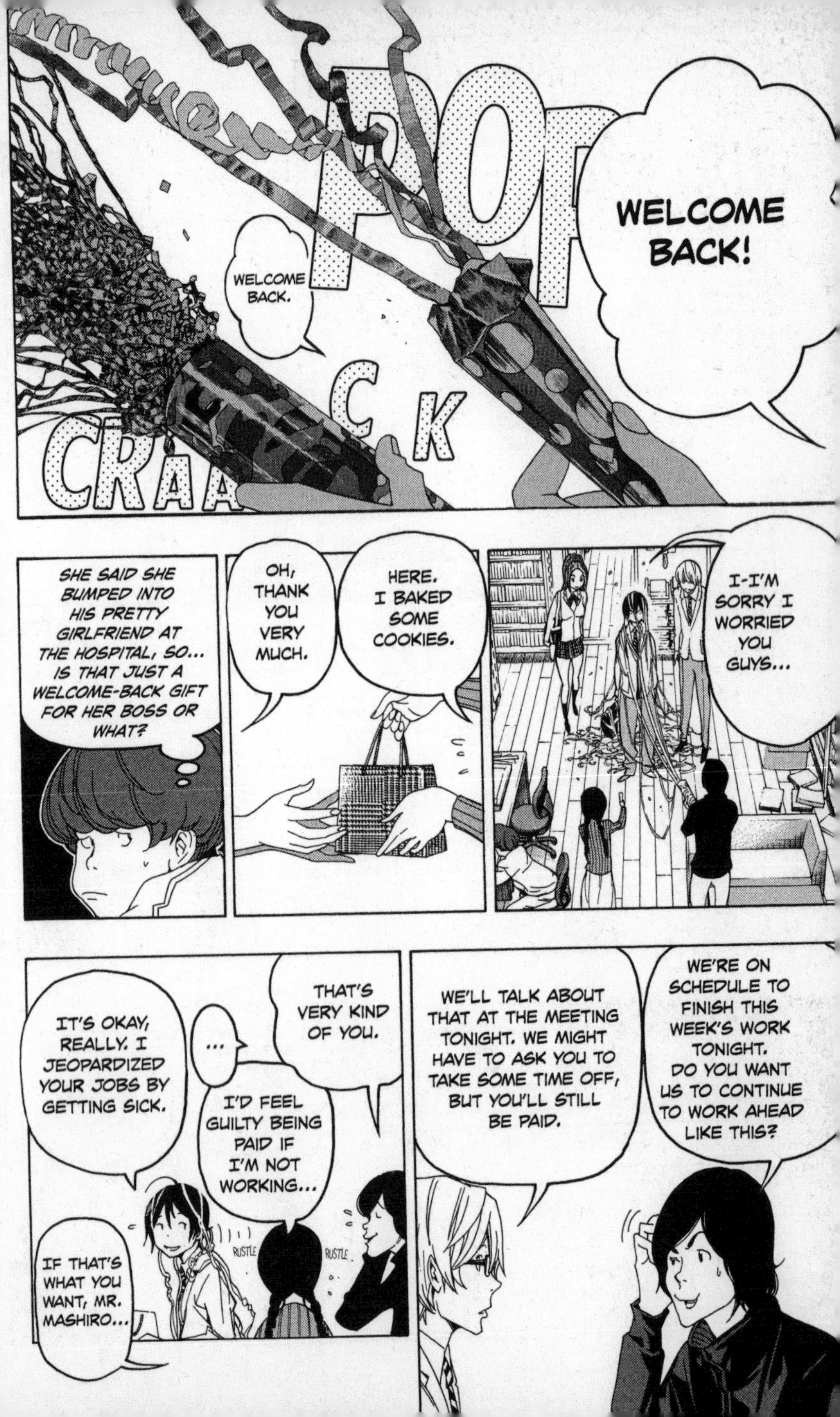
POP
WELCOME BACK!
WELCOME BACK.
CRAACK
I-I'M SORRY I WORRIED YOU GUYS...
HERE. I BAKED SOME COOKIES.
OH, THANK YOU VERY MUCH.
SHE SAID SHE BUMPED INTO HIS PRETTY GIRLFRIEND AT THE HOSPITAL, SO... IS THAT JUST A WELCOME-BACK GIFT FOR HER BOSS OR WHAT?
WE'RE ON SCHEDULE TO FINISH THIS WEEK'S WORK TONIGHT. DO YOU WANT US TO CONTINUE TO WORK AHEAD LIKE THIS?
WE'LL TALK ABOUT THAT AT THE MEETING TONIGHT. WE MIGHT HAVE TO ASK YOU TO TAKE SOME TIME OFF, BUT YOU'LL STILL BE PAID.
THAT'S VERY KIND OF YOU.
...
IT'S OKAY, REALLY. I JEOPARDIZED YOUR JOBS BY GETTING SICK.
I'D FEEL GUILTY BEING PAID IF I'M NOT WORKING...
RUSTLE
RUSTLE
IF THAT'S WHAT YOU WANT, MR. MASHIRO...

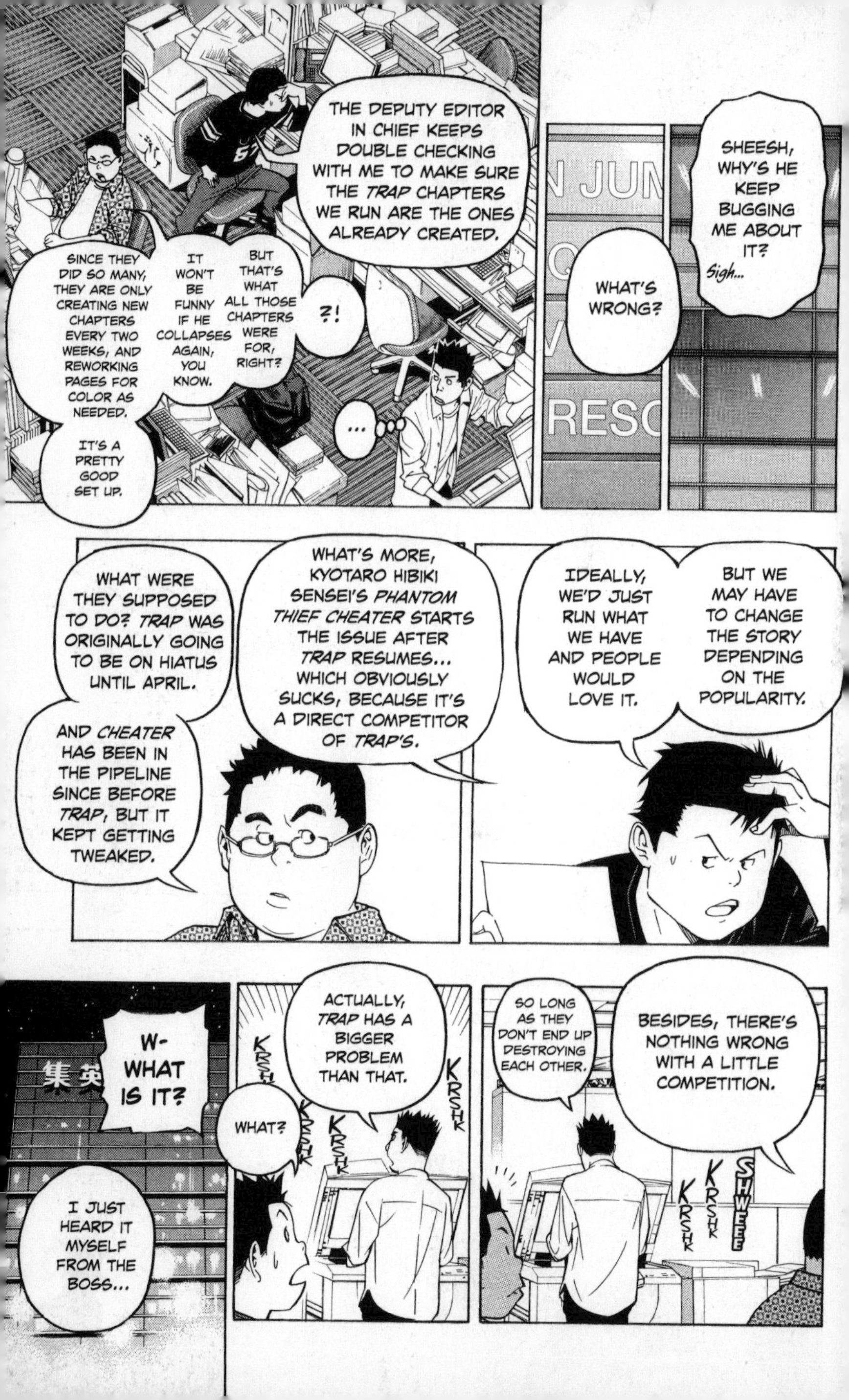
SHEESH, WHY'S HE KEEP BUGGING ME ABOUT IT?
Sigh...
WHAT'S WRONG?
N JUN
RESC
THE DEPUTY EDITOR IN CHIEF KEEPS DOUBLE CHECKING WITH ME TO MAKE SURE THE TRAP CHAPTERS WE RUN ARE THE ONES ALREADY CREATED.
?!
BUT THAT'S WHAT ALL THOSE CHAPTERS WERE FOR, RIGHT?
IT WON'T BE FUNNY IF HE COLLAPSES AGAIN, YOU KNOW.
SINCE THEY DID SO MANY, THEY ARE ONLY CREATING NEW CHAPTERS EVERY TWO WEEKS, AND REWORKING PAGES FOR COLOR AS NEEDED.
IT'S A PRETTY GOOD SET UP.
...
IDEALLY, WE'D JUST RUN WHAT WE HAVE AND PEOPLE WOULD LOVE IT.
BUT WE MAY HAVE TO CHANGE THE STORY DEPENDING ON THE POPULARITY.
WHAT'S MORE, KYOTARO HIBIKI SENSEI'S PHANTOM THIEF CHEATER STARTS THE ISSUE AFTER TRAP RESUMES... WHICH OBVIOUSLY SUCKS, BECAUSE IT'S A DIRECT COMPETITOR OF TRAP'S.
WHAT WERE THEY SUPPOSED TO DO? TRAP WAS ORIGINALLY GOING TO BE ON HIATUS UNTIL APRIL.
AND CHEATER HAS BEEN IN THE PIPELINE SINCE BEFORE TRAP, BUT IT KEPT GETTING TWEAKED.
BESIDES, THERE'S NOTHING WRONG WITH A LITTLE COMPETITION.
SO LONG AS THEY DON'T END UP DESTROYING EACH OTHER.
SHWEEE
KRSHK
KRSHK
ACTUALLY, TRAP HAS A BIGGER PROBLEM THAN THAT.
KRSHK
KRSHK
KRSHK
WHAT?
W-WHAT IS IT?
I JUST HEARD IT MYSELF FROM THE BOSS...

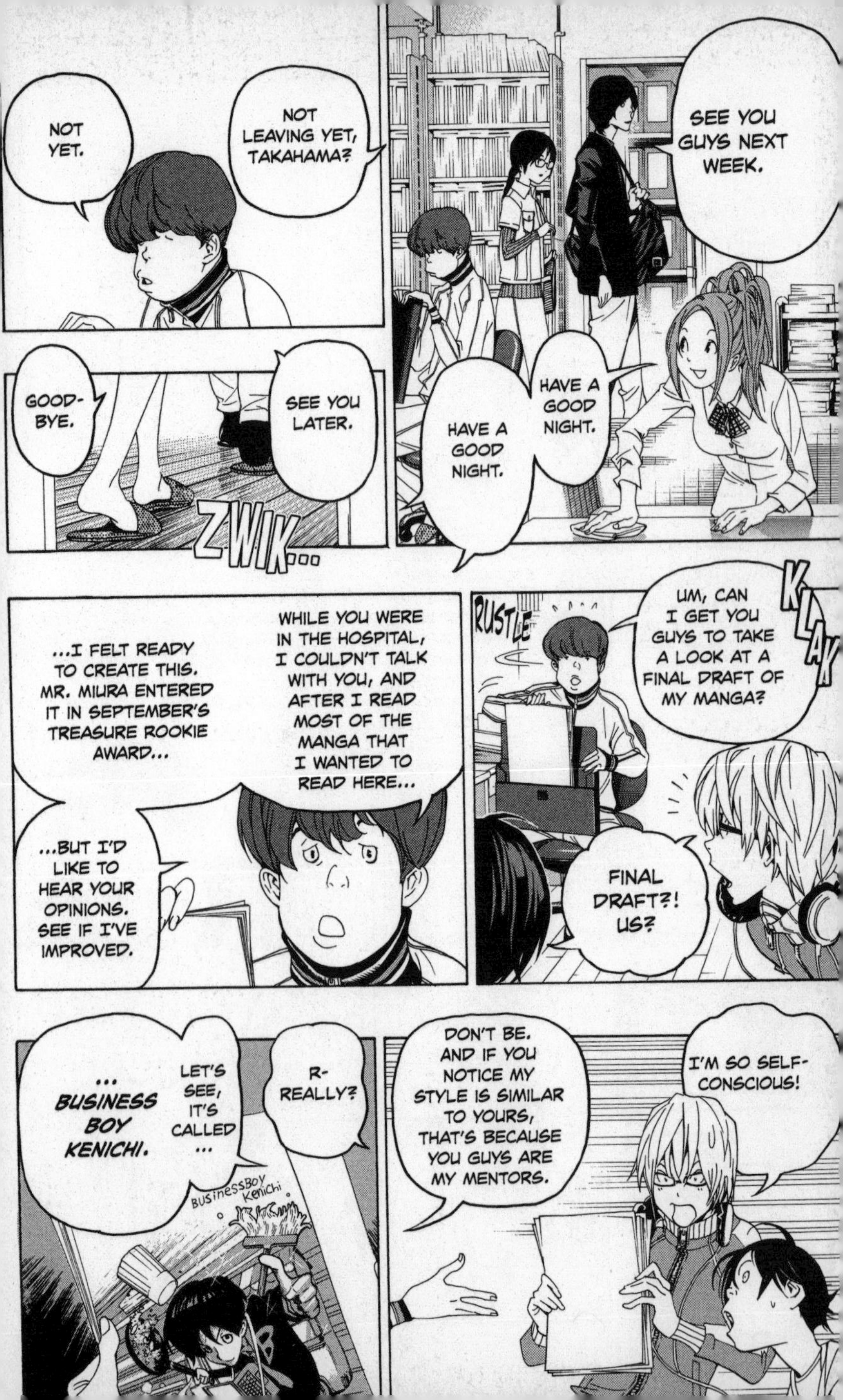
SEE YOU GUYS NEXT WEEK.
HAVE A GOOD NIGHT.
HAVE A GOOD NIGHT.
NOT LEAVING YET, TAKAHAMA?
NOT YET.
SEE YOU LATER.
GOOD-BYE.
ZWIK...
KLAK
UM, CAN I GET YOU GUYS TO TAKE A LOOK AT A FINAL DRAFT OF MY MANGA?
RUSTLE
FINAL DRAFT?! US?
WHILE YOU WERE IN THE HOSPITAL, I COULDN'T TALK WITH YOU, AND AFTER I READ MOST OF THE MANGA THAT I WANTED TO READ HERE...
...I FELT READY TO CREATE THIS. MR. MIURA ENTERED IT IN SEPTEMBER'S TREASURE ROOKIE AWARD...
...BUT I'D LIKE TO HEAR YOUR OPINIONS. SEE IF I'VE IMPROVED.
I'M SO SELF-CONSCIOUS!
DON'T BE. AND IF YOU NOTICE MY STYLE IS SIMILAR TO YOURS, THAT'S BECAUSE YOU GUYS ARE MY MENTORS.
R-REALLY?
LET'S SEE, IT'S CALLED...
... *BUSINESS BOY KENICHI*.
BusinessBoy Kenichi

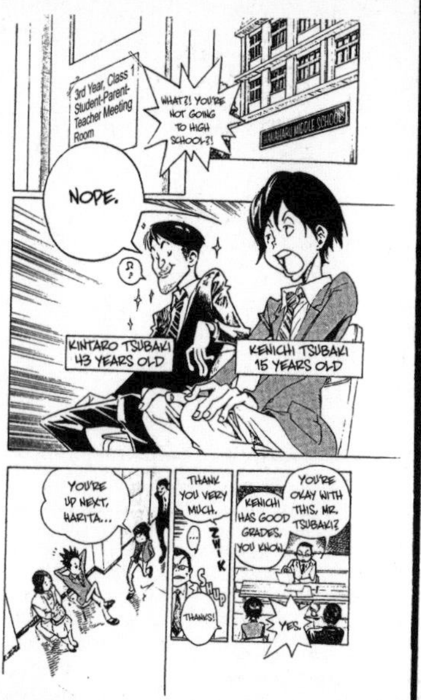
3rd Year, Class 1 Student-Parent-Teacher Meeting Room
WHAT?! YOU'RE NOT GOING TO HIGH SCHOOL?!
NOPE.
KENICHI TSUBAKI 15 YEARS OLD
KINTARO TSUBAKI 43 YEARS OLD
YOU'RE OKAY WITH THIS, MR. TSUBAKI?
KENICHI HAS GOOD GRADES, YOU KNOW.
YES.
THANK YOU VERY MUCH.
...
ZWIK
SHUP
THANKS!
YOU'RE UP NEXT, HARITA...

2

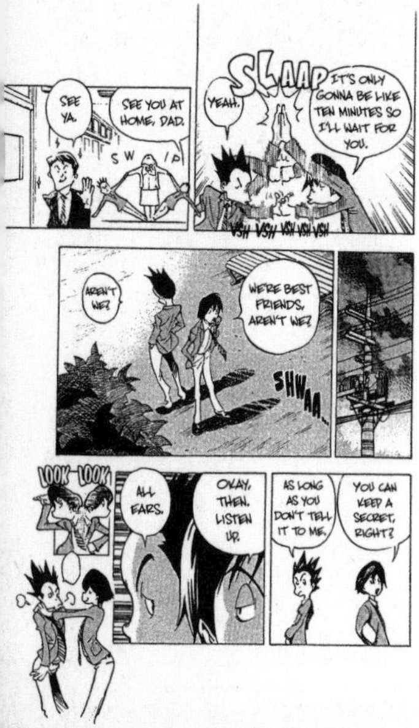
SLAAP
IT'S ONLY GONNA BE LIKE TEN MINUTES SO I'LL WAIT FOR YOU.
YEAH.
VSH VSH VSH VSH VSH
SEE YOU AT HOME, DAD.
SEE YA.
SWIP
WE'RE BEST FRIENDS, AREN'T WE?
AREN'T WE?
SHWAA...
YOU CAN KEEP A SECRET, RIGHT?
AS LONG AS YOU DON'T TELL IT TO ME.
OKAY, THEN. LISTEN UP.
ALL EARS.
LOOK LOOK

3

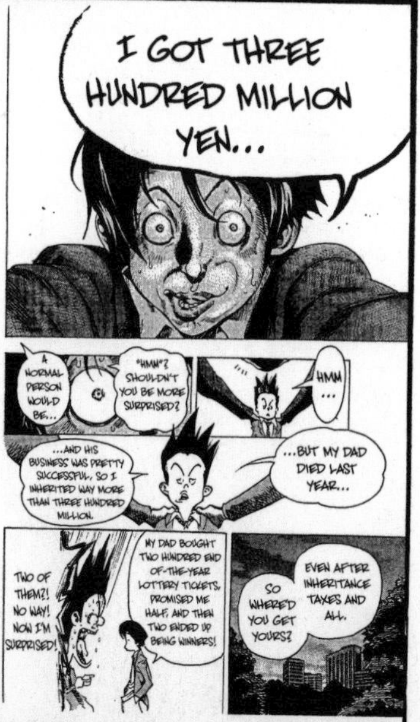
I GOT THREE HUNDRED MILLION YEN...
HMM...
"HMM"? SHOULDN'T YOU BE MORE SURPRISED?
A NORMAL PERSON WOULD BE...
...BUT MY DAD DIED LAST YEAR...
...AND HIS BUSINESS WAS PRETTY SUCCESSFUL, SO I INHERITED WAY MORE THAN THREE HUNDRED MILLION.
EVEN AFTER INHERITANCE TAXES AND ALL.
SO WHERE'D YOU GET YOURS?
MY DAD BOUGHT TWO HUNDRED END-OF-THE-YEAR LOTTERY TICKETS, PROMISED ME HALF, AND THEN TWO ENDED UP BEING WINNERS!
TWO OF THEM?! NO WAY! NOW I'M SURPRISED!

4

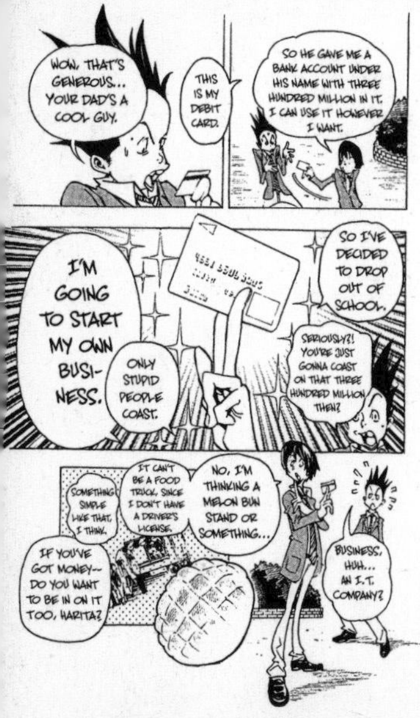
SO HE GAVE ME A BANK ACCOUNT UNDER HIS NAME WITH THREE HUNDRED MILLION IN IT. I CAN USE IT HOWEVER I WANT.
THIS IS MY DEBIT CARD.
WOW, THAT'S GENEROUS... YOUR DAD'S A COOL GUY.
SO I'VE DECIDED TO DROP OUT OF SCHOOL.
SERIOUSLY?! YOU'RE JUST GONNA COAST ON THAT THREE HUNDRED MILLION THEN?
ONLY STUPID PEOPLE COAST.
I'M GOING TO START MY OWN BUSINESS.
BUSINESS, HUH... AN I.T. COMPANY?
NO, I'M THINKING A MELON BUN STAND OR SOMETHING...
IT CAN'T BE A FOOD TRUCK, SINCE I DON'T HAVE A DRIVER'S LICENSE.
SOMETHING SIMPLE LIKE THAT, I THINK.
IF YOU'VE GOT MONEY-- DO YOU WANT TO BE IN ON IT TOO, HARITA?

5

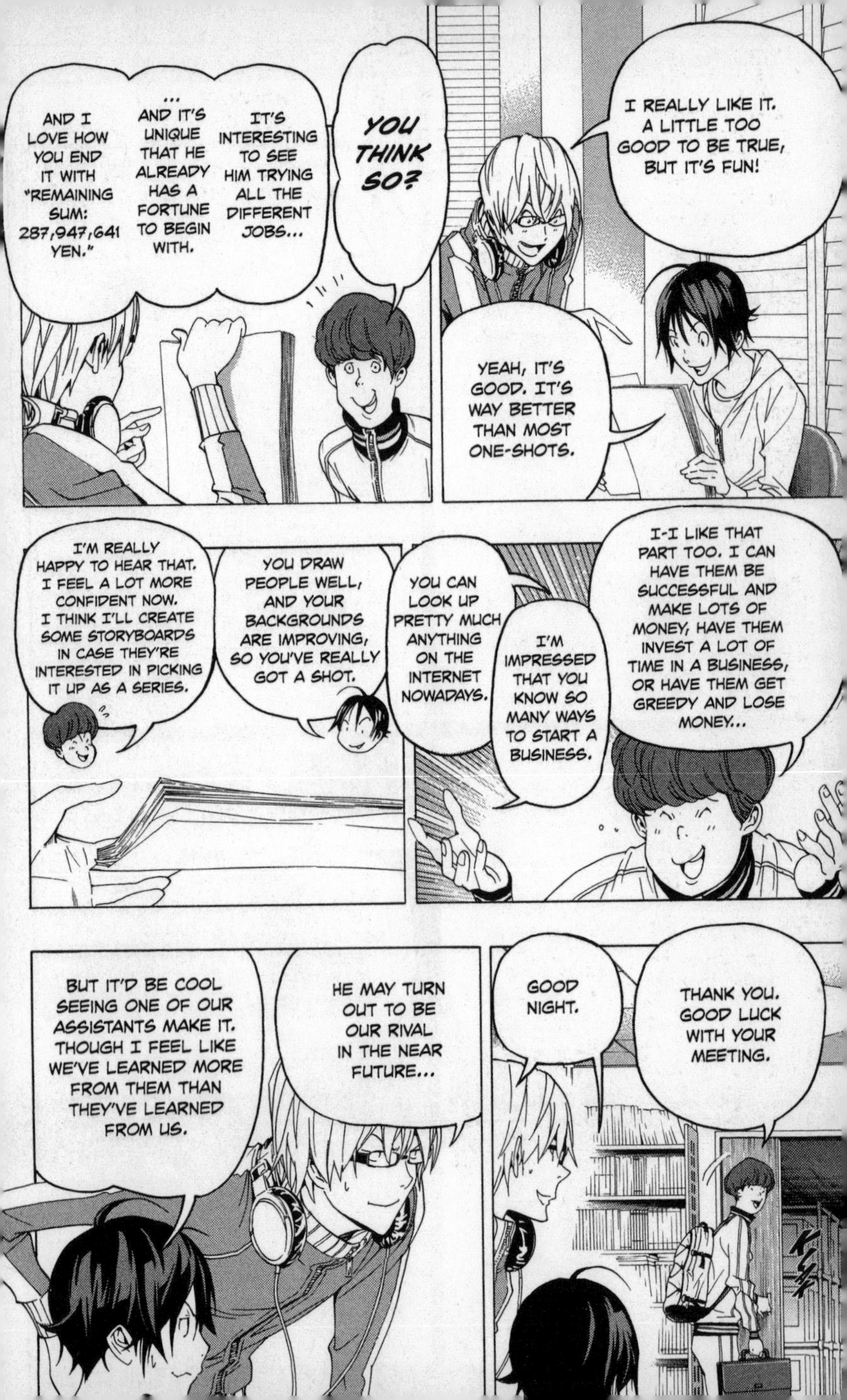
I REALLY LIKE IT. A LITTLE TOO GOOD TO BE TRUE, BUT IT'S FUN!
YEAH, IT'S GOOD. IT'S WAY BETTER THAN MOST ONE-SHOTS.
YOU THINK SO?
IT'S INTERESTING TO SEE HIM TRYING ALL THE DIFFERENT JOBS...
...AND IT'S UNIQUE THAT HE ALREADY HAS A FORTUNE TO BEGIN WITH.
AND I LOVE HOW YOU END IT WITH "REMAINING SUM: 287,947,641 YEN."
I-I LIKE THAT PART TOO. I CAN HAVE THEM BE SUCCESSFUL AND MAKE LOTS OF MONEY, HAVE THEM INVEST A LOT OF TIME IN A BUSINESS, OR HAVE THEM GET GREEDY AND LOSE MONEY...
I'M IMPRESSED THAT YOU KNOW SO MANY WAYS TO START A BUSINESS.
YOU CAN LOOK UP PRETTY MUCH ANYTHING ON THE INTERNET NOWADAYS.
YOU DRAW PEOPLE WELL, AND YOUR BACKGROUNDS ARE IMPROVING, SO YOU'VE REALLY GOT A SHOT.
I'M REALLY HAPPY TO HEAR THAT. I FEEL A LOT MORE CONFIDENT NOW. I THINK I'LL CREATE SOME STORYBOARDS IN CASE THEY'RE INTERESTED IN PICKING IT UP AS A SERIES.
THANK YOU. GOOD LUCK WITH YOUR MEETING.
GOOD NIGHT.
KLIK
HE MAY TURN OUT TO BE OUR RIVAL IN THE NEAR FUTURE...
BUT IT'D BE COOL SEEING ONE OF OUR ASSISTANTS MAKE IT. THOUGH I FEEL LIKE WE'VE LEARNED MORE FROM THEM THAN THEY'VE LEARNED FROM US.

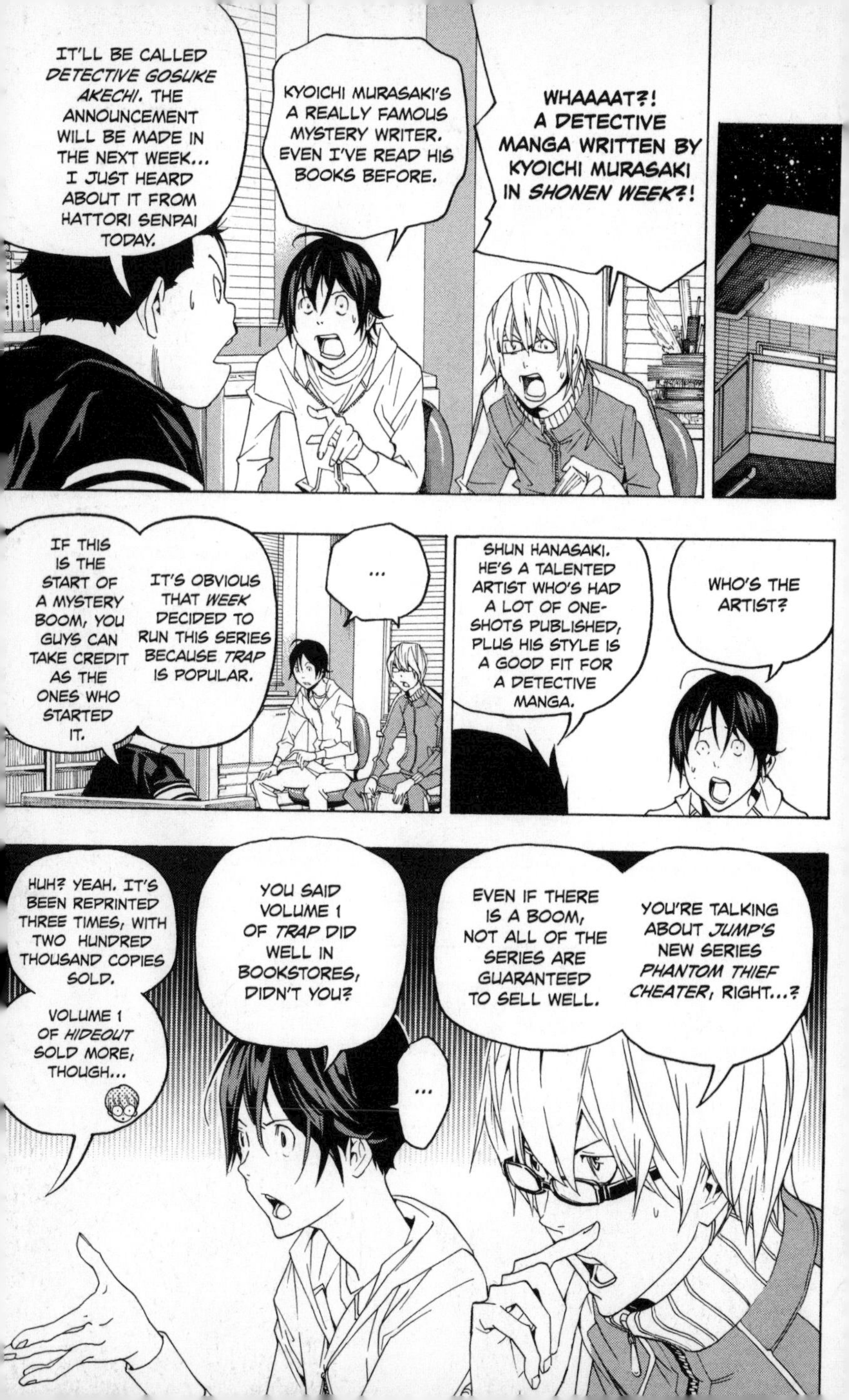
WHAAAAT?! A DETECTIVE MANGA WRITTEN BY KYOICHI MURASAKI IN SHONEN WEEK?!
KYOICHI MURASAKI'S A REALLY FAMOUS MYSTERY WRITER. EVEN I'VE READ HIS BOOKS BEFORE.
IT'LL BE CALLED DETECTIVE GOSUKE AKECHI. THE ANNOUNCEMENT WILL BE MADE IN THE NEXT WEEK... I JUST HEARD ABOUT IT FROM HATTORI SENPAI TODAY.
WHO'S THE ARTIST?
SHUN HANASAKI. HE'S A TALENTED ARTIST WHO'S HAD A LOT OF ONE-SHOTS PUBLISHED, PLUS HIS STYLE IS A GOOD FIT FOR A DETECTIVE MANGA.
...
IT'S OBVIOUS THAT WEEK DECIDED TO RUN THIS SERIES BECAUSE TRAP IS POPULAR.
IF THIS IS THE START OF A MYSTERY BOOM, YOU GUYS CAN TAKE CREDIT AS THE ONES WHO STARTED IT.
YOU'RE TALKING ABOUT JUMP'S NEW SERIES PHANTOM THIEF CHEATER, RIGHT...?
EVEN IF THERE IS A BOOM, NOT ALL OF THE SERIES ARE GUARANTEED TO SELL WELL.
...
YOU SAID VOLUME 1 OF TRAP DID WELL IN BOOKSTORES, DIDN'T YOU?
HUH? YEAH. IT'S BEEN REPRINTED THREE TIMES, WITH TWO HUNDRED THOUSAND COPIES SOLD.
VOLUME 1 OF HIDEOUT SOLD MORE, THOUGH...

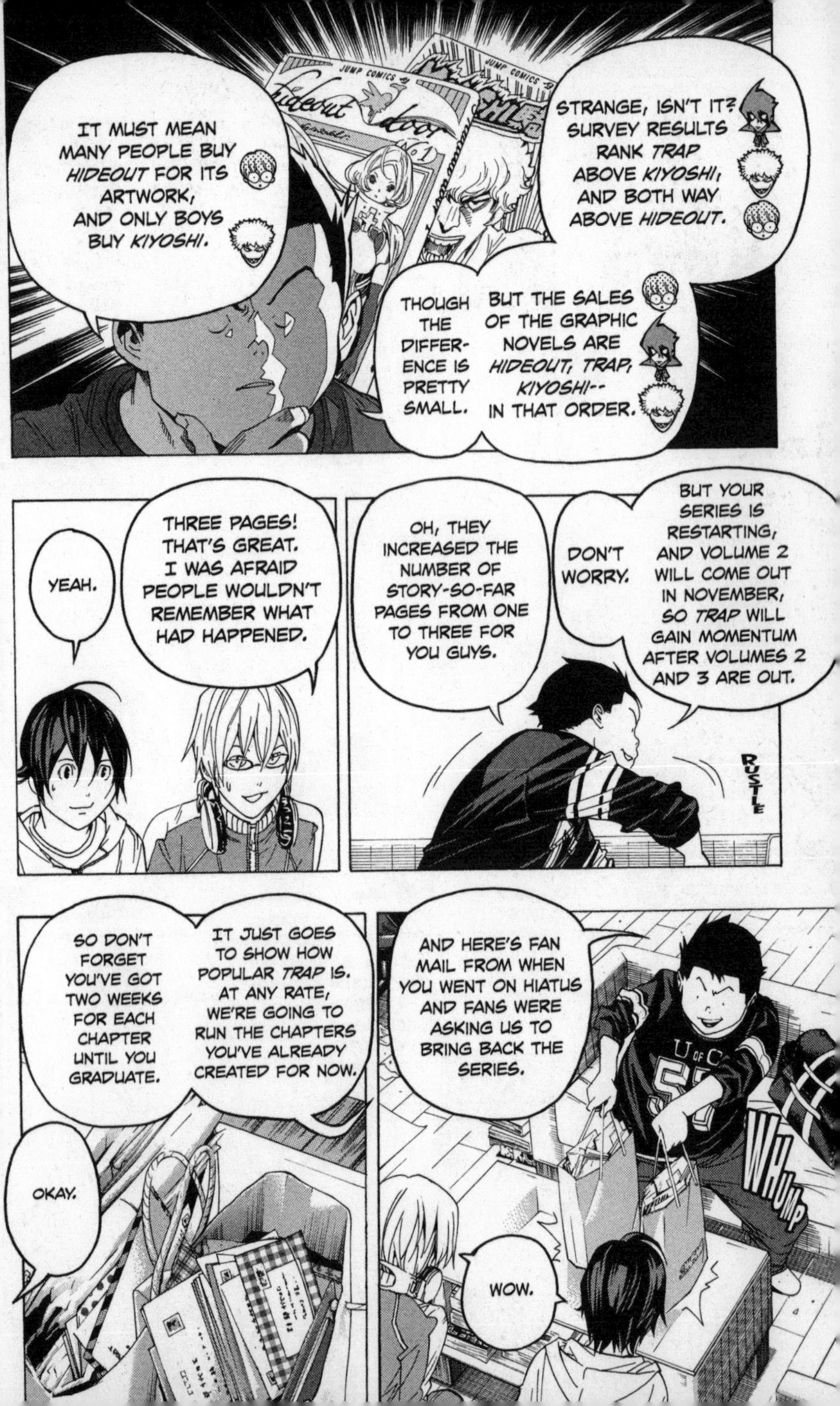
STRANGE, ISN'T IT? SURVEY RESULTS RANK TRAP ABOVE KIYOSHI, AND BOTH WAY ABOVE HIDEOUT.
BUT THE SALES OF THE GRAPHIC NOVELS ARE HIDEOUT, TRAP, KIYOSHI-- IN THAT ORDER.
THOUGH THE DIFFER-ENCE IS PRETTY SMALL.
IT MUST MEAN MANY PEOPLE BUY HIDEOUT FOR ITS ARTWORK, AND ONLY BOYS BUY KIYOSHI.
JUMP COMICS
hideout door
JUMP COMICS
BUT YOUR SERIES IS RESTARTING, AND VOLUME 2 WILL COME OUT IN NOVEMBER, SO TRAP WILL GAIN MOMENTUM AFTER VOLUMES 2 AND 3 ARE OUT.
DON'T WORRY.
OH, THEY INCREASED THE NUMBER OF STORY-SO-FAR PAGES FROM ONE TO THREE FOR YOU GUYS.
RUSTLE
THREE PAGES! THAT'S GREAT. I WAS AFRAID PEOPLE WOULDN'T REMEMBER WHAT HAD HAPPENED.
YEAH.
AND HERE'S FAN MAIL FROM WHEN YOU WENT ON HIATUS AND FANS WERE ASKING US TO BRING BACK THE SERIES.
WHUMP
WOW.
IT JUST GOES TO SHOW HOW POPULAR TRAP IS. AT ANY RATE, WE'RE GOING TO RUN THE CHAPTERS YOU'VE ALREADY CREATED FOR NOW.
SO DON'T FORGET YOU'VE GOT TWO WEEKS FOR EACH CHAPTER UNTIL YOU GRADUATE.
OKAY.

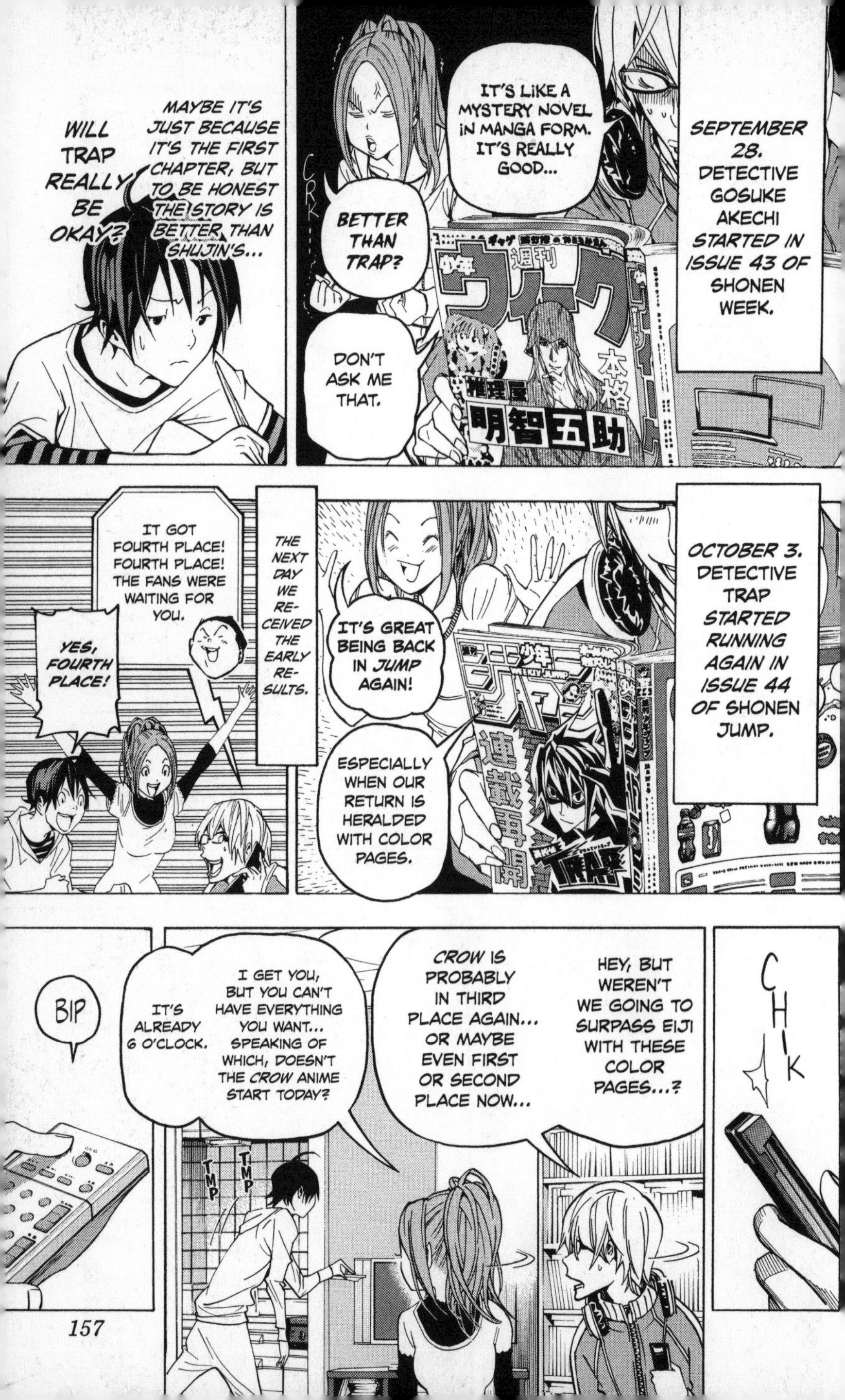
SEPTEMBER 28. DETECTIVE GOSUKE AKECHI STARTED IN ISSUE 43 OF SHONEN WEEK.
IT'S LIKE A MYSTERY NOVEL IN MANGA FORM. IT'S REALLY GOOD...
CRK
BETTER THAN TRAP?
DON'T ASK ME THAT.
週刊
少年
本格
推理屋
明智五助
MAYBE IT'S JUST BECAUSE IT'S THE FIRST CHAPTER, BUT TO BE HONEST THE STORY IS BETTER THAN SHUJIN'S...
WILL TRAP REALLY BE OKAY?
OCTOBER 3. DETECTIVE TRAP STARTED RUNNING AGAIN IN ISSUE 44 OF SHONEN JUMP.
IT'S GREAT BEING BACK IN JUMP AGAIN!
ESPECIALLY WHEN OUR RETURN IS HERALDED WITH COLOR PAGES.
少年
連載再開
THE NEXT DAY WE RECEIVED THE EARLY RESULTS.
IT GOT FOURTH PLACE! FOURTH PLACE! THE FANS WERE WAITING FOR YOU.
YES, FOURTH PLACE!
CHIK
HEY, BUT WEREN'T WE GOING TO SURPASS EIJI WITH THESE COLOR PAGES...?
CROW IS PROBABLY IN THIRD PLACE AGAIN... OR MAYBE EVEN FIRST OR SECOND PLACE NOW...
I GET YOU, BUT YOU CAN'T HAVE EVERYTHING YOU WANT... SPEAKING OF WHICH, DOESN'T THE CROW ANIME START TODAY?
IT'S ALREADY 6 O'CLOCK.
TMP TMP
BIP

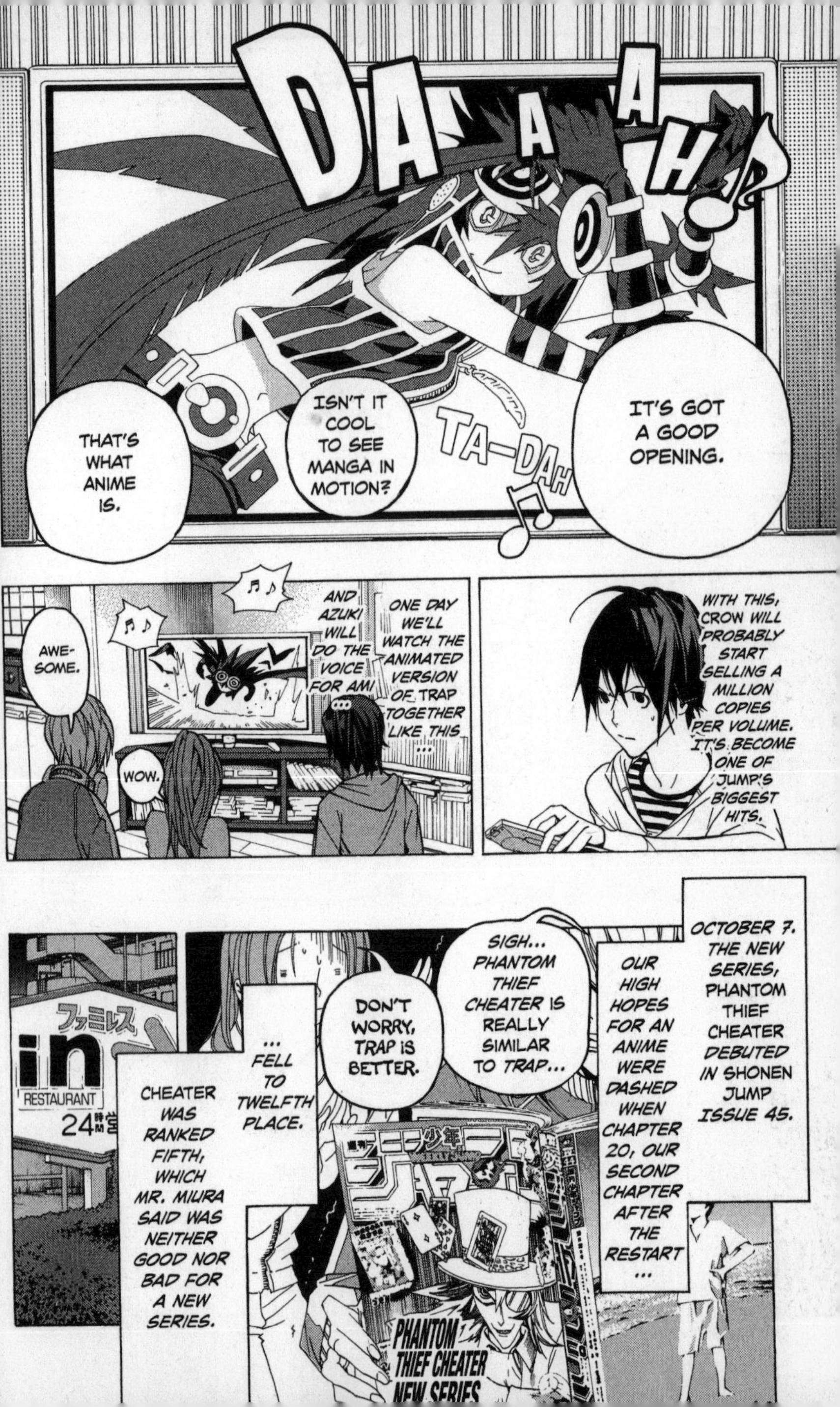
DAAAH!
IT'S GOT A GOOD OPENING.
TA-DAH
ISN'T IT COOL TO SEE MANGA IN MOTION?
THAT'S WHAT ANIME IS.
WITH THIS, CROW WILL PROBABLY START SELLING A MILLION COPIES PER VOLUME. IT'S BECOME ONE OF JUMP'S BIGGEST HITS.
ONE DAY WE'LL WATCH THE ANIMATED VERSION OF TRAP TOGETHER LIKE THIS...
AND AZUKI WILL DO THE VOICE FOR AMI
AWE-SOME.
WOW.
OCTOBER 7. THE NEW SERIES, PHANTOM THIEF CHEATER DEBUTED IN SHONEN JUMP ISSUE 45.
OUR HIGH HOPES FOR AN ANIME WERE DASHED WHEN CHAPTER 20, OUR SECOND CHAPTER AFTER THE RESTART...
SIGH... PHANTOM THIEF CHEATER IS REALLY SIMILAR TO TRAP...
DON'T WORRY, TRAP IS BETTER.
PHANTOM THIEF CHEATER NEW SERIES
...FELL TO TWELFTH PLACE.
CHEATER WAS RANKED FIFTH, WHICH MR. MIURA SAID WAS NEITHER GOOD NOR BAD FOR A NEW SERIES.
ファミレス
in
RESTAURANT

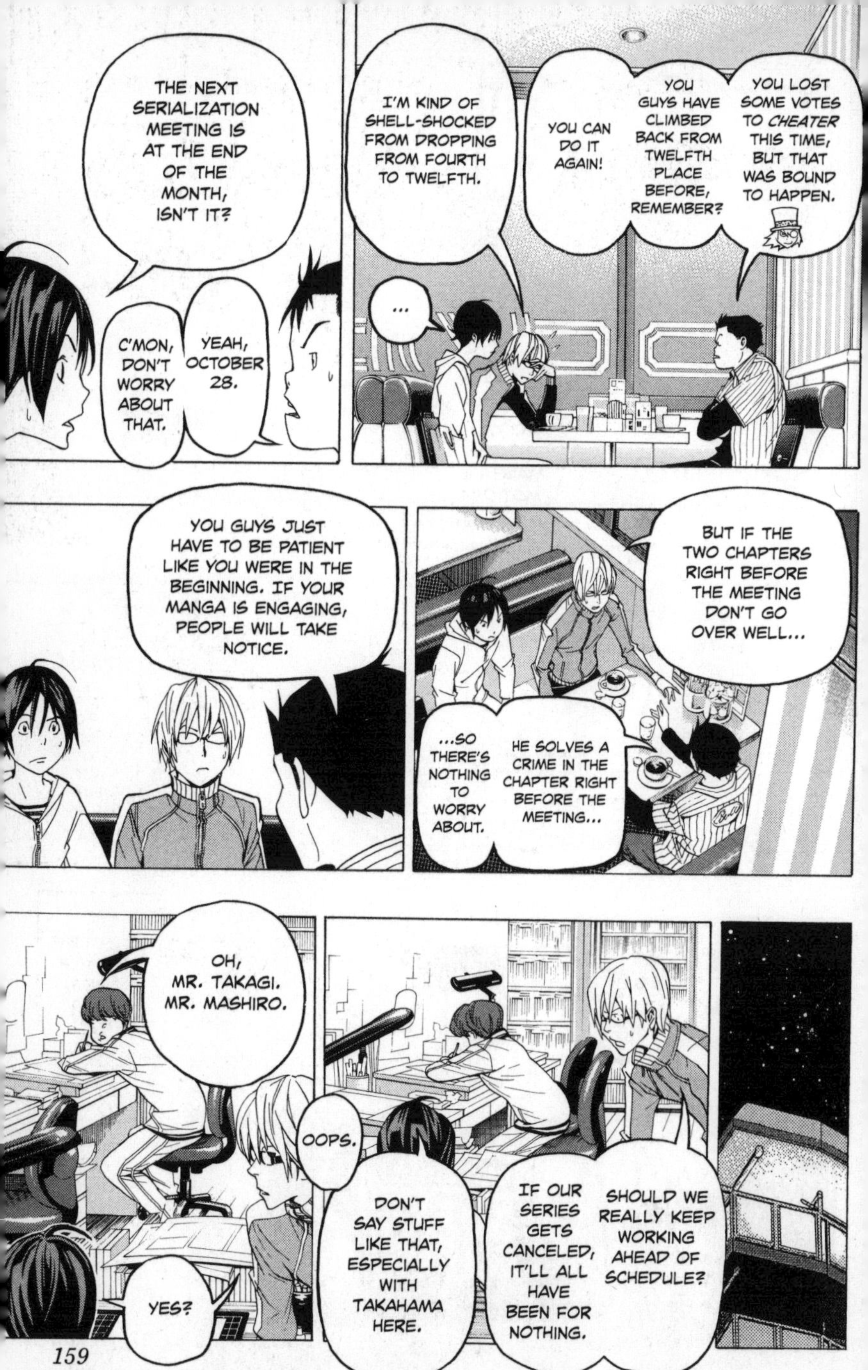
YOU LOST SOME VOTES TO *CHEATER* THIS TIME, BUT THAT WAS BOUND TO HAPPEN.
YOU GUYS HAVE CLIMBED BACK FROM TWELFTH PLACE BEFORE, REMEMBER?
YOU CAN DO IT AGAIN!
I'M KIND OF SHELL-SHOCKED FROM DROPPING FROM FOURTH TO TWELFTH.
...
THE NEXT SERIALIZATION MEETING IS AT THE END OF THE MONTH, ISN'T IT?
YEAH, OCTOBER 28.
C'MON, DON'T WORRY ABOUT THAT.
BUT IF THE TWO CHAPTERS RIGHT BEFORE THE MEETING DON'T GO OVER WELL...
HE SOLVES A CRIME IN THE CHAPTER RIGHT BEFORE THE MEETING...
...SO THERE'S NOTHING TO WORRY ABOUT.
YOU GUYS JUST HAVE TO BE PATIENT LIKE YOU WERE IN THE BEGINNING. IF YOUR MANGA IS ENGAGING, PEOPLE WILL TAKE NOTICE.
SHOULD WE REALLY KEEP WORKING AHEAD OF SCHEDULE?
IF OUR SERIES GETS CANCELED, IT'LL ALL HAVE BEEN FOR NOTHING.
DON'T SAY STUFF LIKE THAT, ESPECIALLY WITH TAKAHAMA HERE.
OOPS.
OH, MR. TAKAGI. MR. MASHIRO.
YES?

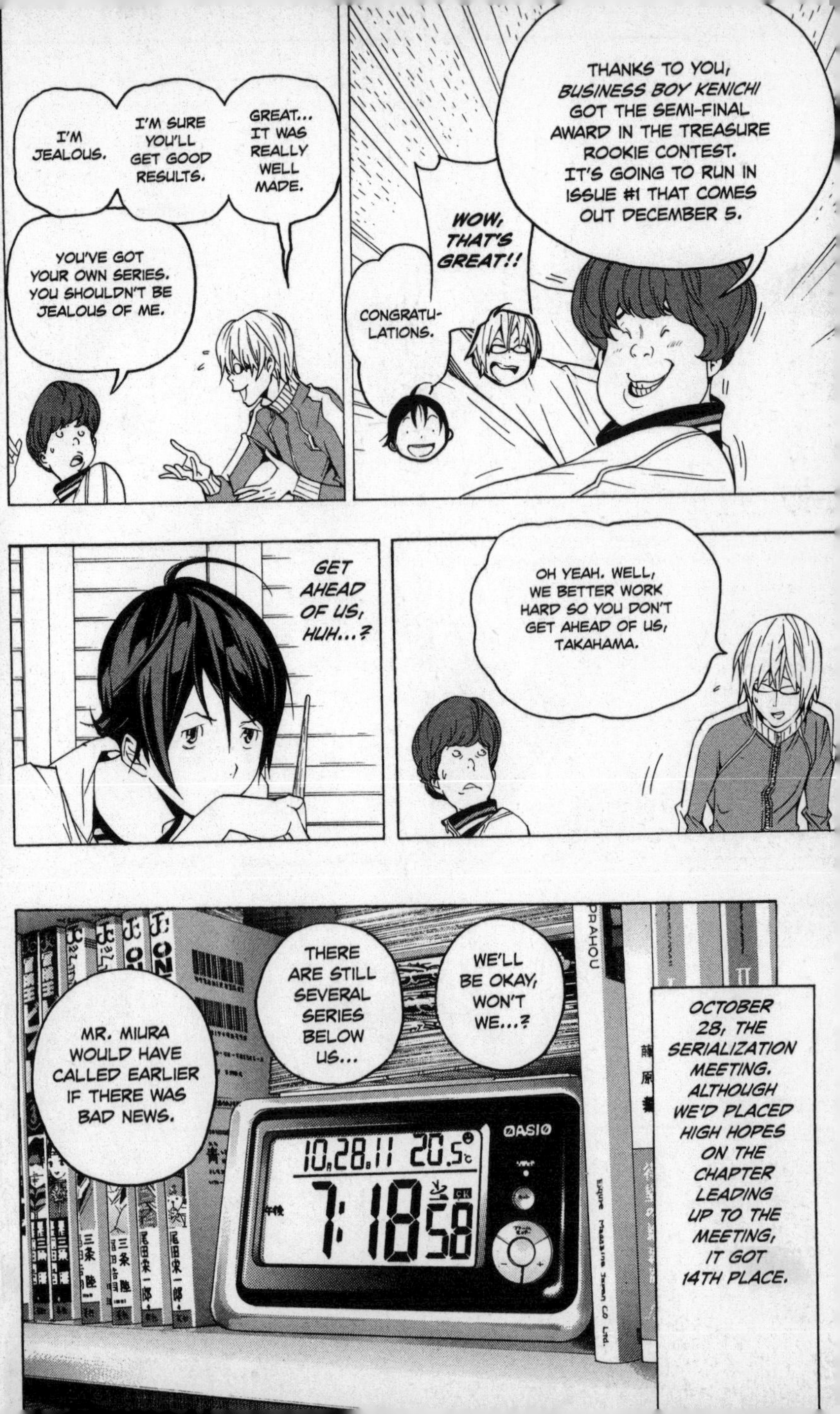
THANKS TO YOU, *BUSINESS BOY KENICHI* GOT THE SEMI-FINAL AWARD IN THE TREASURE ROOKIE CONTEST. IT'S GOING TO RUN IN ISSUE #1 THAT COMES OUT DECEMBER 5.
WOW, THAT'S GREAT!!
CONGRATU-LATIONS.
GREAT... IT WAS REALLY WELL MADE.
I'M SURE YOU'LL GET GOOD RESULTS.
I'M JEALOUS.
YOU'VE GOT YOUR OWN SERIES. YOU SHOULDN'T BE JEALOUS OF ME.
OH YEAH. WELL, WE BETTER WORK HARD SO YOU DON'T GET AHEAD OF US, TAKAHAMA.
GET AHEAD OF US, HUH...?
OCTOBER 28, THE SERIALIZATION MEETING. ALTHOUGH WE'D PLACED HIGH HOPES ON THE CHAPTER LEADING UP TO THE MEETING, IT GOT 14TH PLACE.
WE'LL BE OKAY, WON'T WE...?
THERE ARE STILL SEVERAL SERIES BELOW US...
MR. MIURA WOULD HAVE CALLED EARLIER IF THERE WAS BAD NEWS.

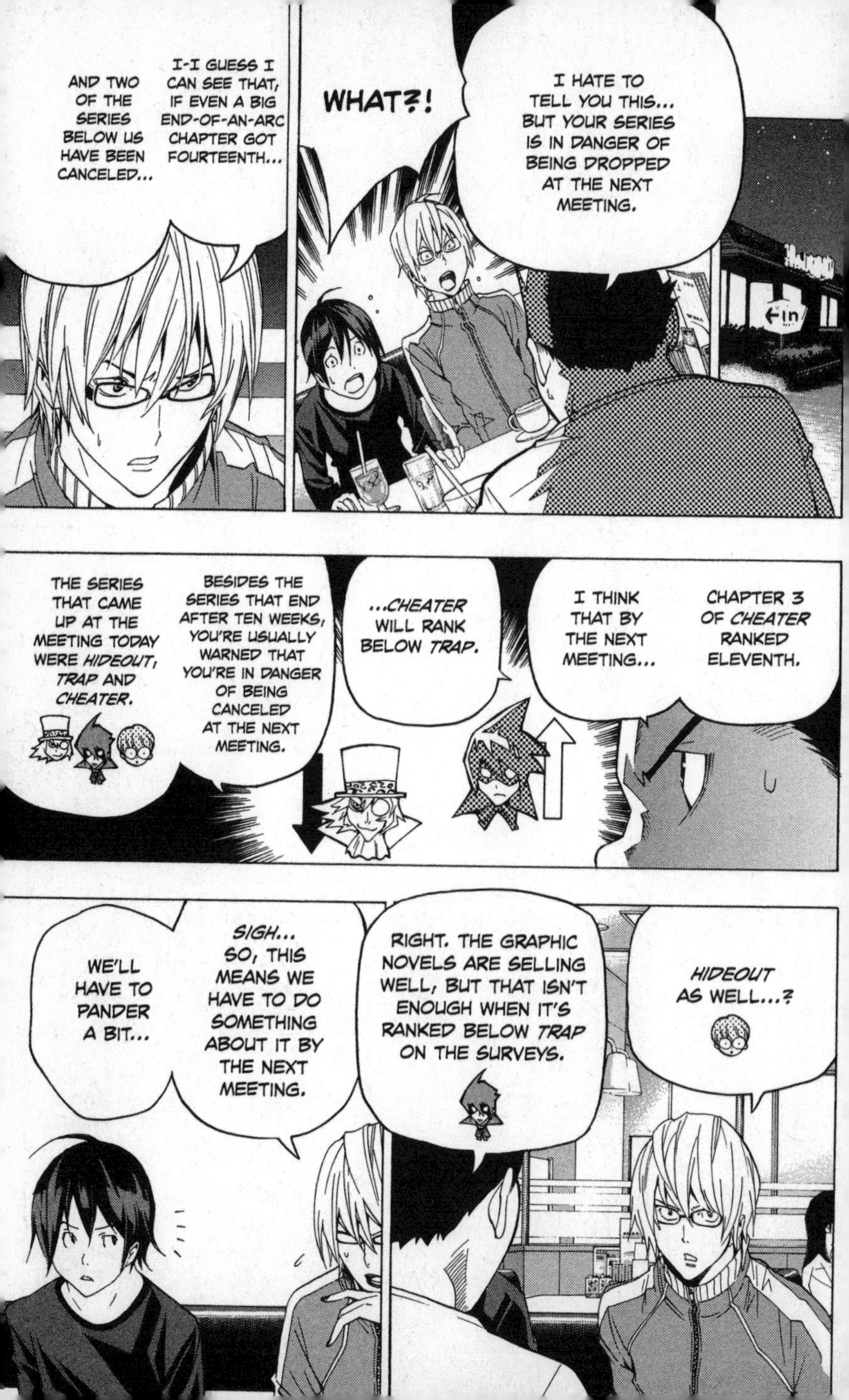
in
I HATE TO TELL YOU THIS... BUT YOUR SERIES IS IN DANGER OF BEING DROPPED AT THE NEXT MEETING.
WHAT?!
I-I GUESS I CAN SEE THAT, IF EVEN A BIG END-OF-AN-ARC CHAPTER GOT FOURTEENTH...
AND TWO OF THE SERIES BELOW US HAVE BEEN CANCELED...
CHAPTER 3 OF *CHEATER* RANKED ELEVENTH.
I THINK THAT BY THE NEXT MEETING...
...*CHEATER* WILL RANK BELOW *TRAP*.
BESIDES THE SERIES THAT END AFTER TEN WEEKS, YOU'RE USUALLY WARNED THAT YOU'RE IN DANGER OF BEING CANCELED AT THE NEXT MEETING.
THE SERIES THAT CAME UP AT THE MEETING TODAY WERE *HIDEOUT*, *TRAP* AND *CHEATER*.
HIDEOUT AS WELL...?
RIGHT. THE GRAPHIC NOVELS ARE SELLING WELL, BUT THAT ISN'T ENOUGH WHEN IT'S RANKED BELOW *TRAP* ON THE SURVEYS.
SIGH... SO, THIS MEANS WE HAVE TO DO SOMETHING ABOUT IT BY THE NEXT MEETING.
WE'LL HAVE TO PANDER A BIT...

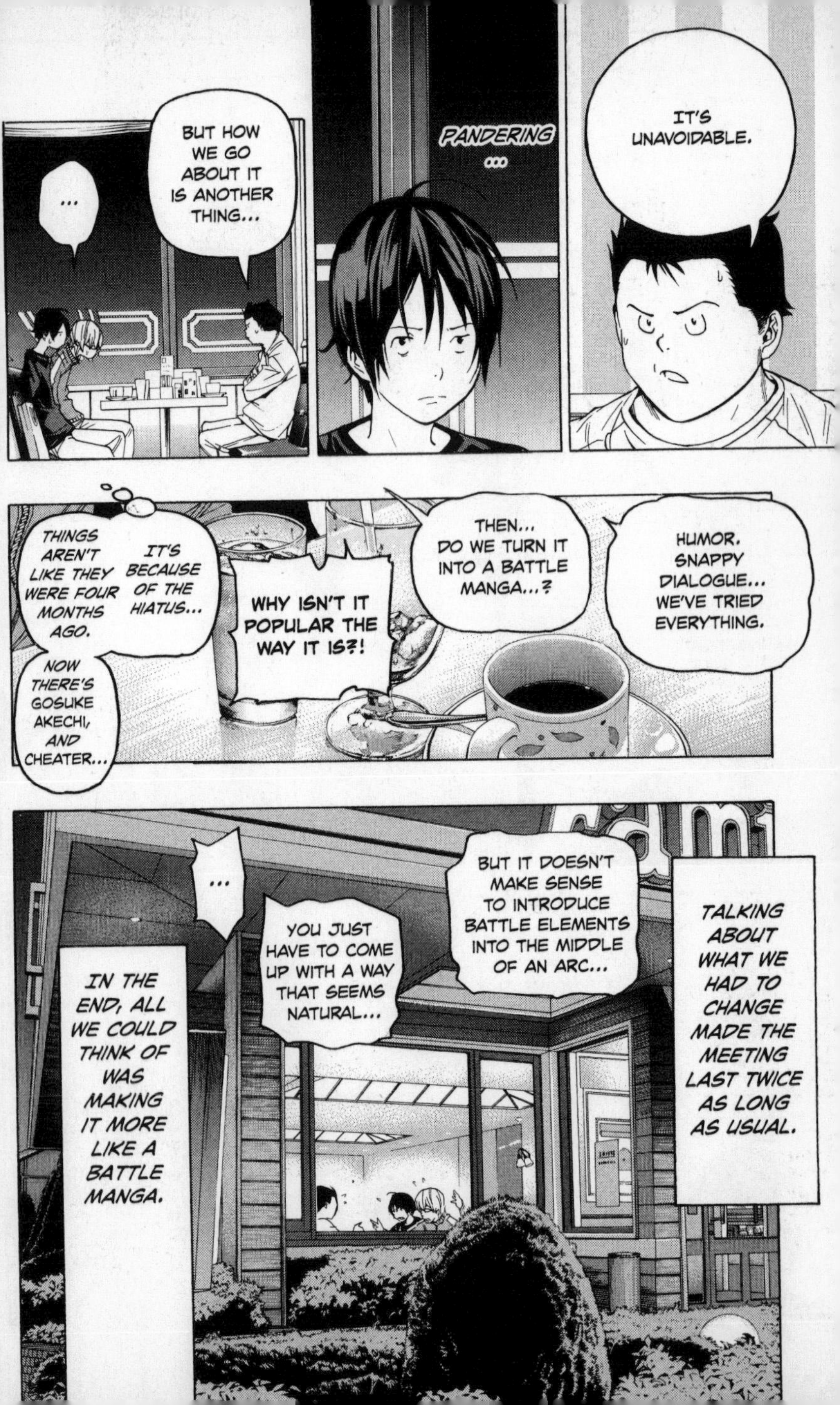
IT'S UNAVOIDABLE.
PANDERING...
BUT HOW WE GO ABOUT IT IS ANOTHER THING...
...
HUMOR. SNAPPY DIALOGUE... WE'VE TRIED EVERYTHING.
THEN... DO WE TURN IT INTO A BATTLE MANGA...?
WHY ISN'T IT POPULAR THE WAY IT IS?!
IT'S BECAUSE OF THE HIATUS...
THINGS AREN'T LIKE THEY WERE FOUR MONTHS AGO.
NOW THERE'S GOSUKE AKECHI, AND CHEATER...
TALKING ABOUT WHAT WE HAD TO CHANGE MADE THE MEETING LAST TWICE AS LONG AS USUAL.
BUT IT DOESN'T MAKE SENSE TO INTRODUCE BATTLE ELEMENTS INTO THE MIDDLE OF AN ARC...
...
YOU JUST HAVE TO COME UP WITH A WAY THAT SEEMS NATURAL...
IN THE END, ALL WE COULD THINK OF WAS MAKING IT MORE LIKE A BATTLE MANGA.

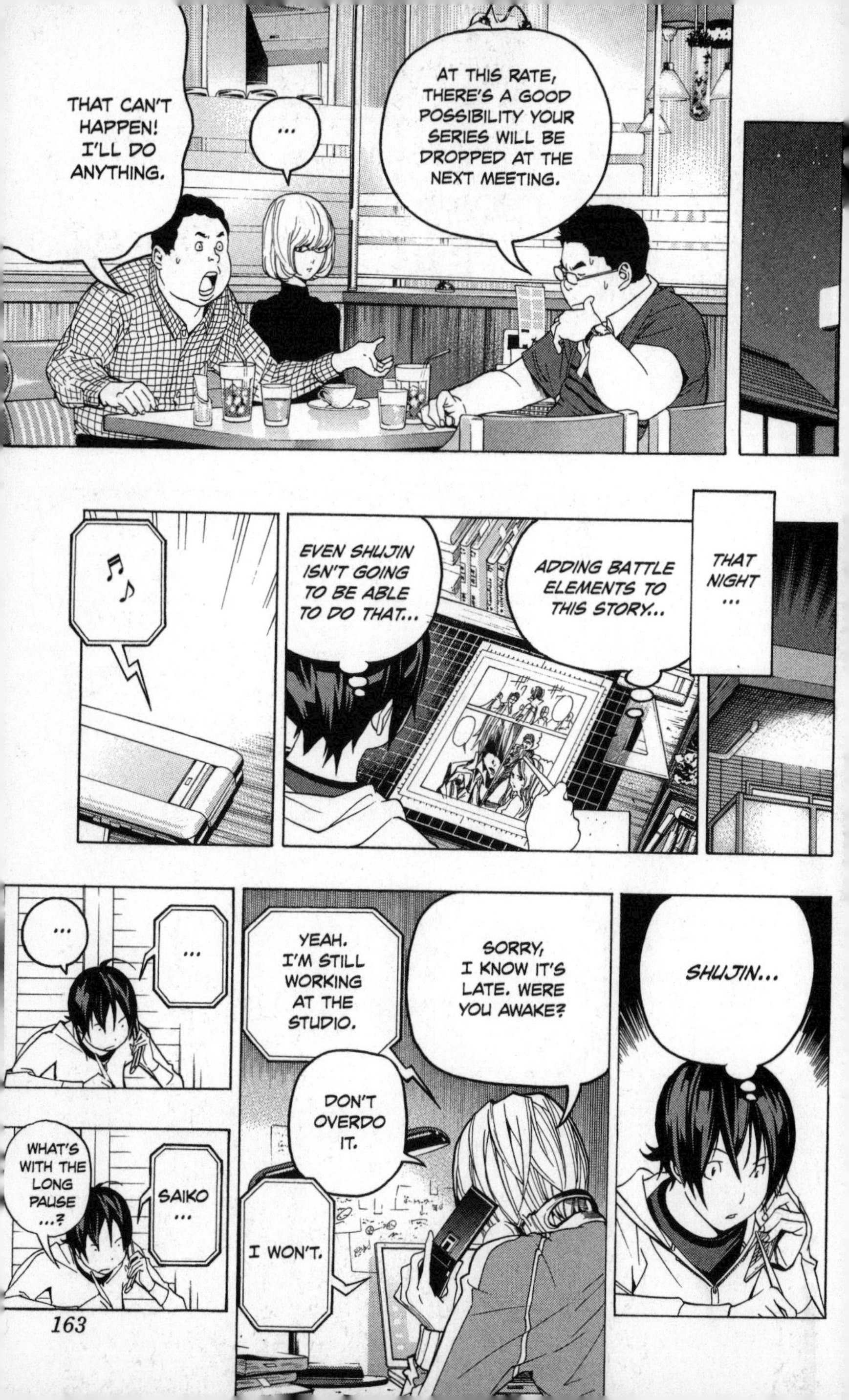
AT THIS RATE, THERE'S A GOOD POSSIBILITY YOUR SERIES WILL BE DROPPED AT THE NEXT MEETING.
...
THAT CAN'T HAPPEN! I'LL DO ANYTHING.
THAT NIGHT ...
ADDING BATTLE ELEMENTS TO THIS STORY...
EVEN SHUJIN ISN'T GOING TO BE ABLE TO DO THAT...
♫ ♪
SHUJIN...
SORRY, I KNOW IT'S LATE. WERE YOU AWAKE?
YEAH. I'M STILL WORKING AT THE STUDIO.
DON'T OVERDO IT.
I WON'T.
...
...
SAIKO ...
WHAT'S WITH THE LONG PAUSE ...?

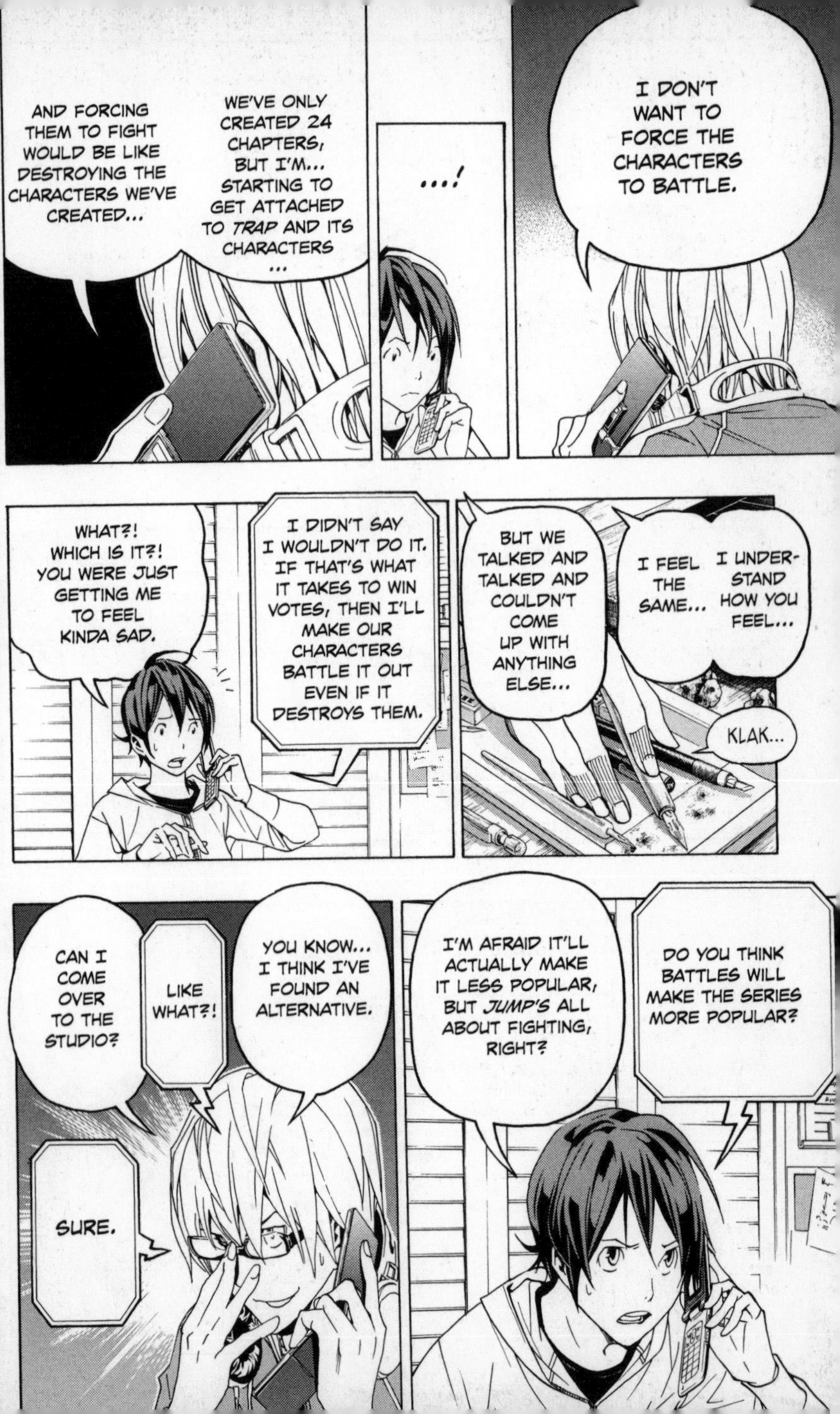
I DON'T WANT TO FORCE THE CHARACTERS TO BATTLE.
...!
WE'VE ONLY CREATED 24 CHAPTERS, BUT I'M... STARTING TO GET ATTACHED TO *TRAP* AND ITS CHARACTERS...
AND FORCING THEM TO FIGHT WOULD BE LIKE DESTROYING THE CHARACTERS WE'VE CREATED...
I UNDER-STAND HOW YOU FEEL...
I FEEL THE SAME...
BUT WE TALKED AND TALKED AND COULDN'T COME UP WITH ANYTHING ELSE...
KLAK...
I DIDN'T SAY I WOULDN'T DO IT. IF THAT'S WHAT IT TAKES TO WIN VOTES, THEN I'LL MAKE OUR CHARACTERS BATTLE IT OUT EVEN IF IT DESTROYS THEM.
WHAT?! WHICH IS IT?! YOU WERE JUST GETTING ME TO FEEL KINDA SAD.
DO YOU THINK BATTLES WILL MAKE THE SERIES MORE POPULAR?
I'M AFRAID IT'LL ACTUALLY MAKE IT LESS POPULAR, BUT *JUMP'S* ALL ABOUT FIGHTING, RIGHT?
YOU KNOW... I THINK I'VE FOUND AN ALTERNATIVE.
LIKE WHAT?!
CAN I COME OVER TO THE STUDIO?
SURE.

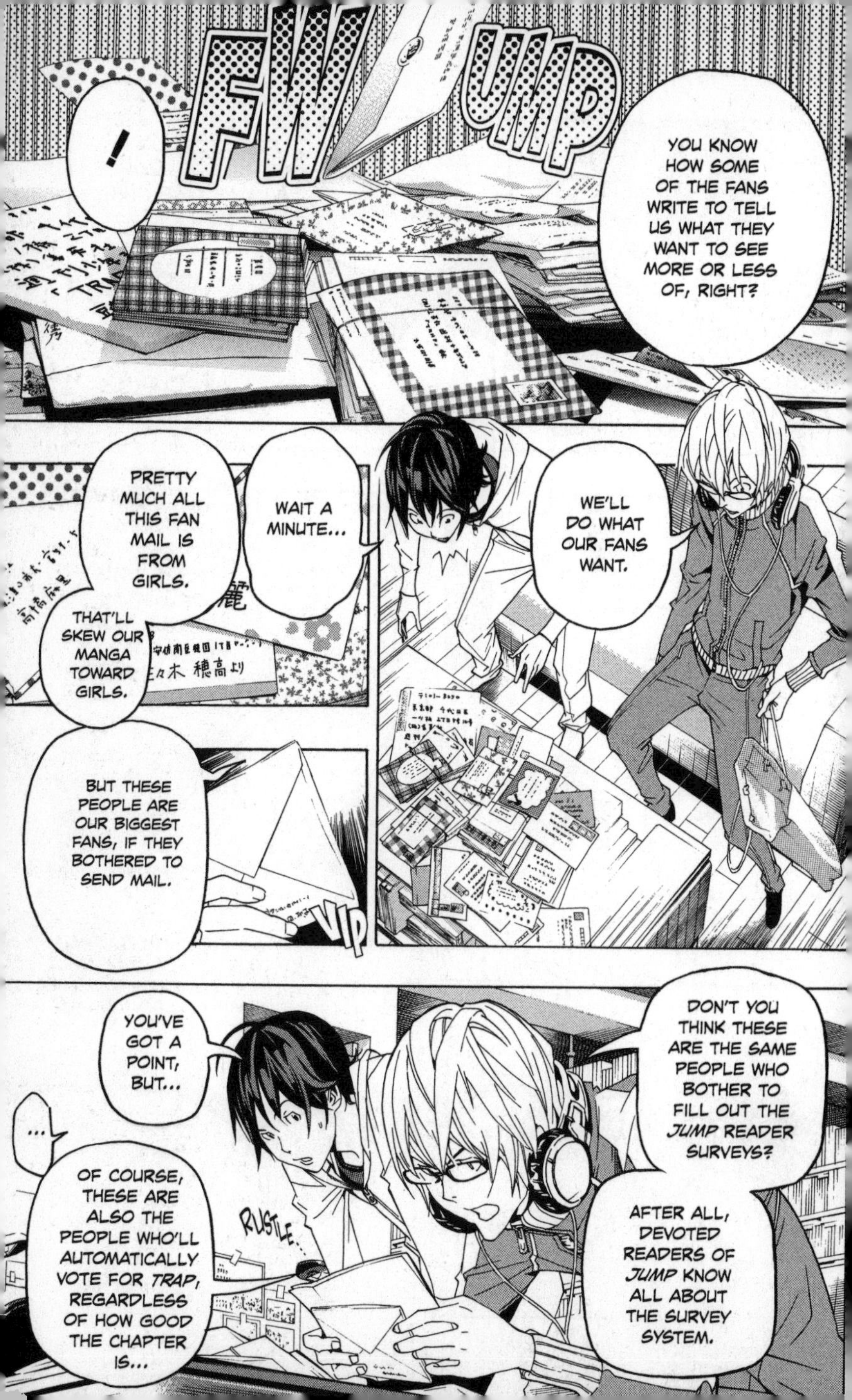
YOU KNOW HOW SOME OF THE FANS WRITE TO TELL US WHAT THEY WANT TO SEE MORE OR LESS OF, RIGHT?
FWUMP
!
WE'LL DO WHAT OUR FANS WANT.
WAIT A MINUTE...
PRETTY MUCH ALL THIS FAN MAIL IS FROM GIRLS.
THAT'LL SKEW OUR MANGA TOWARD GIRLS.
BUT THESE PEOPLE ARE OUR BIGGEST FANS, IF THEY BOTHERED TO SEND MAIL.
VIP
DON'T YOU THINK THESE ARE THE SAME PEOPLE WHO BOTHER TO FILL OUT THE *JUMP* READER SURVEYS?
AFTER ALL, DEVOTED READERS OF *JUMP* KNOW ALL ABOUT THE SURVEY SYSTEM.
YOU'VE GOT A POINT, BUT...
...
OF COURSE, THESE ARE ALSO THE PEOPLE WHO'LL AUTOMATICALLY VOTE FOR *TRAP*, REGARDLESS OF HOW GOOD THE CHAPTER IS...
RUSTLE...

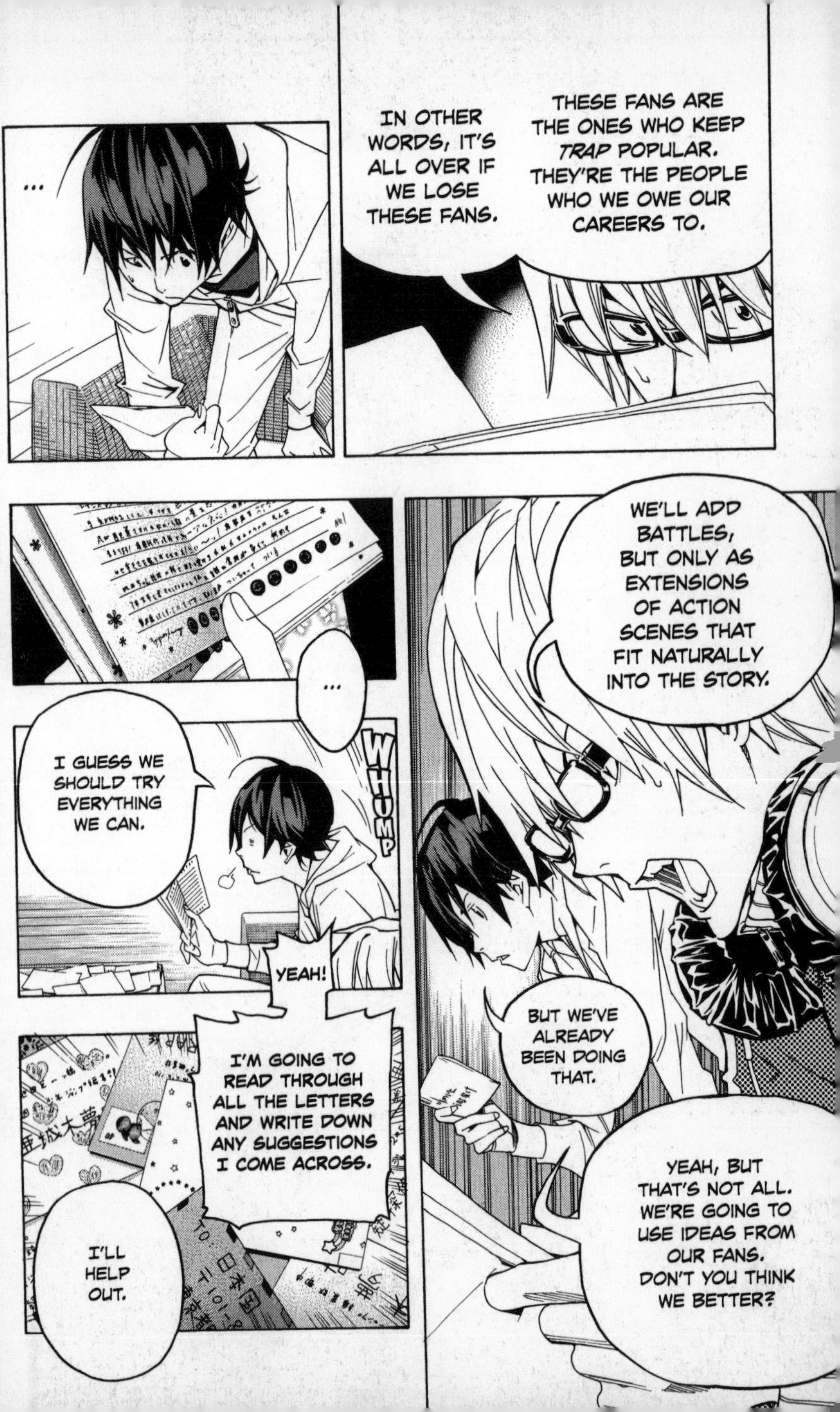
THESE FANS ARE THE ONES WHO KEEP *TRAP* POPULAR. THEY'RE THE PEOPLE WHO WE OWE OUR CAREERS TO.
IN OTHER WORDS, IT'S ALL OVER IF WE LOSE THESE FANS.
...
WE'LL ADD BATTLES, BUT ONLY AS EXTENSIONS OF ACTION SCENES THAT FIT NATURALLY INTO THE STORY.
BUT WE'VE ALREADY BEEN DOING THAT.
YEAH, BUT THAT'S NOT ALL. WE'RE GOING TO USE IDEAS FROM OUR FANS. DON'T YOU THINK WE BETTER?
...
I GUESS WE SHOULD TRY EVERYTHING WE CAN.
WHUMP
YEAH!
I'M GOING TO READ THROUGH ALL THE LETTERS AND WRITE DOWN ANY SUGGESTIONS I COME ACROSS.
I'LL HELP OUT.

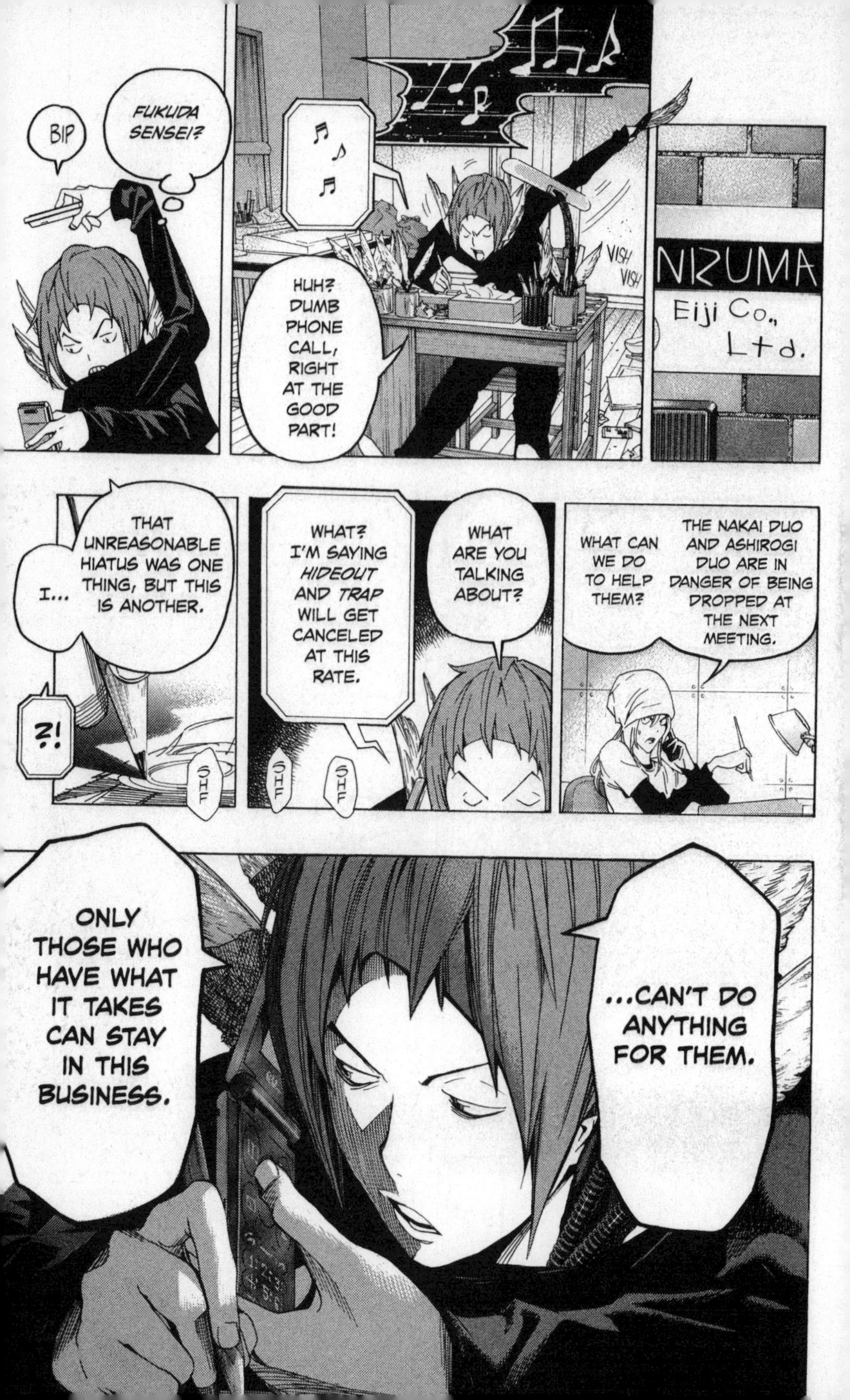
NIZUMA
Eiji Co., Ltd.
♬ ♪ ♬
VISH VISH
HUH? DUMB PHONE CALL, RIGHT AT THE GOOD PART!
FUKUDA SENSEI?
BIP
THE NAKAI DUO AND ASHIROGI DUO ARE IN DANGER OF BEING DROPPED AT THE NEXT MEETING.
WHAT CAN WE DO TO HELP THEM?
WHAT ARE YOU TALKING ABOUT?
WHAT? I'M SAYING *HIDEOUT* AND *TRAP* WILL GET CANCELED AT THIS RATE.
SHF
SHF
THAT UNREASONABLE HIATUS WAS ONE THING, BUT THIS IS ANOTHER.
I...
?!
SHF
...CAN'T DO ANYTHING FOR THEM.
ONLY THOSE WHO HAVE WHAT IT TAKES CAN STAY IN THIS BUSINESS.

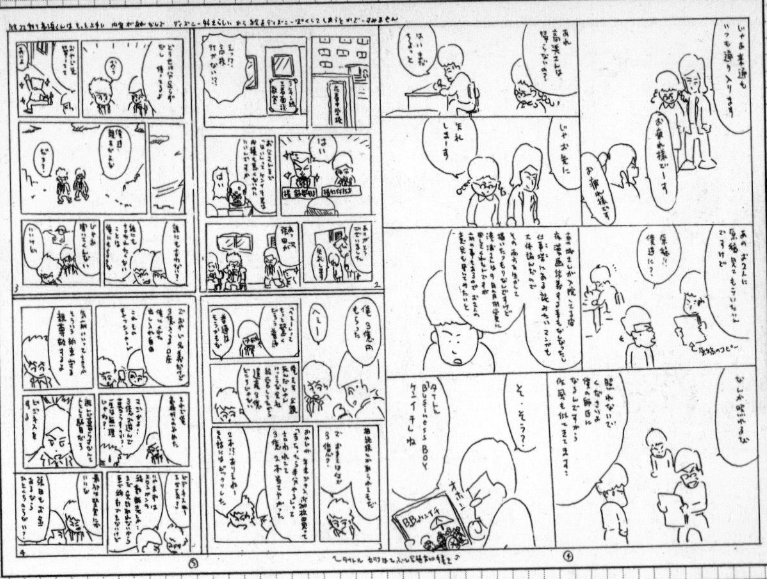

OHBA'S STORYBOARD

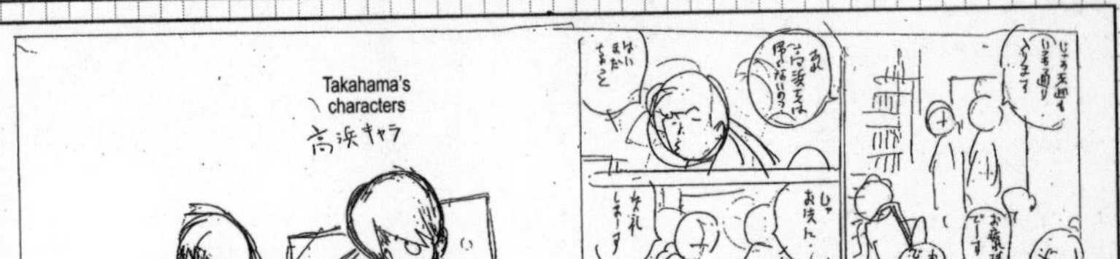
Takahama's characters
高浜キャラ

OBATA'S STORYBOARD

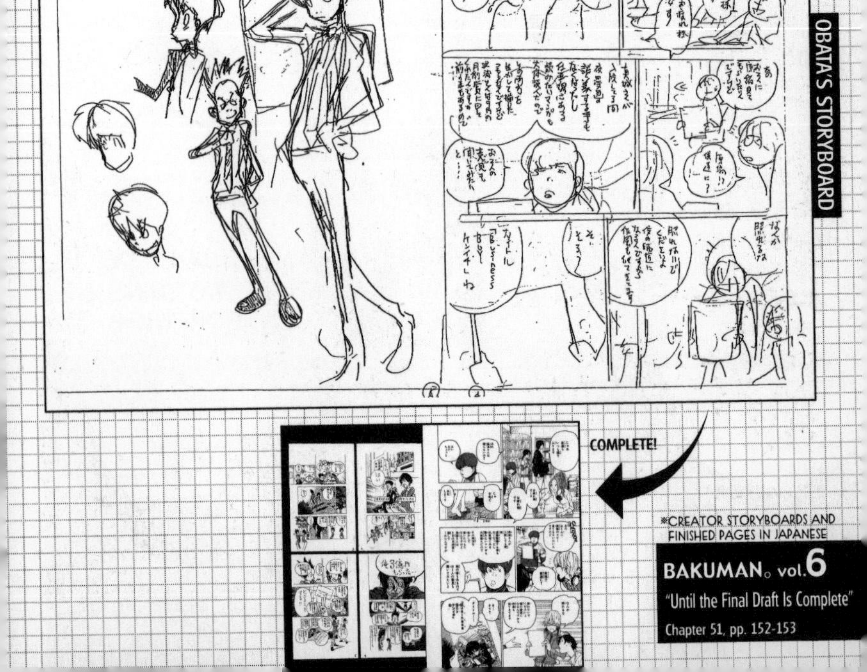

COMPLETE!

※CREATOR STORYBOARDS AND FINISHED PAGES IN JAPANESE

BAKUMAN。 vol.6

"Until the Final Draft Is Complete"

Chapter 51, pp. 152-153

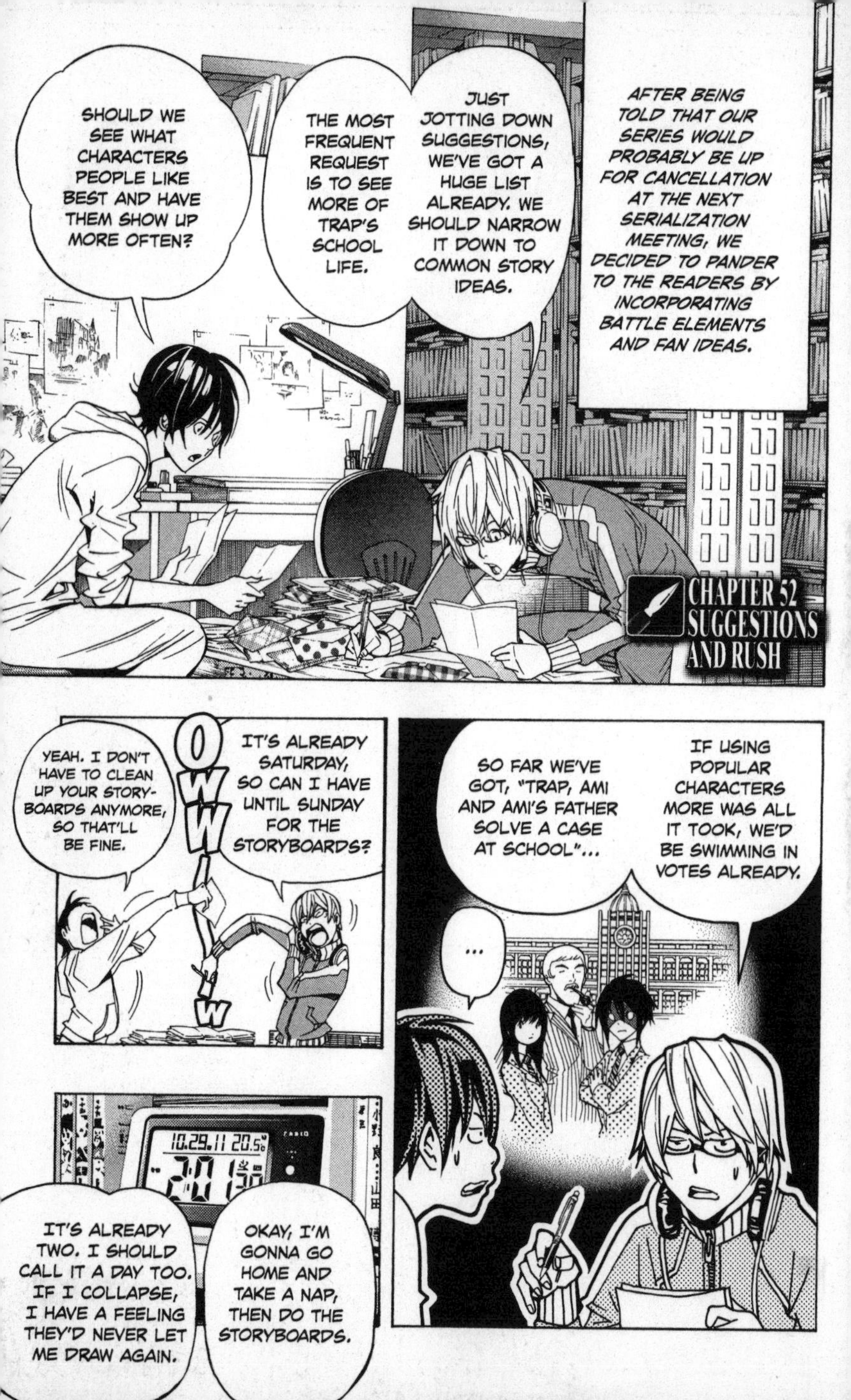
AFTER BEING TOLD THAT OUR SERIES WOULD PROBABLY BE UP FOR CANCELLATION AT THE NEXT SERIALIZATION MEETING, WE DECIDED TO PANDER TO THE READERS BY INCORPORATING BATTLE ELEMENTS AND FAN IDEAS.
JUST JOTTING DOWN SUGGESTIONS, WE'VE GOT A HUGE LIST ALREADY. WE SHOULD NARROW IT DOWN TO COMMON STORY IDEAS.
THE MOST FREQUENT REQUEST IS TO SEE MORE OF TRAP'S SCHOOL LIFE.
SHOULD WE SEE WHAT CHARACTERS PEOPLE LIKE BEST AND HAVE THEM SHOW UP MORE OFTEN?
CHAPTER 52 SUGGESTIONS AND RUSH
IF USING POPULAR CHARACTERS MORE WAS ALL IT TOOK, WE'D BE SWIMMING IN VOTES ALREADY.
SO FAR WE'VE GOT, "TRAP, AMI AND AMI'S FATHER SOLVE A CASE AT SCHOOL"...
...
IT'S ALREADY SATURDAY, SO CAN I HAVE UNTIL SUNDAY FOR THE STORYBOARDS?
OWWW
YEAH. I DON'T HAVE TO CLEAN UP YOUR STORY-BOARDS ANYMORE, SO THAT'LL BE FINE.
OKAY, I'M GONNA GO HOME AND TAKE A NAP, THEN DO THE STORYBOARDS.
IT'S ALREADY TWO. I SHOULD CALL IT A DAY TOO. IF I COLLAPSE, I HAVE A FEELING THEY'D NEVER LET ME DRAW AGAIN.

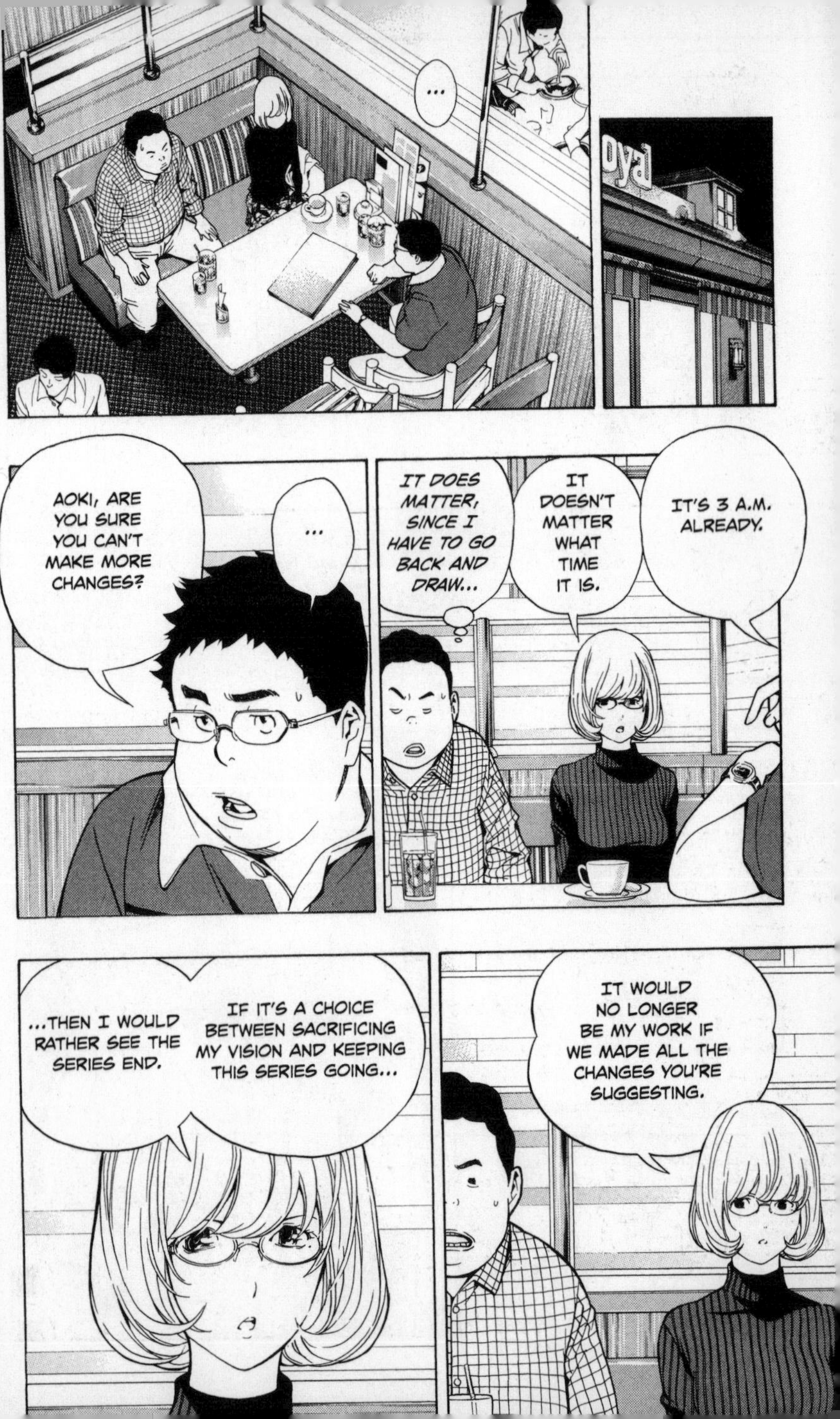
...
IT'S 3 A.M. ALREADY.
IT DOESN'T MATTER WHAT TIME IT IS.
IT DOES MATTER, SINCE I HAVE TO GO BACK AND DRAW...
...
AOKI, ARE YOU SURE YOU CAN'T MAKE MORE CHANGES?
IT WOULD NO LONGER BE MY WORK IF WE MADE ALL THE CHANGES YOU'RE SUGGESTING.
IF IT'S A CHOICE BETWEEN SACRIFICING MY VISION AND KEEPING THIS SERIES GOING...
...THEN I WOULD RATHER SEE THE SERIES END.

READ THIS WAY

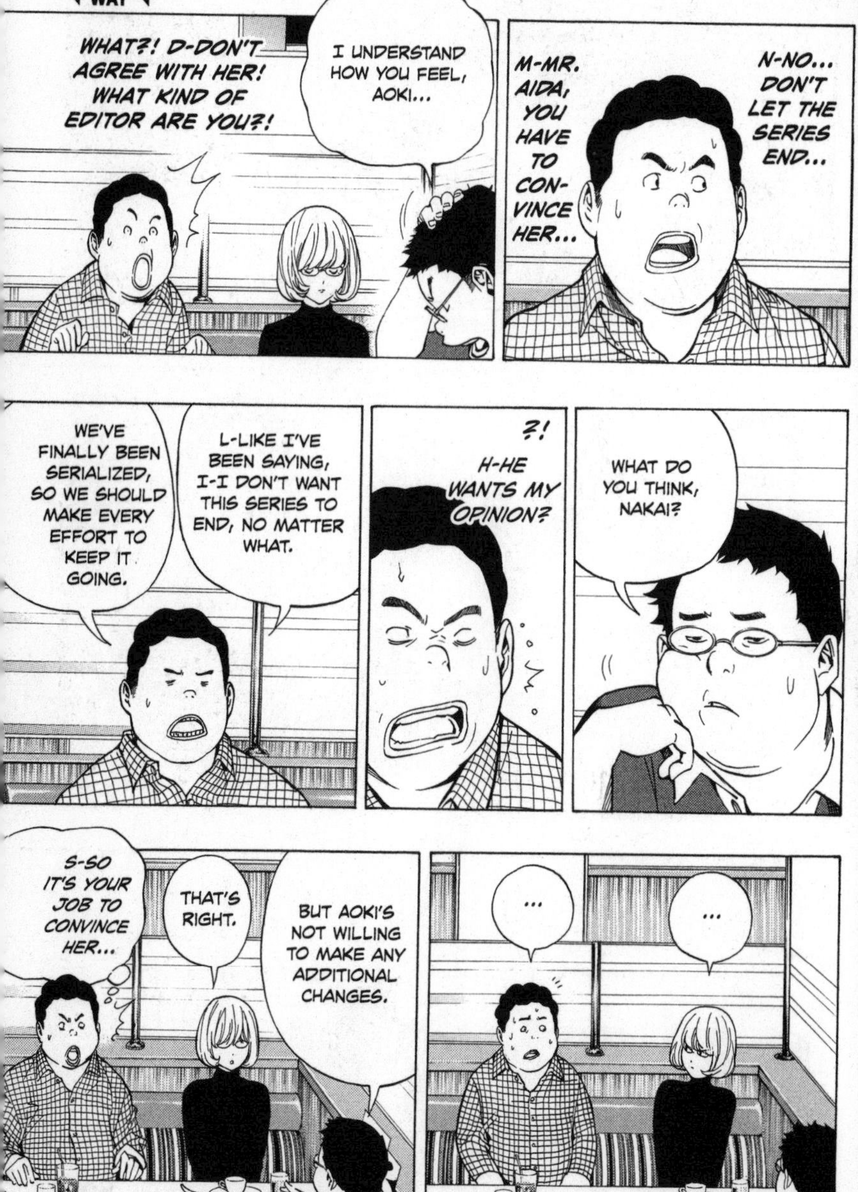
N-NO... DON'T LET THE SERIES END...
M-MR. AIDA, YOU HAVE TO CONVINCE HER...
I UNDERSTAND HOW YOU FEEL, AOKI...
WHAT?! D-DON'T AGREE WITH HER! WHAT KIND OF EDITOR ARE YOU?!
WHAT DO YOU THINK, NAKAI?
?!
H-HE WANTS MY OPINION?
L-LIKE I'VE BEEN SAYING, I-I DON'T WANT THIS SERIES TO END, NO MATTER WHAT.
WE'VE FINALLY BEEN SERIALIZED, SO WE SHOULD MAKE EVERY EFFORT TO KEEP IT GOING.
...
...
BUT AOKI'S NOT WILLING TO MAKE ANY ADDITIONAL CHANGES.
THAT'S RIGHT.
S-SO IT'S YOUR JOB TO CONVINCE HER...

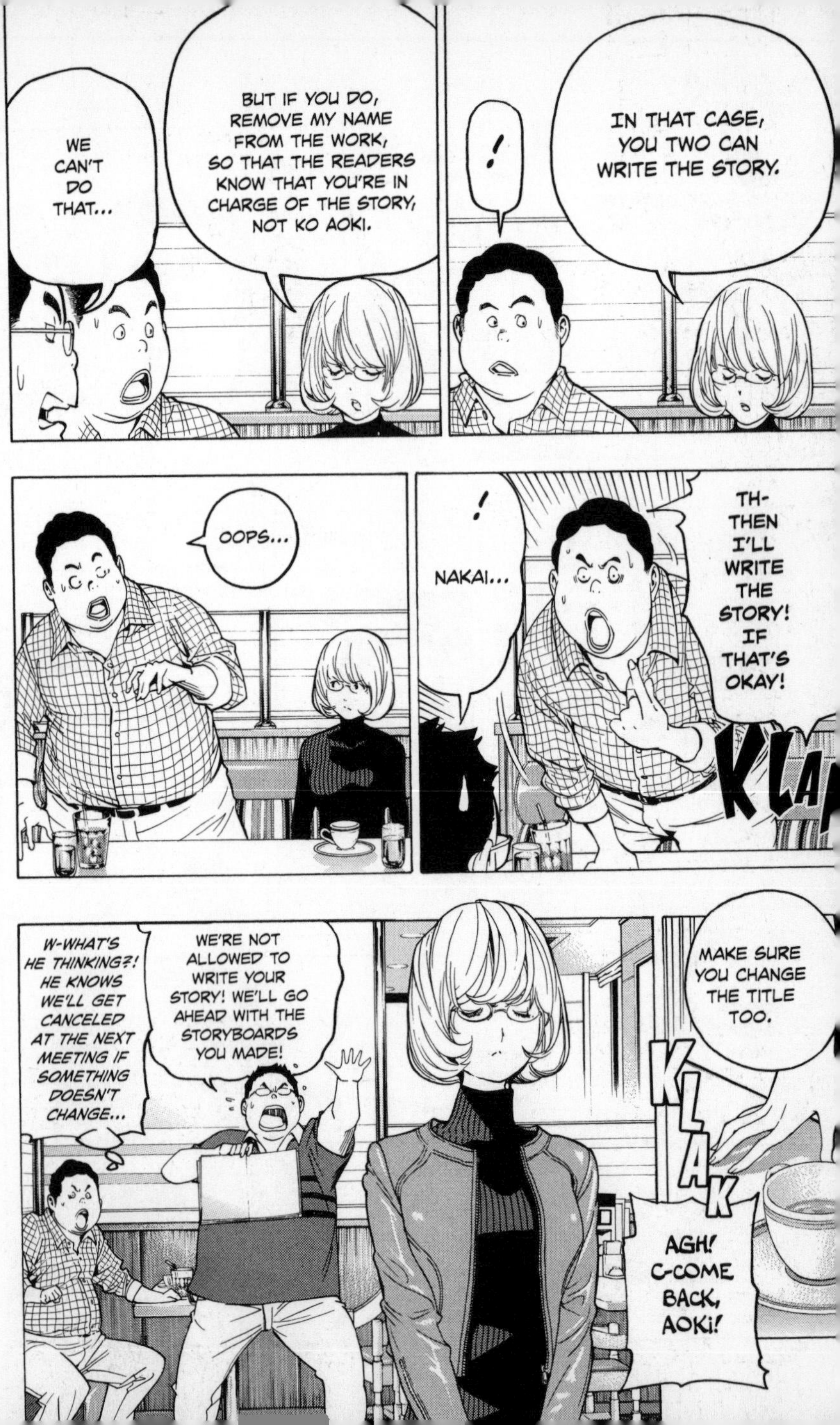
IN THAT CASE, YOU TWO CAN WRITE THE STORY.
!
BUT IF YOU DO, REMOVE MY NAME FROM THE WORK, SO THAT THE READERS KNOW THAT YOU'RE IN CHARGE OF THE STORY, NOT KO AOKI.
WE CAN'T DO THAT...
TH-THEN I'LL WRITE THE STORY! IF THAT'S OKAY!
!
NAKAI...
KLA
OOPS...
MAKE SURE YOU CHANGE THE TITLE TOO.
KLAK
AGH! C-COME BACK, AOKI!
WE'RE NOT ALLOWED TO WRITE YOUR STORY! WE'LL GO AHEAD WITH THE STORYBOARDS YOU MADE!
W-WHAT'S HE THINKING?! HE KNOWS WE'LL GET CANCELED AT THE NEXT MEETING IF SOMETHING DOESN'T CHANGE...

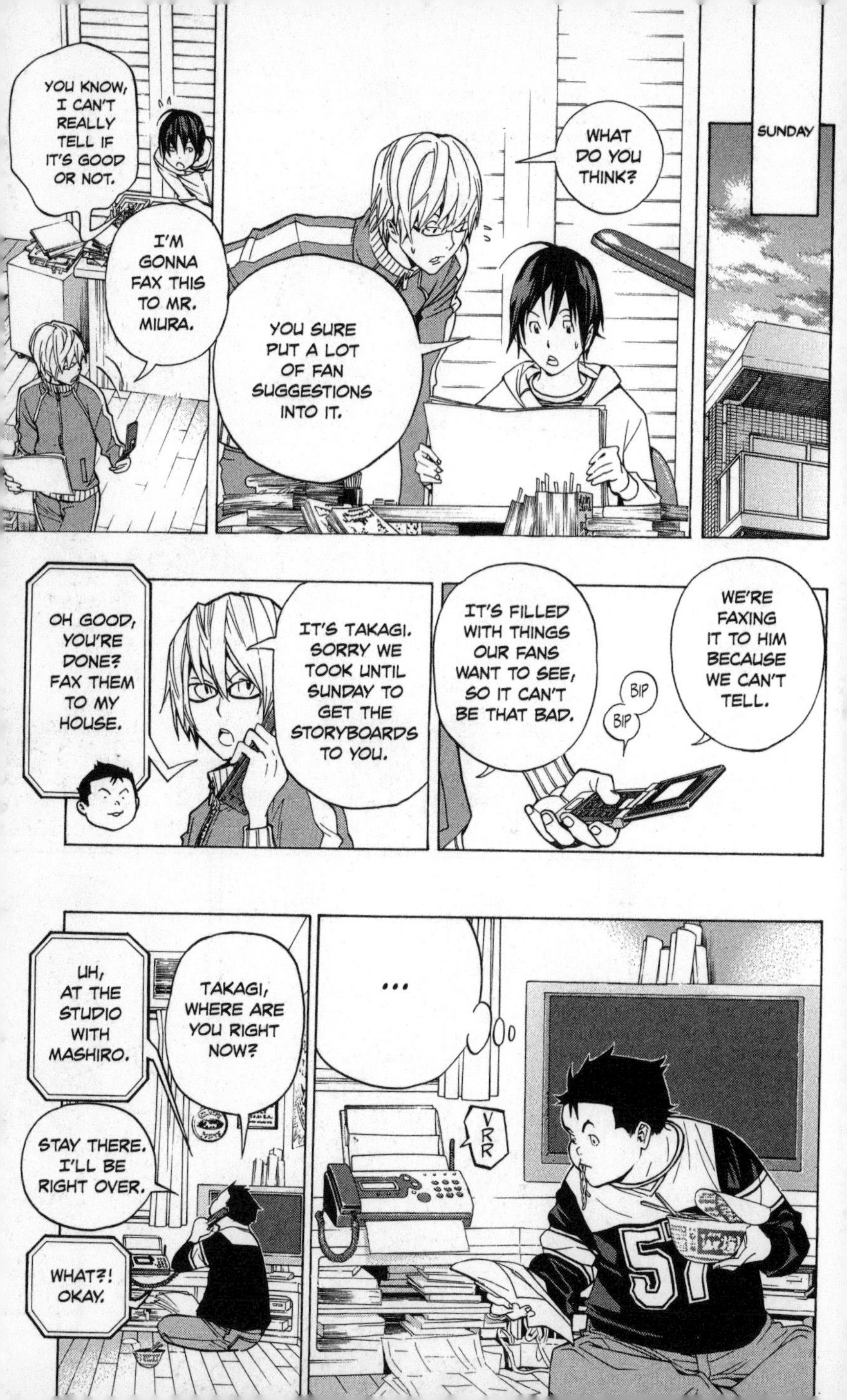
SUNDAY
WHAT DO YOU THINK?
YOU SURE PUT A LOT OF FAN SUGGESTIONS INTO IT.
YOU KNOW, I CAN'T REALLY TELL IF IT'S GOOD OR NOT.
I'M GONNA FAX THIS TO MR. MIURA.
WE'RE FAXING IT TO HIM BECAUSE WE CAN'T TELL.
BIP
BIP
IT'S FILLED WITH THINGS OUR FANS WANT TO SEE, SO IT CAN'T BE THAT BAD.
IT'S TAKAGI. SORRY WE TOOK UNTIL SUNDAY TO GET THE STORYBOARDS TO YOU.
OH GOOD, YOU'RE DONE? FAX THEM TO MY HOUSE.
...
VRR
TAKAGI, WHERE ARE YOU RIGHT NOW?
UH, AT THE STUDIO WITH MASHIRO.
STAY THERE. I'LL BE RIGHT OVER.
WHAT?! OKAY.

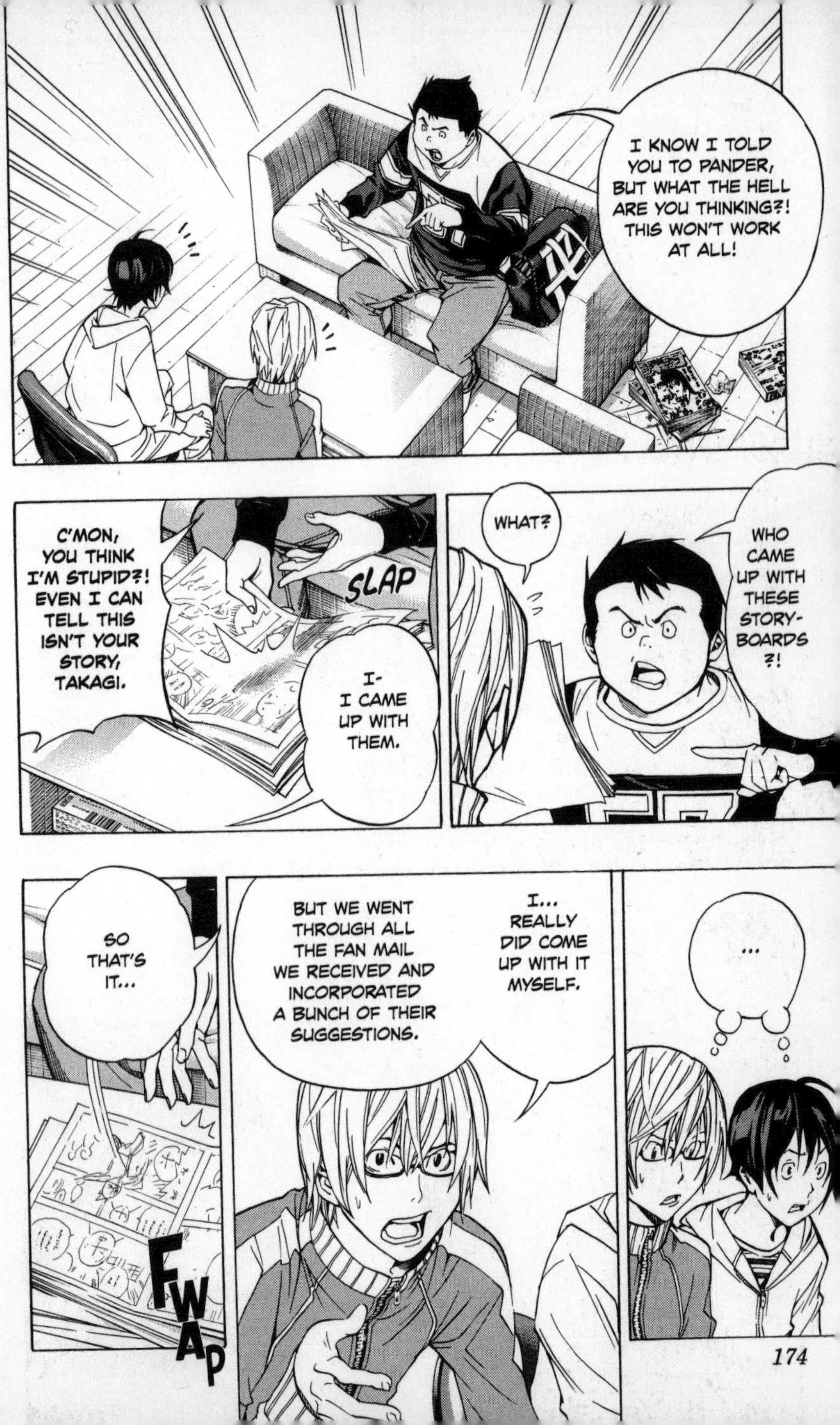
I KNOW I TOLD YOU TO PANDER, BUT WHAT THE HELL ARE YOU THINKING?! THIS WON'T WORK AT ALL!
WHO CAME UP WITH THESE STORY-BOARDS?!
WHAT?
I- I CAME UP WITH THEM.
C'MON, YOU THINK I'M STUPID?! EVEN I CAN TELL THIS ISN'T YOUR STORY, TAKAGI.
SLAP
...
I... REALLY DID COME UP WITH IT MYSELF.
BUT WE WENT THROUGH ALL THE FAN MAIL WE RECEIVED AND INCORPORATED A BUNCH OF THEIR SUGGESTIONS.
SO THAT'S IT...
FWAP

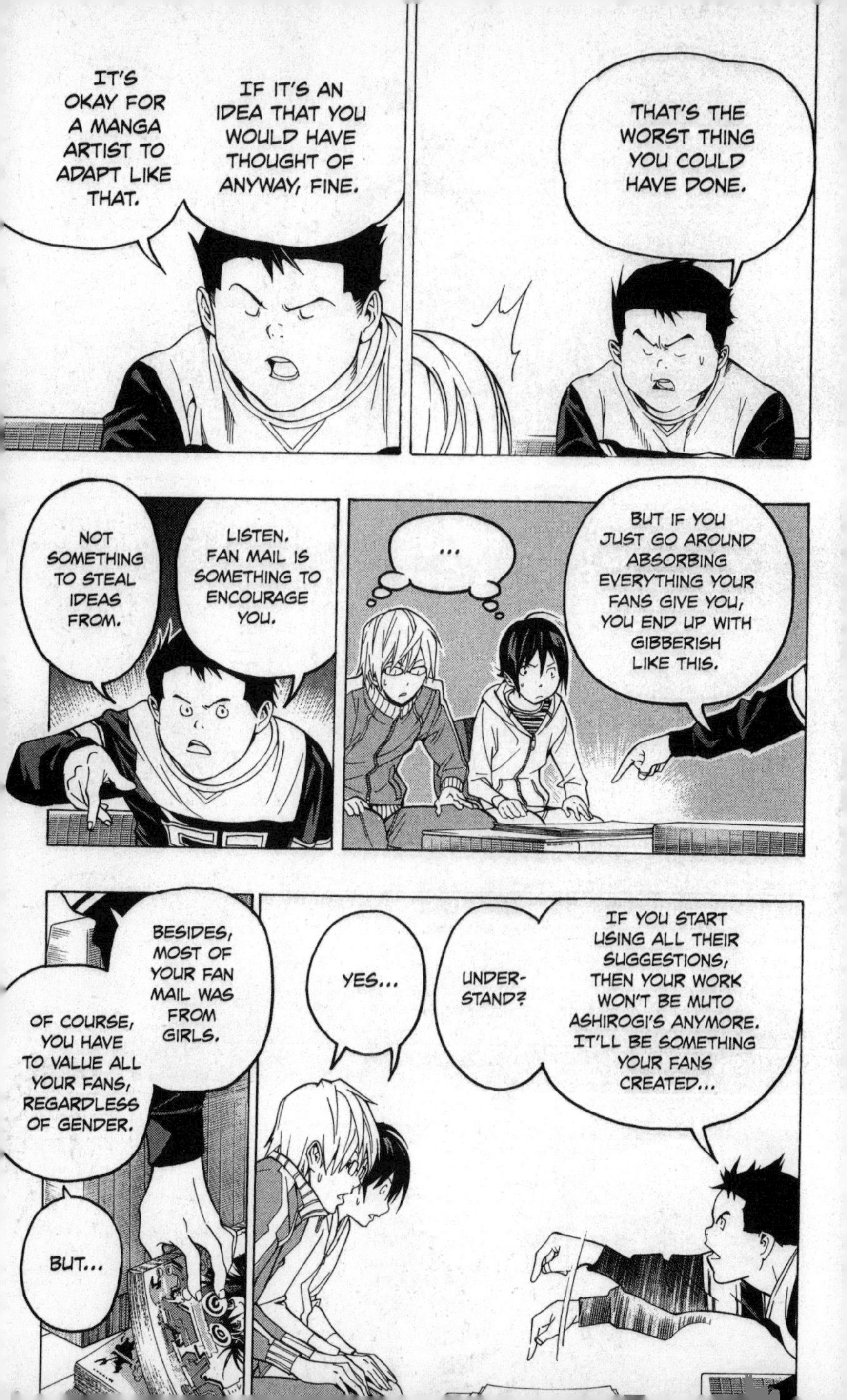
THAT'S THE WORST THING YOU COULD HAVE DONE.
IF IT'S AN IDEA THAT YOU WOULD HAVE THOUGHT OF ANYWAY, FINE.
IT'S OKAY FOR A MANGA ARTIST TO ADAPT LIKE THAT.
BUT IF YOU JUST GO AROUND ABSORBING EVERYTHING YOUR FANS GIVE YOU, YOU END UP WITH GIBBERISH LIKE THIS.
...
LISTEN. FAN MAIL IS SOMETHING TO ENCOURAGE YOU.
NOT SOMETHING TO STEAL IDEAS FROM.
IF YOU START USING ALL THEIR SUGGESTIONS, THEN YOUR WORK WON'T BE MUTO ASHIROGI'S ANYMORE. IT'LL BE SOMETHING YOUR FANS CREATED...
UNDER-STAND?
YES...
BESIDES, MOST OF YOUR FAN MAIL WAS FROM GIRLS.
OF COURSE, YOU HAVE TO VALUE ALL YOUR FANS, REGARDLESS OF GENDER.
BUT...

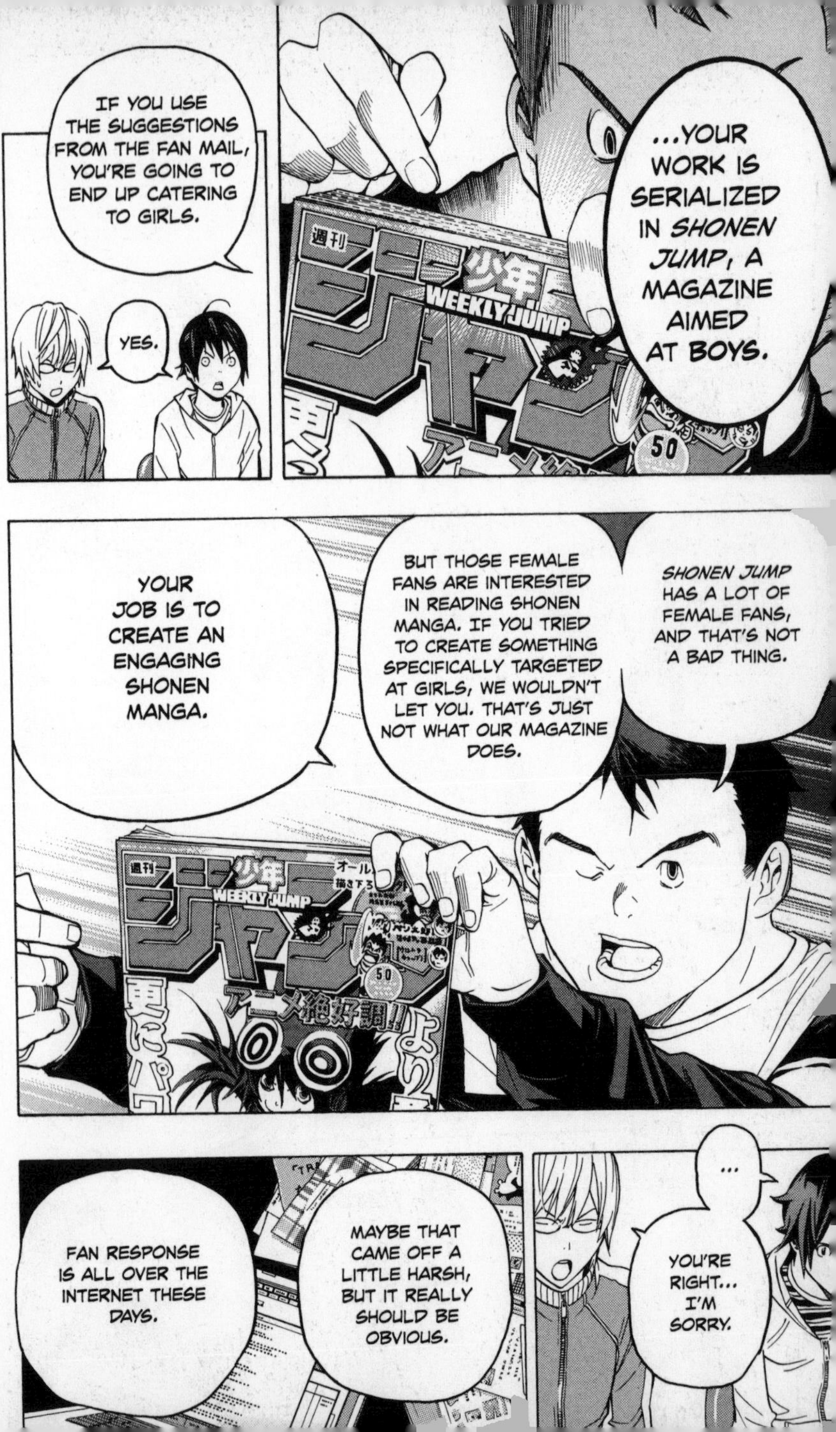
...YOUR WORK IS SERIALIZED IN *SHONEN JUMP*, A MAGAZINE AIMED AT BOYS.
WEEKLY JUMP
50
IF YOU USE THE SUGGESTIONS FROM THE FAN MAIL, YOU'RE GOING TO END UP CATERING TO GIRLS.
YES.
SHONEN JUMP HAS A LOT OF FEMALE FANS, AND THAT'S NOT A BAD THING.
BUT THOSE FEMALE FANS ARE INTERESTED IN READING SHONEN MANGA. IF YOU TRIED TO CREATE SOMETHING SPECIFICALLY TARGETED AT GIRLS, WE WOULDN'T LET YOU. THAT'S JUST NOT WHAT OUR MAGAZINE DOES.
YOUR JOB IS TO CREATE AN ENGAGING SHONEN MANGA.
WEEKLY JUMP
50
...
YOU'RE RIGHT... I'M SORRY.
MAYBE THAT CAME OFF A LITTLE HARSH, BUT IT REALLY SHOULD BE OBVIOUS.
FAN RESPONSE IS ALL OVER THE INTERNET THESE DAYS.

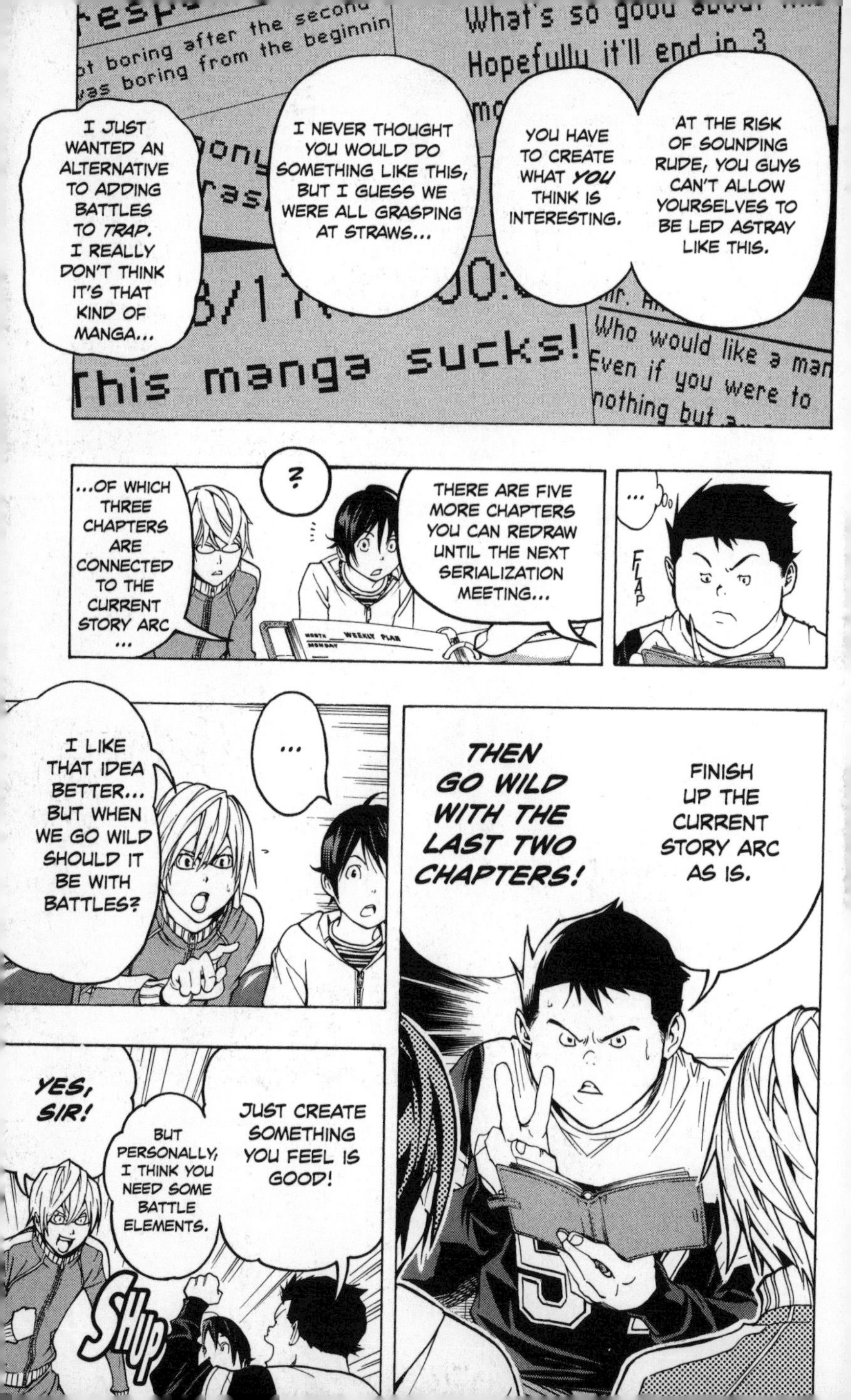
Hopefully it'll end in 3
AT THE RISK OF SOUNDING RUDE, YOU GUYS CAN'T ALLOW YOURSELVES TO BE LED ASTRAY LIKE THIS.
YOU HAVE TO CREATE WHAT *YOU* THINK IS INTERESTING.
I NEVER THOUGHT YOU WOULD DO SOMETHING LIKE THIS, BUT I GUESS WE WERE ALL GRASPING AT STRAWS...
I JUST WANTED AN ALTERNATIVE TO ADDING BATTLES TO *TRAP.* I REALLY DON'T THINK IT'S THAT KIND OF MANGA...
Who would like a man
Even if you were to
This manga sucks!
...
FLAP
THERE ARE FIVE MORE CHAPTERS YOU CAN REDRAW UNTIL THE NEXT SERIALIZATION MEETING...
?
...OF WHICH THREE CHAPTERS ARE CONNECTED TO THE CURRENT STORY ARC...
WEEKLY PLAN
FINISH UP THE CURRENT STORY ARC AS IS.
THEN GO WILD WITH THE LAST TWO CHAPTERS!
...
I LIKE THAT IDEA BETTER... BUT WHEN WE GO WILD SHOULD IT BE WITH BATTLES?
JUST CREATE SOMETHING YOU FEEL IS GOOD!
BUT PERSONALLY, I THINK YOU NEED SOME BATTLE ELEMENTS.
YES, SIR!
SHUP

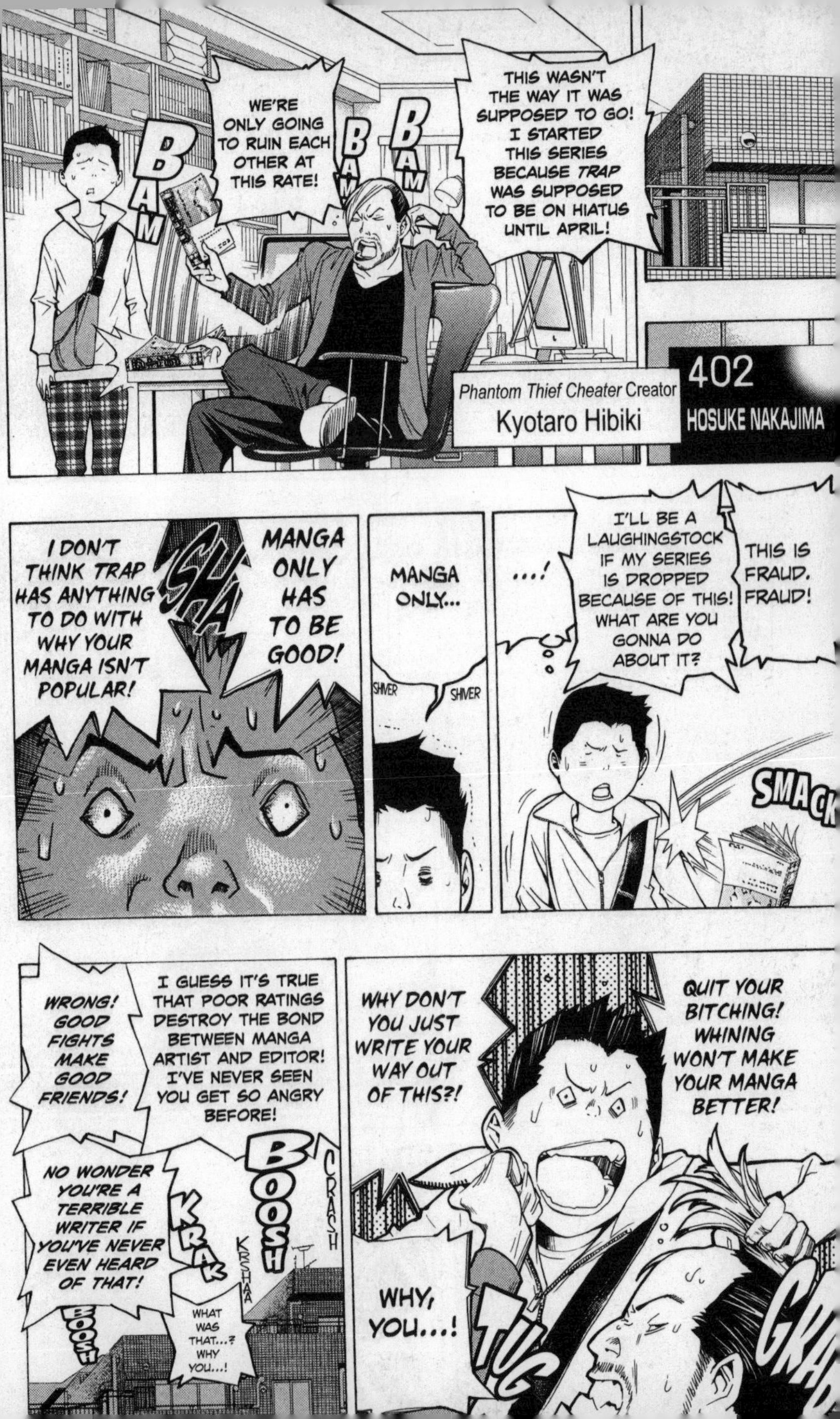
402
HOSUKE NAKAJIMA
THIS WASN'T THE WAY IT WAS SUPPOSED TO GO! I STARTED THIS SERIES BECAUSE TRAP WAS SUPPOSED TO BE ON HIATUS UNTIL APRIL!
Phantom Thief Cheater Creator
Kyotaro Hibiki
BAM
BAM
WE'RE ONLY GOING TO RUIN EACH OTHER AT THIS RATE!
BAM
THIS IS FRAUD. FRAUD!
I'LL BE A LAUGHINGSTOCK IF MY SERIES IS DROPPED BECAUSE OF THIS! WHAT ARE YOU GONNA DO ABOUT IT?
...!
SMACK
MANGA ONLY...
SHIVER
SHIVER
MANGA ONLY HAS TO BE GOOD!
SHA
I DON'T THINK TRAP HAS ANYTHING TO DO WITH WHY YOUR MANGA ISN'T POPULAR!
QUIT YOUR BITCHING! WHINING WON'T MAKE YOUR MANGA BETTER!
WHY DON'T YOU JUST WRITE YOUR WAY OUT OF THIS?!
WHY, YOU...!
TUG
I GUESS IT'S TRUE THAT POOR RATINGS DESTROY THE BOND BETWEEN MANGA ARTIST AND EDITOR! I'VE NEVER SEEN YOU GET SO ANGRY BEFORE!
WRONG! GOOD FIGHTS MAKE GOOD FRIENDS!
BOOSH
CRASH
KRAK
KRSHAA
NO WONDER YOU'RE A TERRIBLE WRITER IF YOU'VE NEVER EVEN HEARD OF THAT!
WHAT WAS THAT...? WHY YOU...!
BOOSH

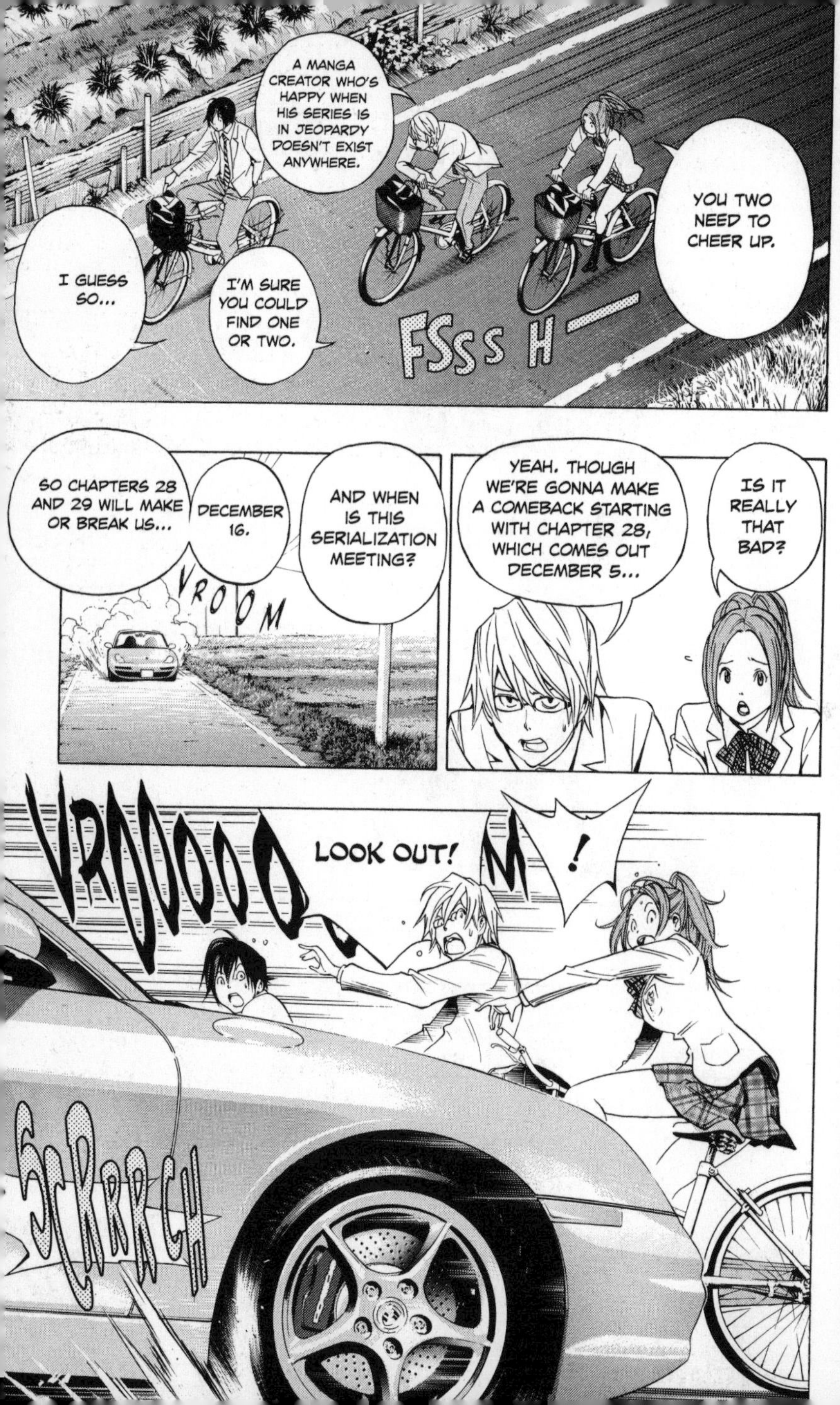
YOU TWO NEED TO CHEER UP.
A MANGA CREATOR WHO'S HAPPY WHEN HIS SERIES IS IN JEOPARDY DOESN'T EXIST ANYWHERE.
FSSS H
I'M SURE YOU COULD FIND ONE OR TWO.
I GUESS SO...
IS IT REALLY THAT BAD?
YEAH. THOUGH WE'RE GONNA MAKE A COMEBACK STARTING WITH CHAPTER 28, WHICH COMES OUT DECEMBER 5...
AND WHEN IS THIS SERIALIZATION MEETING?
DECEMBER 16.
SO CHAPTERS 28 AND 29 WILL MAKE OR BREAK US...
VROOM
!
LOOK OUT!
VROOOOOM
SCRRRCH

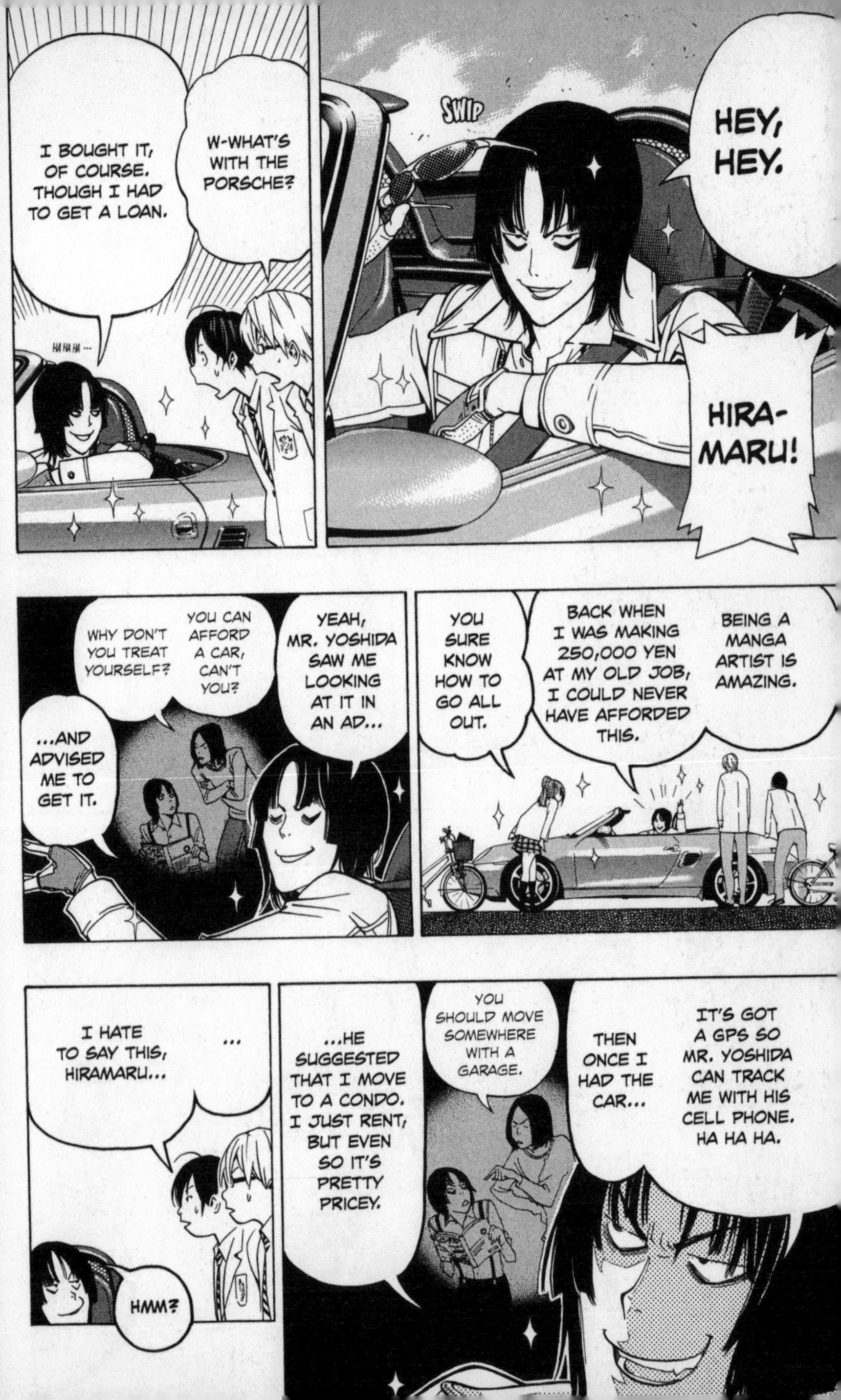
HEY, HEY.
SWIP
HIRA-MARU!
W-WHAT'S WITH THE PORSCHE?
I BOUGHT IT, OF COURSE. THOUGH I HAD TO GET A LOAN.
HA HA HA ...
BEING A MANGA ARTIST IS AMAZING.
BACK WHEN I WAS MAKING 250,000 YEN AT MY OLD JOB, I COULD NEVER HAVE AFFORDED THIS.
YOU SURE KNOW HOW TO GO ALL OUT.
YEAH, MR. YOSHIDA SAW ME LOOKING AT IT IN AN AD...
YOU CAN AFFORD A CAR, CAN'T YOU?
WHY DON'T YOU TREAT YOURSELF?
...AND ADVISED ME TO GET IT.
IT'S GOT A GPS SO MR. YOSHIDA CAN TRACK ME WITH HIS CELL PHONE. HA HA HA.
THEN ONCE I HAD THE CAR...
YOU SHOULD MOVE SOMEWHERE WITH A GARAGE.
...HE SUGGESTED THAT I MOVE TO A CONDO. I JUST RENT, BUT EVEN SO IT'S PRETTY PRICEY.
...
I HATE TO SAY THIS, HIRAMARU...
HMM?

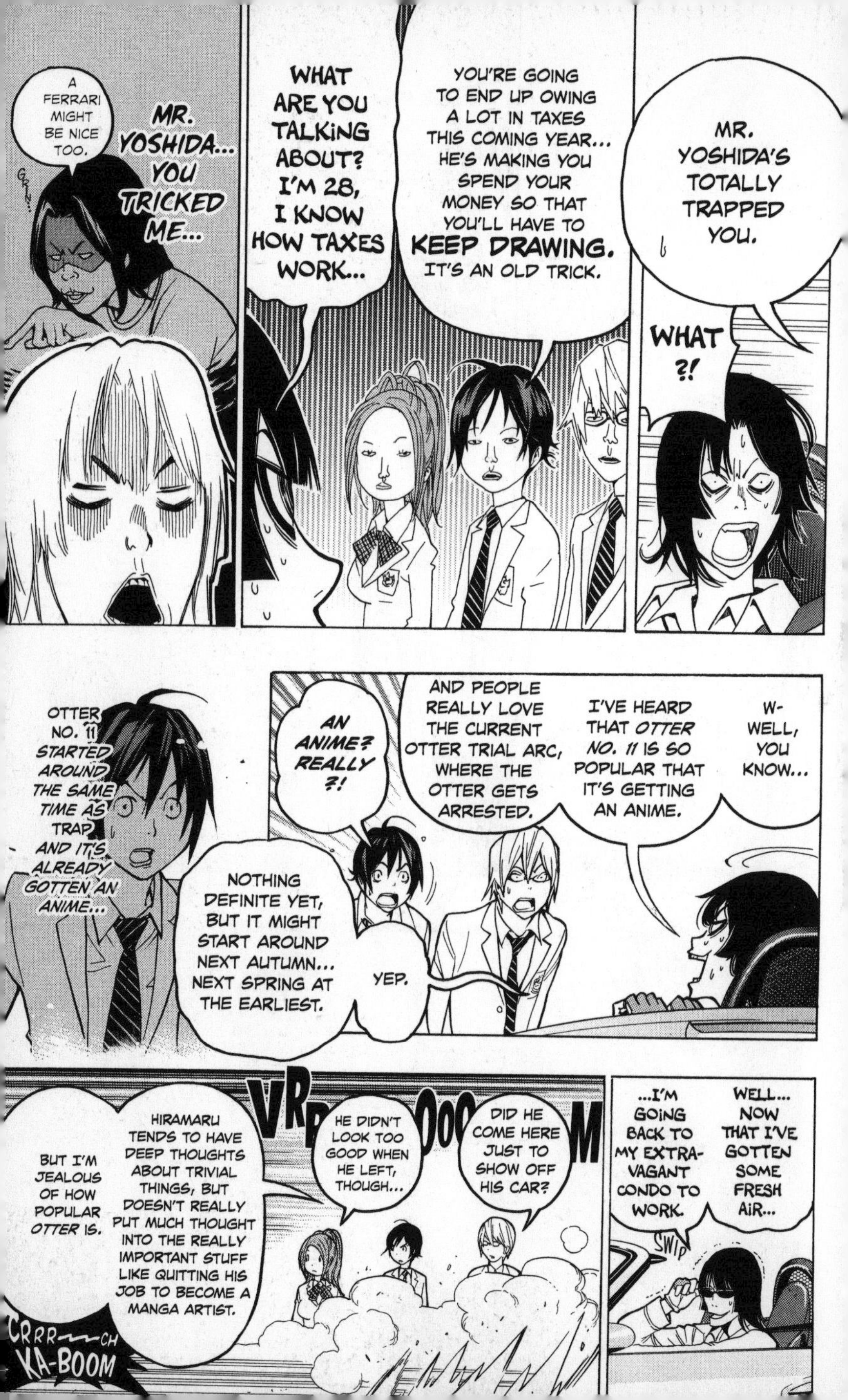
MR. YOSHIDA'S TOTALLY TRAPPED YOU.
WHAT ?!
YOU'RE GOING TO END UP OWING A LOT IN TAXES THIS COMING YEAR... HE'S MAKING YOU SPEND YOUR MONEY SO THAT YOU'LL HAVE TO KEEP DRAWING. IT'S AN OLD TRICK.
WHAT ARE YOU TALKING ABOUT? I'M 28, I KNOW HOW TAXES WORK...
A FERRARI MIGHT BE NICE TOO.
MR. YOSHIDA... YOU TRICKED ME...
W-WELL, YOU KNOW...
I'VE HEARD THAT OTTER NO. 11 IS SO POPULAR THAT IT'S GETTING AN ANIME.
AND PEOPLE REALLY LOVE THE CURRENT OTTER TRIAL ARC, WHERE THE OTTER GETS ARRESTED.
AN ANIME? REALLY?!
NOTHING DEFINITE YET, BUT IT MIGHT START AROUND NEXT AUTUMN... NEXT SPRING AT THE EARLIEST.
YEP.
OTTER NO. 11 STARTED AROUND THE SAME TIME AS TRAP AND IT'S ALREADY GOTTEN AN ANIME...
WELL... NOW THAT I'VE GOTTEN SOME FRESH AIR...
...I'M GOING BACK TO MY EXTRA-VAGANT CONDO TO WORK.
SWIP
DID HE COME HERE JUST TO SHOW OFF HIS CAR?
HE DIDN'T LOOK TOO GOOD WHEN HE LEFT, THOUGH...
HIRAMARU TENDS TO HAVE DEEP THOUGHTS ABOUT TRIVIAL THINGS, BUT DOESN'T REALLY PUT MUCH THOUGHT INTO THE REALLY IMPORTANT STUFF LIKE QUITTING HIS JOB TO BECOME A MANGA ARTIST.
BUT I'M JEALOUS OF HOW POPULAR OTTER IS.
CRRR-NCH KA-BOOM

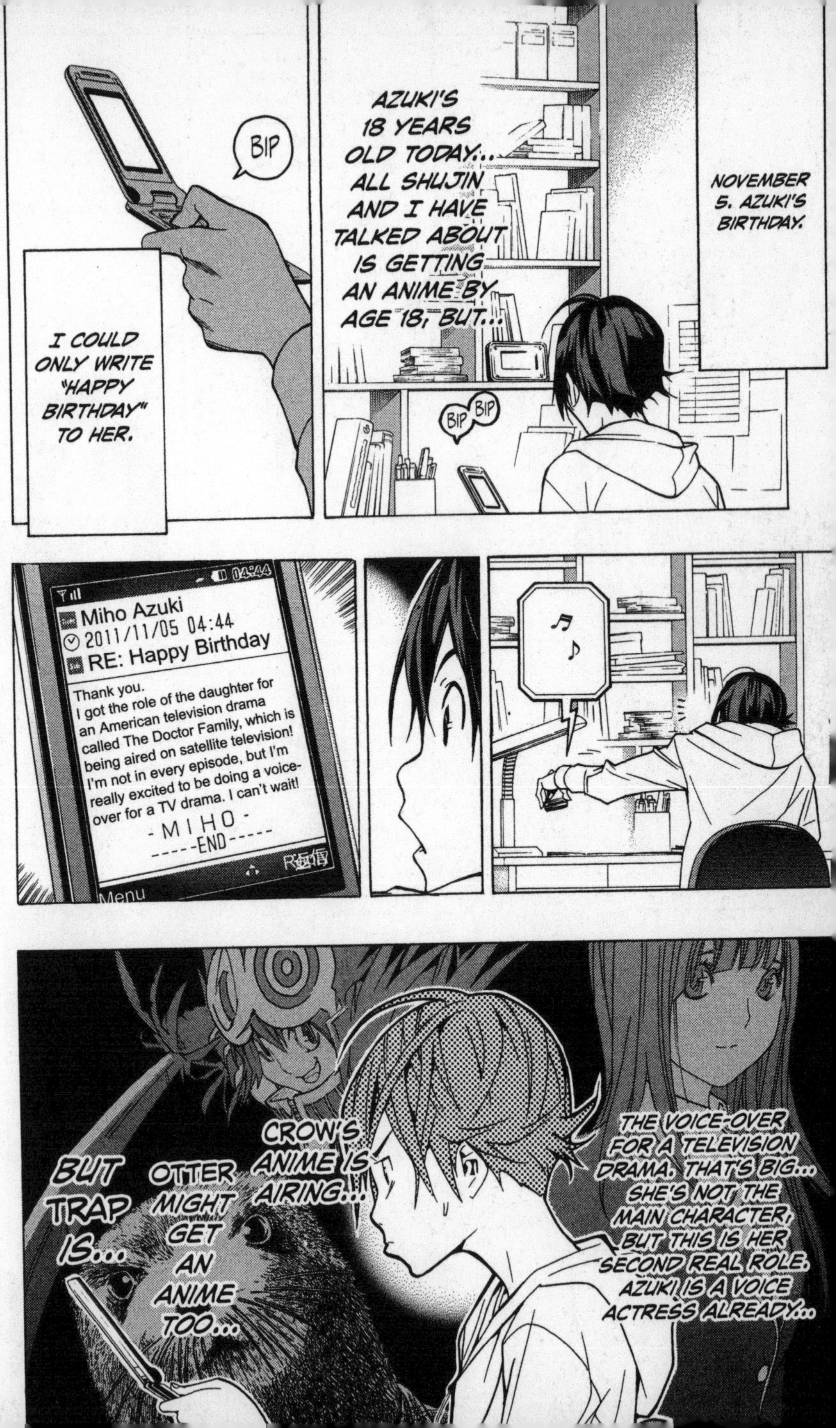
NOVEMBER 5. AZUKI'S BIRTHDAY.
AZUKI'S 18 YEARS OLD TODAY... ALL SHUJIN AND I HAVE TALKED ABOUT IS GETTING AN ANIME BY AGE 18, BUT...
BIP BIP
BIP
I COULD ONLY WRITE "HAPPY BIRTHDAY" TO HER.
04:44
Miho Azuki
2011/11/05 04:44
RE: Happy Birthday
Thank you.
I got the role of the daughter for
an American television drama
called The Doctor Family, which is
being aired on satellite television!
I'm not in every episode, but I'm
really excited to be doing a voice-
over for a TV drama. I can't wait!
-MIHO-
-----END-----
Menu
THE VOICE-OVER FOR A TELEVISION DRAMA. THAT'S BIG... SHE'S NOT THE MAIN CHARACTER, BUT THIS IS HER SECOND REAL ROLE. AZUKI IS A VOICE ACTRESS ALREADY...
CROW'S ANIME IS AIRING...
OTTER MIGHT GET AN ANIME TOO...
BUT TRAP IS...

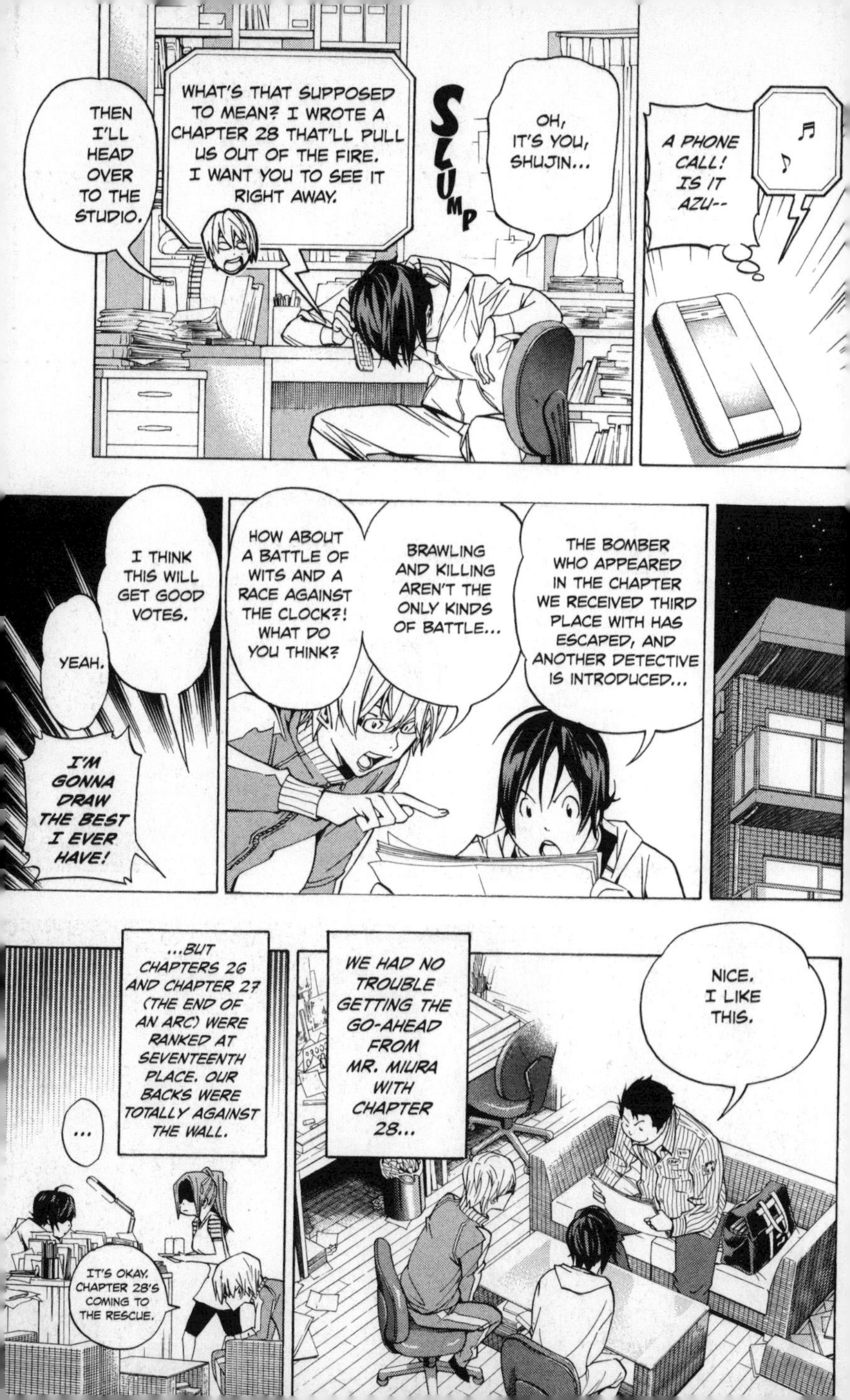
A PHONE CALL! IS IT AZU--
SLUMP
OH, IT'S YOU, SHUJIN...
WHAT'S THAT SUPPOSED TO MEAN? I WROTE A CHAPTER 28 THAT'LL PULL US OUT OF THE FIRE. I WANT YOU TO SEE IT RIGHT AWAY.
THEN I'LL HEAD OVER TO THE STUDIO.
THE BOMBER WHO APPEARED IN THE CHAPTER WE RECEIVED THIRD PLACE WITH HAS ESCAPED, AND ANOTHER DETECTIVE IS INTRODUCED...
BRAWLING AND KILLING AREN'T THE ONLY KINDS OF BATTLE...
HOW ABOUT A BATTLE OF WITS AND A RACE AGAINST THE CLOCK?! WHAT DO YOU THINK?
I THINK THIS WILL GET GOOD VOTES.
YEAH.
I'M GONNA DRAW THE BEST I EVER HAVE!
NICE. I LIKE THIS.
WE HAD NO TROUBLE GETTING THE GO-AHEAD FROM MR. MIURA WITH CHAPTER 28...
...BUT CHAPTERS 26 AND CHAPTER 27 (THE END OF AN ARC) WERE RANKED AT SEVENTEENTH PLACE. OUR BACKS WERE TOTALLY AGAINST THE WALL.
...
IT'S OKAY. CHAPTER 28'S COMING TO THE RESCUE.

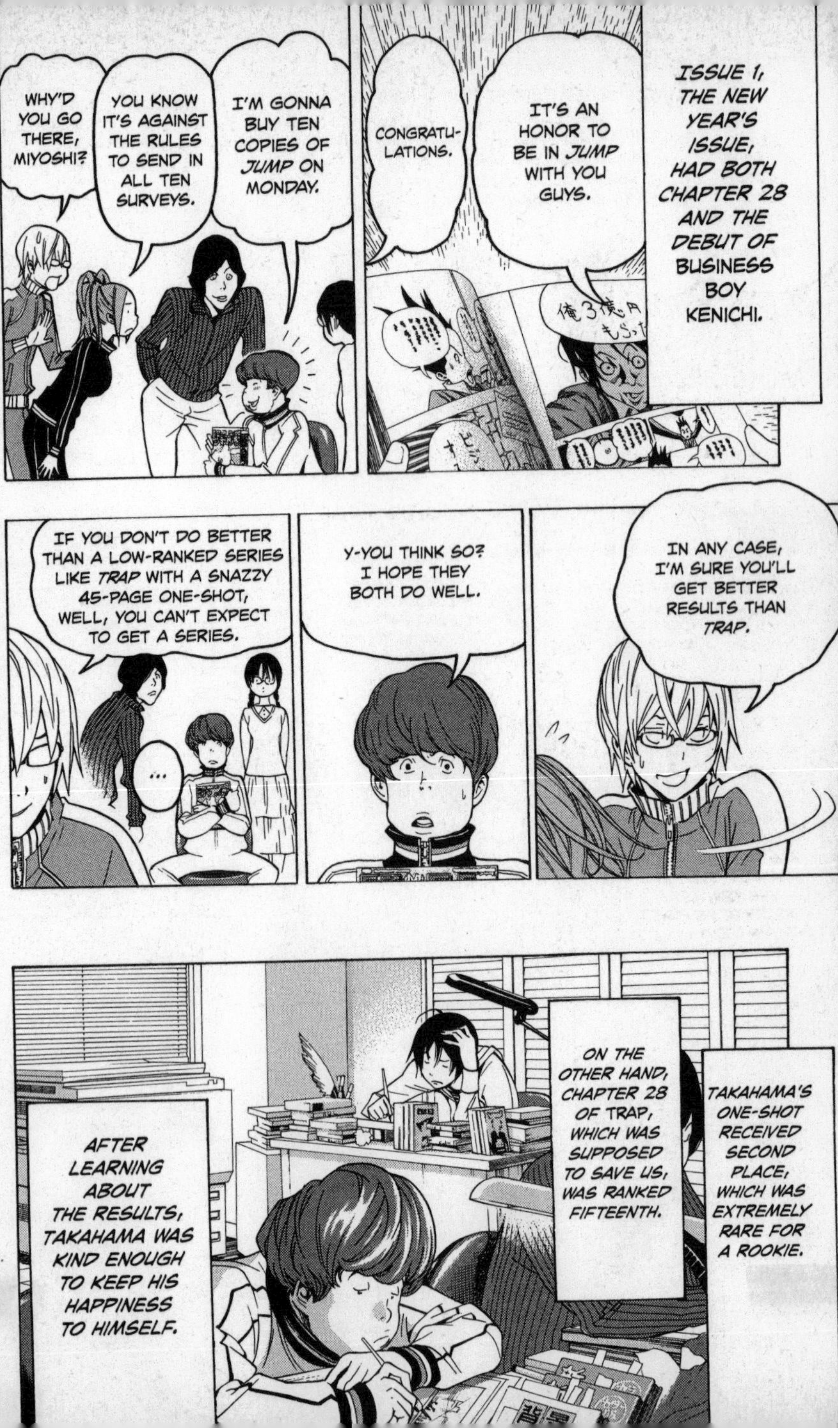

ISSUE 1, THE NEW YEAR'S ISSUE, HAD BOTH CHAPTER 28 AND THE DEBUT OF BUSINESS BOY KENICHI.
IT'S AN HONOR TO BE IN JUMP WITH YOU GUYS.
CONGRATU-LATIONS.
I'M GONNA BUY TEN COPIES OF JUMP ON MONDAY.
YOU KNOW IT'S AGAINST THE RULES TO SEND IN ALL TEN SURVEYS.
WHY'D YOU GO THERE, MIYOSHI?
IN ANY CASE, I'M SURE YOU'LL GET BETTER RESULTS THAN TRAP.
Y-YOU THINK SO? I HOPE THEY BOTH DO WELL.
IF YOU DON'T DO BETTER THAN A LOW-RANKED SERIES LIKE TRAP WITH A SNAZZY 45-PAGE ONE-SHOT, WELL, YOU CAN'T EXPECT TO GET A SERIES.
...
TAKAHAMA'S ONE-SHOT RECEIVED SECOND PLACE, WHICH WAS EXTREMELY RARE FOR A ROOKIE.
ON THE OTHER HAND, CHAPTER 28 OF TRAP, WHICH WAS SUPPOSED TO SAVE US, WAS RANKED FIFTEENTH.
AFTER LEARNING ABOUT THE RESULTS, TAKAHAMA WAS KIND ENOUGH TO KEEP HIS HAPPINESS TO HIMSELF.

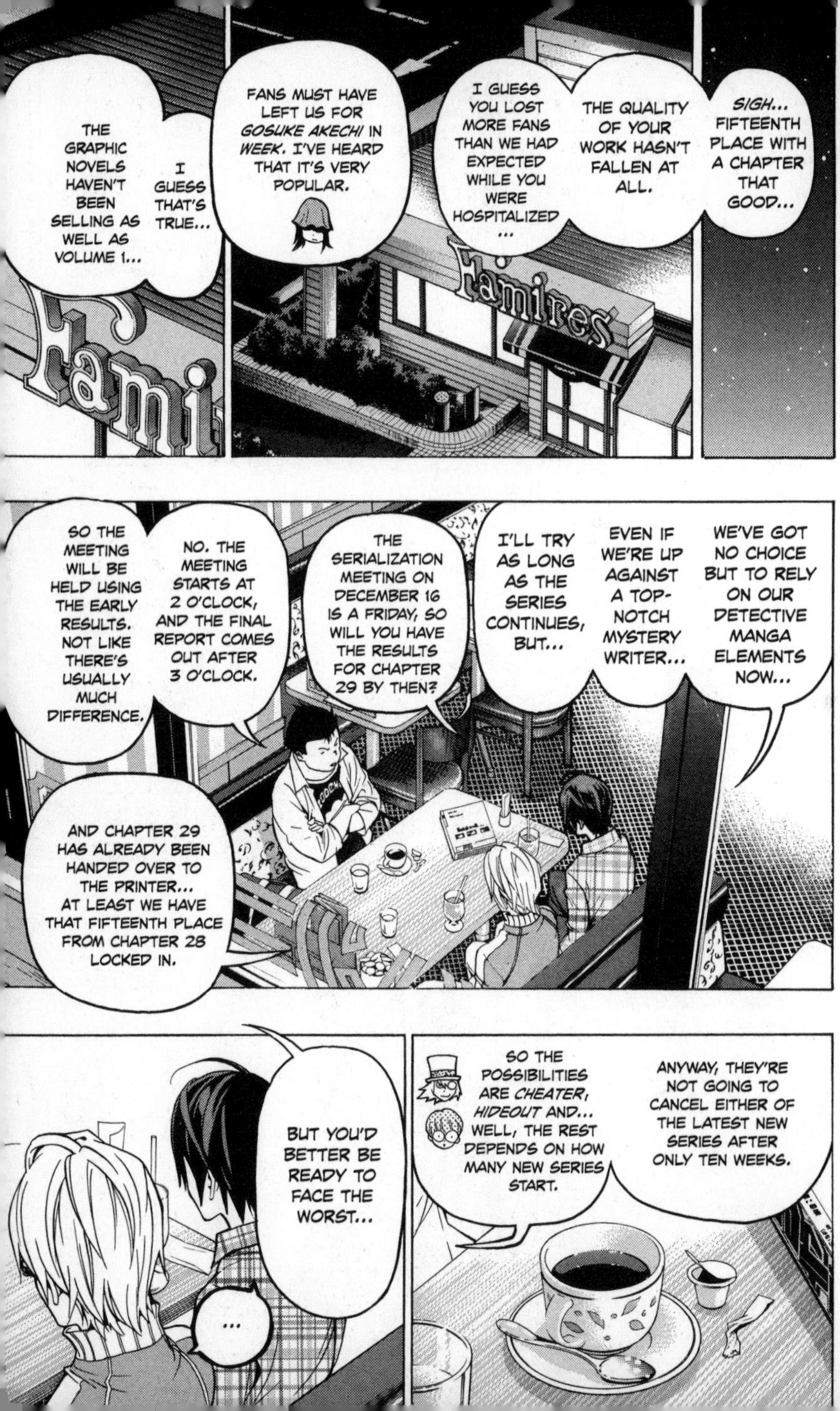
SIGH... FIFTEENTH PLACE WITH A CHAPTER THAT GOOD...
THE QUALITY OF YOUR WORK HASN'T FALLEN AT ALL.
I GUESS YOU LOST MORE FANS THAN WE HAD EXPECTED WHILE YOU WERE HOSPITALIZED...
FANS MUST HAVE LEFT US FOR *GOSUKE AKECHI* IN *WEEK*. I'VE HEARD THAT IT'S VERY POPULAR.
I GUESS THAT'S TRUE...
THE GRAPHIC NOVELS HAVEN'T BEEN SELLING AS WELL AS VOLUME 1...
WE'VE GOT NO CHOICE BUT TO RELY ON OUR DETECTIVE MANGA ELEMENTS NOW...
EVEN IF WE'RE UP AGAINST A TOP-NOTCH MYSTERY WRITER...
I'LL TRY AS LONG AS THE SERIES CONTINUES, BUT...
THE SERIALIZATION MEETING ON DECEMBER 16 IS A FRIDAY, SO WILL YOU HAVE THE RESULTS FOR CHAPTER 29 BY THEN?
NO. THE MEETING STARTS AT 2 O'CLOCK, AND THE FINAL REPORT COMES OUT AFTER 3 O'CLOCK.
SO THE MEETING WILL BE HELD USING THE EARLY RESULTS. NOT LIKE THERE'S USUALLY MUCH DIFFERENCE.
AND CHAPTER 29 HAS ALREADY BEEN HANDED OVER TO THE PRINTER... AT LEAST WE HAVE THAT FIFTEENTH PLACE FROM CHAPTER 28 LOCKED IN.
ANYWAY, THEY'RE NOT GOING TO CANCEL EITHER OF THE LATEST NEW SERIES AFTER ONLY TEN WEEKS.
SO THE POSSIBILITIES ARE *CHEATER*, *HIDEOUT* AND... WELL, THE REST DEPENDS ON HOW MANY NEW SERIES START.
BUT YOU'D BETTER BE READY TO FACE THE WORST...
...

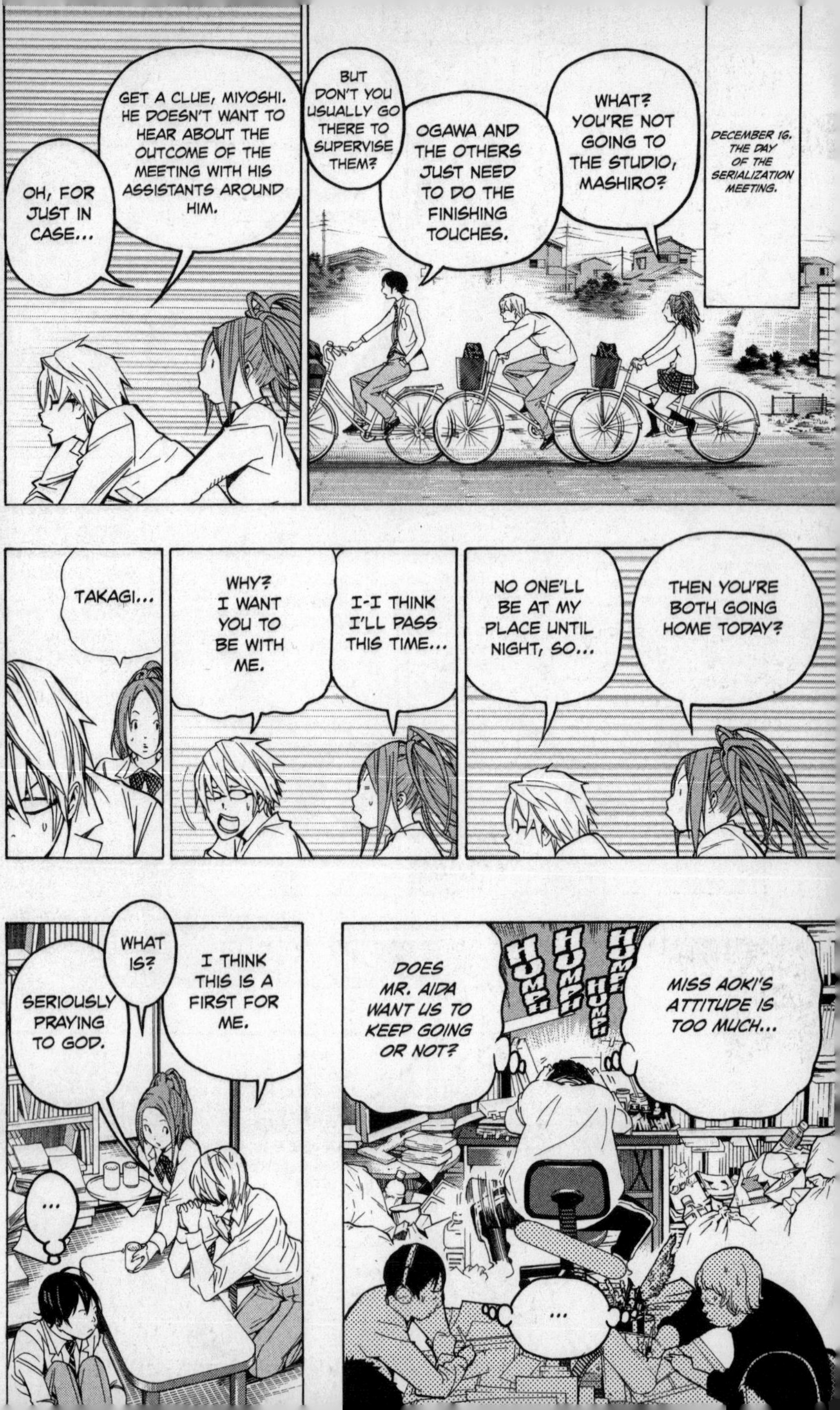
DECEMBER 16. THE DAY OF THE SERIALIZATION MEETING.
WHAT? YOU'RE NOT GOING TO THE STUDIO, MASHIRO?
OGAWA AND THE OTHERS JUST NEED TO DO THE FINISHING TOUCHES.
BUT DON'T YOU USUALLY GO THERE TO SUPERVISE THEM?
GET A CLUE, MIYOSHI. HE DOESN'T WANT TO HEAR ABOUT THE OUTCOME OF THE MEETING WITH HIS ASSISTANTS AROUND HIM.
OH, FOR JUST IN CASE...
THEN YOU'RE BOTH GOING HOME TODAY?
NO ONE'LL BE AT MY PLACE UNTIL NIGHT, SO...
I-I THINK I'LL PASS THIS TIME...
WHY? I WANT YOU TO BE WITH ME.
TAKAGI...
MISS AOKI'S ATTITUDE IS TOO MUCH...
HUMPH! HUMPH! HUMPH! HUMPH!
DOES MR. AIDA WANT US TO KEEP GOING OR NOT?
...
I THINK THIS IS A FIRST FOR ME.
WHAT IS?
SERIOUSLY PRAYING TO GOD.
...

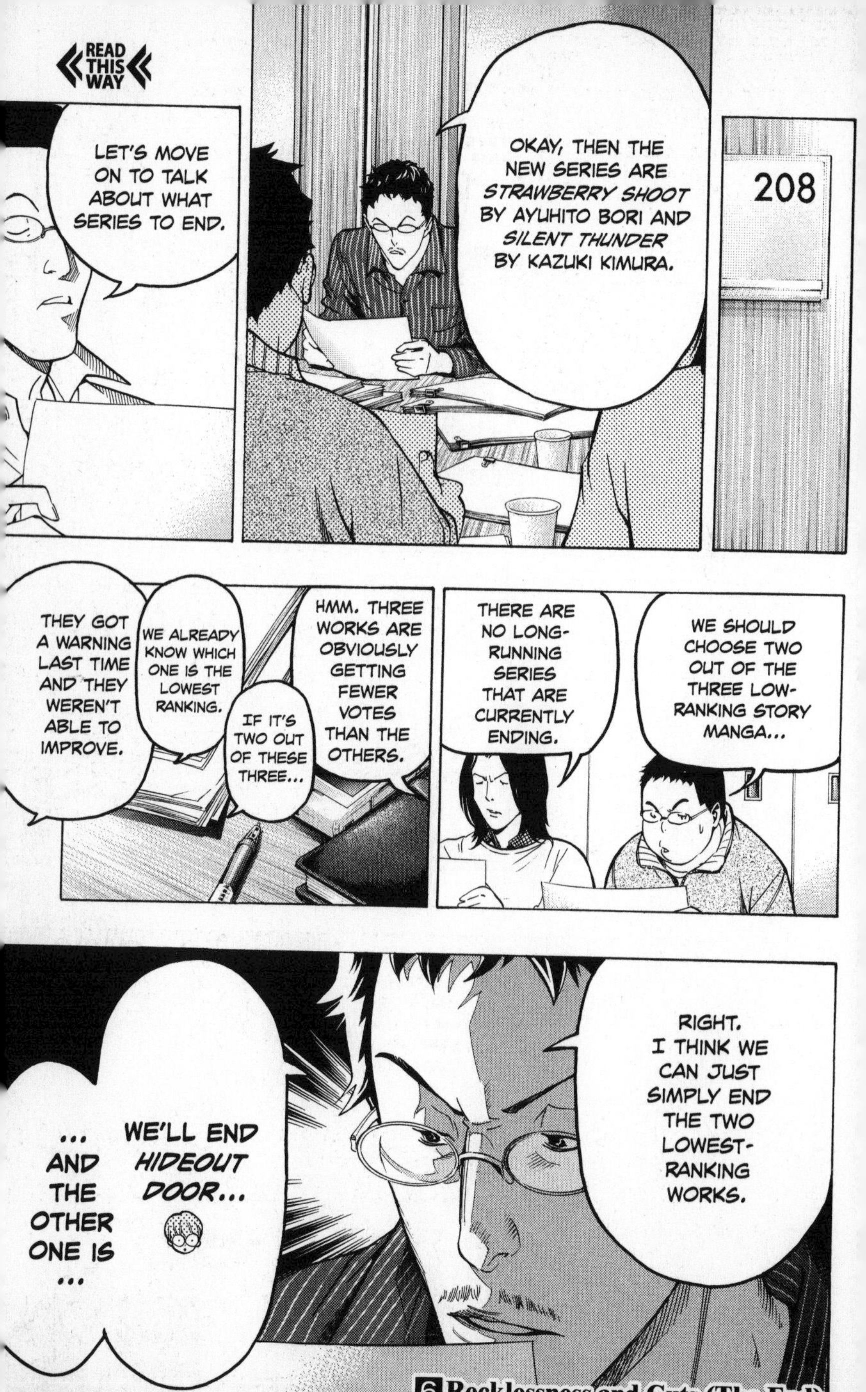
READ THIS WAY
208
OKAY, THEN THE NEW SERIES ARE *STRAWBERRY SHOOT* BY AYUHITO BORI AND *SILENT THUNDER* BY KAZUKI KIMURA.
LET'S MOVE ON TO TALK ABOUT WHAT SERIES TO END.
WE SHOULD CHOOSE TWO OUT OF THE THREE LOW-RANKING STORY MANGA...
THERE ARE NO LONG-RUNNING SERIES THAT ARE CURRENTLY ENDING.
HMM. THREE WORKS ARE OBVIOUSLY GETTING FEWER VOTES THAN THE OTHERS.
IF IT'S TWO OUT OF THESE THREE...
WE ALREADY KNOW WHICH ONE IS THE LOWEST RANKING.
THEY GOT A WARNING LAST TIME AND THEY WEREN'T ABLE TO IMPROVE.
RIGHT. I THINK WE CAN JUST SIMPLY END THE TWO LOWEST-RANKING WORKS.
WE'LL END *HIDEOUT DOOR*...
... AND THE OTHER ONE IS ...

6 **Recklessness and Guts (The End)**

OHBA'S STORYBOARD

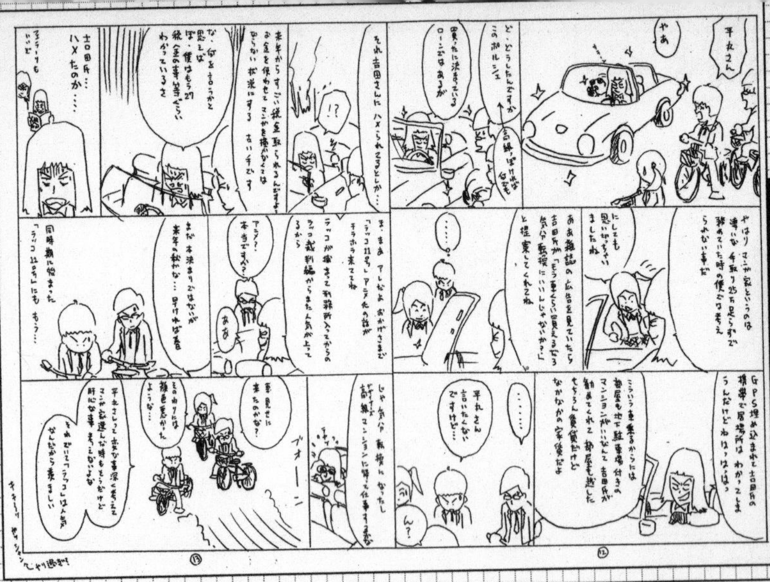

平丸さん
やあ
ど、どうしたんですか このポルシェ
買ったに決まっている ローンではあるが
やはりマンガ家というのは凄いな 手取り25万足らずで勤めていた時の僕が考えられない事だ
にしても思いきりましたね
ああ雑誌の広告を見ていたら吉田氏が「もう車くらい買えるだろう 気分転換にいいんじゃないか」と提案してくれてね
・・・・・・
GPS埋め込まれて吉田氏の携帯で居場所はわかってしまうんだけどね はっはっはっ
・・・・・・
平丸さん 言いたくないですけど…
ん?
それ吉田さんにハメられてるとしか…
!?
来年からすごい税金取られるんですよ お金を使わせてマンガを描かざるをえない状況にする古い手です
な、何を言うかと思えば 僕・僕はもう27 税金の事等ぐらいわかっているさ
吉田氏… ハメたのか…
ま、まあ アレなよ おかげさまで「ラッコ11号」アニメ化の話がチラホラ来てるね
ラッコが捕まって刑務所入ってからのラッコ裁判編からまた人気が上ってるから
アニメ? 本当ですか?
ああ
まだ本決まりではないが来年の秋かな… 早ければ春
同時期に始まった「ラッコ11号」にも もう…
じゃ 気分転換になったし 高級マンションに帰って仕事するよ
ブォーーン
車見せに来たのかな?
そのわりには顔色悪かったような…
平丸さんって変な事深く考えてマンガ家運いい時もあるけど 肝心な事考えないよな
それでいて「ラッコ」は人気なんだから羨ましい

OBATA'S STORYBOARD

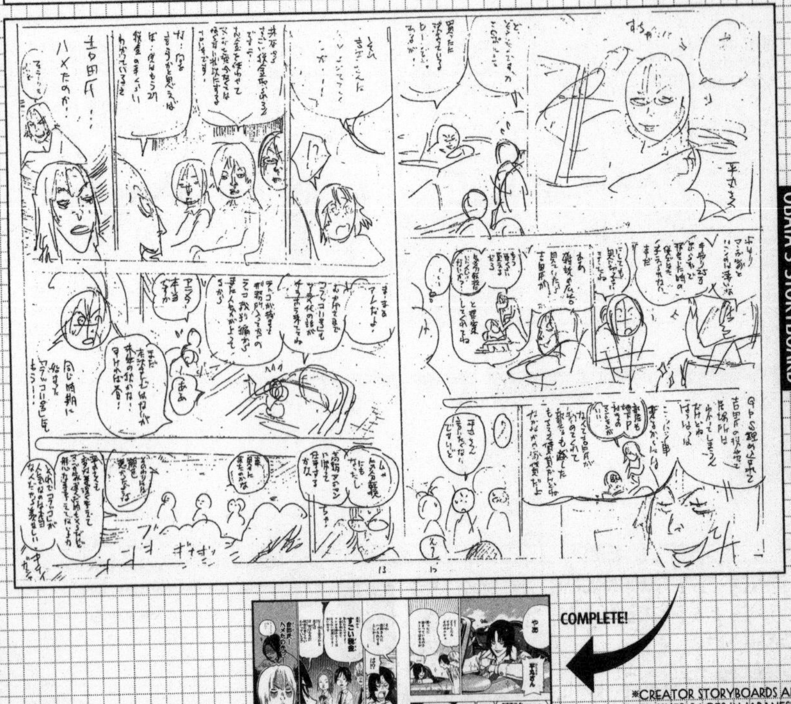

COMPLETE!

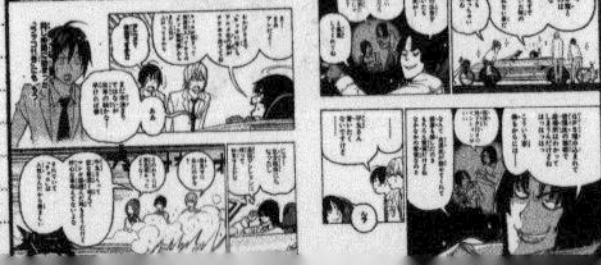

※CREATOR STORYBOARDS AND FINISHED PAGES IN JAPANESE

BAKUMAN。vol.6

"Until the Final Draft Is Complete"

Chapter 52, pp. 180-181

BAKUMAN

In the NEXT VOLUME

Huge changes are in store when the *Jump* editor in chief announces which series will be canceled. Meanwhile, when Moritaka and Akito enroll in college, they start running into some old friends.

Available October 2011!

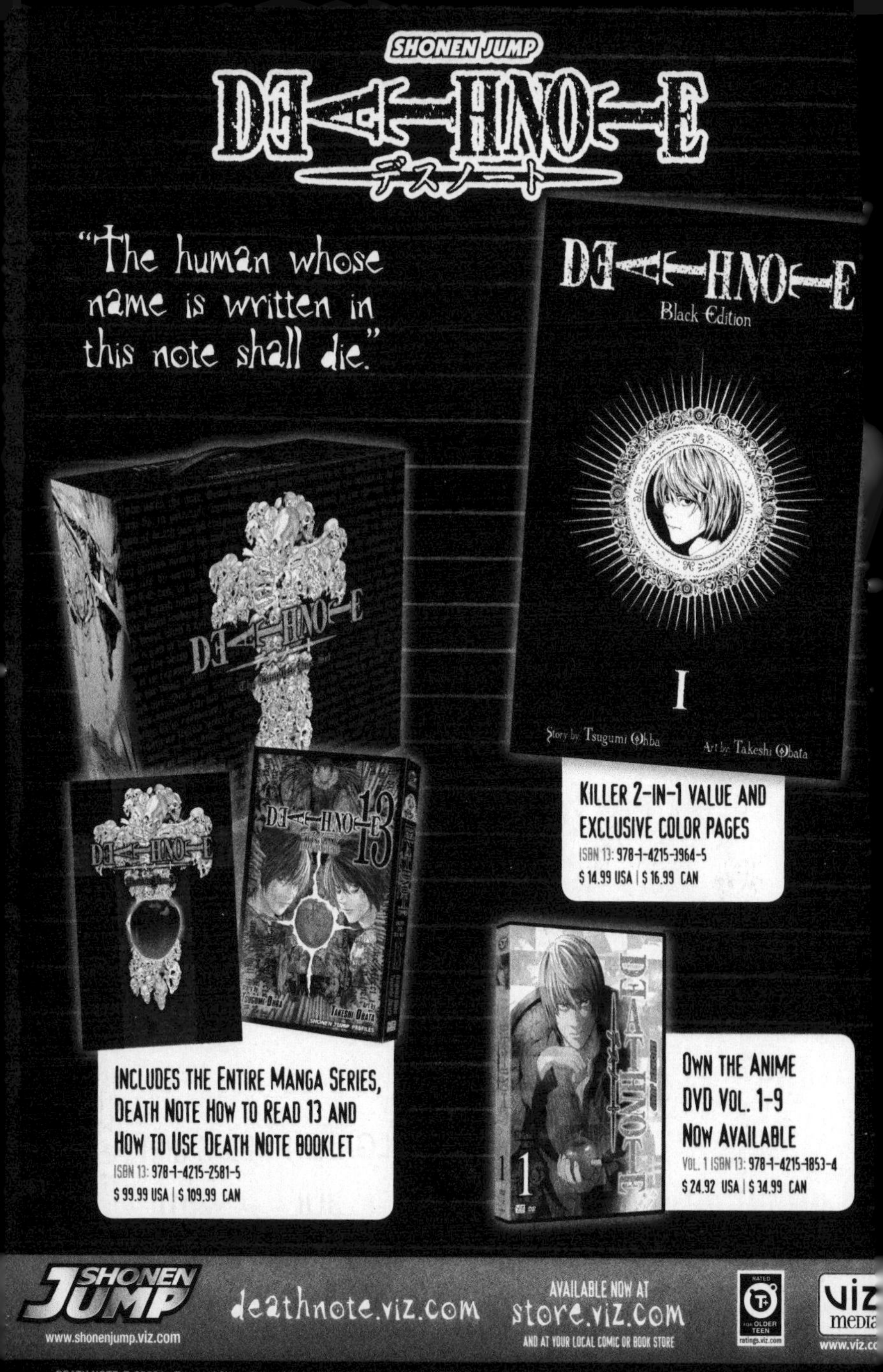
SHONEN JUMP
DEATH NOTE
デスノート
"The human whose name is written in this note shall die."
DEATH NOTE
Black Edition
I
Story by Tsugumi Ohba
Art by Takeshi Obata
KILLER 2-IN-1 VALUE AND EXCLUSIVE COLOR PAGES
ISBN 13: 978-1-4215-3964-5
$ 14.99 USA | $ 16.99 CAN
INCLUDES THE ENTIRE MANGA SERIES, DEATH NOTE HOW TO READ 13 AND HOW TO USE DEATH NOTE BOOKLET
ISBN 13: 978-1-4215-2581-5
$ 99.99 USA | $ 109.99 CAN
OWN THE ANIME DVD VOL. 1-9 NOW AVAILABLE
VOL. 1 ISBN 13: 978-1-4215-1853-4
$ 24.92 USA | $ 34.99 CAN
SHONEN JUMP
www.shonenjump.viz.com
deathnote.viz.com
AVAILABLE NOW AT
store.viz.com
AND AT YOUR LOCAL COMIC OR BOOK STORE
RATED T+ FOR OLDER TEEN
ratings.viz.com
viz media
www.viz.co

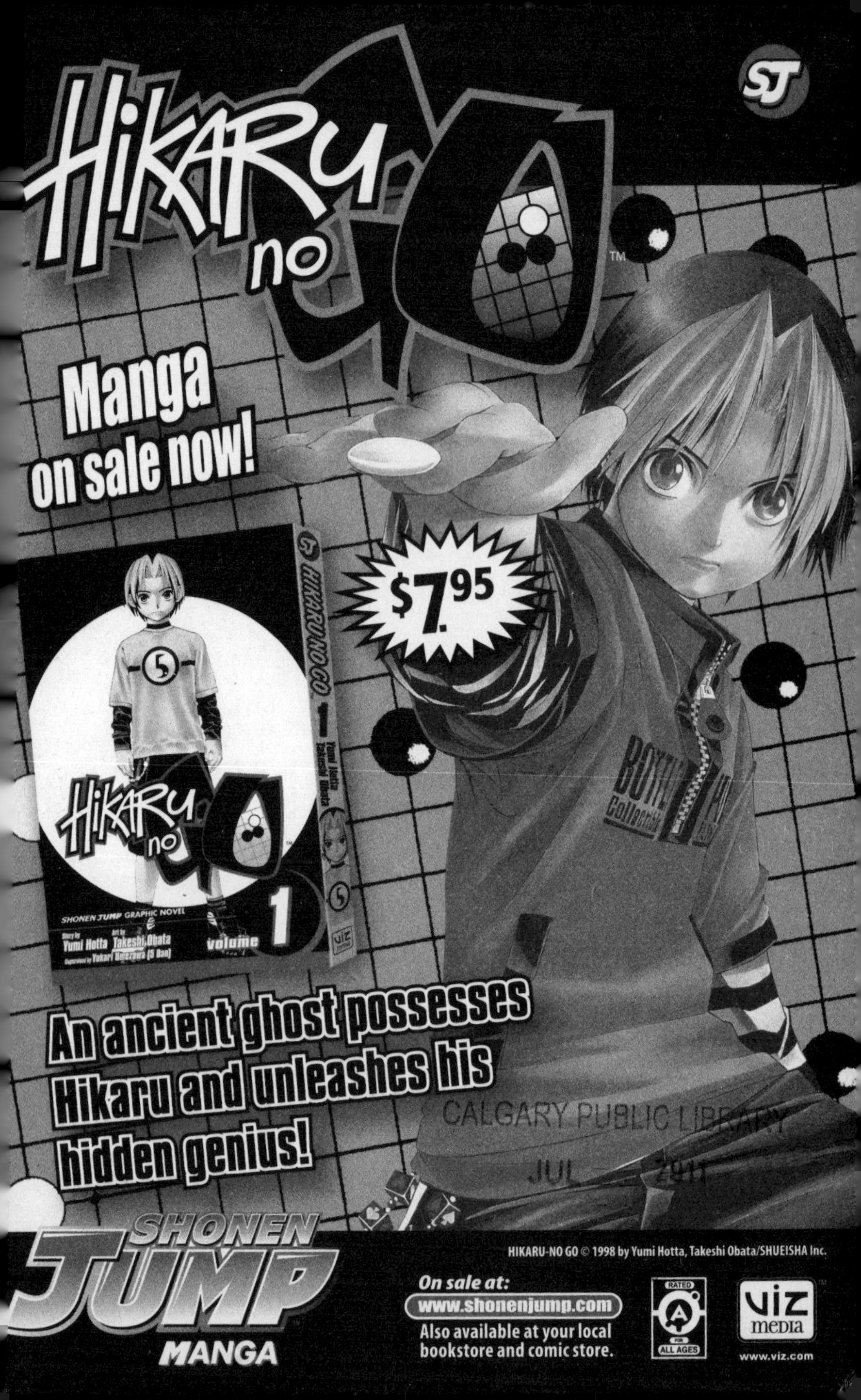
SJ
HIKARU NO GO™
Manga on sale now!
$7.95
SHONEN JUMP GRAPHIC NOVEL
Story by Yumi Hotta
Art by Takeshi Obata
volume 1
SJ HIKARU NO GO 1 Yumi Hotta Takeshi Obata
An ancient ghost possesses Hikaru and unleashes his hidden genius!
SHONEN JUMP MANGA
HIKARU-NO GO © 1998 by Yumi Hotta, Takeshi Obata/SHUEISHA Inc.
On sale at:
www.shonenjump.com
Also available at your local bookstore and comic store.
RATED A FOR ALL AGES
VIZ media
www.viz.com